AGEING OF FISH

419

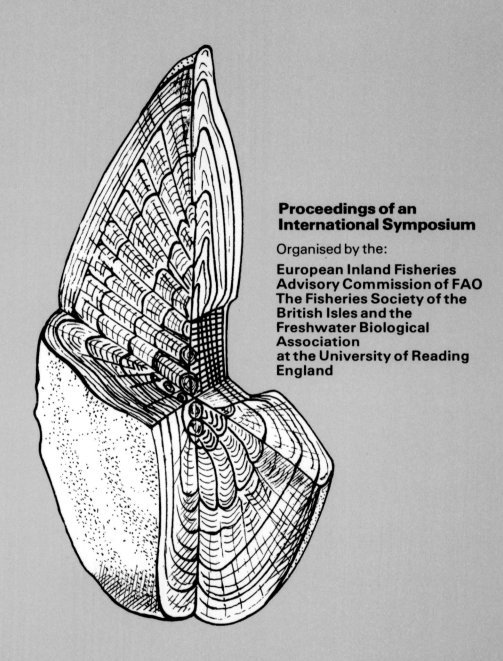

Proceedings of an International Symposium

Organised by the:

European Inland Fisheries Advisory Commission of FAO The Fisheries Society of the British Isles and the Freshwater Biological Association at the University of Reading England

Edited by **T B Bagenal**

UNWIN BROTHERS LIMITED

The Proceedings of an International Symposium on

THE AGEING OF FISH

Sponsored by
The European Inland Fisheries Advisory Commission of F.A.O.,
The Fisheries Society of the British Isles and
The Freshwater Biological Association

and held at
The University of Reading, England
on 19 and 20 July, 1973

Edited by
T. B. BAGENAL
The Freshwater Biological Association

UNWIN BROTHERS LIMITED
The Gresham Press, Old Woking, Surrey, England

First printed and published 1974

by

UNWIN BROTHERS LIMITED

The Gresham Press, Old Woking, Surrey, England GU22 9LH

ISBN 0 9502121 1 3

Contents

page

Introduction: by T. B. Bagenal.   v

List of Chairmen   vi

SOME CONSIDERATIONS OF THE SCIENTIFIC BASIS OF AGE DETERMINATION

Calcium metabolism of fish in relation to ageing: by K. Simkiss   1

Analysis of hard tissue of pike *Esox lucius* L. with special reference to age and growth: by
    J. M. Casselman   13

Otolith growth patterns: an aid in age determination in temperate and tropical fishes: by
    G. Pannella   28

Effects of starvation and feeding on circulus formation on scales of young sockeye salmon
    of four racial origins, and of one race of young kokanee, coho and chinook salmon: by
    H. T. Bilton   40

Age determination in *Tilapia melanotheron* (Ruppell) in the Lagos Lagoon, Nigeria, with a
    discussion of the environmental and physiological basis of growth markings in the
    tropics: by S. O. Fagade   71

The sources of errors in ageing fish and considerations of the proofs of reliability: by
    R. Sych   78

MECHANICAL AIDS TO AGE DETERMINATION

A semi-automatic machine for counting and measuring circuli on fish scales: by
    J. E. Mason   87

The use of image analysis in the ageing of fish: by J. K. Fawell   103

ELIMINATION OF ERRORS IN AGE DETERMINATION

    A—BY COOPERATIVE EFFORTS

The ICNAF cod otolith photograph exchange scheme: by R. W. Blacker   108

The use of otoliths for age determination: by T. Williams and B. C. Bedford   114

    B—WITH FISH OF KNOWN AGE

Age determination of American eels based on the structure of their otoliths: by
    P. K. L. Liew   124

Studies on growth, ageing and back-calculation of roach *Rutilus rutilus* (L.), and dace
    Leuciscus leuciscus (L.): by A. E. Hofstede   137

Scale reading and back-calculation of bream *Abramis brama* (L.) and rudd *Scardinius
    erythrophthalmus* (L.): by B. Steinmetz   148

    C—BY GRAPHICAL METHODS

An account of some methods of overcoming errors in ageing tropical and subtropical fish
    populations when hard tissue growth markings are unreliable and the data sparse:
    by C. P. Mathews   158

SOME SOURCES OF AGE READING ERRORS

The errors likely in ageing roach *Rutilus rutilus* (L.), with special reference to stunted
    populations: by R. S. J. Linfield   167

The problems of protracted check formation and the validity of the use of scales in age
    determination exemplified by two populations of dace *Leuciscus leuciscus* (L.): by
    J. M. Hellawell   173

THE EFFECTS OF ERRORS IN AGE DETERMINATION ON SUBSEQUENT STUDIES

The effect of age reading errors on the statistical reliability of marine fishery modelling:
by K. Brander   181

The effects of different age ranges on estimated Bertalanffy growth parameters in three
fishes and one mollusk of the northeastern Pacific Ocean: by G. Hirschhorn   192

Difficulties in ageing fish in relation to inland fisheries management: by K. D. Carlander   200

The application of age determination in fishing management: by A. E. Hofstede   206

The effects of errors in ageing in production studies: by E. D. Le Cren   221

List of Participants at the symposium meeting   225

List of Demonstrations at the symposium meeting   227

Index   229

Introduction

The ability to tell the age of a fish accurately from its otoliths, scales, fin rays or other structures is one of the most useful features available in fish biology and fishery science. In almost every biological study of fish use is made of this, and age determination is a central part of all work directed to the rational exploitation of a fishery. Yet, even though age determination is so basic to ichthyology and fishery science, the physiological processes leading to the structures that are used are almost unkown. For many years I have marvelled that such a volume of science rests on these relatively unknown processes. I do not doubt for a moment that all this knowledge is correct; but there can be few other branches of science which use such basic techniques without knowing the principles underlying them. Furthermore, if so much can be obtained while we do not know the basic physiological processes, how much more might be gained if we did understand them better.

It was thoughts such as these that led me first to try and interest those who are influencial in British fisheries, and then, in desperation, to organize a symposium which would draw attention to the situation. It is difficult to organize a symposium alone, but after I had got the support of the Fisheries Society of the British Isles and later of the European Inland Fisheries Commission of F.A.O., and of my employer, the Freshwater Biological Association, I could write in my letters 'We think......' instead of 'I think......', and everyone became more enthusiastic. For the most part my sponsors had little idea of what I was doing, but no one objected, and after a few frightful moments of anxiety, the Symposium took place on the 19th and 20th of July 1973, at the University of Reading.

Was the Symposium a success? Financially it was not a failure; I made ends meet and paid for all that I had committed myself to pay for. A total of 120 people attended and any criticisms they may have had will pass with time. The scientific contributions on the other hand are now published in this volume and are one of the two criteria by which the success or failure of the Symposium will be judged.

In this introduction it would be out of place for me to review the papers. Time alone will tell which are grain and which, if any, are chaff. However there are some aspects which can be mentioned.

One particularly gratifying aspect of the meeting was the presence of both marine and freshwater fish biologists. Because fishery scientists of different countries often work on the same stocks, international cooperation comes naturally, and, even though the British attitude at the meeting came across as that of a benevolent despot, marine fisheries have benefited enormously from the international cooperation. EIFAC on the other hand, dealing as much with ponds and lakes as with trans-national rivers, and often with national restrictions to prevent the spread of disease, has less incentive to adopt a dynamic international approach. The marine fishery scientists, particularly the contingent from Lowestoft, showed the enormous benefits of cooperative efforts. This came out more clearly in the meeting than it does in the papers. I think it also became apparent that freshwater fish biologists work under very restrictive conditions. Whereas marine market sampling allows enormous numbers of fish to be sampled, and fish in research vessel samples can be examined to any degree of detail, conditions for sampling from freshwater are sometimes very restrictive. In the first place every freshwater fish (in Britain) has an owner whose permission must be sought before the fish is caught. This sometimes means that the fish may be examined and a scale or two removed, but it must not be killed and it must be returned to the water; so this precludes ageing with otoliths. Secondly in many small water bodies even if the fish may be killed, adequate samples cannot be taken without changing the population in several ways. These different aspects were aired at the meeting after which there was a basis for a more profitable interchange of ideas.

The second criterion by which I will personally judge the success of the Symposium is if it leads to further work. An examination of some of the basic physiological processes on which the huge edifice of fishery science rests (as was behind the conceptual origins of the meeting) is not exactly like digging up the foundations of a Cathedral stone by stone to make sure it is safe; it is more like making a survey to see if the foundations can be extended and used to support an even finer edifice. Therefore I will judge the success of the Symposium to have been a success if the papers, or this volume, stimulate a little more work into the physiological basis of age determination and into error elimination.

One of the gratifying aspects of the Symposium was the support from ichthyologists from overseas. The meeting was attended by a total of 120 participants who represented 18 countries outside the United Kingdom.

Thanks are due to many people for the success of the meeting at Reading. I would particularly like to thank the sponsors of the Symposium especially EIFAC and Professor Backiel, the F.S.B.I. and the F.B.A. I am very grateful to Professor Simkiss for his cooperation and the use of the Zoology Department for the Demonstrations. Thanks are also due to the Huntingdon Research Centre for a financial guarantee. Much of the success of the meetings themselves is due to the chairmen for keeping the meetings on time. I am particularly grateful to my wife Mary for her invaluable help during the meeting at Reading; it would have been a disaster without her.

September 1973.
T. B. BAGENAL

Freshwater Biological Association
Windermere Laboratory
Ambleside
Westmorland
England

List of Chairmen

19th July 1973

E. D. Le CREN, M.A., M.S., Windermere Laboratory
      Freshwater Biological Association, Ambleside, Westmorland, England.

    Morning Session: Consideration of the Scientific Basis of Age Determination

J. W. JONES, O.B.E., D.Sc., Freshwater Fisheries Unit, Life Sciences
      Building, Liverpool University, England.

    Afternoon Session: Cooperative Efforts in Age Determination

20th July 1973

Professor Dr. T. BACKIEL, Inland Fisheries Institute, Piaseczno, Poland

    Morning Session: Mechanical aids to Age Determination

Professor K. SIMKISS, Ph.D., Zoology Department Reading University, England.

    Afternoon Session: The Effects of Errors in Subsequent Studies.

Calcium metabolism of fish in relation to ageing

by K. SIMKISS

Zoology Department, University of Reading, England

The title of this paper is deceptive. It gives no hint of the interpretation to be put on the terms 'calcium metabolism', 'fish' or 'ageing'. Furthermore as I hope to show it demands conclusions in advance of the evidence and poses problems that are only just being appreciated. It is, therefore, a very apt title for this symposium for it instantly exposes the theoretical difficulties underlying the use of mineralized tissues in ageing studies on fish.

The usual meaning of metabolism is 'the changes undergone by nutritive substances in the body'. In this pure sense therefore calcium is not metabolized for it enters and leaves the body without fundamental changes to its substance. During its passage through the body it may, however, exist in various combined forms and the term 'calcium metabolism' will therefore be thought of as involving these three main processes, i.e. its entry into the body, the extent to which it is trapped in the body and the routes by which it is excreted.

These processes will be briefly considered for all the animals in the superclass Pisces. These include

(a)   the Class Agnatha or jawless fish
(b)   the Class of fossil Placoderms
(c)   the Chondrichthyes (Selachii) or sharks and their relatives
(d)   the Class Osteichthyes or higher bony fish.

Most of the research done on calcium metabolism in fish has been confined to the Osteichthyes but by considering the other types of fish it is possible to see the results in a broad context. Thus, in a review of this sort one soon recognizes that the fish were the first and in many ways the last of the great modifiers of calcium metabolism in the vertebrates. During the evolution of the modern fish from the primitive Agnatha one finds evidence for the following innovations

(i)   the origin of bone (in Ordovician ostracoderms). In most vertebrates bone contains cells or osteocytes, embedded in the mineral material. This cellular bone persists in only a few primitive groups of living osteichthyes and most of the bony fish have abandoned it in favour of acellular bone, devoid of osteocytes.

(ii)   the formation of an endoskeleton of cartilage. In many of the Placodermi and Chondrichthyes this is all that remains of the skeleton although it may become calcified and persist as the adult skeleton. In other fish the cartilage is replaced by bone by the process of endochondral ossification.

(iii) the formation of a dermal skeleton by a different process of intra-membraneous ossification. Many bones of fish are formed by this process and a variety of specialized scales also persist in the dermal layers of the skin.

(iv) the control of calcium uptake and loss by a variety of epithelia including the gills, integument, intestine and kidneys. Superimposed upon this is the discovery of vitamin D as a modifier of calcium metabolism and a variety of hormones influencing the uptake and retention of calcium ions. The most recently discovered hormone is calcitonin synthesized by and released from the ultimobranchial glands.

The diversity and possible combinations of these mechanisms can produce a great variety of metabolic systems. Consequently most investigators have limited themselves either to studies of isolated organ systems or to relatively simple descriptions of whole animal situations. The result is that one still has almost no idea about for example, how calcium ions enter a fish. Furthermore in the context of this paper neither of these approaches is entirely valid. It is implicit in the subject matter that one has to consider integrated schemes in order to involve the time relationships of the whole organism.

In biology ageing is normally taken to indicate 'a decline in function with the passage of time'. The 'ageing of fish' however is more a question of trying to provide a basis for explaining the variations in calcium metabolism which provide cyclical events useful in determining age. The two concepts clearly carry the possibility of self contradiction—an attempt to use a degenerating timepiece to measure time. It is as well to remember, therefore, that what one is attempting to do is provide some theoretical basis for an operational exercise which is already in common use.

With this in mind an attempt will be made to review the information available to answer 6 main questions.

(1)   What is the state of the body fluids of fish as indicated by the calcium content of the blood?
(2)   Which membranes of fish transport calcium and how is it controlled?
(3)   Which organs are involved in the storage and recycling of minerals?
(4)   How is the calcium metabolism of the fish regulated?
(5)   Is the calcium metabolism of fish an open or closed system?
(6)   How are these phenomena related to ageing problems?

(1)   THE CALCIUM CONTENT OF THE BLOOD

Comparisons of the ionic composition of the plasma and the external medium enable one to distinguish which ions are being regulated and maintained in an animal in non-equilibrium conditions. It will be apparent from Table 1, which summarizes these data, that there are no fish which show a simple equilibrium situation between environmental and plasma calcium levels. Marine cyclostomes such as the hagfish appear to be roughly isotonic with sea water but their calcium level is only half that of the sea. Similar calcium levels are found in the cartilaginous Chondrichthyes although the total ion situation there is complicated as regards isotonicity by the ability of these fish to retain urea. The osteichthyes which typically have mineralized skeletons are characterized by having total ion concentrations greatly below those of sea water and above those of fresh water. Most

Table 1. Concentrations of calcium and total ions in the plasma of various groups of fish [data from Pickford and Grant (1967); Robertson (1954); Urist and Van de Putte (1967) and Urist, Uyeno, King, Okada and Applegate (1972)].

	Plasma calcium (m. mol/l.)	Total ions (m. mol/l.)
Agnatha		
Order Cyclostomata		
Petromyzon tridentata (lamprey)	2.8 ± 0.3	186 ± 41
Polistotrema stoutii (hagfish)	5.4 ± 0.1	1026 ± 55
Chondrichthyes		
Subclass Elasmobranchii		
Heterodontus francisa (horn shark)	5.0 ± 0.2	490 ± 20
Carcharhinus leucas (bull shark)	4.5 ± 0.5	483
Subclass Holocephali		
Hydrolagus colliei (ratfish)	4.8 ± 0.3	558 ± 15
Osteichthyes		
Subclass Actinopterygii		
Chondrostei		
Acipenser transmontanus (sturgeon)	1.8 ± 0.4	256
Polypterus weeksi (bichir)	2.3 ± 0.1	201
Polyodon spathula	2.2 ± 0.1	250
Holostei		
Lepisosteus platystomus (gar pike)	2.6 ± 0.2	318
Amia calva (bowfin)	2.9 ± 0.2	275
Teleostei		
Oncorhynchus tschawytscha (Pacific salmon)	2.9 ± 0.2	281 ± 26
Coregonus clupeoides	2.7	275
Megalops atlantica	2.5 ± 0.1	267 ± 35
Paralabrax clathratus	3.2 ± 0.	353 ± 24
Subclass Choanichthyes		
Coelacanthini		
Latimeria chalumnae (coelacanth)	3.4	*c.*454
Dipnoi		
Neoceratodus forsteri (Australian lungfish)	1.6	—
Protopterus annectens (African lungfish)	1.8 ± 0.2	210
Lepidosiren paradoxa (S. American lungfish)	2.0 ± 0.3	224
SEA WATER (PACIFIC)	10.0 ± 0.1	1168 ± 60
'FRESH WATER' (LAKE HURON)	0.9 ± 0.1	5 ± 2

marine forms are in the range of 300-350 m. mol/l. of total ions while fresh water species are mainly in the range of 250-275 m. mol/l. Corresponding calcium levels are 2.5-3.5 m. mol/l. for marine Actinopterygians with slightly lower levels for fresh water species. The calcium levels of the sturgeon *A. transmontanus* (1.8 m. mol/l.) are among the lowest of any known vertebrate and the Dipnoi also show surprisingly hypocalcaemic plasma when compared with higher vertebrates. The inter-relationships between plasma levels of calcium, phosphate and total ionic strength are complex especially when attempts are made to correlate them with the saturation levels of secondary calcium phosphate or with the solubility products of bone mineral (Burton, 1973).

It is clear from Table 1 that the variations between individual analyses of specific fish are small and it appears therefore that all fish regulate their plasma calcium levels within narrow limits.

There is a major rider to this, however, which arises from the fact that the plasma calcium of all vertebrates consists of two fractions variously determined as diffusible (or free) and non-diffusible (or protein-bound) calcium. It is the free or more specifically the ionic calcium which is physiologically active in most situations and this normally accounts for about half the plasma calcium content. In reproducing verte-

brates which have bony skeletons and lay yolky eggs there is an additional phenomenon. The yolk proteins are synthesized in the female by the liver and transported to the ovary as calcium complexes in the plasma. Thus female osteichthyes frequently show very elevated plasma calcium levels during the breeding season (Urist and Schjeide, 1961). The phenomenon is, however, almost entirely due to the increase in protein-bound calcium and ionic calcium levels remain normal during this process.

(2) MEMBRANES TRANSPORTING CALCIUM AND THEIR CONTROL

The intestine and kidney are the main organs involved in absorbing and excreting calcium ions in most vertebrates. In fish large ion movements also occur across the gills and the skin in general has also been considered to be involved in calcium ion movements. Each of these organs will therefore be considered.

(a) Intestine

In all the tetrapod vertebrates the intestine is the sole avenue for calcium uptake and the source of this calcium is usually the food. Apparently, however, neither of these conditions necessarily applies to fish.

The situation is perhaps most easily understood by considering first the sparse data available for fresh-water fish. In a neatly argued set of experiments Berg (1968) used [85]Sr as a tracer added to either the food or water of non-growing goldfish *Carassius auratus*. Using various Ca/Sr ratios of supplied material he was able to deduce a number of equations.

Two of these are given below.

$$CDE_{Sr} = \frac{ERW_{Sr}}{ERW_{Sr} + ERF_{Sr}} \qquad (1)$$

where CDE_{Sr} = contribution of direct exchange (from water) of strontium

ERW_{Sr} = exchange rate of stable strontium from water

$$= \frac{cpm\ ^{85}Sr/g\ fish}{sp.\ activity\ Sr\ in\ water \times days}$$

ERF_{Sr} = exchange rate of stable strontium from food

$$= \frac{cpm\ ^{85}Sr/g\ fish}{sp.\ activity\ Sr\ in\ food \times days}.$$

These quantities can be converted into calcium exchanges if the Sr/Ca discrimination factors can be determined (or mathematically eliminated)

i.e. $$ERW_{Ca} = \frac{1}{D.F._w} \times \frac{cpm\ ^{85}Sr/g\ fish}{(cpm\ ^{85}Sr/\mu g\ Sr)\ days}$$

where $D.F._w$ = discrimination factor against strontium

$$= \frac{Sr/Ca\ exchanged\ from\ water\ to\ fish}{Sr/Ca\ in\ water}$$

Sr/Ca discrimination by the intestine appears to be much greater than across the general body surface (page 5).

Using equations of this type in situations where varying levels of calcium were provided from the water and food Berg was able to produce a number of graphs, one of which is shown in Fig. 1. Thus under natural water conditions of 0.5 m.mol Ca/l (as in Lake Maggiore) and with dietary sources of about 100 m.mol Ca/Kg food (as in plankton) the goldfish obtains only about 20% of its total calcium requirements from the food. If the calcium content of the water is lowered to 0.1 m.mol/l the fish still only obtains 35% of its calcium uptake from its food.

It is apparent therefore that although the intestine can absorb calcium ions only small quantities are normally obtained from the food in freshwater animals. Marine fish differ however in two ways. First they drink considerable amounts of water whereas freshwater fish are generally thought to drink only occasionally or not at all. Second, the calcium content of sea water is enormously higher than fresh water since it is about 9 m.mol/l.

Homer Smith (1930) first demonstrated that marine teleosts swallowed considerable quantities of sea water by keeping them in water containing phenol red. The dye was found in a concentrated form in the lumen of the intestine indicating that sea water had been swallowed and that most of the salts and water had

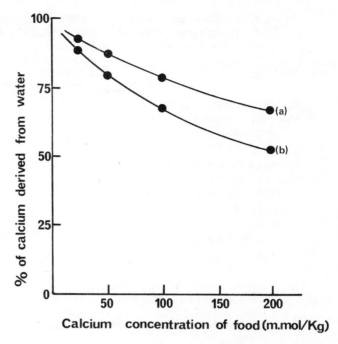

Fig. 1. Percentage of the total calcium exchange that is derived from the water at different concentrations of dietary calcium. Curve (a) is for natural lake water at a calcium concentration of about 0.5 m.mol/l. Curve (b) represents water at 0.1 m.mol/l. (Data from Berg, 1968).

been absorbed. He noted that as the fluid passed along the intestine there was a fall in the concentration of monovalent ions and a rise in the divalent ions, especially magnesium and sulphate.

It is now recognized that most marine teleosts drink sea water at a rate of between 0.2 and 2.0% body weight/h. The rate of drinking, at least in the rainbow trout *Salmo gairdneri* appears to be related to the salinity of the water and Shehadeh and Gordon (1969) found that whereas freshwater forms did not drink, those maintained in 50% sea water drank 95 ml/kg. fish/d. and full marine forms 129 ml/kg fish/d. This is in keeping with the accepted interpretation that sea water is drunk as part of the osmoregulatory process of marine fish.

The fluids in the intestines of rainbow trout and southern flounders *Paralichthys lethostigma* have been analysed in detail and Table 2 shows the relevant data for calcium. The quantity of calcium absorbed can be deduced if measurements of drinking rate, fluid absorption and excretion rates are available. By accepting a number of approximations it is possible to calculate these values as shown in Table 3.

In the case of the rainbow trout it was also shown that the intestine normally produces a mucus tube which envelopes the faeces. This tube may contain large quantities of calcium carbonate apparently derived directly from calcium in the sea water. In starved specimens this accounted for about 64% of the ingested load of calcium.

It is apparent therefore that considerable quantities of calcium may be absorbed by the intestine of marine fish from swallowed sea water. Additional quantities are presumably also available from the food. These results are rather surprising since the intestine of marine fish has usually been considered, since H. Smith's (1930) work, to be relatively impermeable to

3

Table 2. Calcium concentrations of sea water, intestinal fluid and urine. (Data from Shehadeh and Gordon, 1969; Hickman, 1968; and Smith, 1930).

Medium	Calcium concentration (m. mol/l.)			
	Sea water	Ant. intestine	Rectal fluid	Urine
Rainbow trout (*Salmo gairdneri*)				
50% sea water	5	4.0	2.0	4.0
100% sea water	9	5.0	2.0	4.0
Southern flounder (*Paralichthys lethostigma*)				
100% sea water	10	—	12.1	18.6
Angler fish (*Lophius*)				—
100% sea water	6.9	20.6	21.5	7.2

Table 3. Fate of ingested calcium (μ mol/h) in marine fish. (Data partly recalculated from Shehadeh and Gordon (1969) and Hickman (1968).)

	Rainbow trout (*S. gairdneri*)	Southern flounder (*P. lethostigma*)
Swallowed	12.5	42.6
Absorbed	4.5 (35%)	29.2 (68%)
Rectal excretion	0.5 (5%)	13.4 (32%)
+ mucus tube	7.5 (60%)	—
Renal excretion	—	3.3 (11%)

divalent ions. The work of Hickman (1968) shows however that the intestine absorbs calcium at about 5 times the rate of magnesium or sulphate ions.

Calcium may also be re-secreted into the intestine. This so-called endogenous intestinal calcium is known to occur in a number of vertebrates and is at least partly attributable to the calcium present in some of the digestive juices. In the crucian carp *Carassius carassius* Mashiko and Jozuka (1964) found that ^{45}Ca injected into the dorsal musculature appeared in increasing quantities in the intestinal contents during the next 2-6 hours. Such a calcium 'excretion' across the intestinal epithelium may be a continuous process in natural conditions.

From the experiments quoted it will be clear that freshwater fish appear to be relatively independent of dietary sources of calcium. Values of from 2 to 10% are commonly quoted for the dietary contribution to total calcium metabolism (Simmonds, 1971). Nutri-

tional experiments in which trout have been raised for 12 weeks on calcium deficient diets of beef liver confirm this (Table 4). The situation in marine fish is more difficult to assess since relatively fewer experiments have been performed upon them. The experiments of Boroughs, Townsley and Hiatt (1957) and Reid, Townsley and Ego (1959) using sea water adapted *Tilapia* showed that these fish absorbed almost no calcium through the intestines and animals with a blocked or ligatured oesophagus could still absorb calcium from the environment at similar rates to starved control fish (Reid, Ego and Townsley, 1959). Unfortunately the experiments upon which these conclusions have been based are only sparsely reported and they have to be judged against the balance data of Hickman (1968) which involves a large number of estimates. It appears highly likely however that marine fish also absorb relatively little calcium from ingested food and water.

(b) Kidney

The evolution of the fish kidney is characterized by its role in the clearance of free water and by the excretion of bivalent ions. As might be imagined there are major differences in these functions between marine and freshwater forms.

In marine cyclostomes magnesium and sulphate ions are secreted into the tubular fluids but calcium is resorbed and the liver apparently also functions as a major excretory pathway for calcium and magnesium ions via the gall bladder. In marine elasmobranchs calcium is reabsorbed by the kidney although other divalent ions are secreted into the lumen and the rectal gland, of course, acts as a major excretory organ for sodium and chloride ions.

In teleosts the excretion of magnesium and sulphate ions is the dominant activity of the kidney although

Table 4. Calcium absorption from the food of trout kept for 12 weeks on a beef liver diet (data from McCay, Tunison, Crowell and Paul, 1936).

Wt. of fish at start	Gain in wt. during 12 weeks	Calcium content 25 fish		Calcium fed/fish	Non-dietary calcium
		Start	End		
3.65 g	0.85 g	352 mg	502 mg	27 mg (18%)	123 mg (82%)

calcium may also be concentrated in the urine especially in marine species. Freshwater fish have a typically high rate of urine production. The fluid is nearly free of sodium and chloride ions and calcium is strongly resorbed from the urine against concentration gradients (Hickman and Trump, 1969).

Some typical urine and plasma analyses of calcium are shown in Table 5. The urine/plasma ratios indicate the basic differences between freshwater and marine teleosts but it is obviously necessary to know volume and time relationships as well as concentrations if one is to make overall assessments on the renal handling of calcium. There are some data on inulin clearances and urine flow rates (Hickman and Trump, 1969) but the only attempt at a calcium balance is Hickman's (1968) study of the southern flounder *Paralichthys lethostigma*. This analysis produced the rather surprising result that the kidney was responsible for excreting only 11.4% of the absorbed calcium.

Table 5. Plasma calcium and urine analyses for a variety of fish. Concentration in m.mol/l. (Data from many sources summarized by Hickman and Trump (1969)).

	Plasma Ca	Urine Ca	U/P
Cyclostomes			
Eptatretus stoutii (hagfish)	4.5	3.6	0.8
Elasmobranchs			
Squalus acanthias (dogfish)	3.5	3.0	0.86
Marine teleosts			
Paralichthys lethostigma (Southern flounder)	2.73	19.3	7.07
Lophius americanus (goosefish)	3.2	7.2	2.25
Freshwater teleosts			
Fundulus kansae	2.65	1.48	0.56
Anguilla anguilla	2.37	0.63	0.27
Salmo gairdneri	2.65	0.65	0.24
Salvelinus namaycush	2.05	0.95	0.46
Esox lucius	2.55	0.14	0.05
Channa argus	3.06	0.79	0.26

*euryhaline forms adapted to fresh water.

The evidence is sparse but tends to suggest that renal losses of calcium are normally small and the kidney is not a major organ in regulating calcium metabolism.

(c) Uptake by the general body surface and gills

In recent years an enormous number of studies have been performed which show that calcium (and strontium) can be absorbed by fish from the water in which they live (Boroughs, Townsley and Hiatt, 1956, 1957; Mashiko and Jozuka, 1962; Ophel and Judd, 1967; Podoliak and Holden, 1965; Rosenthal, 1956, 1957, 1960). Typically such experiments use radio-isotopes which are added to the water containing the fish. When the results are expressed in the logarithmic form of a concentration factor

i.e. $\dfrac{\log \text{counts/min./100 mg tissue/day}}{\log \text{counts/min./ml water}}$

most freshwater fish show an accumulation which is linear with time (Simmons, 1971). Similar results for ^{45}Ca and ^{90}Sr indicate that there is virtually no discrimination in the relative uptake of these ions in these fish (Rosenthal, 1963) provided that sodium ion concentrations do not fall too low (Rosenthal, 1960).

Unfortunately there have been relatively few attempts to extend these studies by either determining ion fluxes or by attempting to identify specific sites of ion uptake. A few attempts have been made to keep fish in compartmentalized tanks or to attach small bags to various regions and these experiments will be referred to later. Most investigators have assumed that calcium uptake must be due to the gills since these are well known sites of ion uptake and exchange in both marine and freshwater teleosts. The only direct study is, however, Schiffman's (1961) experiment on the perfused gills of the rainbow trout *Salmo gairdneri*. The isotope ^{85}Sr was used, since it can be continuously monitored during an experiment, but since the Sr/Ca discrimination factor seems to be close to unity the results are probably indicative of normal calcium movements. The results indicate that during perfusion the outflux rate is about 30 times greater than the influx and can be maintained against concentration gradients. It is difficult to assess the full significance of this result since it has not been repeated independently and other workers have variously interpreted it as indicating the importance of the gills in excreting calcium from the plasma or in taking calcium up from water. Taken at its face value it demonstrates a clear excretion of calcium and it would be of interest to know if this excretion is under any form of control.

(d) Skin

The evidence for the movement of calcium across part or all of the integument of fish is largely circumstantial. If fish are kept in a compartmentalized tank so that the anterior and posterior halves are in separate solutions then the fish can still accumulate calcium from the posterior half. Thus it is clear that calcium uptake is not restricted to the mouth and gill region and Reid, Townsley and Ego (1959) concluded from experiments of this sort on *Tilapia* that ^{45}Ca could be taken up uniformly by the body surface.

At variance with these results are those of Mashiko and Jozuka (1964) who consider that there are specialized regions for the cutaneous uptake of calcium. Their argument is based on 3 facts. (i) Fish treated with ^{45}Ca by adding it to the water in which they are swimming show the same distribution of isotope around the body as fish injected with ^{45}Ca into the body. (ii) Autoradiographic studies of scales indicated that the ^{45}Ca accumulated by the scale had not penetrated directly through the skin but had been carried to it via the bloodstream. (iii) Enclosing the caudal fin within a rubber sac containing ^{45}Ca resulted in a large uptake of isotope. On the basis of (i) and (ii) they considered that there was no special significance to the amount of ^{45}Ca accumulated at particular sites, i.e. these sites were not necessarily involved in active uptake. Instead they consider on the basis of experiments similar to (iii) that the fins and gills are major sites for the uptake of calcium and that this ion penetrates only sparsely through most of the skin of the fish. Using similar techniques but with radioactive animals and normal water the same authors concluded that these surfaces were probably also involved in the excretion of calcium from the animal.

(3) MINERAL STORES

(a) Skeletons and bones

In most vertebrates the skeleton represents a massive reservoir of calcium, phosphate and other ions which are in a state of continual interchange with the electrolytes of the blood and extracellular fluids. Three processes are recognized in this phenomenon namely (i) accretion, or the deposition of new bone by osteoblast cells; (ii) resorption, or the removal of bone by osteoclast cells; and (iii) exchange, or the equal and opposite movements of ions from the body fluids onto and away from crystal surfaces. The phenomenon of exchange is thus not dependent upon any particular cell type. The characteristic osteocyte cells which normally occur throughout the substance of normal bone are thought to be involved in the 'maintenance' of the bone substance although recent evidence has suggested they may also be capable of resorbing minerals by the somewhat poorly understood process of osteolysis. The skeleton of most vertebrates is thus able to exert a massive buffering effect upon changes in plasma electrolyte values.

Among the fish a variety of very different skeletal systems perform some of these functions. In the elasmobranchs the skeleton consists of calcified cartilage. Growth occurs by a one-way process of deposition and there is no internal remodelling or resorption of this store of mineral. Experiments with ^{45}Ca have shown the remarkable fact that virtually all the calcium in this skeleton is exchangeable. This suggests that a relatively simple equilibrium must exist between the blood and most of the apatite mineral of the skeleton (Urist, 1961). Such a system is in stark contrast to the bones of other vertebrates where, for example, only about 2% of the skeleton may be available for exchange.

The skeletal tissue of the higher orders of teleost fish is very variable but it is unique among vertebrates in that it lacks osteocyte cells. This so-called acellular bone is formed from osteoblast cells which move away from the site of mineralization as bone deposition occurs. Only a few families of the lower orders of Clupeiformes and Scopeliformes remain with the primitive form of cellular bone (Moss, 1961 a, b).

It is by no means clear why most of the modern fish should have abandoned the ancestral and more normal cellular bone. A comparison of the two types of bone was undertaken by Moss (1962) who studied the repair of fractures in the goldfish *Carassius auratus* which has cellular bone and the cichlid *Tilapia macrocephala* which has acellular bone. The fish were variously fed on a normal diet, a calcium deficient diet or starved in an attempt to see if this influenced bone repair. Some were maintained in normal water and some in calcium-free water. The results are shown in Table 6 and from these Moss concluded that cellular bone could maintain a greater calcium homeostasis as measured by the ability to form bone callus material. He considered that acellular bone was conceptually 'dead bone' in that it could not be resorbed or made available to the other organs of the fish. This conclusion is not completely convincing since it is largely dependent upon the interpretation of the complexities of bone healing. Furthermore Norris, Chavin and Lombard (1963) in their study of the Nassau grouper *Epinephelus striatus* found considerable evidence for bone resorption and remodelling even though no osteoclasts or osteocytes could be identified in the acellular bone of this fish. Perhaps the most rigorous investigation into the physiology of acellular bone is, however, the study of Simmons, Simmons and Marshall (1970) on the toadfish *Opsanus tau*. Specimens were injected with ^{45}Ca and tetracycline and investigated by microradiography and autoradiography. The results revealed first, that most of the radiocalcium was retained at sites of bone growth and that the calcium at these new bone surfaces appeared to be unavailable for exchange with blood calcium. Second, there appeared to be no detectable diffuse exchange of radioisotope into the deeper parts of the skeleton such as is found in normal bone. A similar phenomenon had been noted by Hevesy (1945) using radiophosphorus on sticklebacks *Gasterosteus aculeatus*. His calculations indicated that only 3-5% of the skeleton could be replaced over a period of several weeks and if one allowed for the possibility of growth during the experiment the value fell to almost zero.

Table 6. Repair of fractures in fish bone under normal and calcium deficient conditions (from Fleming (1967), after Moss (1962)).

Treatment		C. auratus (cellular bone)	T. macrocephala (acellular bone)
Normal water	Normal diet	+	+
	Acalcemic diet	+	+
	Starvation	−	−
Acalcemic water	Normal diet	+	−
	Acalcemic	+	−
	Starvation	−	−

Given this metabolic inactivity of acellular bone it is difficult to appreciate the influences of its widespread occurrence. Two suggestions have been made. Moss (1962) suggests that there is an energetic saving by the loss of osteocytes but no estimates have been made of the extent of this saving. A second comment by Norris, Chavin and Lombard (1963) suggests that since minerals are rapidly deposited in bone with little recycling then fish must have limited and carefully controlled mechanisms for absorbing calcium and phosphate ions.

(b) Scales

In most fishes much of the connective tissue of the dermis is replaced by a series of scales forming the dermal skeleton. The cosmoid scale was present in primitive crossopterygians and lungfish but has been lost from all living forms. The ganoid scale was found in the older actinopterygians and is sometimes considered to persist in a modified form in some primitive Chondrostei. Among modern fish there are three main types of scale. The placoid is mainly restricted to the Chondrichthyes whilst cycloid and ctenoid scales are found in most teleosts. Details of the structure and distribution of these scales are given by van Oosten (1957) and the rest of this discussion will be restricted to the scales of teleosts.

Cycloid and ctenoid scales are distinguished primarily on the basis of their surface sculpture and their origin and development are fundamentally very similar. It is generally accepted that these scales consist of two layers, a more superficial mineralized 'bony' or 'hyalodentine' layer which is deposited over a deeper fibrous sheet variously described as the 'lamellar' or 'fibrillar plate'. The scales are formed in dermal papillae derived by the mitotic division of fibroblasts. The scale originates in this region as a secretion between two layers of investing cells which are variously described as osteoblasts or scleroblasts and which lead to the deposition and mineralization of the bony or hyalodentine layer. Subsequently the fibrillar plate appears as a thin sheet between the bony scale and the inner osteoblastic layer. Descriptions of this process are confused as are subsequent accounts of the growth of the scale in difference species. It is usually accepted that the hyalodentine layer only grows at its edge so that the scale shows little increase in thickness but deposits rings of mineral allowing age determinations to be made from these structures. The fibrous plate however deposits continuous sheets beneath the scale so that this region is thinner at the outer margins and thicker at the centre. This fibrillar plate is described as being largely uncalcified and without vascular canals.

Undoubtedly there are many variations in the details of these processes in different species and it has been suggested that in some fish, such as the goldfish, the region of new calcification is not restricted to the periphery of the scale but may occur throughout the entire scale between the bony and fibrillar layers (Hiyama and Ichikawa, 1952). Of much greater importance, however, is the possibility that the mineralization process can be reversed. This was originally described in detail by Crichton (1935) in what is sometimes referred to as the 'Crichton effect'. The phenomenon has been best studied in salmon and sea trout during their spawning migrations. Scales are resorbed when the fish stops feeding in the deeper sea waters and the process continues until feeding resumes when the fish returns to the sea after spawning. If the fish is held up at the river mouth before spawning, resorption may be very pronounced before the actual ascent of the river occurs. Conversely if a salmon or sea trout enters the river late in the season and spawns almost immediately there may be little trace of any resorption process. On return to the sea and resumption of feeding fresh scale material is added filling up the absorbed regions and new growth ridges are laid down forming the basis of the spawning mark.

During resorption it is the hyalodentine layer which is mainly affected. It is not possible to distinguish any special cells associated with the resorption process and Crichton concluded that the cells involved 'appear to be identical with those that cause normally the growth of the scale'. Further investigations of this problem have raised the question as to whether 'osteoclast' cells can be identified in these scales (van Someren, 1937) but the question is to some extent academic in view of the general problem of identifying mineral resorbing cells in fish bone. Of greater importance is the possibility that scale resorption may occur in many fish but is most conspicuous in salmon and sea trout because of their particular life cycles. Thus goldfish (Yamada, 1956) and carp (Ichikawa, 1953) also resorb scales if starved and Wallin (1957) was able to induce scale resorption in roach *Rutilus rutilus* if the fish were kept on rachitogenic diets. Resorption started at the anterolateral corners and spread to the cranial edge characteristically attacking the exposed region. The phenomenon also occurs in wild populations of roach especially in mid summer.

The implications of the possibility of scale resorption are obviously great both for understanding the calcium metabolism of fish and for the use of scales in age dating. Scales represent a massive deposit of calcium and Simkiss and Yarker (unpublished) found that the skin contained about 40% of the total calcium in the trout. Injections of ^{45}Ca resulted in about 50% of the injected dose being retained in the skin after even 1 week. Similar results were obtained by Podoliak and Holden (1965) and indicate that the scales are well supplied by the blood system. The radioactivity associated with different scales along the length of the fish body is remarkably constant regardless of position (Simkiss and Thompson, unpublished) and the isotope appears to be firmly attached, although Mashiko, Jozuka and Morita (1964) found that it was slowly released from scales of the crucian carp if the fish were kept in water of over 60 ppm or alternatively injected with $CaCl_2$ solutions.

A number of suggestions have been made that scales might be resorbed to provide a source of calcium during periods of deficiency. Perhaps the best documented of these is the data of Garrod and Newell (1958) which showed a fall in the calcium content of the scales associated with the development of the ovary (Table 7). The implication is clearly that the scales can be partly demineralized to provide calcium for the formation of oocytes.

(c) Otoliths

The otoliths found in the labyrinths of fish ears are very variable structures. In the living cyclostomes the otoliths are the only mineralized structures found in the whole animal. X-ray diffraction of the deposits found in *Lampreta fluviatilis* shows that they are non-crystalline but on heating them to 700°C they give an apatite pattern similar to bone. In

Table 7. Changes in calcium content
(% dry weight) of scales of
Tilapia esculenta in relation
to egg production (from
Garrod and Newell, 1958).

	Ca content scales
Immature	22.5
Ripening	24.2
Mature	19.0
Spent, brooding	18.7
Spent, quiet	19.0
Spent, starting	24.0

Myxine glutinosa the otoliths are crystalline and again composed of apatite. In this characteristic the Agnatha are unique for all other vertebrates have otoliths composed of calcium carbonate.

In elasmobranchs the otoliths are composed of the aragonite form of calcium carbonate. Among the Actinopterygii the Chondrostei have otoliths of pure vaterite, the least stable form of calcium carbonate. The Holostei have otoliths composed of a mixture of vaterite and aragonite whilst teleosts have a pure crystalline form of aragonite as do the coelacanth *Latimeria chalumnae* and the Dipnoi fish. These findings are to some extent surprising since the birds and mammals have calcite otoliths and these represent the most stable of the three polymorphic forms of calcium carbonate (Carlstrom, 1963).

The otoliths are deposited from the endolymphatic fluid of the labyrinth. The ionic composition of this fluid and the membrane potentials across its walls have been investigated by Enger (1964). Little is known, however, of the physiology of otolith formation. The deposition of daily and annual layers has however been investigated in some detail by Pannella (1971). The occurrence of annual rings appears to be associated with the secretion of protein material into the endolymphatic fluid (Mugiya, 1964).

There is no evidence for any resorption of otoliths although other calcareous deposits in the endolymphatic fluid may be resorbed in other vertebrates (Simkiss, 1967).

(4) CONTROL OF CALCIUM METABOLISM

The calcium metabolism of higher vertebrates is dominated by the influences of three substances, parathyroid hormone, calcitonin and vitamin D. Other endocrine systems may influence calcium metabolism but rarely in the direct way that these do. Parathyroid hormone is released when plasma calcium levels fall and it has two main target organs. It induces bone resorption thereby raising plasma levels of calcium and phosphate ions. It also affects the kidney by increasing phosphate excretion and reducing calcium loss. The overall effect is to raise blood calcium levels. Calcitonin is secreted by the cells of the ultimobranchial tissue when plasma calcium levels are high. Its main effect is to depress bone resorption and perhaps increase bone deposition so that the concentration of blood calcium falls. These two hormones, one responding to hypocalcaemia and one to

hypercalcaemia control blood calcium levels at a constant level largely by their influence on the stores of bone mineral in the higher vertebrates.

There is currently considerable interest in whether vitamin D should be considered as a steroid hormone. Its main influences in mammals are upon the intestine and the skeleton and characteristically its action in the healthy animal is to control the rate of calcium absorption from the intestine.

The information on the role of these three compounds in fish is complicated. No parathyroid tissue or glands have ever been identified in any fish and phylogenetically the amphibians are the first animals to possess these endocrine glands. Numerous attempts have been made to demonstrate a response in a fish to injections of mammalian parathyroid hormone but almost without exception this has produced no effect on plasma calcium levels (Moss, 1963; Urist, 1964; Fleming, Stanley and Meier, 1964; Urist, Uyeno, King, Okado and Applegate, 1972).

The presence of ultimobranchial glands in fish has been known for almost a century but they have become of great interest in the past decade since D. H. Copp demonstrated that they were the source of the hormone calcitonin. The structure of the glands and the evidence that they produce a calcium lowering hormone in elasmobranchs and teleosts has been reviewed by Copp, Brooks, Low, Newsome, O'Dor Parkes, Walker and Watts (1970). The cyclostomes do not appear to possess ultimobranchial glands.

Although elasmobranchs, teleosts and all the higher vertebrates produce calcitonin they often show very limited responses to the hormone. The first evidence that the glands were active in fish came from Rasquin and Rosenbloom (1954) who observed that the ultimobranchials of Mexican cave fish *Astyanax mexicanus* became hypertrophied when they were kept for long periods in complete darkness. Associated with this were skeletal deformities and demineralization of the bones. This is evidence for an upset in calcium metabolism but, as Rasquin and Rosenblock pointed out, it was more like a parathyroid response. At the present time the evidence concerning the responses of fish to calcitonin injections are inconsistent. Calcium lowering responses have been claimed by Chan, Chester Jones and Smith (1968) using mammal hormone injected into the eel *Anguilla anguilla* but Pang and Pickford (1967) using a similar preparation failed to obtain any hypocalcaemic response in the killifish *Fundulus heteroclitus*. Injections into the catfish *Ictaberus melas* produced hypocalcaemia but with an attendant hypophosphaturia (Louw, Sutton and Kenny, 1967). Neither salmon nor mammalian calcitonin produced any effect upon plasma calcium levels in the lungfish *Lepidosiren paradoxa* (Urist, Uyeno, King, Okado and Applegate, 1972). The hormone has been detected, by a bioassay, in the plasma of a number of fish. The circulating levels are very high but in the bowfin *Amia* there is evidence for a further large rise following calcium gluconate injections (Dacke, Fleming and Kenny, 1971).

In the elasmobranchs the situation is similarly confused. According to Copp *et al.* (1970) injections of salmon calcitonin into the shark *Squalus suckleyi* produced no response although Urist, Applegate, Wagner and Southwick (1970) found that shark calcitonon raised the serum calcium level in *Pronace glauca* from from 3.4 to 5.4 m. mol/l. This is the reverse of the result expected and it should be remembered of course that these fish have no bony skeletons.

The situation with vitamin D is also complex. The liver of cyclostomes and elasmobranchs contains little if any vitamin D and oral or intramuscular administration has no effect upon plasma calcium levels (Urist, 1964). The liver of teleosts is, however, a rich source of vitamin D especially in marine forms. Balance experiments and metabolic studies have shown that at least part of the vitamin found in the cod comes from non-dietary sources and is synthesized by the fish (Blondin, Kulkarni and Nes, 1967). Its exact function however is not known and fish show little response to its administration (Moss, 1963; Urist *et al.,* 1972).

If one attempts to simplify this difficult situation it appears that fish are deficient in parathyroid glands and this is at least partly in keeping with the low level of bone recycling found in these animals. Ultimobranchial glands are present and release a hormone, calcitonin, which has a potent calcium lowering influence upon the plasma calcium levels of rats by influencing their skeletal system. It is not, however, clear what its exact function is in fish although a control over bone formation rates would be the expected response. Other target organs should obviously not be ruled out, however, especially if it can be shown that 'calcium removal' is the main basis of calcium control in the fish. Vitamin D is present in the teleosts but its physiological effects are not clear. Its distribution, however, shows a rough correlation with the importance of the intestine in calcium absorption. A number of other endocrine systems have also been implicated in the calcium metabolism of fish. These include the pituitary, adrenals, thyroid and Corpuscles of Stannius. The interesting results of the experiments on these organs have been reviewed by Fleming (1967) and Simmons (1971).

Despite the fact that fish show poor responses to the substances that control calcium metabolism in the higher vertebrates it is clear from Table 1 that fish do control the calcium level of their body fluids and maintain them reasonably constant. A number of experiments have been undertaken keeping fish in abnormally high or low calcium environments. Under these situations plasma calcium levels do rise or fall significantly but only slowly and it is clear that the animals are exerting a lot of control over their body composition (Fleming, Stanley and Meier, 1964, on *Fundulus kansae*; Montskó, Tigyi, Lissak and Duraczky, 1964, on *Cyprinus carpio*; Urist, 1963, on cyclostomes; Urist *et al.*, 1972, on Dipnoi). In the case of the lamprey this occurs in an animal with a non-functional gut, without a calcified skeleton and in the absence of parathyroid or ultimobranchial tissue. In the Dipnoi bone remodelling is absent and the gill membranes are also not functional. It is generally assumed that calcium homeostasis is maintained by ion regulation across membranes but the properties or localities of these membranes are obviously still not clear and it is therefore not surprising that the mechanisms of control are so poorly understood.

(5) OPEN AND CLOSED SYSTEMS OF CALCIUM METABOLISM

It will be apparent from the information in sections 2, 3 and 4 that the calcium metabolism of fish is characterized by very different properties from those of other vertebrates. A number of schemes have been proposed to encompass these peculiarities but Urist's discussions are perhaps the clearest. He

suggests that the cyclostomes which have no mineralized endoskeleton regulate their plasma calcium levels by controlling the uptake and loss of ions across the membranes of the gills, intestine, skin and kidney (Urist, 1963). The animal is therefore considered to be part of an 'open system' with calcium ions continually passing in and out of it from the surrounding water. The living elasmobranchs demonstrate what is variously interpreted as being a degenerate or primitive system of storing minerals in the calcified cartilage of the endoskeleton. These mineral stores are available to the animal but there appears to be no controlled mechanism for resorbing or recycling these ions. This important aspect of the 'closed system' is not seen until one studies the osteichthyes (Urist, 1964). The marine teleosts tend to have acellular bone which is very poorly remodelled but Urist relates the invasion of fresh water to the evolution of cellular bone which is capable of resorption and accretion. 'In fresh water streams and rivers bone tissue is absolutely essential for the instaneous turnover and regulation of calcium, phosphate and other electrolytes found in the blood' (McLean and Urist, 1968).

This series of suggestions has led to the idea that during evolution the fish have passed from an open system (in which they continually absorbed and excreted calcium ions so as to maintain themselves in a dynamic steady state) to a closed system (in which the actual control of blood calcium levels was affected by skeletal remodelling). The two schemes are illustrated in Fig. 2 and have the advantage of great clarity. It should be realized, however, that this is

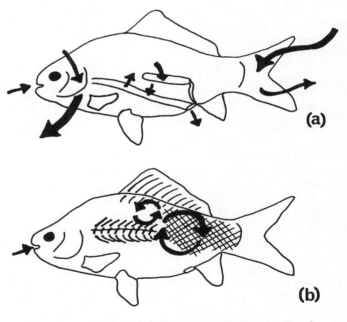

Fig. 2. (a) A fish considered as an 'open system'. Calcium mainly enters and leaves via the fins and gills. A small amount of calcium is absorbed via the intestine and the kidneys exert some control over calcium loss. In its most extreme form this concept considers that the surrounding water acts as an extension of the body fluids. (b) A fish considered as a 'closed system'. Calcium is stored in the scales and skeleton and continually recycled in and out of the structures so as to maintain a steady state in the animal. (a) and (b) represent extreme forms and most teleosts probably have both systems which are clearly not mutually exclusive.

very deceptive for the schemes conceal an enormous ignorance of supporting data. The major problems that remain to be resolved are

(a) which are the actual sites involved in ion movement?
(b) what are the control mechanisms regulating relative rates of uptake and loss?
(c) what are the quantitative values to be placed upon the various components of these systems?
(d) to what extent are environmental influences reflected in the two schemes—bearing in mind of course that the 'open and closed systems' are not mutually exclusive concepts.

(6) HOW ARE THESE PHENOMENA RELATED TO AGEING PROBLEMS?

Otoliths, scales and bones are all mineralized structures which show regular annual rings useful in detecting the age of fish. The suggestion that the calcium metabolism of fish may be interpreted as having some of the properties of 'open and closed systems' is a useful concept in this respect for it focuses attention upon several facts.

First, an open system implies a fairly direct interaction between environmental variables and fish metabolism. The main environmental variables that have been thought likely to influence the deposition of annual rings are temperature, salinity, food and light, but there are virtually no suggestions in the literature that availability of calcium is a limiting factor in forming growth rings.

Second, a closed system implies some feedback control whereby, for example, there is some interrelationship between the relative rates of calcium deposition and calcium resorption. One of the problems of calcium metabolism in fish is the complete ignorance of the control mechanisms. All feedback systems, have, however, a tendency to oscillate so that one might expect such a system to show alternating periods of activity and inactivity. Even among the homeostatic mammals teeth are known to grow in pulses of 3-4 days (Neville, 1967) and bone often shows weekly depositions (Sissons, 1949). It is not surprising therefore that the mineralized structures of fish also show rhythmic depositions. The periodicity of these depositions is likely, however, to be mainly a property of the responsiveness of the feedback system rather than an annual ring.

Third, it will be apparent that in both the open and closed systems the calcium metabolism of the fish is interrelated through a general calcium pool. Any organ making demands upon this pool is likely to influence the availability of calcium to other organs. This means first that oscillating feedback systems could interact to produce longer periodicities. It also implies that any single organ with intermittent demands could impose its primary rhythm upon other mineralized structures. This may explain why for example scales are better structures than otoliths or vice versa in determining the age of some fish. In order to elaborate upon this, however, one needs to know the relative metabolic activities of the different mineralized tissues. Some evidence of this type is available (Table 8) but it cannot be completely analysed in this way. To some extent related to the problem of relative calcium demand is the question of whether some mineralized tissues can be resorbed as well as deposited. The possibility that scales may be able to be demineralized is obviously of importance here when compared with for example the fact that there are no similar suggestions for otoliths.

The question of the relative calcium requirements of the different mineralized tissues is also of importance in considering the other aspect of ageing, namely the decline in physiological efficiency. The accumulation of ^{45}Ca in scales taken from carp of different ages declines with age (Mashiko and Jozuka, 1962) and the uptake of ^{45}Ca by guppies is greater in young than mature fish (Rosenthal, 1956). Do mineralizing tissues all age in similar ways?

Table 8. Hierarchies in the extent to which different tissues concentrate radio-isotopes in different fish. (From Simmons (1971) after Tomiyama *et al.* (1956)).

Limanda herzensteini	*Scomber japonicus*	*Sardinia melanosticta*
Fin	Gut	Scale
Scale	Fin	Fin
Gill	Gill	Gill
Gut	Vertebra	Viscera
Skin	Skin	Vertebra
Vertebra		Skin

Finally one should perhaps reconsider the basic postulate that problems in deriving age data from scales, otoliths and bones have any primary relationship with calcium metabolism. There are two reasons for doing this. First the whole relationship of body/scale growth is clearly an example of an allometric phenomenon. The growth of fish appears to be under the control of the pituitary gland and hypophysectomy stops growth while injections of growth hormone cause its resumption. The scale behaves in a similar way to the whole body, stopping and resuming the formation of rings as growth hormone is removed and replaced (Ball, 1969). In fact bioassays of growth hormone in perch have shown that there is a good correlation between hormone levels and scale and fish growth under normal conditions (Swift and Pickford, 1965). The secretion of growth hormone is influenced particularly by the presence of food and this seems also to be the greatest variable influencing scale growth (Bhatia, 1932). Is the reading of scales therefore really just a bioassay of fluctuating levels of growth hormone which itself simply reflects environmental variables? Secondly it is perhaps worth noting that annual rings are deposited in many apparently stable and inanimate systems such as submerged glass in the sea. The rings are again used to age the bottles although nothing is known of the influences which produce these dating systems (Brill, 1963).

REFERENCES

Ball, J. N. (1969). Prolactin (fish prolactin or paralactin) and growth hormones *in,* Hoar, W. S. and Randall, D. T. Fish Physiology. Acad. Press, London. **Vol. 2,** 207-240.

Berg, A. (1968). Studies on the metabolism of calcium and strontium in freshwater fish. I. Relative contribution of direct and intestinal absorption. Mem. Ist. ital. Idrobiol., 23, 161-96.

Bhatia, D. (1932). Factors involved in the production of annual zones on the scales of the rainbow trout (Salmo irideus). II. J. exp. Biol., 9, 6-14.

Blondin, G. A., Kulkarni, B. D. and Nes, W. R. (1967). A study of the origin of vitamin D from 7 dehydrocholesterol in fish. Comp. Biochem. Physiol., 20, 379-90.

Boroughs, H., Townsley, S. J. and Hiatt, R. W. (1956). The metabolism of radionuclides by marine organisms. I. The uptake accumulation and loss of strontium by fishes. Biol. Bull. mar. biol. Lab., Woods Hole, 111, 336-51.

Boroughs, H., Townsley, S. J. and Hiatt, R. W. (1957). The metabolism of radionuclides by marine organisms. III. Uptake of ^{45}Ca in solution by marine fish. Limnol. Oceanogr., 2, 28-32.

Brill, R. H. (1963). Ancient glass. Scient. Am., 209, (5), 120-130.

Burton, R. F. (1973). The significance of ionic regulation in the internal media of animals. Biol. Rev., 48, 195-231.

Carlstrom, D. (1963). A crystallographic study of vertebrate otoliths. Biol. Bull. mar. biol. Lab., Woods Hole., 125, 441-463.

Chan, D. K. O., Chester-Jones, I. and Smith, R. N. (1968). The effect of mammalian calcitonin on the plasma levels of calcium and inorganic phosphate in the European eel (Anguilla anguilla). Gen. comp. Endocr., 11, 243-245.

Copp, D. H., Brooks, C. E., Low, B. S., Newsome, F., O'Dor, R. K., Parkes, C. O., Walker, V. and Watts, E. G. (1970). Calcitonin and ultimobranchial function in lower vertebrates, in, Taylor, S. (ed.) Calcitonin 69. Heinemann, London. 281-294.

Crichton, M. I. (1935). Scale resorption in salmon and sea trout. Salm. Fish., Edinb. No. 4, 1-8.

Dacke, C. G., Fleming, W. R. and Kenny, A. D. (1971). Plasma calcitonin levels in fish. Physiologist, Washington, 14, (abstract).

Enger, P. S. (1964). Ionic composition of the cranial and labyrinthine fluids and saccular D. C. potentials in fish. Comp. Biochem. Physiol., 11, 131-137.

Fleming, W. R. (1967). Calcium metabolism in teleosts. Am Zool., 7, 835-42.

Fleming, W. R., Stanley, J. G. and Meier, A. H. (1964). Seasonal effects of external calcium, estradial and ACTH on the serum calcium and sodium levels of Fundulus kansae. Gen. comp. Endocr., 4, 61-67.

Garrod, D. and Newell, B. S. (1958). Ring formation in Tilapia esculentia. Nature, Lond., 181, 1411-1412

Hevesy, G. (1945). Rate of renewal of the fish skeleton. Acta physiol. scand., 9, 234-247.

Hickman, C. (1968). Ingestion, intestinal absorption and elimination of sea water and salts in the southern flounder (Paralichthys lethostigma). Can. J. Zool., 46, 457-466.

Hickman, C. and Trump, B. E. (1969). The kidney, in, Hoar, W. S. and Randall, D. J. (ed.) Fish Physiology. Acad. Press. London. Vol. 1, 91-239.

Hiyama, Y. and Ichikawa, R. (1952). A method to mark the time in the scale and other hard tissues of fish to see their growth. Jap. J. Ichthyol., 2, 156-157.

Ichikawa, R. (1953). Absorption of fish scale caused by starvation. Rec. oceanogr. Wks Japan. 1, 101-104.

Louw, G. N., Sutton, W. W. and Kenny, A. D. (1967). Action of thyrocalcitonin in the teleost fish Ictalurus melas. Nature, Lond., 215, 888.

Mashiko, K and Jozuka, K. (1962). Studies on the calcium uptake by teleost fishes I. ^{45}Ca uptake by the crucian carp. Scient. Rep. Kanazawa Univ., 8, 107-126.

Mashiko, K. and Jozuka, K. (1964). Absorption and excretion of calcium by the teleost fishes with special reference to the routes followed. Annotnes. zool. jap., 37, 41-50.

Mashiko, K., Jozuka, K. and Morita, O. (1964). Turnover of ^{45}Ca by the scale of the crucian carp. Ann. Rep. Noto. Mar. Lab. Univ. Kanazawa., 4, 53-58.

McCay, C. M., Tunison, A. V., Cromwell, M. and Paul, H. (1936). The calcium and phosphorus content of the body of the brook trout in relation to age, growth and food. J. biol. Chem., 114, 259-263.

McLean, F. C. and Urist, M. R. (1968). Bone. Univ. Chicago Press, 3rd ed. 314 pp.

Montskó, T., Tigyi, A., Lissak, K. and Duraczky, J. (1964). Calcium regulation in Teleostei. Acta physiol. hung., 23, suppl., 63.

Moss, M. L. (1961a). Studies of the acellular bone of teleost fish. I. Morphological and systematic variations. Acta anat., 46, 343-426.

Moss, M. L. (1961b). Osteogenesis of acellular fish bone. Am. J. Anat., 108, 99-110.

Moss, M. L. (1962). Studies of the acellular bone of teleost fish. II. Response to fracture under normal and acalcemic conditions. Acta anat., 48, 46-60.

Moss, M. L. (1963). The biology of acellular teleost bone. Ann. N.Y. Acad. Sci., 109, 337-350.

Moss, M. L. and Freilich, M. (1963). Studies of the acellular bone of teleost fish. IV. Inorganic content of calcified tissues. Acta anat., 55, 1-8.

Mugiya, Y. (1964). Calcification in fish and shell fish. III. Seasonal occurrence of a prealbumin fraction in the otolith fluid of some fish corresponding to the period of opaque zone formation in the otolith. Bull. Jap. Soc. scient. Fish., 30, 955-967.

Neville, A. C. (1967). Daily growth layers in animals and plants. Biol. Rev., 42, 421-441.

Norris, W. P., Chavin, W. and Lombard, L. S. (1963). Studies of calcification in a marine teleost. Ann. N.Y. Acad. Sci., 109, 312-336.

Ophel, I. L. and Judd, J. M. (1967). Skeletal distribution of strontium and calcium and strontium/calcium ratios in various species of fish, in, Lenihan, J. M. A., Loutit, J. F. and Martin, J. H. (ed.) Strontium Metabolism., Acad. Press, London. 103-109.

Pang, P. K. T. and Pickford, G. E. (1967). Failure of hog thyrocalcitonin to elicit hypocalcemia in the teleost fish Fundulus heteroclitus. Comp. Biochem. Physiol., 21, 573-578.

Pannella, G. (1971). Fish otoliths: Daily growth layers and periodical patterns. Science, N.Y., 173, 1124-1126.

Pickford, G. E. and Grant, F. B. (1967). Serum osmolarity in the coelacanth Latimeria chalumnae urea retention and ion regulation. Science, N.Y. 155, 568-570.

Podoliak, H. A. and Holden, H. K. (1965). Distribution of dietary calcium to the skeleton and skin of fingerling brown trout. Cartland Hatchery Report No. 33, 64-70.

Rasquin, P. and Rosenbloom, L. (1954). Endocrine imbalance and tissue hyperplasia in teleosts maintained in darkness. Bull. Am. Mus. nat. Hist., **104**, 362-425.

Reid, D. F., Ego, W. T. and Townsley, S. J. (1959). Ion exchange through epithelia of freshwater and seawater adapted teleost studied with radioactive isotopes. Anat. Rec., **134**, 628 (abstract).

Reid, D. F., Townsley, S. J. and Ego, W. T. (1959). Uptake of [85]Sr and [45]Ca through epithelia of freshwater and seawater adapted *Tilapia mossambica*. Proc. Hawaii Acad. Sci., **34**, 32 (abstract).

Robertson, J. D. (1954). The chemical composition of the blood of some aquatic chordates including members of the Tunicata, Cyclostomata and Osteichthyes. J. exp Biol., **31**, 424-442.

Rosenthal, H. L. (1956). Uptake and turnover of Ca[45] by the guppy. Science, N.Y., **124**, 571-574.

Rosenthal, H. L. (1957). Uptake of Ca[45] and Sr[90] from water by freshwater fishes. Science, N.Y., **126**, 699-700.

Rosenthal, H. L. (1960). Accumulation of Sr[90] and Ca[45] by freshwater fishes. Proc. Soc. exp. Biol. Med., **104**, 88-91.

Rosenthal H. L. (1963). Uptake, turnover and transport of bone-seeking elements in fishes. Ann. N.Y. Acad. Sci., **109**, 278-293.

Schiffman, R. H. (1961). A perfusion study of the movement of strontium across the gills of rainbow trout. Biol. Bull. mar. lab., Woods Hole, **120**, 110-117.

Shehadeh, Z. H. and Gordon, M. S. (1969). Role of the intestine in salinity adaptation of the rainbow trout *Salmo gairdnerii*. Comp. Biochem. Physiol., **30**, 397-418.

Simkiss, K. (1967). Calcium in reproductive physiology; A comparative study of vertebrates. Chapman and Hall, Lond. 264 pp.

Simmons, D. J. (1971). Calcium and skeletal tissue physiology in teleost fishes. Clin. Orthopaedics, **76**, 244-280.

Simmons, D. J., Simmons, N. B. and Marshall, J. H. (1970). The uptake of Ca[45] in the acellular-boned toadfish. Calc. Tiss. Res., **5**, 206-221.

Sissons, H. A. (1949). Intermittent periosteal activity. Nature, Lond., **163**, 1001-1002.

Smith, H. M. (1930). The absorption and excretion of water and salts by marine teleosts. Am. J. Physiol., **93**, 480-505.

Swift, D. R. and Pickford, G. E. (1965). Seasonal variations in the hormone content of the pituitary gland of the Perch (*Perca fluviatilis*). Gen. comp. Endocr., **5**, 354-365.

Tomiyama, T., Ishio, S. and Kobayashi, K. (1956). Absorption of dissolved [45]Ca by marine fishes, *in,* Research in the effects and influences of the nuclear bomb test explosions. II. Tokyo Japan. Soc. Promo. Sci., 1181-1187.

Urist, M. R. (1961). Calcium and phosphorus in the blood and skeleton of the Elasmobranchii. Endocrinology, **69**, 778-801.

Urist, M. R. (1963). The regulation of calcium and other ions in the serum of hagfish and lampreys. Ann. N.Y. Acad. Sci., **109**, 294-311.

Urist, M. R. (1964). Further observations bearing on the bone-body fluid continuum: composition of the skeleton and serum of cyclostomes, elasmobranchs and bony vertebrates, *in* Frost, H.M. (ed.) Bone Biodynamics. Little Brown, 151-179

Urist, M. R., Applegate, S., Wagner, S. H. and Southwick, F. (1970). Comparative blood chemistry and calcitonin in the basking shark *Cetorhinus maximus*. Shark research panel. Am. Inst. Biol. Fish. 61-62.

Urist, M. R. and Schjeide, A. O. (1961). The partition of calcium and protein in the blood of oviparous vertebrates during estrous. J. gen. Physiol., **44**, 743-56.

Urist, M. R., Uyeno, S., King, E., Okado, M. and Applegate, S. (1972). Calcium and phosphorus in the skeleton and blood of the lungfish *Lepidosiren paradoxa* with comment on humoral factors in calcium homeostasis in the osteichthyes. Comp. Biochem. Physiol., **42A**, 393-408.

Urist, M. R. and Van de Putte, K. A. (1967). Comparative biochemistry of the blood of fishes, *in*, Gilbert, P. W., Mathews, R. F. and Rall, D. P. (ed.) Sharks, Skates and Rays. John Hopkins Press, Baltimore, 271-285.

Van Oosten, J. (1957). The skin and scales, *in* Brown, M. E. (ed.) The physiology of fishes. Acad. Press. Lond. **Vol. 1**. 207-244.

Van Someren, V. (1937). A preliminary investigation into the causes of scale absorption in salmon (*Salmo salar*). Salm. Fish., Edinb., **No. II**, 1-12.

Wallin, O. (1957). On the growth, structure and developmental physiology of the scale of fishes. Rep. Inst. Freshwat. Res. Drottningholm., **38**, 385 447.

Yamada, J. (1956). On the mechanism of the appearance of the scale structure. VI. Some observations associated with the absorption of scale in the goldfish. Bull. Fac. Fish. Hokkaido Univ., **7**, 202-207.

Analysis of hard tissue of pike *Esox lucius* L. with special reference to age and growth

JOHN M. CASSELMAN

Department of Zoology, University of Toronto, Toronto, Ontario, Canada M5S 1A1

SUMMARY

(1) Pike from a natural population were injected with tetracycline antibiotics to examine appositional growth of opaque and translucent zones in cleithra. Macroanalysis of cleithra from three populations was conducted to determine specific gravity, ash, and nitrogen content. Microanalysis with an electron microprobe X-ray analyser was used to examine elemental composition in relation to zonation.

(2) Tetracycline labelled cleithra indicated that an average of 80% of the annual linear growth, representing the opaque zone, was deposited during 22% of the calendar year. The remaining 20% of the cleithral growth, which contains the translucent zone, formed during 78% of the year, confirming that the opaque zone forms at a much faster rate of growth than the translucent zone. Sexual maturity is reflected in time of annulus formation which is delayed with increasing age.

(3) The three populations examined had different growth rates. Cleithra from the slower growing Wickett Lake population were not only significantly smaller at any specific body length but also contained relatively more annuli.

(4) Slower growing cleithra transmit more light than faster growing ones of the same size because they not only contain relatively more translucent annuli which are often wider but also have opaque zones that are optically less dense. Wickett Lake cleithra which were slower growing had at least two times as many *pseudoannuli* as those of the other two populations which were faster growing.

(5) In reflected light hard tissue has broad white growth zones, called *reflective zones,* and narrow darker annuli, called *absorptive zones.*

(6) Specific gravity and ash residue of whole and sectioned parts of cleithra from all three populations increased with increasing age and decreasing growth rate. This difference was observed not only between parts of cleithra but also between individuals and populations.

(7) Nitrogen content was inversely related to specific gravity and ash, was highest in younger cleithra, and increased with increasing growth rate.

(8) The electron microprobe X-ray analyser related these results directly to differential calcification of the zones and confirmed that the translucent zone contained a higher calcium and total inorganic content. Calcium and total mineral content of both zones increased with increasing age and decreasing growth rate. Calcium was uniformly high in the translucent zone but was lower and more variable in the opaque zone. The lowest calcium content, especially noticeable in older slower growing cleithra, often was observed near the beginning of the opaque zone and then gradually increased across the opaque zone to the next translucent zone. Calcium and total mineral content were inversely related to optical density.

(9) Changes in the relative amounts of both organic and inorganic material in the calcified tissue influence the transmission and reflection of light causing optically different zones. Transmission of light through the more compact translucent zone is enhanced by increased calcium content which is considerably more abundant when equal volumes of material are compared. The relatively more abundant collagen fibres of the opaque zone probably cause increased dispersion and refraction with an attenuating effect on light transmission, increasing the relative opacity.

(10) It is postulated that any factor which influences appositional proteinaceous growth of the matrix will be registered in the calcified tissue by differential calcification which is inversely related to the rate of growth of the expanding edge. General protein anabolism which results in protein somatic growth concurrently influences appositional growth by synthesis of a protein matrix. If a change in protein metabolism results in a decrease in appositional growth with continued calcification of the possibly reduced matrix, then a check or translucent zone will be formed in the calcified tissue.

INTRODUCTION

Pike *Esox lucius* L. were among the first fish used to examine the fundamental problem of age and growth assessment which has received much attention from fisheries scientists. Hederström in 1759 questioned the age of Heibrun's pike, alleged to have been 267 years old. He proposed that vertebrae reflected accurate age and growth assessment of pike and several other species. He left this proposition to all students of natural science to determine to what extent his endeavours were successful; 214 years later we still have not completely resolved this age-old problem.

Since Hederström's astute observation of vertebrae, several other hard structures have been intensively investigated to assess age and growth of pike. Scales have been examined in detail (Williams 1955; Frost and Kipling 1959; Casselman 1967) since zones were first detected on them by Hoffbauer in 1905 (Graham 1929). Other hard tissues have been used: opercula (Svetovidov 1929; Frost and Kipling 1959, 1961), teeth (Astanin 1947), fin rays (Johnson 1959), otoliths (Hatfield *et al.* 1972), metapterygoids (Filipsson 1972), and cleithra (Casselman, in preparation).

Although calcified tissue of many fish species has been frequently used for age and growth assessment, no general theory is available to explain annulus formation, and the factor or factors controlling their occurrence in hard tissue are not yet fully understood (De Bont 1967; Balon 1972). A systematic study of the surface configurations on pike scales, assisted by marked-recaptured samples, elucidated factors influencing annulus and *pseudoannulus* formation (Casselman 1967). From that study I concluded that

13

in immature pike temperature is the most important factor controlling linear growth and annulus formation. In mature pike annulus formation represents a combination of a cessation in growth related to decreasing water temperature, accumulation of reproductive products, and an interruption in the resumption of growth caused by spawning.

Pike were chosen for a general study of calcified tissue growth of fish because considerable data had been accumulated on their biology and several detailed age and growth studies were available (Williams 1955; Frost and Kipling 1959, 1961). Quantitative and qualitative growth of pike calcified tissue and their relation to body growth were investigated to obtain more knowledge of the growth of calcified tissue which could subsequently be used to interpret more accurately age and growth of the fish. Because the quality of the translucent and opaque zones found in fish hard tissue is optically quite different, a direct analysis of these zones was conducted. Direct evidence concerning qualitative and quantitative composition of the zones presumably would lead to a better understanding of the factors influencing growth of fish calcified tissue and the mechanism controlling check and zone formation. With few exceptions (Mugiya 1965) a direct analysis of the elemental composition of zones in fish calcified tissue has not been attempted.

Most hard structures that had been used in age and growth assessment of pike were not suitable for all phases of this general study. Because Frost and Kipling (1959) concluded that 'the opercular bone provides a valid method of determining the age and growth (but not the age without the growth)' a search was undertaken to find an alternative hard-tissue tool which independently would express both age and growth. As a result of this search the cleithrum, a flat bone from the pectoral girdle, was used throughout this study. A more detailed description of its application in age and growth assessment of esocids will be presented elsewhere (Casselman, in preparation).

This paper presents an analysis of quantitative linear growth of cleithra in relation to the rate of formation of opaque and translucent zones and a qualitative and quantitative analysis of their physical and chemical properties using macrotechniques and microtechniques. Quantitative growth data were derived from cleithra from a natural population labelled during midsummer with tetracycline compounds. Macroanalysis was conducted on whole bone and sectioned parts of cleithra from three pike populations to determine specific gravity, ash, and nitrogen content. Microanalysis of the elemental composition of the zones in cleithra was obtained with an electron microprobe X-ray analyser.

MATERIALS AND METHODS

Quantitative linear growth of zones in cleithra

Pike used in this phase of the study were collected from Wickett Lake (45° 54'N, 83° 08'W) a shallow, 100-hectare lake on Manitoulin Island, Ontario. Native pike were captured with trap and fyke nets, tagged, injected with tetracycline hydrochloride (Polyotic, powder; Cyanamid of Canada Limited), and released. Data used here were obtained from 138 pike released between May and August, 1969 and 1970, and recaptured at least one year later. Cleithra were

removed from recaptured fish, cleaned, and stored in 65% glycerol at 2 C. Cleithra were washed immediately prior to analysis in distilled water and air dried.

The tetracycline labels not only validated the translucent zone as an annulus, but also were time-markers relative to adjacent annuli. Tetracycline antibiotics are deposited in the zone of calcification, and fluoresce as a yellow line or band when excited with ultraviolet light (Kobayashi et al. 1964). Cleithra were illuminated with ultraviolet light, and the position of the tetracycline label between the two adjacent translucent annuli was measured to the nearest 0.1 mm along the ventral edge of the rib (medial costa). For age assessment the annulus is acceptably described as a zone or band of translucent calcified tissue. But for more precise purposes, such as mensuration, the annulus is more accurately located at the point where the distal edge of the translucent zone meets the proximal edge of the opaque zone. Annual growth of calcified tissue usually includes one wide, opaque and one narrow, translucent zone. Fig. 1 shows a sectioned cleithrum with a longitudinal cut along the ventral edge of the medial costa along the line used to obtain cleithral measurements. The fluorescent tetracycline label on this cleithrum from a tagged-recaptured pike not only validated the annulus but also indicated that on 27 May 1969, 17% of the annual linear cleithral growth had been completed.

Percentages of annual growth completed at time of labelling were calculated, grouped according to age at time of injection, and plotted against the date of labelling. Regression analysis was used to obtain the line of best fit which was extrapolated to the point of zero growth to determine the approximate time of annulus formation. The time required to form the opaque zone was determined by computing the time when 80% of the annual linear cleithral growth was completed. An average of 80% of the annual growth is opaque, although the proportional amount of growth occupied by this zone decreases with age.

Macroanalysis of cleithra

Macroanalysis was conducted on cleithra from 203 pike from three Ontario populations. Cleithra were used from 121 Wickett Lake fish collected between January and April, 1971 and 1972, and from 42 pike captured during the same period from Smoky Hollow Lake (45° 38'N, 82° 04'W) a shallow, 30-hectare lake on Manitoulin Island. Cleithra were also used from 40 pike collected during October and November 1969 from the 1000 Islands section of the St. Lawrence River (42° 80'N, 75° 50'W). Approximately equal numbers of males and females were used from each population. Cleithra were used from fish which were captured during late fall and winter, at least before spawning, to insure that all individuals were in a similar state of growth and differed only in relation to sexual maturity. Cleithra from these collections were, to some extent, similarly translucent on the edge and were considered to be in the growth cessation that results in annulus formation.

Initially the cleithra were removed from the pike, cleaned of all muscle and connective tissue with hot water and a fine brush, and rinsed in clean water. The bones were air dried and stored in envelopes. When they were selected for macroanalysis one cleithrum from each fish was soaked in distilled water for 12 hours, then vigorously scrubbed with a fine brush, rinsed in distilled water, and wiped dry. These cleithra were then air dried and viewed with an ultra-

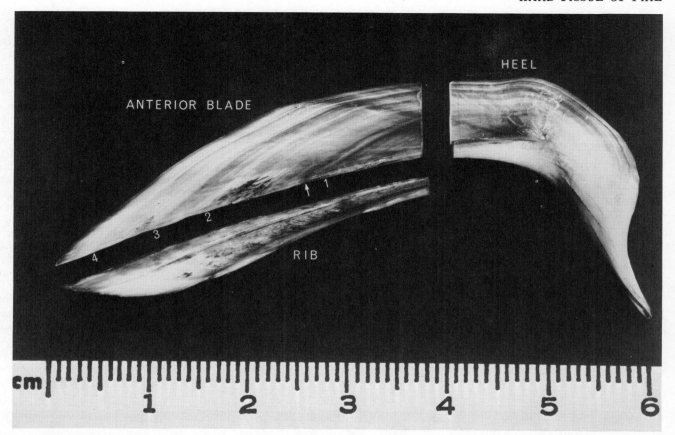

Fig. 1. Sectioned left cleithrum from a tagged Wicket Lake female pike showing the parts used for macroanalysis. Pike was tagged and injected with tetracycline hydrochloride 27 May 1969, 280 mm T.L., and recaptured 20 August 1972, 582 mm T.L. Age 4+. Point where the fluorescent line in the anterior blade meets the medial costa indicated by arrow. Reflected white light.

violet light to insure that no soft tissue remained in the fossa or striae. Under these conditions soft tissue appears yellow against the bluish autofluorescent background of the bone. Relative opacity of the cleithra was then examined in transmitted and reflected white light and occurrences of annuli and pseudoannuli were recorded. Age assigned was that of the annulus which was forming on the edge of the bone and would have been completed and demarcated when new growth resumed. This condition was designated by a small circle 'o' after the number of the annulus forming at the edge. The bone therefore had one annulus less than the age assigned, which was equal to the number of growing seasons or opaque zones in the bone.

As emphasized by Mina (1968) and Blacker (1969), there is considerable confusion in the literature describing the relative appearance of the zones in fish calcified tissue. The interpretation of results has been complicated by ambiguous terminology such as 'light and dark', 'black and white' when the method of illumination was not described. When the method of illumination is not specified, I recommend the terms *translucent* and *opaque* because in each the type of illumination is implicit.

The anterior cleithral radius was then measured from the origin to the point where the tip of the anterior blade intersects the medial costa. The relationships between the anterior cleithral radius and total body length at time of capture for the three samples of cleithra were compared.

Specific gravity was determined by the displacement method. Whole bones were dried at 60 C to a con-

stant weight and, suspended from a fine wire, were weighed first in air and then in 95% ethyl alcohol. Preliminary determinations with water, which is highly polar, indicated that its large surface tension causes air bubbles to be trapped on the irregular surface of the bone. Alcohol was used to eliminate this problem and its effect on the results (Woodard 1962) and their reproducibility. A pyconometer flask was used to standardize determinations for variations in operating temperature and changes in specific gravity of the ethanol.

Moss (1961) reported that vascular channels occur in compact fish bone. Test-sectioning of cleithra revealed that the rib contains some vascularization and that a trabeculated cavity develops in the heel. To eliminate possible effects resulting from variation in porosity, cleithra were sectioned (Fig. 1) to obtain the compact, avascular mass of acellular bone in the anterior blade. A jewellers' saw was used to separate the heel from the anterior part by a transectional cut through the middle of the first growth zone. The blade was separated from the rib by a longitudinal cut along the ventral edge of the medial costa.

Fat was then extracted from the sections by refluxing with diethyl ether in a soxhelet apparatus for 14 hours.

Specific gravity was determined on the fat-free sections dried to a constant weight at 60 C.

The samples were then divided into two similar subsamples. Ash residue was determined on the sections by placing them in a muffle furnace at 640 C for 24 hours. Usually ash content of the parts was determined separately and the results were combined to calculate the total inorganic content of the bone expressed as per cent oxide on a dry weight basis. Before and after ashing, samples were oven dried to a constant weight at 100 C. Variations between runs were standardized with $CaCO_3$. To reduce the hygroscopic problems encountered in ashing (Joslyn 1970) the crucibles containing the samples were covered and transferred to a dessicator to cool to a constant weight.

The other subsample of fat-free bone sections was dried to a constant weight at 60 C and nitrogen was determined by the micro-kjeldahl technique (Horwitz 1970). Variations between runs were standardized with urea. Nitrogen content of the parts was determined separately, then combined to give a whole bone value expressed as per cent dry weight.

Microanalysis of cleithra

Microanalysis was conducted to determine qualitative and quantitative information on the distribution of elements in the zones of hard tissue. An Applied Research Laboratories Electron Microprobe X-ray Analyser was used for this analysis. A fine beam of electrons averaging 5μ in diameter was focussed on a highly polished carbon-coated specimen surface.

The electron bombardment causes characteristic X-rays to be emitted by the atoms affected by electron excitation. Wave length and intensity of the X-rays were analysed and converted through computer facilities to an elemental analysis (Rucklidge 1967) expressed as per cent dry weight, using the calibrations of X-ray production from standards of known analysis.

Cleithral specimens were obtained by removing a transectional slice (Fig. 2-a) from the middle of the first growth zone with a jewellers' saw. The slice was then mounted on its edge (Fig. 2-b) and the surface was prepared for microprobe analysis. Thin sections (150 to 250 μ) of the cleithral slices were probed in transmitted light. The portion outlined at Fig. 2-b is one of the regions analysed. Because zonation is usually examined on the surface of the intact bone, the region analysed on the slice was projected onto the intact tip of the blade and is demarcated by arrows (Fig. 2-c). The tip of the anterior blade permits a more detailed interpretation of zonation because this part grows at a faster rate than other parts of the cleithrum and the zones are more widely spaced where they intersect the medial costa. Exact details of specimen preparation and operating conditions for an accurate elemental analysis of fish

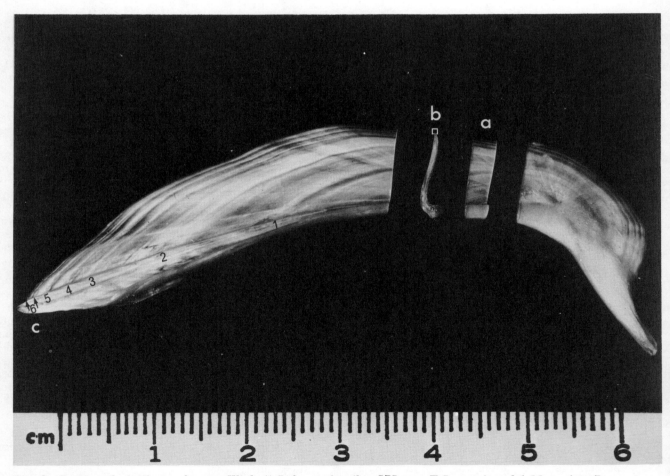

Fig. 2. Sectioned cleithrum from a Wickett Lake male pike, 575 mm T.L., captured 1 May. Age 7o. Cleithrum contains six annuli with a translucent zone along the outer edge indicating that it was in the growth cessation that would result in annulus formation when linear growth resumed. Annuli, except sixth, are labelled on the medial costa. Reflected light. a—Transectional slice removed from the cleithrum and prepared for microprobe analysis. b—Sliced section showing surface analysed. Tip of the section outlined by square indicates one portion probed. c—Projection between arrows of the region analysed and outlined at b, illustrating the appearance of the zones at intersection of the medial costa on the intact tip of the anterior blade.

hard tissue will be presented elsewhere (Casselman *et al.*, in preparation).

Line scan analysis of the calcium content was photographed from a computer plotted graph. The graph was then contact printed on a photograph of the zones of the specimen subjected to line scan analysis. Correct registry of the analysis on the photograph of the specimen was insured by marking the specimen and the mounting medium at the beginning and end of the scan.

RESULTS AND DISCUSSION

Quantitative linear cleithral growth

Cleithra labelled with tetracycline showed that the approximate time of annulus formation ranged over a period of nearly one month (Table 1). Time of annulus formation depended upon age and occurred earlier in young, sexually immature pike. All pike from Wickett Lake were mature at the end of their third growing season, and all subsequent ages formed the annulus at approximately the same time. In other pike populations a delay in time of annulus formation on the scales was associated with sexual maturity (Casselman 1967). Because other species form annuli later with increasing age (Backiel 1962; Chugunova 1968), time of annulus formation in hard tissue of at least some species reflects sexual maturity.

ceases (Simmons *et al.* 1970), then the opaque zone is formed at a much faster rate of growth than the translucent zone.

Description of samples used for macroanalysis

Cleithra used in this study were taken from three populations with two distinctly different growth rates (Fig. 3). Growth curves were fitted by regression analysis; the correlation coefficients ranged from $r = 0.853$ for St. Lawrence River females to $r = 0.977$ for Smoky Hollow Lake males. Smoky Hollow Lake and St. Lawrence River populations had somewhat similar growth rates but were represented by samples with different age distributions. Wickett Lake pike had a much slower growth rate during the first 2 years. In older age groups average body length of the faster growing Wickett Lake females was well below that of the slower growing males from the other two populations. At any given age Wickett Lake pike were noticeably smaller than fish sampled from the other two populations.

A comparison of the relation between anterior cleithral radius and total body length showed differences between the three populations (Fig. 4). Regression analysis indicated that highly significant straight-line relationships described these variables. Because age was obtained from cleithra, this relationship proved that growth of the body and cleithrum could be compared synonymously.

Table 1. Extrapolated time of annulus formation and average time when 80% of annual linear bone growth was complete. Calculated using tetracycline hydrochloride labelled cleithra from Wickett Lake pike tagged, injected, and released between May and August, 1969 and 1970, and recaptured at least 12 months later.

Annulus	Approximate time of annulus formation[1]	Growth zone	Average time when 80% of annual bone growth was completed	Time in weeks to complete 80% of annual bone growth[2]	Sample size
1	4th week, April	2	1st week, August	14	26
2	1st week, May	3	3rd week, July	11	29
3	2nd week, May	4	2nd week, July	9	26
4	2nd week, May	5	2nd week, July	9	38
5	2nd week, May	6	3rd week, July	10	19

[1]Extrapolated using the line of best fit.

[2]Calculated from extrapolated time of annulus formation.

An average of 80% of the annual linear cleithral growth was completed by midsummer (Table 1). Although young pike attained this percentage of cleithral growth later than older pike, the relative rate of growth of the younger fish is higher, as indicated by the width of their annual zones. Mature pike of all ages not only formed the annulus at approximately the same time but also formed the opaque zone over the same 9- to 10-week period.

Although extrapolation is probably not the most accurate method of determining the exact time of annulus formation, 80% of the annual appositional cleithral growth which represents the opaque zone was deposited during 22% of the calendar year. The remaining 20% of the cleithral growth, which contains the translucent zone, formed during 78% of the year. Assuming that appositional growth of fish bones never

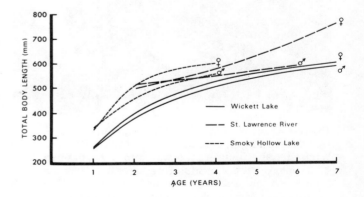

Fig. 3. Curves of mean total body length at age for pike used in macroanalysis of cleithra from three Ontario populations.

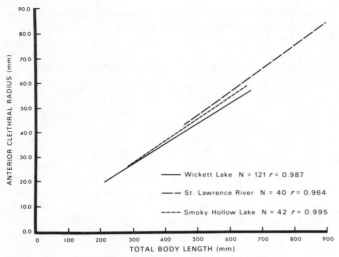

Fig. 4. Regression of anterior cleithral radius on total body length for pike used in the macroanalysis of cleithra from three populations. N = number of cleithra measured. r = correlation coefficient of regression lines.

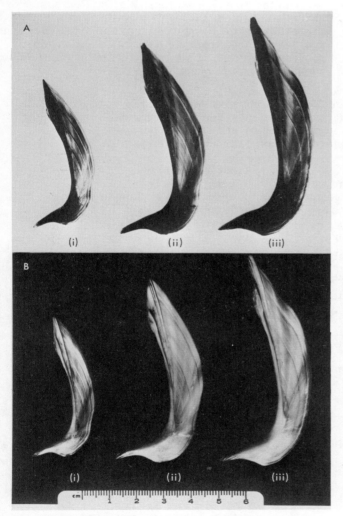

Fig. 5. Cleithra from three pike populations: A—transmitted light; B—reflected light. (i) From a Wickett Lake female pike, 522 mm T.L., captured 23 January 1972, contains five annuli. (ii) From a Smoky Hollow Lake female pike, 667 mm T.L., captured 12 March 1973, contains two annuli. (iii) From a St. Lawrence River female pike, 700 mm T.L., captured 20 December 1972, contains four annuli.

An analysis of covariance was used to test the regression lines and proved that cleithra from the slower growing Wickett Lake pike were significantly smaller than those from the other two populations. A preliminary test of the variability between the sexes within populations revealed no significant difference ($P > 0.05$). A comparison of the slopes of the regression lines between populations over the range of overlapping lengths (455 to 650 mm) indicated that the slopes were not quite significantly different at the 5% level ($P = 0.07$ for Wickett and St. Lawrence), permitting an analysis of their elevations. A test of elevations substantiated that, at any specific body length over the range tested, cleithra from slower growing Wickett Lake pike were significantly smaller than those from Smoky Hollow Lake fish ($P < 0.01$) and St. Lawrence River fish ($P < 0.01$). Smoky Hollow Lake pike also had smaller cleithra than St. Lawrence River pike ($P < 0.01$).

General appearance of the cleithra was compared at time of age assessment. These three samples of cleithra were visibly different when viewed in transmitted and reflected white light (Fig. 5).

In transmitted light cleithra contain wide, opaque, optically dense zones which are growth zones, and narrow, translucent, optically less dense zones which are annuli or pseudoannuli. Slow growing cleithra (Fig. 5A-(i)) transmit more light than faster growing ones of the same size not only because they contain relatively more translucent annuli, which are often wider, but also because they have opaque zones that are optically less dense. Faster growing cleithra (Fig. 5A-(ii) and (iii)) are uniformly more opaque and usually contain less distinct, translucent zones, with only a slight difference in the relative transmission of light from zone to zone.

In reflected light cleithra contain broad, white growth zones which reflect light, referred to here as *reflective zones*. They also contain narrow, relatively darker zones or annuli which result from the passage of light into, and its absorption by, the hyaline-like material and the background, and are referred to here as *absorptive zones*. Slow growing cleithra (Fig. 5B-(i)) are generally darker than fast growing cleithra (Fig. 5B-(ii) and (iii)), with relatively more light being absorbed than reflected. Annuli of faster growing cleithra, especially in the heels, are relatively white (Fig. 5B-(ii) and (iii)).

The occurrence of pseudoannuli, usually diffuse translucent bands in the growth zones, confirmed that slow growing cleithra were generally more translucent than faster growing cleithra. Cleithra from Wickett Lake pike used in this analysis had almost twice as many annual zones with pseudoannuli (17%) as did Smoky Hollow Lake pike (9%) and nearly three times as many as St. Lawrence River pike (6%).

Macroanalysis of cleithra

In all three populations specific gravity of the cleithra and their sections increased with increasing age (Fig. 6). The 201 whole cleithra analysed had an average age of 3.2 years and an average specific gravity of 1.83, whereas specific gravity of 142 anterior blade sections from these cleithra averaged 1.96. This substantial difference indicated that vascularization probably influenced the results from whole cleithra. Increased density of the slow growing heel was apparent because, although it contained a large central vascular cavity, it had the same specific gravity as the faster growing, less vascular rib.

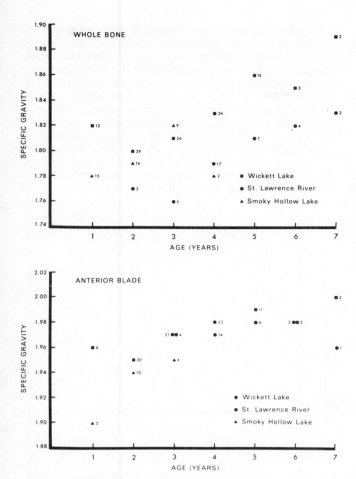

Fig. 6. Relation between specific gravity and age for whole bone and anterior blade of cleithra from three pike populations. Mean values for each age are plotted with the number of individuals analysed.

Slower growing cleithra from the Wickett Lake population were optically least dense and had the highest specific gravity. Whole cleithra, and to a lesser extent compact anterior blades, from the faster growing populations, especially from the St. Lawrence River, were optically more dense and had lower specific gravities at all ages. Usually deviations from the general trend were related to small sample size. One-year-old Wickett Lake fish had a relatively high specific gravity which is unexplained.

Specific gravity of the compact anterior blade is probably typical of acellular fish bone. Woodard (1962) presented specific gravity values for compact cellular human cortical bone which ranged from 1.79 to 1.93 with a mean value of 1.90. However, anterior blades from cleithra with an average age of 3.3 years had a range of mean values from 1.88 to 2.02 and a total mean value of 1.96. The slightly more dense acellular fish bone demonstrates one of the basic differences between acellular bone and cellular bone with osteocytes and Haversian systems. Similarly, an increase in specific gravity with increasing age and development has been reported for human bone (Woodard 1962).

Additional proof is available that the density of fish hard tissue is inversely related to optical density. Irie (1955) used an X-ray technique to examine relative densities of $CaCO_3$ in the zones of otolith slices of the fish *Pseudosciaena*. He demonstrated that X-rays penetrated the opaque zone more easily than

they did the translucent zone and concluded that the $CaCO_3$ in the opaque layer was 'lighter' than in the translucent layer. In a preliminary study using an isodensimetric technique (Casselman, unpublished) small sections (approximately 1 mg) of zones from pike cleithra ranged in specific gravity from 1.75 to 2.10. All opaque zones had a lower specific gravity than the adjacent translucent zones. These results substantiated that the general trends shown by specific gravity were related to the relative increase in the percentage of hard tissue occupied by the translucent zone with increasing age and decreasing growth (Fig. 5A-(i)).

Ash residue increased with increasing age, supporting the specific gravity results and confirming that inorganic content of cleithra increased with age (Fig. 7). This trend was apparent in whole bone values of all populations, although the youngest and oldest samples showed some deviation, especially from the Wickett Lake population. A similar relationship was obvious for the compact anterior blade, although the increase was not gradual. Ash content was slightly higher in the slower growing heel than in the other two faster growing sections of the cleithrum. With few exceptions the whole bone and anterior blade from the faster growing populations had a lower ash value. The slower growing Wickett Lake population showed a noticeably higher ash content in older age groups.

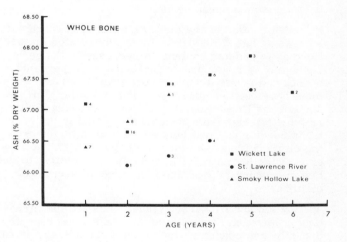

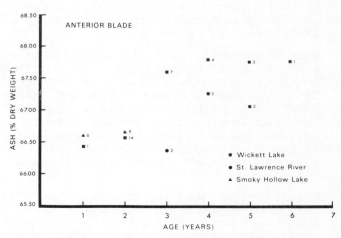

Fig. 7. Relation between ash residue and age for whole bone and anterior blade of cleithra from three pike populations. Mean values for each age are plotted with the number of individuals analysed. Ash expressed as per cent dry weight determined at 100 C.

Dannevig (1956) found differences in the calcium content of cod *Gadus morhua* otoliths and reported that for fish captured in the same locality large otoliths contained 54.86% CaO whereas small otoliths contained 52.5% CaO. Although ages of the cod were not given, presumably the larger individuals were older. Because otoliths are essentially calcic bodies comprised of $CaCO_3$ in the form of aragonite (Degens *et al.* 1969), the inorganic content of cod otoliths probably increases with increasing age.

Ashing substantiated that vascularization caused the lower specific gravity of whole bones. Exactly the same average value (66.94%) was obtained for the ash weight of 65 whole cleithra with an average age of 2.6 years and their sectioned anterior blades. Because there was no difference in the mineral content of these two groups, the difference in specific gravity was due to porosity.

Moss and Freilich (1963) used ethylenediamine extraction to analyse the bones of fish. They reported that opercula, which are structurally similar to cleithra, had an average inorganic content of 67.2%; very similar to the value for cleithra reported here, 66.94%.

Dollerup (1964) showed that the increase in inorganic content of normal human bone with increasing age was correlated with an increase in calcium content. This relationship occurs in different classes of animals (Dickerson 1962a, 1962b), substantiating that it is a common phenomenon.

Nitrogen content of the cleithra, which decreased with increasing age (Fig. 8), was inversely related to specific gravity and ash content. A decrease in the percentage of nitrogen and an increase in the percentage of inorganic constituents during growth and development have been reported for other animals (Widdowson and Dickerson 1964). Slower growing cleithra from Wickett Lake, which were optically the most translucent, contained less nitrogen than faster growing cleithra from the other two populations. The slower growing heel had 7.0% less calcium relative to the faster growing rib and anterior blade of sectioned cleithra.

Widdowson and Dickerson (1964) reviewed the literature of nitrogen content in animal bones and reported that nitrogen concentrations ranged from 3.19% in rat to 4.57% in human bone. Similarly, 41 whole pike cleithra with an average age of 3.3 years averaged 4.36% nitrogen.

Bone consists of two major components; one a proteinaceous organic matrix, and the other a mineral in the form of hydroxyapatite (McLean and Urist 1968). The organic phase is comprised of collagen, a unique fibrillar protein which forms 90% of the organic matrix, and ground substance made up of protein-polysaccharides and glycoproteins (Vaughan 1970). At least 90% of the organic phase is measured if the nitrogen is converted to protein by using the usual factor 6.25.

Results from anterior blades of cleithra from Wickett Lake pike were used to test completeness of the analysis. Nitrogen content was converted from dry weight at 60 C to dry weight of the ash weights at 100 C by correcting for an additional water loss of 2.52%. A protein content of 29.23% was calculated from the average nitrogen value and was added to the inorganic content of 67.09%, giving a total of 96.32%. Whole cleithra from the same population gave a total of 94.78%. Because

only one cleithrum from each fish was analysed, variation between individuals would influence a comparison of these two phases. To test this effect both cleithra from five Wickett Lake pike were analysed, one for nitrogen and one for ash. The combined results totalled 97.53%. Woodard (1962) reported that 6.5% was not accounted for after this summation, and calculated totals from data presented by Dollerup (1964) left a difference of 4.07%. The difference for pike cleithra ranged from 2.47 to 5.22% and probably resulted from the loss during ashing of non-proteinaceous organic matter such as carbohydrates and trace fats, as well as bound water.

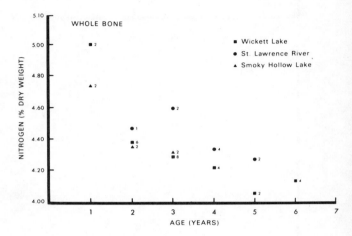

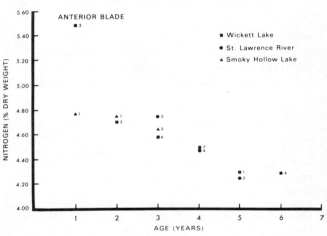

Fig. 8. Relation between nitrogen content and age for whole bone and anterior blade of cleithra from three pike populations. Mean values for each age are plotted with the numbers of individuals analysed. Nitrogen content expressed as per cent dry weight determined at 60 C.

Odland *et al.* (1972) concluded that as humans grow older skeletal growth slackens and bone nutrients are used to increase density. The decreased growth rate of cleithra with increasing age probably accounts for the increased specific gravity, ash content and lower nitrogen values for older fish. The opaque zone becomes narrower with increasing age and the relative amount of translucency of the zone gradually increases. Older and slower growing fish not only have more translucent zones per unit area, but also form translucent zones that are wider and relatively more hyaline. The slower growing Wickett Lake fish had cleithra with a higher specific gravity and ash content, and usually less nitrogen. In addition, cleithra from that sample were significantly smaller at any specific body length than those of the faster growing samples, were generally more translucent, and contained more pseudoannuli when compared with the optically more dense St. Lawrence River and Smoky Hollow Lake cleithra.

Microanalysis of cleithra

A microprobe X-ray analyser was used to examine the differences in mineral content not only from zone to zone but also within zones. Initially crystal spectrometer scans were used to qualitatively analyse the elemental composition of cleithra. Under the operating conditions employed, nine elements heavier than nitrogen were readily detected (Casselman *et al.*, in preparation). To obtain results which would be closer to a total analysis of the zones in cleithra, 14 elements were examined. This analysis was representative of the inorganic components of the bone because it excluded oxygen and all lighter elements, such as nitrogen, carbon, and hydrogen which combine to form the organic component. A computer program was used to calculate oxide weights, which were totalled and compared with calcination. Calcium and phosphorus accounted for 95% of the inorganic phase. Calcium, which was the most abundant element, showed different concentrations from zone to zone. Under the operating conditions employed no other element, with the possible exception of sulphur, showed noticeable differences with zonation. Differential calcification with zonation was examined in detail by analysis of individual points (point analysis) and analysis by systematic scanning (line scan analysis). Specific values presented here are from cleithral slices of two of the 19 pike which were analysed in detail from the three populations.

Point analysis revealed a gradual increase in mean calcium content of the opaque and translucent zones with increasing age. The translucent zone usually had a higher calcium content than the adjacent opaque zones. Mean calcium concentrations for the rib of the cleithrum illustrated in Fig. 2 showed a gradual increase from 26.3% in the first opaque zone to 30.4% in the seventh opaque zone, and from 27.4% in the first translucent zone to 32.1% in the seventh translucent zone on the edge of the bone. These values for the slower growing rib near the heel had an average absolute difference of 2.6% more calcium than the corresponding zone on the faster growing blade. Total inorganic composition of the zones reflected by the 14-element analysis closely paralleled the calcium content. These results were similar to those obtained in macroanalysis, substantiating that not only inorganic content, but also calcium content, increased with increasing age and decreased growth rate.

Results of the microprobe analysis were compared to results obtained by macroanalytic technique. When microprobe values were weighted for the size of the zones they represented, a mean calcium concentration of 27.4% was obtained for the transectional slice of the cleithrum illustrated in Fig. 2-b. A value of 27.8% calcium was obtained from an adjacent similar section of bone (Fig. 2-a) by ashing and determining the calcium content by a fluorometric method with calcein. The absolute difference of 0.4% between these methods is considered to be insignificant. The total inorganic content for this section of bone (Fig. 2-b) as obtained by oxide calculation from a 14-element analysis on the microprobe was 67.6% as compared with 68.2% obtained by ashing at 640 C.

The exclusion of some minor elements in the probe analysis would in part account for the difference. A test was conducted to determine if higher temperature would result in more complete oxidation. The average ash content of five cleithra decreased from 66.44% at 640 C to 66.01% at 800 C, proving that temperature influenced the results.

Line scan analysis on the cleithrum illustrated in Fig. 2 demonstrated differences in the calcium content across the zones. Differences in calcium concentrations across the two translucent and one opaque zone (Fig. 9) are typical of those seen throughout the analysis especially in older, slower growing cleithra. Differences between zones were much less obvious during the first 2 years of growth. The translucent zone contained a higher, usually more uniform, calcium concentration than the opaque zone on either side. The lowest concentration often appeared at the beginning of the opaque zone and then gradually increased across the zone, but showed considerably more variation than the translucent zone. The abrupt decrease in calcium concentration at the beginning of the opaque zone was most extreme in older, slower growing cleithra where an absolute difference of 5 to 6% calcium was occasionally measured.

The differences between the calcium concentration in adjacent zones were not as great in St. Lawrence River cleithra (Fig. 10A) although the general trends were similar to those obtained for Wickett Lake cleithra. The appearance of the region analysed on the intact tip of the blade (Fig. 10B) and the whole cleithrum with the transectional slice removed (Fig. 10C) are illustrated. The transectional slice (Fig. 10A) is extremely thick, occluding much of the optical detail; however, the relationship between optical density and calcium content is obvious if the results are compared with Fig. 10B. Calcium concentration was high in the third translucent zone, decreased at the beginning of the fourth opaque zone, and gradually increased across the zone. The concentration was high in the fourth translucent zone and low at the beginning of the fifth opaque zone. The current year's growth of this pike, captured in August, contained a pseudoannulus with a high calcium content and had a small amount of new growth after this check at the edge of the bone (Fig. 10B) with a low calcium content. The mean calcium concentration obtained by point analysis of zones of this cleithrum weighted according to their percentage of the transectional slice gave a value of 26.2% calcium as compared to 25.9% obtained by the macroanalytical technique.

The electron microprobe was used to examine calcium content in relation to zonation in hard tissue from other species of fish (Casselman *et al.*, in preparation). Calcium values determined by line scan analysis across cross-sectional slices of cod otoliths indicated that the calcium content was higher in the translucent than in the opaque zone and ranged from 44 to 32% respectively. Mugiya (1966) reported that in flatfish *Kareius bicoloratus* during the period of opaque zone formation the diffusible calcium in the otolith fluid decreased to 65.4% of the total calcium, but reached a maximum of 79.1% during the period of translucent zone formation. Results of the current study also agree with those of Irie (1955, 1960) who examined otoliths of fish and deduced that the translucent zone was more dense, and contained larger microcrystals of $CaCO_3$.

Several workers have considered the organic component in zones. They concluded that the opaque zone

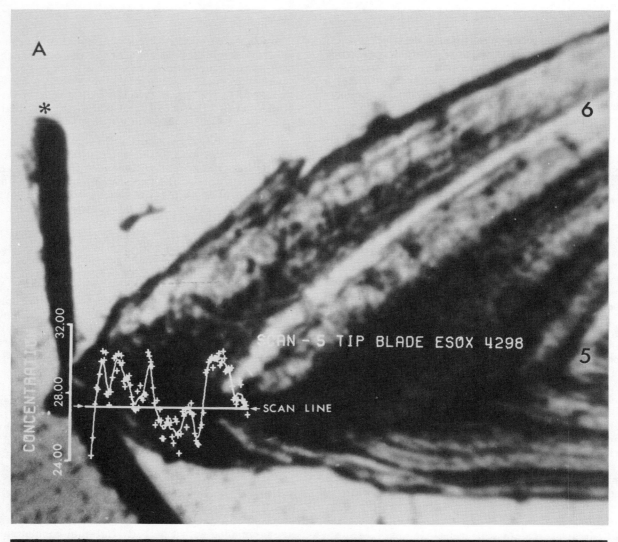

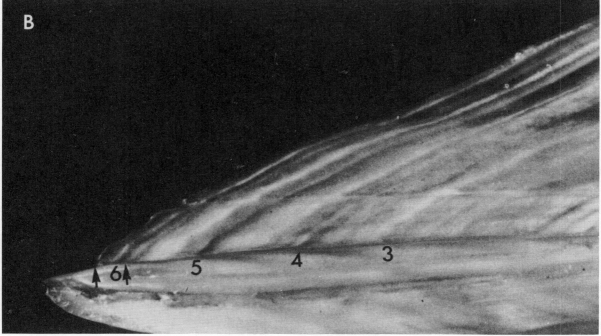

Fig. 9. Microanalysis of calcium content across the tip of a cleithrum from a Wickett Lake male pike. Analysis conducted across the region outlined in Fig. 2-b. A—calcium concentration determined by line scan analysis expressed as per cent dry weight across the sixth annulus and seventh growth zone on the tip of a thin transectional slice of the blade. Arrows mark beginning and end of analysis—actual distance 150 μ. Transmitted light. Asterisk marks a crack in the mounting medium at the tip of the section and is an artifact of the method of mounting, independent of the section. B—Projection between arrows of the region analysed illustrating the appearance of the zones at intersection of the medial costa on the intact tip of the anterior blade. Actual distance between arrows 900 μ. Reflected light.

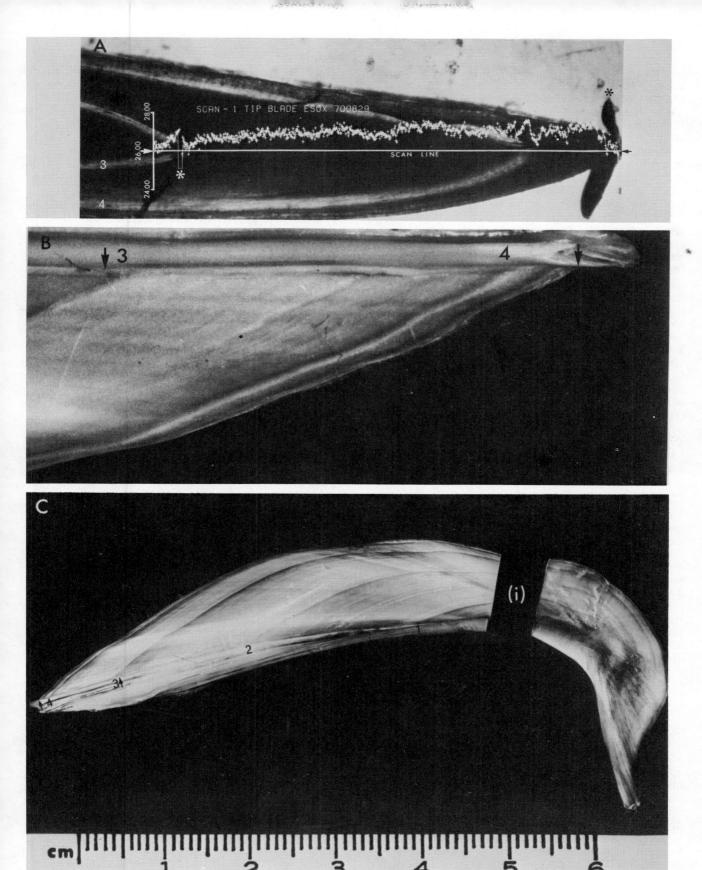

Fig. 10. Microanalysis of calcium content in a cleithrum from a St. Lawrence River female pike, 680 mm T.L., captured 29 August 1970. Age 4+. A—calcium concentration determined by line scan analysis expressed as per cent by dry weight commencing near the end of the third growth zone on the surface transectional slice and ending at the tip of the section. Arrows mark the beginning and end of the analysis-actual distance 1.05 mm. Transmitted light. Black asterisk marks a crack in mounting medium same as Fig. 9A. White asterisk marks a decrease in calcium concentration related to a crack across the specimen. B—Projection between arrows of the region analysed illustrating the appearance of the zones at intersection of the medial costa on the intact tip of the anterior blade. Actual distance between arrows 9.50 mm. Reflected light. C—Sectioned cleithrum illustrating at (i) location where transectional slice was removed for analysis. Reflected light.

contains more organic material than the translucent zone. Because the relationship between the organic and the inorganic content is inverse, their results agree with those of the present study. Hickling (1931) demineralized hake *Merluccius merluccius* otoliths and observed a predominance of thick organic lamellae in the opaque zone, and thinner lamellae in the translucent zone. Dannevig (1956) examined cod otoliths, identified the organic material as a protein, conchiolin, and concluded that it was more abundant in the opaque zone and in the center of the otolith. Irie (1960) used electron microscopy to view otoliths and found that the opaque zone contained much more protein than the translucent zone. Mugiya (1965) conducted a direct analysis on small samples from the otoliths of several species and demonstrated that the opaque zone contained more nitrogen (0.24%) than did the translucent zone (0.16%). He concluded that the amount of protein deposited in the otolith is an important factor which determines the differences between opaque and translucent zones. On this matter we concur, however, the difference in calcium content between zones, although relatively small on a weight basis, probably influences the transmission of light. Specific gravity was used to demonstrate that the translucent zone in cleithra was more compact, containing a considerably greater weight of calcium on a volume basis, which enhances its translucency. Preliminary results of specific gravity of small samples of the zones indicated that the translucent zone may contain as much as 25% more calcium than the opaque zone when the same volumes are compared.

The mineral form of the calcium may also have an important influence on optical density. The relative amounts of amorphous calcium phosphate, apparently the first type of calcium deposited in clouds in the collagen matrix (Budy 1970), and crystalline apatite may vary between zones, influencing optical density. Relative opacity of the opaque zone is probably related to increased dispersion and refraction of light resulting from a greater abundance of collagen fibres. The type of protein deposited in the zone may also play an important role. Mugiya (1964) demonstrated that the otolith fluid of two species of fish contained an additional prealbumin fraction at the time of opaque zone formation.

CONCLUSIONS

Macroanalysis of pike cleithra demonstrated that specific gravity and ash content increased, whereas nitrogen content decreased with increasing age, and that these changes were correlated with the relative increase of the translucent zone and decreased growth rate. These trends were observed not only between different sections of the bone, but also between individuals and populations. The electron microprobe was used to relate these results directly to differential calcification of the zones and to confirm that the translucent zone had a higher calcium and total inorganic content. Calcium and total mineral content of both zones increased with increasing age and decreasing growth rate. Calcium content was uniformly high in the translucent zone but was lower and more variable in the opaque zone. The lowest calcium content, especially in older pike, often was observed near the beginning of the opaque zone and then gradually increased across the opaque zone to the next translucent zone.

Although the relationship between quantity of inorganic and organic components in hard tissue is inverse, continued work with an electron microprobe X-ray analyser equipped to detect lighter elements such as nitrogen and carbon, could be used to examine the distribution of protein and the organic component in relation to zonation. However, direct evidence supplied by Mugiya (1965) and reciprocal evidence from the current study indicate that the opaque zone contains more protein than does the translucent zone.

Appositional bone growth results from the initial deposition of a protein matrix and its subsequent calcification. It is postulated that any factor which influences appositional proteinaceous growth of this matrix will be registered in the tissue by differential calcification of the matrix which is inversely related to the rate of growth of the expanding edge. However, during decreased appositional bone growth the quantity of matrix deposited per unit volume may also be reduced. Appositional growth of the opaque zone, which contains more protein than the translucent zone, occurs at a faster rate than that of the translucent zone and during the period of most rapid body growth. It is postulated that general protein anabolism which results in protein somatic growth concurrently influences appositional calcified tissue growth by synthesis of a protein matrix.

Other workers have considered a decrease in protein production important in annulus formation in the calcified tissue of fish. Wallin (1957) demonstrated that calcification of the protein matrix on scales continues even after termination of protein synthesis and deposition. Under these conditions previously formed circuli are calcified and circuli terminate freely on the osseous layer while calcification continues towards the edge of the scale. Keeton (1965) showed that marginal growth on scales may not be reduced while the rate of protein deposition is retarded or completely stopped, but that calcification of the edge continues.

Studies conducted on bone growth in other animals indicate that the degree of calcification may also be related to the rate of appositional growth of the protein matrix. Appleton (1929, cited by Widdowson and Dickerson 1964) concluded that the level of nutrition had a greater influence on rate of bone growth than on degree of ossification. Dickerson (1962a) noted that under certain conditions appositional growth of the matrix may proceed at a faster rate than calcification of the matrix, and result in new bone that is less calcified. Frost's work (1967, cited by Vaughan 1970) possibly supplies a partial explanation for this difference. Frost considered that initial calcification of the matrix occurs very rapidly in lamellar bone, attains 70% of total mineralization in about 4 days, and is entirely dependent upon the presence of osteoblasts. He maintained that the final 30% mineralization is a much slower process and is probably not associated with osteoblastic activity.

Extremely fast rate of growth of the expanding front might seal off the matrix from further calcification and result in a zone that contains relatively more protein and less calcium. During extremely slow growth the amount of protein available for appositional growth is reduced although calcium would still be available from the environmental water. Direct uptake of calcium by fish from environmental water has been well documented (Philips *et al.* 1960; Mashiko and Jozuka 1962, 1964; Moss 1963; Irie *et al*, 1967; Berg 1968, 1970).

Hormonal control and osmoregulation may also be important in increasing the calcium content in the translucent zone. Estrogens have been associated with increased plasma calcium levels in the cod (Woodhead 1968); however, the source of this bound calcium is most likely the environment (Simmons 1971).

Evidence exists that protein metabolism is related to check and zone formation in calcified tissue of fish. Holden (1955) noted that 'ring formation is dependent upon the condition of the fish and that there is a threshold level of condition above which no ring formation will occur, but below which ring formation is continuous' and the width of the ring depends upon the length of time the fish remains below this condition. In otoliths of marine fish the opaque zone was formed during the period of heaviest feeding (Trout 1958) and highest protein ingestion. Hogman (1968) postulated that a physiological protein-demand cycle existed which caused periodic diversion of scale protein to support other metabolic functions. Similarly, Coble (1970) concluded that a decline in growth rate of the scale and fish resulted when food energy was used for functions other than growth.

Many factors which have been associated with check and translucent zone formation are related to reduced protein anabolism and even catabolism. Decreased food ingestion to maintenance levels, and even starvation would greatly influence available protein for appositional matrix growth. High, low, or rapidly changing temperature would affect activity, feeding, and general metabolism. Extreme starvation which causes general protein catabolism might result in resorption of the protein matrix at the edge of the calcified tissue especially of the more proteinaceous scales which in pike contain 59% protein. Resorption of scales has been reported for fish which were starved (Yamada 1956), in extremely poor condition (Regier 1962), and precociously mature (Ouchi *et al.* 1972). Accumulation of gonadal products in mature fish, influenced by photoperiod, probably represents a major protein demand, resulting in a shift of ingested protein from somatic to reproductive growth, and possibly causing mobilization of body protein. Any condition which affects general body metabolism can be expected to be reflected in a change in protein metabolism. If this change results in a reduction in the amount of protein available for matrix production and appositional growth, with continued calcification of this possibly reduced matrix, then a check or translucent zone will be formed in the calcified tissue.

The relationship between protein metabolism and matrix production in calcified tissue growth should be examined more fully, possibly with amino acids labelled with radioisotopes.

ACKNOWLEDGMENTS

I am especially indebted to Drs. H. H. Harvey and E. J. Crossman for their advice and interest in my study. I wish to thank them, along with Drs. F. E. J. Fry and H. A. Regier, for their helpful review of the manuscript. Dr. J. C. Rucklidge gave me access to an electron microprobe; his advice and assistance and those of Dr. R. Hewins are gratefully acknowledged.

This research was supported by the Fisheries Research Board of Canada and the Canadian National Sportsmen's Show.

REFERENCES

Appleton, A. B. 1929. The relation between the rate of growth and the rate of ossification in the foetus of the rabbit. Compt. Rend. Assoc. Anat., 24th Meeting, Bordeaux, p. 3. [Original not seen].

Astanin, L. P. 1947. On the determination of the age of fishes [in Russian, English summary]. Zool. Zh., 26, 287-288.

Backiel, T. 1962. Determination of time of annulus formation on fish scales. Acta Hydrobiol., 4, 393-411.

Balon, E. K. 1972. Possible fish stock size assessment and available production survey as developed on Lake Kariba. Afr. J. Trop. Hydrobiol. Fish., 1, 45-73.

Berg, A. 1968. Studies on the metabolism of calcium and strontium in freshwater fish. I.—Relative contribution of direct and intestinal absorption. Mem. Ist. ital., Idrobiol., 23, 161-196.

Berg, A. 1970. Studies on the metabolism of calcium and strontium in freshwater fish. II.—Relative contribution of direct and intestinal absorption in growth conditions. Mem. Ist. ital. Idrobiol., 26, 241-255

Blacker, R. W. 1969. Chemical composition of the zones in cod (*Gadus morhua* L.) otoliths. J. Cons. perm. int. Explor. Mer, 33, 107-108.

Budy, A. M., ed. 1970. Proceedings of the third conference on biology of hard tissue. Gordon and Breach, Science Publishers, New York, N.Y. 566 pp.

Casselman, J. M. 1967. Age and growth of northern pike, *Esox lucius* Linnaeus, of the upper St. Lawrence River. M. S. thesis, Univ. Guelph, Guelph, Ontario. 219 pp.

Casselman, J. M. (In preparation). Cleithral method of determining age and growth of northern pike *Esox lucius* Linnaeus and other esocids.

Casselman, J. M., R. Hewins, and J. C. Rucklidge. (In preparation). Electron microprobe X-ray analysis of the seasonal growth zones in fish calcified tissue.

Chugunova, N. I. 1968. Employment of scales, bones and otoliths of fishes for the study of growth, age and other aspects of their biology, pages 3-17. *In* International conference on ageing and growth of fishes, Smolenice [mimeographed]. 143 pp.

Coble, D. W. 1970. False annulus formation in bluegill scales. Trans. Am. Fish. Soc., 99, 363-368.

Dannevig, E. H. 1956. Chemical composition of the zones in cod otoliths. J. Cons. perm. int. Explor. Mer, 21, 156-159.

De Bont, A. F. 1967. Some aspects of age and growth of fish in temperate and tropical waters, pages 67-88. *In* S. D. Gerking, ed. The biological basis of freshwater fish production. Blackwell Scientific Publications, Oxford. 495 pp.

Degens, E. T., W. G. Deuser, and R. L. Haedrich. 1969. Molecular structure and composition of fish otoliths. Mar. Biol., 2, 105-113.

Dickerson, J. W. T. 1962a. The effect of development on the composition of a long bone of the pig, rat and fowl. Biochem. J., 82, 47-55.

Dickerson, J. W. T. 1962b. Changes in the composition of the human femur during growth. Biochem. J., 82, 56-61.

Dollerup, E. 1964. Chemical analyses and microradiographic investigations on bone biopsies from cases of osteoporosis and osteomalacia as compared with normal. Part I. Calcium, phosphorus and nitrogen content of normal and osteoporotic human bone, pages 399-404. *In* H. J. J. Blackwood, ed. Bone and tooth. The Macmillan Company, New York, N.Y.

Filipsson, O. 1972. Sötvattenslaboratoriets provfiske-och provtagningsmetoder. Information från Sötvattenslaboratoriet Drottningholm, **16,** 24 pp.

Frost, H. M. 1967. The dynamics of osteoid tissue. *In* L'osteomalacie (Tours 1965) (editor D. J. Hioco), pp. 3-18. Mason. Paris. [original not seen].

Frost, W. E., and C. Kipling. 1959. The determination of the age and growth of pike (*Esox lucius* L.) from scales and opercular bones. J. Cons. perm. int. Explor. Mer, **24,** 314-341.

Frost, W. E., and C. Kipling. 1961. Some observations on the growth of pike, *Esox lucius*, in Windermere. Verh. int. Verein. theor. angew. Limnol., **14,** 776-781.

Graham, M. 1929. Studies of age-determination in fish. Part II--A survey of the literature. Fishery. Invest., Lond., Ser. II, **11,** 50 pp.

Hatfield, C. T., J. N. Stein, M. R. Falk, and C. S. Jessop. 1972. Fish resources of the Mackenzie River Valley. Environment Canada, Fisheries Service, Interim Rep. 1, 1, 247 pp.

Hederström, H. 1759. Rön om Fiskars Ålder. Handl. Kungl. Vetenskapsakademin (Stockholm) 20: 222-229. Re-published in Rep. Inst. Freshwat. Res. Drottningholm, **40,** 161-164 (1959) as Observations on the age of fishes.

Hickling, C. F. 1931. The structure of the otolith of the hake. Q. Jl. microsc. Sci., New Ser., **74,** 547-562.

Hogman, W. J. 1968. Annulus formation on scales of four species of coregonids reared under artificial conditions. J. Fish. Res. Bd. Can., **25,** 2111-2122.

Holden, M. J. 1955. Ring formation in the scales of *Tilapia variabilis* Boulenger and *Tilapia esculenta* Graham from Lake Victoria. East Afr. Fish. Res. Organ. Ann. Rep. 1954-1955, 36-40.

Horwitz, W., ed. 1970. Official methods of analysis of the Association of Official Analytical Chemists. 11th ed. Association of Official Analytical Chemists, Washington, D.C. 1015 pp.

Irie, T. 1955. The crystal texture of the otolith of a marine teleost *Pseudosciaena*. J. Fac. Fish. Anim. Husb. Hiroshima Univ., **1,** 1-13.

Irie, T. 1960. The growth of the fish otolith. J. Fac. Fish. Anim. Husb. Hiroshima Univ., **3,** 203-221.

Irie, T., T. Yokoyama, and T. Yamada. 1967. Calcification of fish otolith caused by food and water. Bull. Jap. Soc. scient, Fish., **33,** 24-26.

Johnson, L. D. 1959. Story of a thousand stomachs. Wis. Conserv. Bull., **24,** 7-9 .

Joslyn, M. A. 1970. Ash content and ashing procedures, pages 109-140. *In* M. A. Joslyn, ed. Methods of food analysis. Physical, chemical, and instrumental methods of analysis. 2nd ed. Academic Press, New York, N.Y. 845 pp.

Keeton, D. 1965. Application of Stoeltzner's method to determine growth of fish scales. Trans. Am. Fish. Soc., **94,** 93-94.

Kobayashi, S., R. Yuki, T. Furui, and T. Kosugiyama. 1964. Calcification in fish and shell-fish—I. Tetracycline labelling patterns on scale, centrum and otolith in young goldfish. Bull. Jap. Soc. scient. Fish., **30,** 6-13.

Mashiko, K., and K. Jozuka. 1962. Studies on the calcium uptake by teleost fishes. I. ^{45}Ca uptake by the crucian carp. Sci. Rep. Kanazawa Univ., **8,** 107-126.

Mashiko, K., and K. Jozuka. 1964. Absorption and excretion of calcium by teleost fishes with special reference to routes followed. Annotnes zool. jap., **37,** 41-50.

McLean, F. C., and M. R. Urist. 1968. Bone. Fundamentals of the physiology of skeletal tissue. 3rd ed. University of Chicago Press, Chicago, Ill. 314 pp.

Mina, M. V. 1968. A note on a problem in the visual qualitative evaluation of otolith zones. J. Cons. perm. int. Explor. Mer, **32,** 93-97.

Moss, M. L. 1961. Studies of the acellular bone of Teleost fish. 1. Morphological and systematic variations. Acta anat., **46,** 343-362.

Moss, M. L. 1963. The biology of acellular Teleost bone. Ann. N.Y. Acad. Sci., **109,** 337-350.

Moss, M. L., and M. Freilich. 1963. Studies of the acellular bone of Teleost fish. IV. Inorganic content of calcified tissues. Acta anat., **55,** 1-8.

Mugiya, Y. 1964. Calcification in fish and shell-fish—III. Seasonal occurrence of a prealbumin fraction in the otolith fluid of some fish, corresponding to the period of opaque zone formation in the otolith. Bull. Jap. Soc. scient. Fish., **30,** 955-967.

Mugiya, Y. 1965. Calcification in fish and shell-fish—IV. The differences in nitrogen content between the translucent and opaque zones of otolith in some fish. Bull. Jap. Soc. scient. Fish., **31,** 896-901.

Mugiya, Y. 1966. Calcification in fish and shell-fish—VI. Seasonal change in calcium and magnesium concentrations of the otolith fluid in some fish, with special reference to the zone formation of their otolith. Bull. Jap. Soc. scient. Fish., **32,** 549-557.

Odland, L. M., R. L. Mason, and A. I. Alexeff. 1972. Bone density and dietary findings of 409 Tennessee subjects. I. Bone density considerations. Am. J. clin. Nutr., **25,** 905-907.

Ouchi, K., J. Yamada, and S. Kosaka. 1972. On the resorption of scales and associated cells in precocious male parr of the *Masu* salmon (*Oncorhynchus masou*) [in Japanese, English summary]. Bull. Jap. Soc. scient. Fish., **38,** 423-430.

Phillips, A. M., Jr., H. A. Podoliak, D. L. Livingston, R. F. Dumas, and R. W. Thoesen. 1960. Cortland Hatchery report No. 28 for the year 1959. Fish. Res. Bull. 23, N.Y. Cons. Dep., Albany, N.Y., 83 pp.

Regier, H. A. 1962. Validation of the scale method for estimating age and growth of bluegills. Trans. Am. Fish. Soc., **91,** 362-374.

Rucklidge, J. C. 1967. A computer program for processing microprobe data. J. Geol., **75,** 126.

Simmons, D. J. 1971. Calcium and skeletal tissue physiology in teleost fishes. Clin. Orthop. Rel. Res., **76,** 244-280.

Simmons, D. J., N. B. Simmons, and J. H. Marshall. 1970. The uptake of calcium-45 in the acellular-boned toadfish. Calc. Tiss. Res., **5,** 206-221.

Svetovidov, A. N. 1929. To the question of age and growth of perch, rudd and pike from the Lake Krugloe [in Russian, English summary]. Russk. zool. Zh. **9,** 3-22.

Trout, G. C. 1958. Otoliths in age determination, pages 207-214. *In* Some problems for biological fishery survey and techniques for their solution. International Commission for the North-West Atlantic Fisheries, Spec. Publ. 1. A symposium held at Biarritz, France, 1-10 March 1956.

Vaughan, J. M. 1970. The physiology of bone. Oxford University Press, London. 325 pp.

Wallin, O. 1957. On the growth structure and developmental physiology of the scale of fishes. Rep. Inst. Freshwat. Res. Drottningholm, **38**, 385-447.

Widdowson, E. M., and J. W. T. Dickerson. 1964. Chemical composition of the body, pages 1-247. *In* C. L. Comar and R. Bronner, eds. Mineral metabolism, an advanced treatise. Vol. II, The elements, Part A. Academic Press, New York, N.Y. 649 pp.

Williams, J. E. 1955. Determination of age from scales of northern pike (*Esox lucius* L.). Ph.D. thesis, Univ. Michigan, Ann Arbor, Mich. 185 pp.

Woodard, H. Q. 1962. The elementary composition of human cortical bone. Hlth Phys., **8,** 513-517.

Woodhead, P. M. J. 1968. Seasonal changes in the calcium content of the blood of Arctic cod. J. mar. biol. Ass. U.K., **48,** 81-91.

Yamada, J. 1956. On the mechanism of the appearance of the scale structure. VI. Some observations associating with the absorption of scale in the goldfish. Bull. Fac. Fish. Hokkaido Univ., **7,** 202-207.

Otolith growth patterns: an aid in age determination in temperate and tropical fishes

by GIORGIO PANNELLA

Department of Geology, University of Puerto Rico in Mayaguez, Puerto Rico

SUMMARY

Age determination by means of otolith growth rings can be accurate if one is able to separate the patterns due to seasonal variations from those due to other causes that do not have annual periodicity. The presence of daily growth layers provides an invaluable help in determining the temporal and, indirectly, physiological meaning of growth patterns.

This paper compares the otolith periodical growth patterns of 25 species of tropical fishes with those of temperate otoliths in an attempt to provide a method of age determination.

Fish living in cold and temperate climates show rather marked seasonal rings which are separable from others due to spawning. The obvious seasonal changes in the environment must affect the calcification and growth rate of otoliths. How physiology and consequently calcification are controlled by environmental changes, is still unclear. Less obvious is the reason for growth rings found in tropical water fishes. Preliminary observations of some fishes living along the Western and Southwestern coast of Puerto Rico (lat. 18°18' and 17°57' N) indicate that otolith growth patterns and growth rate do not appreciably change through the year and that the rings are created by small changes in the ratio of organic matrix and argonite.

A basic bimonthly and monthly pattern is common to all otoliths and is possibly related to lunar influence. The hyaline zones reported from tropical fishes are probably related to reproductive activities. There is a tendency for hyaline zones to recurr with multiples of monthly periodicities.

The monthly or bimonthly bands can provide the precise basis for age determination.

INTRODUCTION

As clearly shown by other papers in this symposium, reading the age of a fish in its scales or otoliths is not a simple and unequivocal process. Although there is a tendency to blame ambiguous records as the only reason for the often contradictory readings, limitations of human experience and variability of growth patterns in different species, populations or individuals can easily account for discrepant results. To standardize the readings beyond the reader's personal experience is very important and many attempts have been made to establish some general criteria to distinguish 'false' from 'true' rings, that is, annual from subannual or random checks. A new possibility of finding such criteria is provided by the discovery of daily growth lines in some fish otoliths (Pannella, 1971). With the help of this basic time unit it is possible to separate the information essential for age determination from the rest. The presence of daily growth lines in otoliths may also help in resolving the long standing debate as to which of the records, the otoliths or the scales, is less ambiguous. Scales present some advantages with respect to otoliths: they are easy to collect, handle and study; furthermore they do not require the sacrifice of the fish for collection. The major advantage of otoliths over scales is the presence of clearly visible daily lines. This is not to say that daily lines do not exist in scales. In fact, there is some evidence that they do but that, because of their extreme thinness and their angular relationship with the structural features, they are not easily detected and studied. Because the daily journal can be followed in otoliths and not in scales, the precision and amount of data are far superior in the former. For practical purposes, the selection of otoliths over scales depends on many considerations. The study of daily lines requires longer time than current ageing techniques, but it could be expedited, and on the other hand used only to supplement the data obtained by common methods when they are equivocal. The discovery of daily increments not only increases manyfold the resolution and precision of the age counts but also promises to provide the fish biologist with an essential source of information since growth patterns are an accurate day by day journal of the fish life history. The usefulness of otoliths can hardly be overstressed.

This paper discusses the periodical growth patterns of otoliths of some temperate fishes and compares them with those found in some tropical fish otoliths, in an attempt to provide a method of age determination.

Determining the age of tropical fishes is difficult because there are no clearly annual rings. There are, however, periodically recurring growth bands which, once their periodicity has been established with the use of daily increments, could be used for age determination.

The basic assumption of this method is that tropical otoliths grow by daily addition similarly to temperate ones. It is a legitimate assumption in view of the fact that most, if not all, organisms tend to synchronize growth pauses with daily astronomical cycles, but it is offered as preliminary before experimental confirmation. It is an assumption that reasonably correlates the periodical patterns with what, however little, is known of the biology of tropical fishes.

MATERIALS AND METHODS

Because this study was intended as a general and not as a systematic survey, no attempts were made to obtain otoliths from specific groups. Most of the tropical material collected in October 1972 and January 1973 along the West and Southwest shores of Puerto Rico was kindly provided by Dr. W. Eger, Mr. J. Prentice, Mr. C. MacDonald, and by a group of fishermen from Mani. The otoliths of twenty-five different tropical species were examined and the largest ones, belonging to the following species, were studied in detail: *Cynoscion jamaicensis, Centropomus undecimalis, Vomer setapinnis, Micropogon furnieri, Lutianus apodus, Haemulon sciurus, Holocentrus rufus.* None of the tropical specimens were more than 4 years old, most of them were one or two years old.

Temperate specimens, collected in the Northwestern Atlantic and kindly provided by Dr. R. L. Wigley, belong to the species: *Merluccius bilinearis, Urophycis chuss, Gadus morhua,* and *Pseudopleuronectes americanus.*

All the specimens were prepared for acetate replicas following the method previously described (Pannella, 1971). Some etched and unetched specimens were also examined with the SEM. Growth patterns are best studied along sections that cut growth surfaces at right angles and where the thickness of increments is maximal. Otoliths increase in size, from one or more central nuclei by concentric increments. Growth gradients are equal in all directions only in the early stage and become unequal later, giving the characteristic laterally compressed shape of the mature otolith. Because of the vectorial growth only the median dorso-ventral surface, which represents the surface of maximum growth (SMG) can bring out the increments. This surface is generally curved and difficult to replicate as a whole on the flat surface obtained by grinding. It is better to break the otolith in the middle along the

dorso-ventral axis and prepare the anterior and the posterior parts separately. It is also recommended to begin grinding from the outer side of the otolith, which is often the closest to the surface of maximum growth. Fig. 1 shows some cross-sections of an idealized otolith: the most detailed patterns are developed only along a dorso-ventral section. All the other sections show the record compressed and incomplete.

The replicas are obtained, after grinding with 2600 grit (American Optical Co.), embedding the otolith in epoxy, and etching with 1% HCl aqueous solution, using thin acetate sheets over the acetone-flooded surface. After drying the replicas are immediately sandwiched between glass slides to keep them flat. For large otoliths that can withstand mechanical stresses, embedding in epoxy is not necessary.

TERMINOLOGY OF GROWTH RINGS

The neophyte finds the use of the terms describing otolith growth bands very confusing. The bands are called rings, zones or, occasionally, annuli. Adjectives like hyaline, transparent, translucent, dark, opaque, white describe the optical appearance of the band. The terms hyaline and opaque are used most frequently, but rather inconsistently. What is the hyaline band of one writer, is the opaque of another. In Table 1 are listed, some examples of inconsistent use of the terms by different writers.

One of the reasons for the conflicting use of the terms is the varying appearance of the bands under different lighting conditions. In incident light a band reflecting light appears white or opaque, whereas a band absorbing light appears dark or translucent. In transmitted light opaque and hyaline bands are those with high and low optical density, respectively. When Irie (1955, 1960), following Dannevig's (1956) misuse (Blacker, 1969), applied the terms translucent to the summer band and opaque to the winter band, one is left to wonder whether this is a semantic or observational mistake. Another reason for the lack of uniformity in the use of the terms can be attributed to the fact that latitudinal differences also involve seasonal differences and shifts in the time of deposition of the opaque and hyaline zone. Most of the literature deals with otolith growth rings of cold and temperate fishes and there is a clear tendency to consider sy-

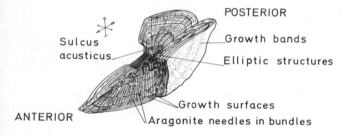

Sulcus acusticus

POSTERIOR

Growth bands

Elliptic structures

ANTERIOR

Growth surfaces

Aragonite needles in bundles

IDEALIZED SECTIONS OF FISH SAGITTA

Fig. 1. Growth patterns develop at right angles to structural patterns, from spherical centres and are best expressed in the anterior and posterior parts of the dorso-ventral sagittal plane. The three axes on the upper left provide a symbolic representation of all the possible sections in an otolith.

Table 1. Terminology of seasonal growth bands as used by different authors.

Author	Fish Name	Geographical Area	Fast-growth Zone	Slow-growth Zone
Molander (1947)	Plaice	Barents Sea	Hyaline	Opaque
Trout (1954)	Cod	Barents Sea	Opaque	Hyaline
Dannevig (1956)	Cod	Norwegian Coast	Transparent	Opaque
Kelly and Wolf (1959)	*Sebastes*	Gulf of Maine	Opaque	Hyaline
Irie (1960)	*Lateolabrax, Argyromus*	Sea of Seto	Translucent	Opaque
Mugiya (1964, 1966b)	*Salmo, Kareius*	Hokkaido	Opaque	Translucent
Mina (1968)	Cod	Barents Sea	Opaque	Hyaline
Pannella (1971)	*Merluccius, Gadus, Urophycis*	Western Atlantic	Fast-growth	Slow-growth

nonymous the terms summer and opaque, winter and hyaline bands. The synomymity has to be demonstrated in each instance, however, rather than be accepted as a general fact.

A third reason for confusion is related to the visual identification of a band, as pointed out by Mina (1968, p. 95): 'we can only observe that a new zone has been laid down when the change in calcium deposition is great enough to produce a change in the optical density of the otolith substance that can be detected easily'. Visual evaluations are relative to contiguous bands and do not depend on an absolute difference in the optical density of the bands. Thus, the conflicting use of the terms essentially arises because one does not make a distinction between a 'forming' and a 'formed' band. Statements like 'opaque zones formed from May to November and hyaline zones from December to April' are in many instances misleading because they imply a continuous growth during the stated months (an unwarranted conclusion, for one can only say the bands were formed before November or May) and do not allow for interruptions in growth which could drastically change conclusions as to the meaning of the zones. Interruptions do occur in biological growth; in some instances, as in fish scales, they are accompanied by resorption. Thus not only is there the possibility of time not being represented in the growth patterns but also of elimination of previously deposited record.

Because of all these considerations, a re-evaluation of all the present and accepted ideas in the field of age determination seems necessary. Also a more universal terminology applicable not only to temperate fishes should be adopted.

Daily growth increments could play an important role in this task. First they allow accurate measurements of the time represented in each band and of the growth rate. Increment thickness is the spatial expression of time. In a continuous process of growth the thicker the increment the more time it represents. Biological growth in general, and otolith deposition in particular, are rhythmic processes with daily frequencies, but only a fraction of the 24 hour period is used for the actual increment formation. We call the spatial expression 'daily'. The thickness of the increments can vary because of changes either in the length of the deposition time or in the rate of deposition. In the case of otolith formation and for our purpose, we can overlook the first possibility and conclude that increment thickness is the faithful expression of the conditions and rate of growth. Thus, it is clear that opaque zones made of thicker increments than hyaline zones represent periods of fast growth and can be called fast-growth zones (Pannella, 1971.) In temperate climates these zones tend to form during warm months, whereas the slow-growth zones are formed either at the end or at the beginning of the fast-growing period. Before accepting the two new terms, however, their applicability to tropical fish otoliths must be demonstrated.

To conclude the section: before we accept or reject new terms we need to know more about zone formation. Meanwhile it will avoid confusion if the meanings of the terms to be used are stated. In this paper the terms opaque and hyaline will be used to indicate zones of fast-growth, that appear light colour in acetate replicas, and ones of slow-growth, which appear dark colour in replicas, respectively, without any implication of seasonality unless so stated.

The last point on terminology problems: the term otolith is commonly, and incorrectly, used to indicate the largest of the 3 otoliths present in fish labyrinth. The appropriate term, however, is sagitta (or the very rarely used *sacculith*) since the largest otolith, with very few exceptions in teleosts, is contained in the sacculus. Because of the general acceptance in the field of age determination of the synonymity of sagitta and otolith, in this paper I will use the two terms as synonymous.

RESULTS

Even with all the pending questions, age determination of temperate fishes appears relatively simple when compared with that of tropical fishes. Growth checks and zones have been reported in bones and otoliths of tropical fishes (Pantulu, 1962, 1963; Eziuzo, 1963; Poinsard and Troadec, 1966) but they have been shown to form not during the same period nor with same regularity as in fishes of higher latitudes. After the preliminary study which reported the presence of daily lines in some temperate fishes (Pannella, 1971), it was an obvious project to investigate growth patterns in tropical fishes in the attempt to find some criteria for age determination. One of the basic problems is that, whereas in the otoliths of higher latitude fishes the accepted seasonality of zone formation was used to prove that the fine growth increments were deposited with daily periodicity, no such argument can be used for tropical growth patterns. The description of the observations must precede the discussion on this problem. The basic working hypothesis is that the smallest, regularly recurrent growth layers, designated as first-order, represent a constant time span and can be used to discover the periodicity of rhythmic growth patterns.

Fishes were collected in two areas: South-west coast (La Parguera), 17°57' lat. N and West coast of Puerto Rico (Mani) 18°18' lat. N. In both areas seasonal temperature fluctuations have a range of about 3°C. The South-Western area has very little rainfall and only few small rivers flow into the Caribbean waters; there are no seasonal salinity changes. Near Mani, however, the rainfall reaches annual values of 100-120 cm. with maximum of precipitation in the months of July, August and September. The Añaseo River flowing into the Mona Passage nea Mani is the major factor controlling salinity changes. Storms and turbidity increase in the same months. Tidal range in both areas is less than 30 cm.

Fishes were collected in October 1972 (Mani area) and in January 1973 (La Parguera area).

Microscopic examination of tropical sagittae, following the standard technique, reveals less sharply defined growth zones than in temperate ones. Small sagittae do not provide any clue to age determination, for they appear optically homogenous. Larger otoliths show some closely-spaced bands. To interpret them as annual would make the age of the fish unreasonably high for its size.

Microscopically many more details are discernible that can help the interpretation of the bands. Acetate replicas of the dorso-ventral sagittal SMG reveal the presence of dark and light periodically-recurrent bands made of thin growth increments (Plate 2, figs. 1, 2).

The smallest growth bandings, developed at right angles to structural aragonitic needles, consist of light layers of inorganic material delimited by thin dark surfaces, similar to those found in higher latitude otoliths (Hickling, 1931; Panella, 1971) (Plate 1, fig. 1; Plate 2, figs. 3, 4; Plate 6, figs. 1, 2, 3, 4). They become visible only after etching with HCl. They are thicker than those in temperate fish otoliths, by at least a factor of 2. Their thickness ranges from 3 to 20 μm. Sagittal and transversal sections show that the concentric first-order layers do not maintain a uniform thickness all around the otolith. Uniformly thick layers are deposited in spherical fashion only in the early stage of the sagittae; in later stages the layers show lateral change in thickness and pinching out (Plate 3, figs. 1, 2). The least incomplete sequence of first-order layers are found in the anterior or posterior areas of dorsoventral sagittal sections crossing the centre. Transversal dorso-ventral sections show very pronounced surfaces of interruption of growth (Plate 5, figs. 1, 2, 3). It is along these surfaces that the structural continuity of aragonitic needles is broken (Plate 5, figs. 3, 4, 6).

Interruptions in the sequences become more frequent in the late stage. Early sequences are very regular and continuous (Plate 4, figs. 1, 2). In some instances interruptions appear to be periodical (Plate 2, figs. 3, 4) but more often seem to be random.

Periodically-recurrent patterns become well developed in some species after the deposition of a central part made of 100-300 first-order layers. They consist of first-order layers progressively decreasing in thickness and in the density of organic fibres until they become almost indistinguishable (Plate 2, figs. 1, 2; Plate 3, fig. 4; Plate 5, figs. 5, 6). In several species (*Centropomus undecimalis, Cynoscion jamaicensis, Haemulon sciurus, Lutjanus apodus*) the succession of thick and thin first-order layers is periodical and the groupings show two pronounced

frequency peaks around 14 and 28. In figure 2 the frequences of groupings are shown. Pattern periodicities compare very close to those of higher latitude growth patterns.

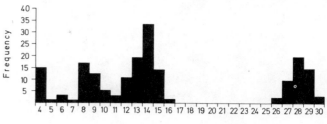

No. of lines / grouping

Fig. 2. Frequency diagram of periodically recurrent groupings of first-order bands in tropical fishes. The basic bimonthly patterns is repeated as multiple and submultiple in the peaks at 8 and 28. The reason for the peak at 4 is still unclear.

Other recurrent bands, not noted in temperate sagittae, with periodicities that are multiples of 28, are well developed in the largest specimens (estimated age from 7 months to 3 years). They consist of relatively undisturbed sequences of thick first-order layers followed after a check by interrupted sequences of thin layers. Microscopically and under reflected light they appear to correspond to the opaque and hyaline bands respectively. Because of their similarity with the spawning rings of higher latitude otoliths, they are interpreted as due to reproductive activities. No seasonal bands or winter checks analogous to those in higher latitude were found.

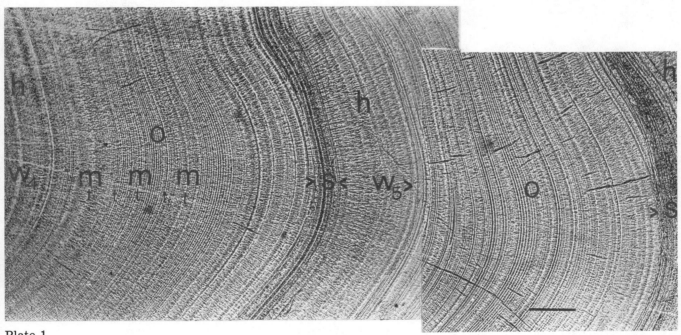

Plate 1

Periodical growth patterns in *Merluccius bilinearis* (Mitchill). Dorso-ventral sagittal secton: posterior part.

The record represents almost two years of growth. From left to right (direction of growth): W_4 the fourth winter band (also representing the fourth hyaline zone h) is followed by O the fourth opaque band deposited during spring, summer and fall months (about six months of thick daily lines) in which lunar month bands (m) and bimonthly bands (t) are well developed. S: spawning breaks (about two-month record); W_5 fifth winter band (about 4-month record) followed by the fifth opaque band, the second spawning break, and the sixth hyaline zone. Scale: 100 μm.

Plate 2

Periodical growth patterns in tropical otoliths of *Cynoscion jamaicensis* (Vaillant and Bocourt). All dorso-ventral sagittal posterior sections.

1. Bimonthly patterns (t). Growth direction from left to right. The patterns are made of thin and optically dense increments alternating with relatively thick less-dense increments. Scale: 500 μm.

2. Detail of one bimonthly band. Scale: 100 μm.

3. Central part of the otolith. Very regular patterns made of 2-4 increments. Clearly developed are the structure, made of aragonitic needles, at right angles to growth surfaces. Scale: 100 μm.

4. High magnification of picture 3. Scale: 50 μm.

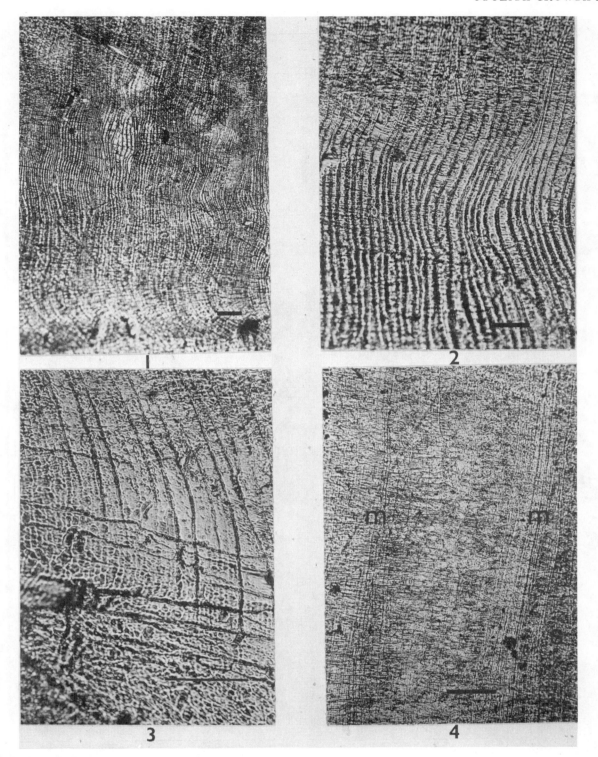

Plate 3

Otolith growth patterns in *Centropomus undecimalis* (Bloch). Dorso-ventral transversal section.

1.   Sequences of growth increments forming no evident patterns. The growth increments are not daily because they are made of smaller possibly diurnal bands as shown in pictures 2 and 3. The sequences in the sulcus acusticus area are highly compressed and incomplete. Scale: 100 μm.

2 and 3.   Detail view of growth increments depicted in picture 1. Scale: 100 μm.

4.   Monthly patterns (from m to m = one month) and spawning band (S). Scale 100 μm.

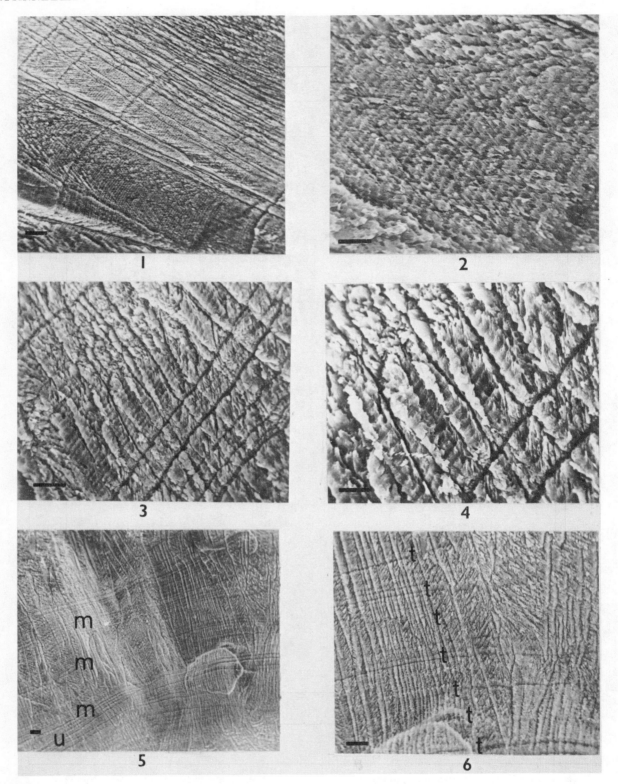

Plate 4

SEM pictures of growth patterns in otoliths of *Centropomus undecimalis* (Bloch).

1. Dorso-ventral transversal section of central part of otolith. Sequences of uniformily-thick growth increments without periodical patterns. Note random interruption surfaces; × 465, scale: 100 μm.

2. Detail of picture 1; × 1837. 5, scale: 50 μm.

3. Daily growth bands. × 900, scale: 100 μm.

4. Detail of picture 3; × 1800, scale 50 μm.

5. Monthly patterns (from *m* to *m* is one month); *U*, unconformity, the surface represents a period of resorption of the otolith, × 184, scale: 100 μm.

6. Detail of picture 5, showing fortnightly patterns (t), × 461, scale 100 μm.

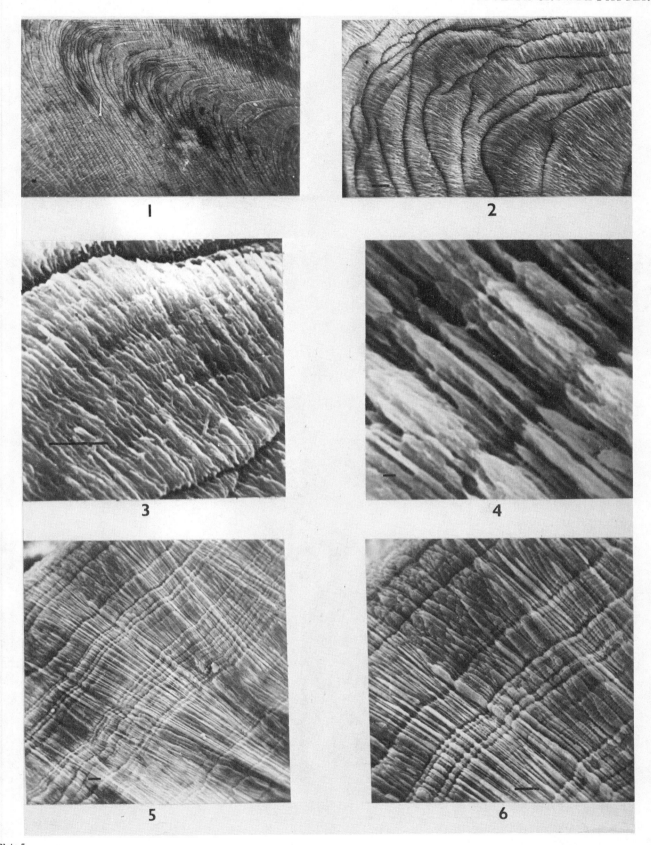

Plate 5

SEM pictures of periodical growth patterns in otoliths of tropical *Cynoscion jamaicensis* (Vaillant and Bocourt). Scale: 100 μm. unless otherwise specified.

1. Etched specimens; specimen no. F0-2. SEM of dorso-ventral transversal section showing the axis of maximum growth (crossing the curved growth surface at right angle). Along this section growth sequences are interrupted and irregular; × 154.

2. Detail of above area showing deep interruption surfaces and aragonitic needles; × 772.5.

3. Detail of above area: The time represented between the two interruption surfaces is about a fortnight; × 3,863.

4. Detail of picture 6, demonstrating that the surfaces of interruption are more deeply etched than the rest; the bridges between aragonitic needles represent organic sheets bounding daily increments; × 7,500, scale: 10 μm.

5. Dorso-ventral transversal section: growth patterns in the area of the sulcus acusticus: long sequences of daily increments are interrupted periodically by surfaces that indicate cessation of growth; × 367

6. Detail of above picture, showing uniformly-thick increments and periodical cessation of growth; × 750.

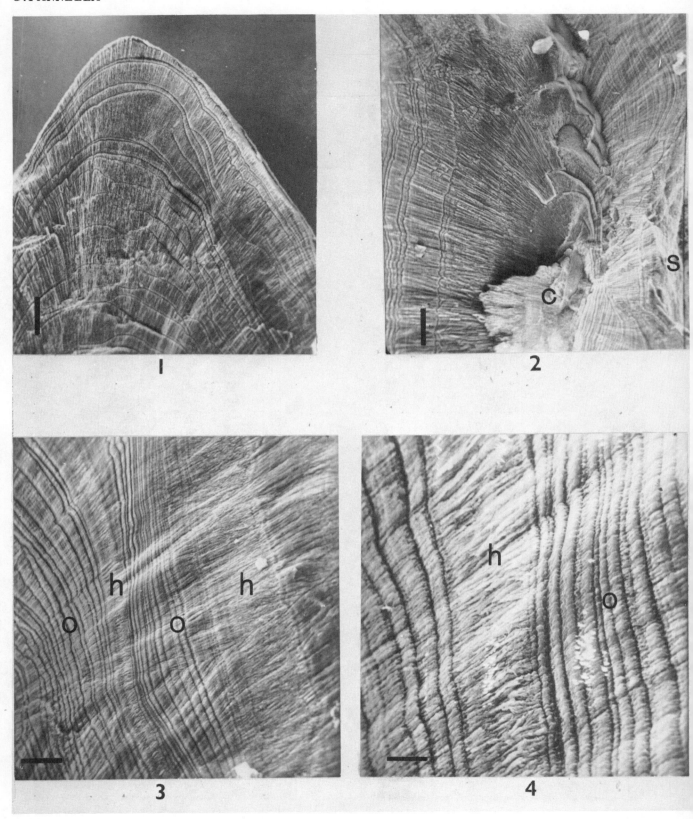

Plate 6

Growth patterns in etched specimen of *Pseudopleuronectes americanus* (Walbaum). Collected in New Haven Harbor, Connecticut on August 30, 1970.

1. Dorsal part of dorso-ventral transversal section showing interruption surfaces; × 184, scale: 500 μm.

2. Central part of same section; *C* is the center of the otolith, *S* is the sulcus acusticus. The line from *C* to *S* is the direction of minimum growth. Along this direction growth record is highly compressed and discontinuous; × 188.6, scale 500 μm.

3. Dorso-ventral transversal section showing two hyaline (*h*) and two opaque (*o*) zones. Note the different structural and growth features between the two zones. The hyaline zone represent a highly compressed record in which no daily lines are detectable, the opaque zone shows daily lines and periodically recurrent growth interruptions. In flatfish most of the interruptions have fortnight periodicity; × 473.8, scale: 200 μm.

4. Detail of picture 3; × 1886, scale: 100 μm.

One pattern is common in both tropical and temperate sagittae. The central part of them is characterized by very regular groupings of 2-4 first-order layers (Plate 2, figs. 3, 4). Only after these patterns have been laid down, do the fortnight and monthly bands become prominent. The change from the central area is not gradual but abrupt and often marked by great disturbance rings or by an organic rich band. This change was observed in all the otoliths, and must correspond to a fundamental physiological transformation that affects the rate and the periodicity of calcium deposition in otoliths. Interesting is the fact that the transformation takes place after the second or third year (depending on the species) in temperate fishes but only after six to eight months in tropical ones.

Using the thickness of first-order layers as an indication of the growth rate of the otolith (and, consequently, of the fish), one has to conclude that tropical fishes grow much faster than temperate ones, at least in the early stage, for the following reasons: the 'daily' growth increments is much higher and there is no seasonal slowing down of growth. After seasonal maturity, however, because the reproductive activity is spread through the year, growth is drastically reduced. This is shown in figure 3 where average maximum thickness of first-order layers is plotted against the age. The much faster tropical growth rapidly tapers off after the second and third year. This conclusion is well in agreement with what is known on the growth of tropical fishes (Edwards *et al.*, 1971; Scholander *et al.*, 1953).

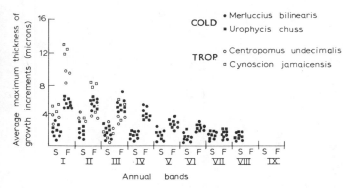

Fig. 3. Thickness of first-order growth bands in tropical and temperate fishes. Tropical fishes grow initially at a much faster rate than temperate ones until they reach sexual maturity. Breeding activities decrease otolith growth.

DISCUSSION AND CONCLUSION

Although it is impossible at this stage to pinpoint the causative factors of the daily lines in the sagittae of temperate fishes and one can only speculate, their existence should not come as a surprise, considering that organic activities are controlled by environmental changes geared to the diurnal astronomical cycle. Whether rhythmic growth is related to diurnal migratory behaviour, rhythmic feeding, or activity and rest, is difficult to say. But as we learn more about animal behaviour and physiology we discover how closely synchronized are the biological rhythms to the external ones.

It is also fair to conclude that, if daily increments exist in otoliths of temperate fishes, there is no strong

reason why they should not be present in otoliths of tropical fishes. After all, both environments show diurnal changes. Once this conclusion is accepted, it becomes possible to compare growth patterns and preliminarily to suggest a method of ageing tropical fishes.

There are patterns in temperate and tropical otoliths that have the same periodicies: the bimonthly (or fortnightly), and the monthly patterns. The environmental rhythms with such periodicies are related to lunar influence. The fact that no winter checks or seasonal bands are recognizable in the otoliths from the tropics where there are not marked seasonal fluctuations in the environment, is to be expected. Table 2 represents an attempt to list and describe the most clearly developed growth patterns in both tropical and temperate fish. This attempt must be considered only preliminary since only an infitesimal small number of representatives were examined. No doubt the table will have to be revised many times before becoming of general application. The first-order bands in tropical sagittae not only are thicker than those of temperate ones but also show differential etching (Plate 4, fig. 2) indicating a general change in inorganic content. Winter checks are not present in tropical fishes. There are frequent checks that abruptly interrupt the crystalline continuity but they are random accidental disturbances. The number of them seems to be inversely proportional to the water depth of fish habitats.

Spawning rings are most frequent with periodicities that appear to be multiples of months, perhaps supporting the idea of lunar influence on the reproductive cycles of certain fishes.

Poinsand and Troadec (1966) related the formation of hyaline bands in some Scianidae otoliths from West Africa to a major warm season that extends from January to May, and that of opaque bands to a major cold season from June to September. However, also during the warm season, spawning occurs. I would like to suggest that, perhaps, the hyaline bands are related to reproductive activities, as in the Scianidae found in Puerto Rico, rather than to seasonal changes. Gonadal development and spawning are in part controlled by seasonal changes but apparently less so in the tropics than in temperate areas. Hyder (1969) found that in *Tilapia leucosticta* from an equatorial lake in Kenia the gonadal development was stimulated by sunlight and high temperature (in the period December to March) and that breeding begins at the onset of the rainy season or, at least, peaks during this season.

The use of hyaline and opaque bands in tropical fishes as indicators of annual periodicity can be misleading. Their periodicity must be checked by means of daily or monthly patterns.

With the help of first-order layers one can establish the periodicity of the bands that are microscopically visible for each species or each population. Once the periodicity has been determined, microscopic observations of the bands can be speedily carried out and the age established.

This preliminary work allows the following conclusions:

1. First-order layers very similar to those found in temperate fish otoliths are present in some tropical fish from West and SW Puerto Rico.
2. If the interpretation of the first-order layers

Table 2. Periodical growth patterns in temperate and tropical fish sagittae

	DAILY (First-order)	FORTNIGHT	MONTHLY	SPAWNING	WINTER CHECK	SEASONAL (Slow-growth)	(Fast-growth)
TEMPERATE	Thin growth bands (0.5-4μm) made of one layer of inorganic material with organic fibers oriented parallel to aragonitic needle long axis and a thinner one with fibers oriented at right angle to the axis.	Groups of 7-8 1st-order bands with densily-packed organic fibers (slow-growth) alternate with 7-8 1st-order bands with loosely-packed fibers (fast-growth).	Consist of two fortnight patterns one with thinner 1st-order layers than the other.	Relatively abrupt change in the thickness and optical density of first-order bands followed by a slow recovery. Generally only one year.	Break in otolith deposition preceded by general slowing down of growth and followed by a general return to previous growth rate.	Hyaline band made by very thin 1st-order layers often indistinguishable. It appears as a dark band in acetate replicas (under transmitted light).	Well defined 1st-order layers. Light band in acetate replicas (under transmitted light).
TROPICAL	Thin growth bands (3-20μm) similar to the above doublets but with less defined boundary between the two differently-oriented organic fiber layers.	Similar to the temperate ones but with stronger contrast between the 7-8 1st-order groups	Generally detectable when the fortnight patterns are not strongly developed.	Same features but more than one per year and spread throughout the year.	None	Not clearly developed.	

being daily is correct, the rhythmically recurrent patterns have bimonthly and monthly periodicities.

3.   No winter checks or defined seasonal bands are detectable.

4.   Spawning rings recurring with periodicity less than annual coincide with hyaline bands, which, thus, have different temporal meaning than those in temperate otoliths and cannot be used for age determination.

5.   It is suggested that age determination in tropical fishes could be carried out by defining the periodicity of regularly-recurrent bands microscopically detectable by means of first-order layers. Multiplying the number of bands by their periodicity one can obtain the precise age in number of days.

ACKNOWLEDGMENTS

The author wishes to express his appreciation to Dr. W. Eger, Mr. J. Prentice, and C. MacDonald for generously providing most of the tropical otoliths and for their identification, to Dr. R. L. Wigley for the temperate otoliths, to Mrs. J. M. Thompson and Mrs. D. Hewett (Physics Department, University of Newcastle) for drawing the illustrations, to Mr. H. Sergent for taking the SEM photographs. I thank Dr. J. D. Weaver for reading the manuscript and Mrs. Nidia T. de Irizarry who kindly deciphered my handwriting.

REFERENCES

Blacker, R. W., 1969.   Chemical composition of the zones in cod (*Gadus morhua L.*) otoliths. J. Cons. perm. int. Explor. Mer, **33**, (1), 107-108.

Dannevig, E. H., 1956.   Chemical composition of the zones in cod otoliths. J. Cons. perm. int. Explor. Mer. **21**, (2), 156-159.

Edwards, R. R. C., J. H. S. Blaxter, V. K. Gopalan, C. V. Mathew and D. M. Finlayson, 1971.   Feeding, Metabolism and growth of tropical flatfish. J. exp. mar. Biol. Ecol., **6**, 279-300.

Eziuzo, E. N. C., 1963.   The identification of otoliths from West African demersal Fish. Bull. Inst. fr. Afr. noire, **25**, (1), 488-512.

Hickling, C. F., 1931.   The structure of the otolith of the hake. Quart. Jl. Microsc. Sci. **74**, 547-563.

Hyder, M., 1969.   Gonadal development and reproductive activity of the cichlid fish *Tilapia leucosticta* (Trewavas) in an equational lake. Nature, Lond., **224**, 1112.

Irie, T., 1955.   The crystal texture of the otolith in a marine teleost, *Pseudosciaena*. J. Fac. Fish. Anim. Husb., Hiroshima Univ., **1**, 1-8.

——, 1960.   The growth of the fish otolith. J. Fac Fish. Anim. Husb., Hiroshima Univ., **3**, 203-221.

Kelly, G. F. and R. S. Wolf, 1959.   Age and growth of the redfish (*Sebastes marinus*) in the Gulf of Maine. Fish. Bull. U.S., **60**, (156), 1-31.

Mina, M. V., 1968.   A note on a problem in the visual qualitative evaluation of otolith zones. J. Cons. perm. int. Explor. Mer, **32**, (1), 93-97.

Molander, A. R., 1947.   Observations on the growth of the plaice and on the formation of annual rings in its otoliths. Svenska hydrogr.-biol. Komma. Skr., N.S. Biol., **2**, (8), 11pp.

Mugiya, Y., 1964.   Calcification in fish and shell-fish III. Seasonal occurrence of a prealbumin fraction in the otolith fluid of some fish, corresponding to the period of opaque zone formation in the otolith. Bull. Jap. Soc. scient. Fish., **30**, (12), 955-961).

——, 1966a.   Calcification in fish and shell-fish V. A study on paper electrophoretic patterns of the acid mucopolysacchanides and PAS-positive materials in the otolith fluid of some fish. Bull. Jap. Soc. scient. Fish., **32**, (2), 117-129.

——, 1966b.   Calcification in fish and shell-fish VI. Seasonal change in calcium and magnesium concentrations of the otolith fluid in some fish, with special reference to the zone formation of their otolith. Bull. Jap. Soc. scient. Fish., **32**, (7), 549-557.

Pannella, G., 1971.   Fish otoliths: daily growth layers and periodical patterns. Science N.Y., **173**, 1124.

Pantulu, V. R., 1962.   On the use of pectoral spines for the determination of age and growth of *Pangasius pangasius* (Ham. Buch.). J. Cons. perm. int. Explor. Mer, **27**, 192-216.

——, 1963.   Studies on the age and growth, fecundites and spawning of *Osteogeneiosus militaris* (Linn.). J. Cons. perm. int. Explor. Mer, **28**, 295-315.

Poinsard, F. and J. P. Troadec, 1966, Détermination de l'age. par la lecture des otolithes chez deux espèces de Sciaenides Ouest-Africains. J. Cons. perm. int. Explor. Mer, **30**, (3), 291-307.

Trout, G. C., 1954.   Otolith growth of the Barents Sea Cod. Rapp. P.-V. Reun Cons. perm. int. Explor. Mer, **136**, 89-102.

Scholander, P. F., W. Flagg, V. Walters & L. Irving., 1953.   Climatic adaptation in artic and tropical poikilotherms. Physiol. Zoöl., **26**, 67-92.

Effects of starvation and feeding on circulus formation on scales of young sockeye salmon of four racial origins, and of one race of young kokanee, coho and chinook salmon

by H. T. BILTON

Fisheries Research Board of Canada, Pacific Biological Station, Nanaimo, B.C.

SUMMARY

1. The effects of alternate periods of starvation and feeding on circulus formation on scales of young sockeye salmon of four different racial origins *(Oncorhynchus nerka)* and of young kokanee *(O. nerka kennerlyi)*, coho *(O. kisutch)* and chinook salmon *(O. tshawytscha)* were examined.

2. Replicate populations of young fish of each species, race, and cross were reared under three treatment regimes: $2S \rightarrow 1F$, $2S \rightarrow 2F$, $2S \rightarrow 3F$; $3F \rightarrow 2S$, $2F \rightarrow 2S$, $1F \rightarrow 2S$; and fed daily for 12 months (for example, 2S equals starved for 2 months and 2F fed daily for 2 months). One half of the replicate populations reared under each of the treatment regimes was sampled up to six times during the 12-month period and the remaining populations were sampled only once at the end of the experiment. As only the effects of ration were to be examined fluctuations in water temperature were held at a minimum and the water flow was held constant. During the 12-month period, water temperatures ranged from means of 5.9°C to 8.7°C. Light period was automatically controlled to provide 12 hr of light in each 24-hr period.

3. Regardless of species, race, or crosses, changes in length and weight of fish and in the scale characters in response to periods of feeding and starvation were generally similar. Circuli formed during periods of feeding but in most cases circuli did not form during periods of starvation. In several instances there were significant decreases in mean number of circuli suggesting resorption of the scale material. Repeated sampling, up to six times throughout a 12-month period, not only affected the length and weight of fish but was also reflected in the increment in number of circuli and the scale radius in almost half the comparisons. In these populations increments in circuli and scale radius were less among populations sampled six times. In virtually all populations the mean number of checks increased during periods of feeding rather than starvation. In most populations repeated sampling of the fish up to six times did not induce the formation of checks. Changes in circulus spacing between individual starvation and feeding periods were insignificant in most comparisons. There did not appear to be a strong relationship between circulus spacing and periods of starvation or feeding. In most populations the size of the scale nucleus was found to decrease significantly over the 12-month period. These changes did not appear to be associated with either feeding or starvation.

4. In a number of populations there were significant positive correlations between the size of the scale nucleus and the length of the fish at the end of the experiment. The treatment regimes had no effect on either the circulus- or scale radius-body length relationships in most comparisons. However, the age

and/or size of the male and female parents appeared to have an effect on both these relationships in a number of comparisons. Fish appeared to grow more in length and weight when fed either for 1 or 3 months near the end of the 12-month period than when they were fed for the same periods of time near the beginning of the period. This was not always reflected in the increments in circuli and scale radius. Quite often there was no difference between the mean increments for the same feeding periods at the beginning and the end.

INTRODUCTION

Starvation, feeding, and light period influence circulus formation and the incidence of checks on scales of young sockeye salmon *(Oncorhynchus nerka)* Bilton and Robins 1971a, b, c). Results indicated that the number and spacing of circuli, the scale radius, and check formation were associated with feeding and not with starvation. Circuli either did not form or were resorbed during periods of starvation. The present paper examines further the effects of starvation and feeding on circulus formation on scales of young sockeye salmon of 4 different racial origins, and of young kokanee *(O. nerka kennerlyi)*, coho *(O. kisutch)*, and chinook salmon *(O. tschawytscha)*. Other factors such as the effects of age and size of the parents and the size of the egg and fry on circulus formation are also examined.

MATERIALS AND METHODS

Experimental stocks

In the fall of 1970 a number of crosses between male and female salmon of either both known ages* and/or lengths (mm) were made (Table 1). These crosses included 4 of sockeye; 2 races from the Fraser River system located in southern British Columbia and 2 crosses of 2 races from the Skeena River system in northern British Columbia. Two crosses of kokanee from Meadow Creek on Kootenay Lake in southern British Columbia, 1 cross of coho, and 1 of chinook from the Big Qualicum River on the east coast of Vancouver Island were also made (Fig. 1). The fertilized eggs from each of the crosses were reared in incubator stacks at the Rosewall Creek station on Vancouver Island.

When each group of fertilized eggs had developed to the 'eyed' stage, 100 eggs from each cross from each donor stock of eggs were selected without known bias

---

* The European system of age designation (Koo, 1962) is used in this paper. Age 1.3 indicates 1 year of freshwater life and three years of sea life.

and each egg in each of the 100-egg lots was weighed in milligrams. These were returned to their respective donor stocks. Then, without known bias, 59 replicate lots of eggs containing from 50 to 100 eggs were selected from the same crosses and donor stocks and placed in individual tanks (Table 1). The number of replicate lots of eggs varied from 3 (coho, Big Qualicum) to 6 (the variation in the number of replications was due to the availability of eggs). These lots of eggs were placed in wire mesh baskets in tanks in the hatchery and the number that hatched each day was recorded. Forty-five days after the date of 90% hatch of each lot of eggs, 10 to 25 of the resultant fry (prior to feeding) (Table 1) were measured for length (fork length in millimeters) and weight (in grams) and then preserved in 10% formalin. Fry in each lot were offered *ad libitum* food according to standard hatchery procedures for a period of 91 days. Ninety-one days after the previous sampling of each lot of fry from the various donor stocks and crosses, totals of 25 to 50 fry were selected without known bias from each, and their fork lengths measured, giving the means and standard deviations as shown in Table 1. On the same dates, as shown in Table 1, groups of from 6 to 25 fry whose lengths fell within one standard deviation of each of their respective means were selected for the experiment and were placed in individual tanks. An additional 25 fry from each were selected on the same basis, killed, and measured for length and weight, and scales removed to serve as the 'starting point' against which subsequent growth data were compared.

Ration

To test the gross effects of ration, fish were offered either an *ad libitum* diet (commercial hatchery food) daily or were starved. The effects of alternate periods of feeding and starving were examined.

Experimental apparatus

As only the effects of ration were to be examined, fluctuations in water temperature were held at a minimum and water flow was held constant. The experimental apparatus was located in a building at the Rosewall Creek facility. Each tank held 10 gallons of water at a mean temperature ranging from 5.8°C for the period April 23-30, 1971 to 8.75°C for September, 1971 (see Table 2). Individual flowmeters ensured equal flow to all tanks. The experimental area was illuminated by incandescent lights automatically controlled to give 12 hours of light in each 24-hour period.

Experimental design

The experimental design is depicted in Table 3. Within each of the 4 races of sockeye and the 1 of chinook, 6 groups of fry from specific crosses were reared for a period of 12 months. In each case, 2 groups were reared under a feeding regime beginning with 2 months of starvation and ending with 3 months of feeding (Table 3) (2S → 3F). One of these groups was sampled for length, weight, and scales at the end of each period of starvation or feeding for a total of

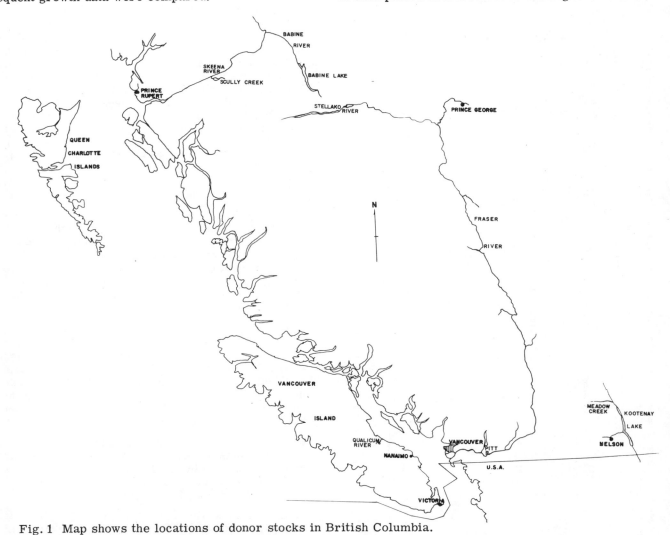

Fig. 1 Map shows the locations of donor stocks in British Columbia.

Table 1. Summary of crosses made by species, race, age, length, dates fertilized, dates measurements of eggs and of fry obtained, and number of eggs and fry in each group.

Species	Race	Cross ♂ Age	♂ Length	♀ Age	♀ Length	Date fertilized	Date eyed eggs measured	No. of replicate lots of eggs	No. eggs each	Date fry measured 45 days after 90% hatch	No. of replicate lots of fry measured	No. fry each	Length of fry N	X̄	SD	Date fry measured 91 days after 90% hatch + 45 days	No. of replicate lots of fry	No. fry in each experimental group
Sockeye	Pitt R.	1.3	576	1.2	454	15/9/70	29/10/70	6	100	22/1/71	6	25	50	47.4	3.30	23/4/71	6	25
		1.3	615	1.3	540	"	"	6	100	"	6	25	50	51.3	3.95	"	6	25
		1.3	615	1.2	499	"	"	6	100	"	6	25	50	47.8	5.71	"	6	25
	Stellako R.	1.2	443	1.3	509	28/9/70	10/11/70	6	100	25/1/71	6	25	50	50.2	5.38	26/4/71	6	25
		1.2	443	1.2	476	"	"	6	100	"	6	25	50	51.7	2.67	"	6	25
	L. Babine R.	1.2	467	1.3	521	24/9/70	5/11/70	6	50[b]	22/1/71	6	25	50	47.7	4.09	23/4/71	6	25
	Scully Cr.	1.2	440	1.2	436	5/9/70	15/10/70	6	100	18/1/71	6	25	25	47.2	2.48	19/4/71	6	6, 22, 25, 25, 25
Kokanee	Meadow Cr.	—	185	—	260	24/9/70	2/11/70	4	50[a]	28/1/71	4	10	27	36.5	1.25	29/4/71	4	19, 25, 25, 25
		—	185	—	176	"	"	4	50[a]	"	4	10	25	37.8	2.12	"	4	25
Coho	B. Qualicum	1.1	461	1.1	452	26/11/70	6/1/71	3	100	12/3/71	3	25	50	49.5	6.82	11/6/71	3	25
Chinook	B. Qualicum	—	675	—	675	29/10/70	12/12/70	6	100	16/2/71	6	25	50	53.8	4.64	20/5/71	6	25

[a] Number of eggs small due to the small number available in each female.
[b] Number of eggs small because of low survival to eyed stage.

TABLE 2 Mean monthly water temperatures and standard deviation

Month		X̄ temp. °C	SD
Apr. 23-30	1971	5.87	0.05
May	1971	7.13	0.49
June	1971	6.51	0.10
July	1971	6.61	0.18
Aug.	1971	7.68	0.48
Sep.	1971	8.75	0.13
Oct.	1971	7.88	0.81
Nov.	1971	7.98	0.58
Dec.	1971	7.63	0.17
Jan.	1972	6.90	0.29
Feb.	1972	6.22	0.21
Mar.	1972	5.79	0.09
Apr.	1972	6.69	0.78
May	1972	5.90	0.17
June 1-14	1972	6.01	0.09
Range	5.79-8.75		
Weighted X̄	6.99		

six times. The second group was sampled only once at the end of the 12-month period. Two other groups were reared under a feeding regime beginning with 3 months of feeding and ending with 2 months of starvation (3F → 2S). One of these groups was sampled at the end of each period of starvation or feeding, for a total of six times. The second group was sampled only once at the end of the 12-month period. A third pair of groups of fry was fed daily throughout the 12-month period. One group was sampled a total of six times and the other sampled only once at the end of 12 months.

The kokanee fry were reared under alternating periods of starvation and feeding, one of each pair was sampled six times, the other only once at the end. None were reared on daily feeding for 12 months. Two groups of coho fry were reared under the two feeding-starvation regimes and were sampled six times. A third group was fed daily for 12 months and sampled only once at the end.

Sampling and scale measurements

Fish were measured for length (fork length measured from tip of nose to fork of tail) and weight (grams) and scales removed from the part of the body just below the insertion of the dorsal fin and two or three rows above the lateral line (see International North Pacific Fisheries Commission 1957).

In the laboratory, impressions of scales were made in acetate plastic cards using the method described by Clutter and Whitesel (1956). Scale impressions were then examined under a Leitz Prado-X 123 micro-projector equipped with plano lenses.

Images of the scale impressions were projected with a magnification of 254 × onto sheets of 1-mm grid

Table 3. Experimental design: group designations and related periods of *ad libitum* feeding and starvation. 2S = two months of starvation; 2F = two months of *ad libitum* food daily

Species	Race	Cross ♂ Age	♂ Length	♀ Age	♀ Length	Group no.	2S	1F	2S	2F	2S	3F	3F	2S	2F	2S	1F	2S	Fed for 12 months
Sockeye	Pitt R.	1.3	576	1.2	454	1			Sampled 6 times										
						2			Sampled at end										
						3									Sampled 6 times				
						4									Sampled at end				
						5													Sampled 6 times
						6													Sampled at end
		1.3	615	1.3	540	1			Sampled 6 times										
						2			Sampled at end										
						3									Sampled 6 times				
						4									Sampled at end				
						5													Sampled 6 times
						6													Sampled at end
		1.3	615	1.2	499	1			Sampled 6 times										
						2			Sampled at end										
						3									Sampled 6 times				
						4									Sampled at end				
						5													Sampled 6 times
						6													Sampled at end
	Stellako R.	1.2	443	1.3	509	1			Sampled 6 times										
						2			Sampled at end										
						3									Sampled 6 times				
						4									Sampled at end				
						5													Sampled 6 times
						6													Sampled at end
		1.2	443	1.2	476	1			Sampled 6 times										
						2			Sampled at end										
						3									Sampled 6 times				
						4									Sampled at end				
						5													Sampled 6 times
						6													Sampled at end
	L. Babine R.	1.2	467	1.3	521	1			Sampled 6 times										
						2			Sampled at end										
						3									Sampled 6 times				
						4									Sampled at end				
						5													Sampled 6 times
						6													Sampled at end
	Scully Cr.	1.2	440	1.2	436	1			Sampled 6 times										
						2			Sampled at end										
						3									Sampled 6 times				
						4									Sampled at end				
						5													Sampled 6 times
						6													Sampled at end
Kokanee	Meadow Cr.	—	185	—	260	1			Sampled 6 times										
						2			Sampled at end										
						3									Sampled 6 times				
						4									Sampled at end				
		—	185	—	176	1			Sampled 6 times										
						2			Sampled at end										
						3									Sampled 6 times				
						4									Sampled at end				
Coho	B. Qualicum	1.1	461	1.1	452	1			Sampled 6 times										
						2									Sampled 6 times				
						3													Sampled at end
Chinook		—	675	—	675	1			Sampled 6 times										
						2			Sampled at end										
						3									Sampled 6 times				
						4									Sampled at end				
						5													Sampled 6 times
						6													Sampled at end

Note: for example, 2S = two months of starvation
2F = two months of *ad libitum* food daily

graph paper. Each scale impression was oriented so that the longest axis (determined by measurement) of the image lay along the lines of the grid, and the centre of the nucleus† was at the edge of the sheet. The outer edges of the images of each circulus from the nucleus to the edge of the scale were then marked on the graph paper, as were all checks.

For each scale, the following counts and measurements were made: N = radius of nucleus (distance along longest axis of scale from centre of nucleus (determined by eye) to outside edge of first circulus); A-N = radius of scale minus radius of nucleus; C = total number of circuli from centre of nucleus to edge of scale; A-N/C-1 = average space between circuli when the radius of the nucleus and the first circulus are not included; check = the last narrowly spaced circulus of two or more closely spaced circuli preceding the first, more widely spaced circulus.

Statistical analyses

Mean increments in body and scale measurements at the end of each feeding and starvation period were compared either with *t*-tests or a Duncan's Multiple Range test (Li 1964). In a number of cases, the slopes

and intercepts of regression lines of number of circuli and scale radius on fish length, using mean values of fish sampled at the end of each feeding and starvation period, were tested for differences between populations with analyses of variance. Simple correlation coefficients were also calculated. Results of statistically testing for differences between mean increments in body and scale measurements at the end of each feeding and starvation period and for the total period for populations sampled six times and only once are shown in Tables 4 to 10. The actual values of mean increments in body and scale measurements at the end of each feeding and starvation period and for the total period of the experiment are shown in Appendix Tables A I to A VII on pages 64 to 70.

RESULTS

A. Feeding regime (2S → 3F)

(a) *Length*

Regardless of species, race, or cross, the direction of change in length associated with the various feeding or starvation periods was similar (Table 4). As

Table 4. Significance at the 5% level of mean increments in length at end of each feeding and starvation period

Species	Race	Cross age ♂	Cross age ♀	X̄ wt./egg	Start point	2S	1F	2S	2F	2S	3F	Sampled 6 times
Sockeye	Babine R.	1.2 × 1.3		0.1549	47.69	*	+	*	+	Missing	+	<a
	Scully Cr.	1.2 × 1.2		0.1203	47.75	*	+	*	+	*	+	<
	Pitt R.	1.3 × 1.2		0.1348	47.84	*	*	*	+	*	+	*
	Pitt R.	1.3 × 1.3		0.1726	50.18	*	+	*	+	*	+	*
	Pitt R.	1.3 × 1.2		0.1607	48.21	*	+	*	+	*	+	*
	Stellako R.	1.2 × 1.3		0.1124	50.27	*	+	*	+	*	+	*
	Stellako R.	1.2 × 1.2		0.1070	51.80	*	+	*	+	*	+	>b
Kokanee	Meadow Cr.	—	—	0.1000	37.80	*	+	Missing	+	*	+	*c
	Meadow Cr.	—	—	0.0742	36.5	*	*	*	+	*	+	*
Chinook	B. Qualicum	—	—	0.3064	53.92	*	+	*	+	*	+	<
Coho	B. Qualicum	1.1 × 1.1		0.3271	50.48	*	+	*	+	*	+	None

Species	Race	Cross age ♂	Cross age ♀	X̄ wt./egg	Start point	3F	2S	2F	2S	1F	2S	Sampled 6 times
Sockeye	Babine R.	1.2 × 1.3		0.1549	47.69	+	*	+	*	*	+	*
	Scully R.	1.2 × 1.2		0.1203	47.75	+	*	+	*	+	*	<
	Pitt R.	1.3 × 1.2		0.1348	47.84	+	*	+	*	+	*	<
	Pitt R.	1.3 × 1.3		0.1726	50.18	+	*	+	*	+	*	*
	Pitt R.	1.3 × 1.2		0.1607	48.21	+	*	+	*	+	*	<
	Stellako R.	1.2 × 1.3		0.1124	50.27	+	*	+	*	+	*	*
	Stellako R.	1.2 × 1.2		0.1070	51.80	+	*	+	*	+	*	*
Kokanee	Meadow Cr.	—	—	0.1000	37.80	+	*	+	*	+	*	*
	Meadow Cr.	—	—	0.0742	36.5	+	*	+	*	+	*	*
Chinook	B. Qualicum	—	—	0.3064	53.92	+	*	+	*	+	*	<
Coho	B. Qualicum	1.1 × 1.1		0.3271	50.48	+	*	+	*	*	*	None

+ Indicates an increase; — indicates a decrease; * indicates no change.
a Indicates total mean increment of fish sampled 6 times was less than that of fish sampled once.
b Indicates total mean increment of fish sampled 6 times was greater than that of fish sampled once.
c Indicates total mean increment of fish sampled 6 times was the same as that of fish sampled once.

---

† The meanings of Nucleus, Circulus, Annulus and Check as used in this paper are given in Bilton and Robins, 1971a.

would be expected, significant increases in mean lengths were indicated at the end of each feeding period. No significant change in length occurred during each of the intervening 2-month periods of starvation. The increment in length at the end of each feeding period was correlated but not directly proportional to the duration of each of the periods (Table A I). Calculation of the estimated grand mean monthly increments in length indicate a change in the rate. These are given below:

	Period					
	2S	1F	2S	2F	2S	3F
All Sockeye	+0.7	+4.7	+0.3	+7.4	+0.3	+11.2
Kokanee	−0.3	+5.8	+0.1	+5.1	−0.3	+ 7.0
Chinook	+0.2	+6.4	+0.1	+7.6	−0.05	+10.3
Coho	+0.4	+6.0	−0.5	+7.4	−1.8	+ 7.5

In general, after feeding for periods of 2 and 3 months, fish had higher monthly length increments than when fed for 1 month. The only exception was the kokanee, where the monthly increment was lower for the 2-month feeding period than that of the 1-month period.

Comparison of mean lengths of populations sampled six times with those of populations sampled only once at the end indicated that in the 10 comparisons the means of 6 were the same, the means of 3 that had been sampled six times were significantly less, and in 1 the mean was significantly larger than those sampled only once (Table 4).

(b) *Weight*

In general, the direction of change in mean weight of fish among all populations was similar (Table 5). In all populations there was no significant change in mean weight of fish from the beginning up to the end of the second 2-month starvation period. Subsequent increases in weight were indicated at the end of the 2-month and the 3-month feeding periods among all populations, except the second cross of kokanee (there was no change in their mean weight at the end of the 2-month feeding period).

Generally, there was no change in weight during each of the starvation periods. In 1 population (1 cross of Stellako River sockeye) there was a significant loss at the end of the third starvation period. The increment in weight at the end of each feeding period was correlated but not directly proportional with the duration of each period (Table A II). Calculation of the estimated grand mean monthly increments in weight indicate a change in rate. These are given below:

	Period					
	2S	1F	2S	2F	2S	3F
All Sockeye	−0.1	+0.4	−0.2	+1.3	−0.4	+3.1
Kokanee	−0.04	+0.3	−0.1	+0.4	−0.2	+1.3
Chinook	−0.1	+1.1	−0.3	+1.6	−0.4	+3.6
Coho	−0.1	+0.9	−0.2	+1.7	−0.7	+2.2

Table 5. Significance at the 5% level of mean increments in weight at end of each feeding and starvation period.

Species	Race	Cross age ♂	♀	Start point	2S	1F	2S	2F	2S	3F	Sampled 6 times
Sockeye	Babine R.	1.2	× 1.3	1.09	*	*	*	+	Missing	+	*
	Scully Cr.	1.2	× 1.2	1.17	*	*	*	+	*	+	<
	Pitt R.	1.3	× 1.2	1.21	*	*	*	+	*	+	*
	Pitt R.	1.3	× 1.3	1.26	*	*	*	+	*	+	*
	Pitt R.	1.3	× 1.2	1.09	*	*	*	+	*	+	*
	Stellako R.	1.2	× 1.3	1.32	*	*	*	+	−	+	*
	Stellako R.	1.2	× 1.2	1.27	*	*	*	+	*	+	>
Kokanee	Meadow Cr.	——	——	0.44	*	*	Missing	+	*	+	*
	Meadow Cr.	——	——	0.39	*	*	*	*	*	+	*
Chinook	B. Qualicum	——	——	1.60	*	*	*	+	*	+	<
Coho	B. Qualicum	1.1	× 1.1	1.60	*	*	*	+	*	+	None

Species	Race	Cross age ♂	♀	Start point	3F	2S	2F	2S	1F	2S	
Sockeye	Babine R.	1.2	× 1.3	1.09	+	*	+	*	+	*	*
	Scully R.	1.2	× 1.2	1.17	+	*	+	*	+	−	<
	Pitt R.	1.3	× 1.2	1.21	+	*	+	*	+	−	<
	Pitt R.	1.3	× 1.3	1.26	+	*	+	−	+	−	<
	Pitt R.	1.3	× 1.2	1.09	+	*	+	*	+	−	*
	Stellako R.	1.2	× 1.3	1.32	+	*	+	−	+	−	<
	Stellako R.	1.2	× 1.2	1.27	+	*	+	−	+	−	<
Kokanee	Meadow Cr.	——	——	0.44	+	*	+	*	+	*	*
	Meadow Cr.	——	——	0.39	+	*	*	*	*	*	*
Chinook	B. Qualicum	——	——	1.60	+	*	+	−	+	−	<
Coho	B. Qualicum	1.1	× 1.1	1.60	+	*	+	−	+	*	None

At the end of 3 months' feeding, fish had higher monthly increments in weight than they had when fed for periods of 1 and 2 months. This was also the case between the 1- and 2-month periods.

Comparison of mean weights of populations sampled six times with those of populations sampled only once at the end indicated that in the 10 comparisons the means of 7 were the same, the means of 2 that had been sampled six times were significantly less, and in 1 the mean was significantly larger than those sampled only once (Table 5).

(c) *Total circuli*

Changes in mean number of circuli generally reflected changes in length and weight associated with periods of feeding and starvation (Table 6). In most populations a significant number of circuli did not form during periods of starvation and in 1 population appeared to be resorbed. (At the end of the second 2-month starvation period, subsequent to 1 month of feeding, there was a significant decrease in circuli on the scales of the 1 population of coho.) By the end of the third starvation period, subsequent to 2 months of feeding, there was a significant increase in circuli for 2 populations (Scully Creek sockeye and the Big Qualicum chinook).

At the end of each feeding period the mean number of circuli increased in most populations. However, there were some exceptions. At the end of 1 month of feeding, the mean number of circuli of 6 populations had increased significantly but had not changed for the

remaining 5 populations. At the end of both the 2- and 3-month feeding periods the mean number of circuli had increased in all populations. The mean increment in circuli was correlated but not directly proportional with the duration of each feeding period (Table A III). Calculation of the estimated grand mean monthly increments in circuli indicate a change in the rate. These are given below:

	Period					
	2S	1F	2S	2F	2S	3F
All Sockeye	+0.2	+1.4	+0.2	+1.5	+0.4	+2.0
Kokanee	+1.1	+1.3	−0.4	+2.0	+0.1	+1.7
Chinook	+0.6	+0.7	+0.5	+1.2	+0.7	+1.3
Coho	+0.3	+1.3	−0.8	+3.0	−0.9	+1.1

For the sockeye, there was little difference between the estimated monthly increment in circuli after 1 and 2 months of feeding. However, there was an increase in the rate of circulus formation after 3 months of feeding. For the other species there was a difference between the rates after 1 and 2 months of feeding, with the latter having a higher rate of circulus formation. During 3 months of feeding, the rate of circulus formation either did not change or

Table 6. Significance at the 5% level of mean increments in total circuli at end of each feeding and starvation period.

Species	Race	Cross age ♂	♀	Start point	Feeding regime 2S	1F	2S	2F	2S	3F	Sampled 6 times
Sockeye	Babine R.	1.2 × 1.3		2.88	*	*	*	+	Missing	+	<
	Scully Cr.	1.2 × 1.2		2.75	*	*	*	+	+	+	<
	Pitt R.	1.3 × 1.2		3.44	*	+	*	+	*	+	*
	Pitt R.	1.3 × 1.3		3.73	*	+	*	+	*	+	*
	Pitt R.	1.3 × 1.2		3.50	*	+	*	+	*	+	<
	Stellako R.	1.2 × 1.3		3.54	*	+	*	+	*	+	*
	Stellako R.	1.2 × 1.2		3.48	*	*	*	+	*	+	>
Kokanee	Meadow Cr.	——	——	None		+	Missing	+	*	+	<
	Meadow Cr.	——	——	None		*	*	+	*	+	*
Chinook	B. Qualicum	——	——	4.69	*	*	*	+	+	+	*
Coho	B. Qualicum	1.1 × 1.1		4.76	*	+	—	+	*	+	None

Species	Race	Cross age ♂	♀	Start point	Feeding regime 3F	2S	2F	2S	1F	2S	
Sockeye	Babine R.	1.2 × 1.3		2.88	+	*	*	*	*	*	<
	Scully Cr.	1.2 × 1.2		2.75	+	*	*	*	+	+	<
	Pitt R.	1.3 × 1.2		3.44	+	*	+	*	+	*	*
	Pitt R.	1.3 × 1.3		3.73	+	*	+	*	+	*	*
	Pitt R.	1.3 × 1.2		3.50	+	*	+	*	+	*	*
	Stellako R.	1.2 × 1.3		3.54	+	*	+	*	+	*	<
	Stellako R.	1.2 × 1.2		3.48	+	*	*	*	*	*	<
Kokanee	Meadow Cr.	——	——	None		*	+	+	+	*	*
	Meadow Cr.	——	——	None		*	+	*	+	*	*
Chinook	B. Qualicum	——	——	4.69	+	*	+	*	*	—	<
Coho	B. Qualicum	1.1 × 1.1		4.76	+	*	+	+	*	—	None

decreased from that during 2 months of feeding. This is contrary to what had been observed for both length and weight of the fish.

Comparison of mean number of circuli on scales of populations sampled six times with that of populations sampled only once at the end indicated that among the 10 comparisons the means of 5 were the same, the means of 4 that had been sampled six times were significantly less, and in 1 the mean was significantly larger than those sampled only once (Table 6).

(d) *Nucleus radius*

In 8 of the 11 populations there was a significant decrease in the mean nucleus radius on scales of fish between that at the beginning and that at the end of the experiment (for the 2 kokanee populations the period of comparison was from the end of the first 2 months of starvation to the end of 3 months of feeding) (Table 7). For the 3 remaining populations there was no change in the nucleus radius.

Most of the change in nucleus radius occurred during the 1-month feeding period (Table A IV). At the end of 1 month of feeding the nucleus radius for 7 populations decreased significantly and for 4 populations it remained unchanged.

Comparison of the mean nucleus radius of scales between populations sampled six times with that of populations sampled only once at the end indicated that among 10 comparisons the means of 7 were the

same, and the means of 3 that had been sampled six times were significantly larger than those sampled only once (Table 7).

(e) *Number of checks*

In most populations the mean number of checks increased significantly during each of the feeding periods and not during the starvation periods (Table 8). At the end of the first 2-month starvation period, none of the 11 populations showed a significant increase in the mean number of checks (in all cases checks were absent at the beginning). At the end of 1 month of feeding, 8 of the 11 populations had a significant increase in the number of checks. At the end of the second 2-month starvation period, scales of 2 populations showed a significant increase, for 5 there was no change, and for 3 there was a significant decrease in the number of checks. At the end of the 2-month feeding period, 9 of the 11 populations had a significant increase in the number of checks and for 2 there was no change. By the end of the third 2-month starvation period there was no change among 7 of the 10 populations, and for the remaining 3 there was a significant decrease in the number of checks. At the end of the 3-month feeding period, for 10 of the 11 populations there was a significant increase in the mean number of checks and for 1 (the coho) the mean number remained unchanged. The mean increment in the number of checks was highest at the end of the 3-month feeding period (Table A V). The

Table 7. Significance at the 5% level of mean increments in nucleus radius at end of each feeding and starvation period.

Species	Race	Cross age ♂	Cross age ♀	Start point	2S	1F	2S	2F	2S	3F	Sampled 6 times	Start and end
Sockeye	Babine R.	1.2 × 1.3		26.1	*	*	*	*	Missing	—	*	—
	Scully R.	1.2 × 1.2		24.9	*	*	*	*	*	*	*	—
	Pitt R.	1.3 × 1.2		24.4	+	—	*	*	*	*	*	*
	Pitt R.	1.3 × 1.3		22.6	+	—	*	*	*	*	*	*
	Pitt R.	1.3 × 1.2		21.5	+	—	*	*	*	*	*	—
	Stellako R.	1.2 × 1.3		24.0	+	—	—	*	*	*	*	—
	Stellako R.	1.2 × 1.2		26.4	*	—	*	*	*	*	>	—
Kokanee	Meadow Cr.	——	——	None	18.0	—	Missing	*	*	*	*	—a
	Meadow Cr.	——	——	None	17.1	—	+	—	*	*	>	—a
Chinook	B. Qualicum	——	——	24.0	*	*	*	—	*	*	>	—
Coho	B. Qualicum	1.1 × 1.1		23.6	*	*	*	—	*	*	None	*

Species	Race	Cross age ♂	Cross age ♀	Start point	3F	2S	2F	2S	1F	2S	Sampled 6 times	Start and end
Sockeye	Babine R.	1.2 × 1.3		26.1	*	*	*	*	*	*	*	—
	Scully Cr.	1.2 × 1.2		24.9	*	*	*	*	*	*	*	*
	Pitt R.	1.3 × 1.2		24.4	*	*	*	*	*	*	*	*
	Pitt R.	1.3 × 1.3		22.6	*	*	*	*	*	*	<	—
	Pitt R.	1.3 × 1.2		21.5	*	*	*	*	*	*	*	*
	Stellako R.	1.2 × 1.3		24.0	+	—	*	*	*	—	*	—
	Stellako R.	1.2 × 1.2		26.4	*	—	*	*	*	*	*	—
Kokanee	Meadow Cr.	——	——	None	19.8*	*	*	*	*	*	*	*b
	Meadow Cr.	——	——	None	18.8*	*	*	*	*	*	*	—b
Chinook	B. Qualicum	——	——	24.0	*	*	*	*	*	—	*	—
Coho	B. Qualicum	1.1 × 1.1		23.6	*	*	*	—	+	+	None	*

a Difference in nucleus radius between end of first 2S and end of 3F.
b Difference in nucleus radius between end of 3F and end of last 2S.

grand mean increment in number of checks for all populations at the end of each feeding and starvation period are shown in Fig. 2.

Comparison of mean number of checks on scales of populations sampled six times with that of populations sampled only once at the end indicated that among 10 comparisons the means of 4 were the same, the means of 4 that had been sampled six times were significantly less, and in 2 the means were significantly larger than those sampled only once (Table 8).

Comparison of the mean circulus spacing on scales of populations sampled six times with that of populations sampled only once indicated that among 10 comparisons the means of 9 were the same, and the mean of 1 sampled six times was significantly larger than the population sampled only once (Table 9).

(g) Scale radius

Changes in mean scale radius did not always reflect significant changes in length of the fish or appear to

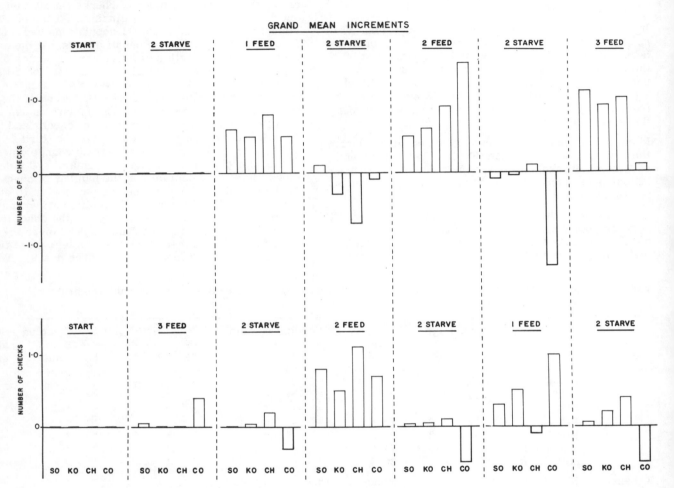

Fig. 2.   The grand mean increments in number of checks on scales of sockeye (SO), kokanee (KO), chinook (CH), and coho (CO) at the end of each feeding and starvation period under regimes 2S → 3F and 3F → 2S.

(f) Circulus spacing

In 5 of the 11 populations the mean circulus spacing decreased significantly, in 3 it increased, and in 3 it remained the same from the beginning to the end of the experiment (for the 2 kokanee populations the period of comparison was from the end of the first 2 months of starvation to the end of 3 months of feeding) (Table 9).

In most populations, changes in spacing between individual starvation and feeding periods were small and generally non-significant statistically. However, there was one exception: at the end of 1 month of feeding there were significant decreases in the mean circulus spacing on scales from 6 populations. The spacing on the remaining 5 remained the same. In Table A VI the actual mean increments and direction of the change of circulus spacing is given for each of the populations.

be always correlated with changes in the number of circuli. Although by the end of 1 month of feeding there were significant increases in the mean length of 9 of the 11 populations and in total circuli for 6 of the populations, the mean scale radius increased significantly only in 1 population (Table 10). After 2 months of feeding and 3 months of feeding there were significant increases in the mean scale radius in all but one case (Babine River sockeye). (For the same periods there were significant increases in both fish length and total circuli in all cases.) During each period of starvation the scale radius did not change significantly except in 2 populations. In 1 population there was a significant increase (Babine River sockeye) and in the other (the second kokanee cross) a decrease in the mean scale radius. The actual mean increment in scale radius was generally correlated but not directly proportional with duration of each feeding period (Table A VII).

Table 8. Significance at the 5% level of mean increments in number of checks at end of each feeding and starvation period.

Species	Race	Cross age ♂	Cross age ♀	Start point	2S	1F	2S	2F	2S	3F	Sampled 6 times
Sockeye	Babine R.	1.2	× 1.3	0.0	*	*	+	*	Missing	+	<
	Scully Cr.	1.2	× 1.2	0.0	*	*	+	*	*·	+	<
	Pitt R.	1.3	× 1.2	0.0	*	+	—	+	*	+	<
	Pitt R.	1.3	× 1.3	0.0	*	+	—	+	*	+	*
	Pitt R.	1.3	× 1.2	0.0	*	+	*	+	—	+	<
	Stellako R.	1.2	× 1.3	0.0	*	+	*	+	*	+	*
	Stellako R.	1.2	× 1.2	0.0	*	+	*	+	—	+	>
Kokanee	Meadow Cr.	——	——	None	0.0	+	Missing	+	*	+	*
	Meadow Cr.	——	——	None	0.0	+	—	+	*	+	*
Chinook	B. Qualicum	——	——	0.0	*	*	*	+	*	+	>
Coho	B. Qualicum	1.1	× 1.1	0.0	*	+	*	+	—	*	None

Species	Race	Cross age ♂	Cross age ♀	Start point	3F	2S	2F	2S	1F	2S	
Sockeye	Babine R.	1.2	× 1.3	0.0	*	*	+	*	*	*	<
	Scully Cr.	1.2	× 1.2	0.0	*	*	+	*	*	+	*
	Pitt R.	1.3	× 1.2	0.0	*	*	+	*	+	+	*
	Pitt R.	1.3	× 1.3	0.0	*	*	+	*	+	*	*
	Pitt R.	1.3	× 1.2	0.0	*	*	+	*	*	*	<
	Stellako R.	1.2	× 1.3	0.0	*	*	+	*	+	—	>
	Stellako R.	1.2	× 1.2	0.0	*	*	+	*	*	*	<
Kokanee	Meadow Cr.	——	——	None	0.0	*	+	*	+	*	*
	Meadow Cr.	——	——	None	0.0	*	+	*	*	+	*
Chinook	B. Qualicum	——	——	0.0	*	*	+	*	*	+	*
Coho	B. Qualicum	1.1	× 1.1	0.0	*	*	+	*	+	—	None

Calculation of the estimated grand mean monthly increments in scale radius indicate a change in the rate. These are given below:

	Period					
	2S	1F	2S	2F	2S	3F
All Sockeye	+0.5	+5.5	+1.0	+ 8.6	+3.0	+14.8
Kokanee	+2.9	+2.8	−7.8	+12.5	+2.0	+10.5
Chinook	+2.8	+4.8	+3.0	+ 6.4	+2.8	+12.1
Coho	+1.0	+4.2	−2.5	+12.3	−2.5	+11.8

For the sockeye, chinook, and coho the rate of increase in scale radius was higher during 3 months of feeding than that during 1 and 2 months' feeding. However, for the kokanee the rate was lower during 3 months of feeding than that observed for 2 months of feeding. In all populations the rate was higher during 2 months' than 1 month of feeding.

Comparison of the mean scale radius of scales of populations sampled six times with that of populations sampled only once indicated that among 10 comparisons the means of 6 were the same, the means of 3 that had been sampled six times were significantly less, and the mean of 1 was significantly larger than those sampled only once (Table 10).

B. Feeding regime (3F → 2S)

(a) *Length*

Significant increases in mean length were indicated at the end of each of the three feeding periods in all but 2 populations (Table 4). In the 2 populations the lengths did not change significantly after 1 month of feeding. The greatest increments in length occurred during the 3 months of feeding. Increments in length were generally correlated but not directly proportional with the duration of the feeding period (Table A I).

Calculation of the estimated grand mean monthly increments in length indicate a change in the rate. These are given below:

	Period					
	3F	2S	2F	2S	1F	2S
All Sockeye	+9.0	+0.4	+4.5	+0.6	+7.4	+0.4
Kokanee	+7.3	+0.2	+3.5	−0.1	+5.8	−0.1
Chinook	+9.0	0.0	+6.3	−0.8	+8.6	+0.05
Coho	+7.4	−0.4	+5.7	−0.9	+2.9	−0.2

Table 9. Significance at the 5% level of mean increments in circulus spacing (A-N/C-1) at end of each feeding and starvation period.

Species	Race	Cross age ♂	Cross age ♀	Start point	Feeding regime 2S	1F	2S	2F	2S	3F	Sampled 6 times	Start and end
Sockeye	Babine R.	1.2 × 1.3		6.0	*	*	*	*	Missing	*	*	—
	Scully Cr.	1.2 × 1.2		7.2	*	—	*	*	*	*	*	—
	Pitt R.	1.3 × 1.2		7.9	*	—	*	*	*	*	*	—
	Pitt R.	1.3 × 1.3		6.3	*	*	*	*	*	*	*	*
	Pitt R.	1.3 × 1.2		7.3	*	—	*	*	*	*	*	—
	Stellako R.	1.2 × 1.3		7.0	—	—	*	*	*	*	*	*
	Stellako R.	1.2 × 1.2		6.4	*	—	*	*	*	+	>	+
Kokanee	Meadow Cr.	—	—	None	4.4	*	Missing	*	*	*	*	+[a]
	Meadow Cr.	—	—	None	4.3	—	+	—	*	*	*	+[a]
Chinook	B. Qualicum	—	—	7.5	*	*	*	*	*	*	*	—
Coho	B. Qualicum	1.1 × 1.1		6.9	*	*	*	—	*	*	None	*

Species	Race	Cross age ♂	Cross age ♀	Start point	Feeding regime 3F	2S	2F	2S	1F	2S	Sampled 6 times	Start and end
Sockeye	Babine R.	1.2 × 1.3		6.0	*	*	*	*	*	*	*	—
	Scully Cr.	1.2 × 1.2		7.2	*	*	*	*	*	*	<	—
	Pitt R.	1.3 × 1.2		7.9	—	*	*	*	*	*	*	—
	Pitt R.	1.3 × 1.3		6.3	—	*	*	*	—	*	*	—
	Pitt R.	1.3 × 1.2		7.3	—	*	*	*	*	*	*	—
	Stellako R.	1.2 × 1.3		7.0	*	*	*	*	*	*	*	—
	Stellako R.	1.2 × 1.2		6.4	+	—	*	*	*	*	*	*
Kokanee	Meadow Cr.	—	—	None	6.4	*	—	*	*	*	*	—[b]
	Meadow Cr.	—	—	None	6.0	*	*	*	*	*	*	—[b]
Chinook	B. Qualicum	—	—	7.5	—	*	—	*	*	*	<	—
Coho	B. Qualicum	1.1 × 1.1		6.9	—	*	—	*	*	*	None	*

[a] Difference in circulus spacing between end of 2S and end of 3F.
[b] Difference in circulus spacing between end of 3F and end of last 2S.

For all species the rate of increase in length was highest during the 3 months of feeding. With the exception of the coho, the lowest rate of increase among feeding periods occurred during the 2 months of feeding. In all but 1 population lengths did not change during periods of starvation. In this instance, there was a significant increase.

Comparison of mean lengths of populations sampled six times with those of populations sampled only once at the end of the experiment indicated that among the 10 comparisons, the means of 5 were the same, and the means of 5 that had been sampled six times were significantly less than those sampled only once (Table 4).

(b) *Weight*

In all but 2 populations there were significant increases in mean weight at the end of each feeding period (Table 5). At the end of the 2- and 1-month feeding periods the mean weight of the second cross of kokanee had not changed from that at the end of the 3 months of feeding. In general, increments in weight were correlated but not directly proportional with the duration of the feeding period (Table A II).

Calculation of estimated grand mean monthly increments in weight indicate a change in the rate. These are given below:

	Period 3F	2S	2F	2S	1F	2S
All Sockeye	+1.1	−0.3	+1.4	−0.5	+2.8	+0.8
Kokanee	+0.5	−0.1	+0.6	−0.3	+1.2	−0.2
Chinook	+1.3	−0.4	+1.7	−0.6	+3.4	−0.7
Coho	+0.9	−0.4	+1.5	−0.7	+1.6	−0.3

For all species the rate of increase in weight increased from 3 months to 2 months to 1 month of feeding. This trend was almost the opposite to that observed for increments in length between the three feeding periods.

Comparison of mean weights of populations sampled six times with those of populations sampled only once indicated that among the 10 comparisons, the means of 4 were the same, and the means of 6 that had been sampled six times were significantly less than those sampled only once (Table 5).

(c) *Total circuli*

Changes in mean number of circuli generally reflected changes in length and weight associated with

Table 10. Significance at the 5% level of mean increments in scale radius (A-N) at end of each feeding and starvation period.

Species	Race	Cross age ♂	Cross age ♀	Start point	Feeding regime 2S	1F	2S	2F	2S	3F	Sampled 6 times
Sockeye	Babine R.	1.2	× 1.3	11.0	*	*	+	*	Missing	+	<
	Scully Cr.	1.2	× 1.2	12.1	*	*	*	+	*	+	<
	Pitt R.	1.3	× 1.2	19.2	*	*	*	+	*	+	*
	Pitt R.	1.3	× 1.3	22.2	*	+	*	+	*	+	*
	Pitt R.	1.3	× 1.2	18.2	*	*	*	+	*	+	<
	Stellako R.	1.2	× 1.3	17.7	*	*	*	+	*	+	<
	Stellako R.	1.2	× 1.2	15.8	*	*	*	+	*	+	>
Kokanee	Meadow Cr.	—	—	None		*	Missing	+	*	+	*
	Meadow Cr.	—	—	None		*	—	+	*	+	*
Chinook	B. Qualicum	—	—	27.7	*	*	*	+	*	+	*
Coho	B. Qualicum	1.1	× 1.1	26.5	*	*	*	+	*	+	None

Species	Race	Cross age ♂	Cross age ♀	Start point	Feeding regime 3F	2S	2F	2S	1F	2S	Sampled 6 times
Sockeye	Babine R.	1.2	× 1.3	11.0	+	*	*	*	*	*	*
	Scully Cr.	1.2	× 1.2	12.1	+	*	*	*	*	+	<
	Pitt R.	1.3	× 1.2	19.2	+	*	+	*	+	*	<
	Pitt R.	1.3	× 1.3	22.2	+	*	+	*	+	*	<
	Pitt R.	1.3	× 1.2	18.2	+	*	+	*	*	*	*
	Stellako R.	1.2	× 1.3	17.7	+	+	+	*	*	*	<
	Stellako R.	1.2	× 1.2	15.8	+	*	*	*	*	*	<
Kokanee	Meadow Cr.	—	—	None	*	*	*	*	*	*	*
	Meadow Cr.	—	—	None	*	+	*	*	*	*	*
Chinook	B. Qualicum	—	—	27.7	+	*	*	*	*	*	<
Coho	B. Qualicum	1.1	× 1.1	26.5	+	*	+	—	+	*	None

periods of feeding and starvation (Table 6). In all but 2 populations, circuli did not form during periods of starvation. At the end of the second 2-month starvation period, scales of the coho had significantly more circuli and at the end of the third starvation period the number of circuli increased significantly for the Scully Creek sockeye. By the end of the third starvation period, circuli had decreased significantly for the chinook and coho, suggesting resorption. In general, increments in circuli were correlated but not directly proportional with the duration of the feeding period (Table A III).

Calculation of estimated grand mean monthly increments in number of circuli indicate a change in the rate. These are given below:

	Period 3F	2S	2F	2S	1F	2S
All Sockeye	+1.9	+0.4	+0.9	+0.2	+1.9	+0.3
Kokanee	+2.2	+0.02	+1.1	+0.05	+2.3	−0.05
Chinook	+1.9	+0.1	+1.3	+0.3	+1.2	−0.9
Coho	+1.5	−0.1	+1.4	+1.3	+0.7	−1.1

For sockeye and kokanee the rate of increase in circuli was highest during 3 months' and 1 month's feeding, respectively. However, the rate declined during 2 months of feeding. For the chinook and coho, there was a decline in the rate of circulus formation from 3 months to 2 months to 1 month of feeding.

Comparison of mean numbers of circuli on scales of populations sampled six times with that of populations sampled only once indicated that among the 10 comparisons, the means of 5 were the same, and the means of 5 that had been sampled six times were signficantly less than those sampled only once (Table 6).

(d) *Nucleus radius*

In 6 of the 11 populations there was a significant decrease in the mean nucleus radius on scales of fish between that at the beginning and that at the end of the experiment (for the 2 kokanee populations the period of comparison was from the end of 3 months' feeding to the end of the last starvation period) (Table 7). For the 5 remaining populations there was no change in nucleus radius. In most cases the changes in nucleus radius between each of the feeding and starvation periods were insignificant (Table A IV).

Comparison of the mean nucleus radius of scales of populations sampled six times with that of populations sampled only once indicated that among 10 comparisons, the means of 9 were the same, and the mean of 1 that had been sampled six times was significantly smaller than the 1 sampled once (Table 7).

(e) *Number of checks*

Among the 11 populations, none had a significant increase in the mean number of checks at the end of 3 months of feeding from what was present at the beginning (in all cases, checks were absent at the beginning) (Table 8). Only at the end of 2 months of feeding after 2 months of starvation was there a significant increase in checks among all the populations. Number of checks did not change significantly during each of the first 2 periods of starvation. However, at the end of the third starvation period there was a significant increase in checks for 4 populations, a decrease for 2, and no change among the remaining 5 populations. The mean increment in the number of checks was highest at the end of the 2-month feeding period (Table A V). The grand mean increments in number of checks for all populations at the end of each feeding and starvation period are shown in Fig. 2.

Comparison of mean number of checks on scales of populations sampled six times with that of populations sampled only once indicated that among 10 comparisons the means of 6 were the same, the means of 3 that had been sampled six times were significantly less, and in 1 the mean was significantly higher than those sampled only once (Table 8).

(f) *Circulus spacing*

In 9 of the 11 populations the mean circulus spacing at the end of the experiment decreased significantly, and in 2 it remained the same as that at the beginning (for the 2 kokanee populations the period of comparison was from the end of the 3-month feeding period to the last 2-month starvation period) (Table 9).

In most populations, changes in spacing between individual starvation and feeding periods were small and generally non-significant statistically. However, there was one major exception: at the end of 3 months of feeding, at the beginning of the experiment, where in 5 populations there were significant decreases in mean circulus spacing; of the remaining 4, 3 remained the same, and the spacing of 1 increased significantly. In Table A VI the actual mean increments and the direction of the change of circulus spacing are given for each of the populations.

Comparison of the mean circulus spacing on scales of populations sampled six times with that of populations sampled only once indicated that among 10 comparisons, the means of 8 were the same, and the means of 2 sampled six times were significantly less than those sampled only once (Table 9).

(g) *Scale radius*

Changes in mean scale radius did not always reflect significant changes in length of the fish or appear to be always correlated with changes in the number of circuli. At the end of the 1-month feeding period near the end of the experiment, there were significant increases in mean length in 9 of the 11 populations, and for total circuli in 7 populations, whereas the scale radius increased significantly in only 3 populations (Table 10). At the end of the 3-month feeding period there were significant increases in the mean scale radius in all cases, but after 2 months of feeding there were significant increases in radius in only 6 of the 11 populations. During each period of starvation the scale radius did not change significantly, except in 3 populations. In 2 there was a significant increase and in 1 (coho) there was a decrease in the scale radius.

The actual mean increment in scale radius was generally correlated but not directly proportional with duration of each feeding period (Table A VII). Calculation of estimated grand mean monthly increments

on the scale radius indicated a change in the rate. These are given below:

	Period					
	3F	2S	2F	2S	1F	2S
All						
Sockeye	+12.4	+2.4	+6.1	+0.6	+5.6	+2.9
Kokanee	+11.6	−0.3	+5.1	+1.3	+7.1	+0.3
Chinook	+11.8	+3.1	+2.2	+0.2	+4.7	−2.4
Coho	+ 7.5	+0.7	+6.4	+5.2	+5.4	−1.3

For all species the rate of increase in scale radius was highest during 3 months' feeding. Among the three feeding periods, the rate of increase for kokanee and chinook was lowest during 2 months' feeding. On the other hand it was lowest for sockeye and coho during 1 month of feeding.

Comparison of the mean scale radius of scales of populations sampled six times with that of populations sampled only once indicated that among 10 comparisons the means of 4 were the same, and the means of 6 that had been sampled six times were significantly less than those sampled only once (Table 10).

C. **Comparison of mean increments of body and scale measurements between pairs of populations after feeding for 1-month, 2-month, and 3-month periods**

(a) *Fed 1 month*

The results of comparison of the mean increments between populations fed for 1 month near the beginning and near the end of the experiment are given in Table 11. Among 11 comparisons the increment in length was significantly higher for 4 populations fed near the end. There was no difference among the 7 remaining populations. However, for 10 of the 11 comparisons the mean increment in weight of those fed near the end was significantly higher than of those fed near the beginning of the experiment. Among the 11 comparisons only 3 of those fed for 1 month near the end had significantly more circuli. There was no difference between 7 comparisons, and in 1 comparison those fed for 1 month near the beginning had a higher number of circuli. For the scale radius, in 2 comparisons those fed near the beginning had larger scale radius than those fed for 1 month near the end. There was no difference among the 9 remaining comparisons.

In 6 of 11 comparisons the circulus spacing of those fed for 1 month near the beginning and the end did not differ. For the remaining 5 those fed near the beginning had significantly wider spaced circuli. The nucleus radius of 5 of the 11 comparisons was larger for fish fed for 1 month near the beginning than at the end. In 1 comparison it was higher for those fed near the end and in 5 comparisons no difference was indicated.

(b) *Fed 2 months*

The results of comparison of the mean increments between populations fed for 2 months beginning on the fifth month under the two regimes are given in Table 11. For 8 of 10 comparisons the mean increment in length of those populations reared under regime

Table 11. Comparison of the mean increments in body and scale measurements between populations fed for 1 month near the beginning and the end of the experiment; fed for 2 months after 5 months of treatment and fed for 3 months at the beginning and the end of the experiment.

Species	Race	♂	♀	Fed 1 month Length	Weight	No. circuli	Scale radius	Circulus spacing	Nucleus radius	Fed 2 months Length	Weight	No. circuli	Scale radius	Circulus spacing	Nucleus radius	Fed 3 months Length	Weight	No. circuli	Scale radius	Circulus spacing	Nucleus radius
Sockeye	Pitt R.	1.3 576	1.2 454	E	E	E	*	S	S	A	*	A	A	B	*	E	E	E	E	E	*
	Pitt R.	1.3 615	1.3 540	E	E	E	*	*	S	A	*	*	*	*	*	E	E	*	E	S	S
	Pitt R.	1.3 615	1.2 499	E	E	*	*	S	S	A	B	*	*	*	*	E	E	*	*	E	*
	Stellako R.	1.2 443	1.3 509	*	E	*	S	*	S	A	*	A	A	A	*	E	E	*	*	*	S
	Stellako R.	1.2 443	1.2 476	*	E	*	*	S	S	A	*	A	A	*	A	E	E	*	E	*	*
	L. Babine R.	1.2 467	1.3 521	E	E	*	*	*	*	A	*	A	A	*	A	E	E	*	E	*	*
	Scully Cr.	1.2 440	1.2 436	E	E	*	*	S	*	A	*	*	*	B	A	E	E	*	*	E	*
Kokanee	Meadow Cr.	— 185	— 260	*	E	E	*	*	S	*	*	*	*	*	*	E	E	S	S	*	*
	Meadow Cr.	— 185	— 176	*	E	E	*	S	S	A	*	A	A	A	A	E	E	*	*	*	*
Coho	B. Qualicum	1.1 461	1.1 452	*	*	S	S	*	E	*	*	A	*	*	*	*	E	S	*	*	*
Chinook	B. Qualicum	— 675	— 675	E	E	*	*	*	*	*	*	*	A	*	*	E	*	S	*	S	*

Note: A = fish which underwent treatment 2S → 3F and began the 2-month feeding period after 5 months.
B = fish which underwent treatment 3F → 2S and began the 2-month feeding period after 5 months.
S = fish which were fed for a specific period near or at the beginning of the experiment.
E = fish which were fed for a specific period near or at the end of the experiment.

Entry of one of the above letters indicates an increment that was significantly greater at the 5% level.
Entry of * indicates no significant difference at the 5% level.

2S→ 3F was significantly higher. There was no difference between the 2 remaining comparisons. Such differences between populations in the increments in weight were not indicated. In 9 comparisons there was no difference, and in 1 reared under regime 3F → 2S the increment in weight was higher. Comparisons of circuli indicated that in 6, those fed for 2 months under regime 2S → 3F had significantly more circuli than those fed for 2 months under regime 3F → 2S. No difference was indicated for the 5 remaining comparisons. Such was also the case for the scale radius. For circulus spacing there was little difference between populations fed for 2 months under the two treatment regimes. The nucleus radius in 3 comparisons was larger for populations under the regime 2S → 3F. No differences were indicated for the remaining populations.

(c) *Fed 3 months*

The results of comparisons of the mean increments between populations fed for 3 months at the beginning and at the end of the experiment are given in Table 11. Among 10 comparisons the increment in length of 8 of the populations fed at the end was significantly higher than those fed for 3 months at the beginning. Such was also the case for increments in weight where all populations fed at the end for 3 months had gained significantly more in weight. However, the increments in circuli, scale radius, circulus spacing and nucleus radius did not reflect these differences in length and weight of the fish. In more than half the comparisons there was no difference between populations fed for 3 months at the beginning and at the end.

D. **Relationship of scale nucleus to egg size and fish length**

As indicated in Table 4, the mean weight of eggs from different females of different species and races varied from 0.0742 (kokanee) to 0.3271 gr (coho). It was hypothesized that the radius of the scale nucleus is correlated with the size of the eggs from which the progeny originated. Whether this is the case or not cannot be conclusively determined from the present data. The kokanee, which produced the smallest eggs, also had the smallest scale nucleus, thus lending some support to the theory. However, the chinook and coho, which originated from the largest eggs, had small scale nuclei which were similar in size to those of the sockeye. In order to support the hypothesis, the scale nuclei of the chinook and coho should have been larger than that observed for the other species.

The relationship between the scale nucleus radius and fish length at the end of the experiment was examined for 3 crosses of Pitt River and 1 cross of Babine sockeye that had each undergone three feeding regimes for a period of 12 months (Table 12). Half of the populations compared had been sampled six times and the other half only once at the end of the period.

Among the Pitt River sockeye populations, which had been sampled six times, there were significant positive correlations between final fish length and the nucleus radius for 5 of the 9 populations (Table 12). Among those populations which were sampled only once at the end of the experiment, there were significant positive correlations for 7 of the 9 populations. The fewer significant correlations among populations sampled six times suggests that the repeated sampling may have affected the relationship.

Table 12. Relationship between nucleus radius and fish length for populations of sockeye reared under three treatment regimes.

Species	Race	Cross ♂		Cross ♀		Treatment	Nucleus radius and fish length Sampled once r	n	Sampled 6 times r	n
Sockeye	Pitt R.	1.3	576	1.2	454	2S → 3F	0.391[a]	25	0.299	24
						3F → 2S	0.824[d]	23	0.460[b]	24
						Fed 12 months	0.895[d]	20	0.362	25
		1.3	615	1.3	540	2S → 3F	0.668[d]	23	0.821[d]	24
						3F → 2S	0.825[d]	24	0.315	23
						Fed 12 months	0.327	24	0.352	24
		1.3	615	1.2	499	2S → 3F	0.663[d]	25	0.605[c]	23
						3F → 2S	0.126	21	0.612[c]	20
						Fed 12 months	0.665[c]	20	0.690[c]	17
	Babine R.	1.2	467	1.3	521	2S → 3F	0.278	19	0.278	19
						3F → 2S	0.411[a]	25	0.466	18
						Fed 12 months	0.654[b]	15	0.536[a]	15

[a] 5.0% level of significance. r = correlation coefficient
[b] 2.0% level of significance.
[c] 1.0% level of significance.
[d] 0.1% level of significance.

Treatments appeared to have little effect on the relationship between nucleus radius and final fish length. Among those populations reared under treatment 2S → 3F, there were 5 significant correlations, under treatment 3F → 2S there were 4, and for those fed for 12 months there were 3 with significant correlations.

Among the Babine River sockeye populations there were significant positive correlations for 1 of the 3 populations sampled six times and for 2 of the populations sampled only once at the end.

The relationship between the scale nucleus radius and the number of circuli laid down on the scales by the end of the experiment for the same crosses was also examined. Among all the populations examined there were no significant correlations between the number of circuli and the nucleus radius. Correlation coefficients ranged from 0.00 to 0.446 and were all positive.

E. Comparison of the body-scale relationship between populations from the same species, race, and cross subjected to different treatments

(a) Circulus-body length relationship

Among 11 crosses subjected to different feeding and starvation treatments there was a significant difference in the relationship in only one instance. The intercepts of the regression lines of populations from the second cross of Stellako sockeye (1.2, 443 × 1.2, 476) differed between treatments (Table 13 and Fig. 3). The population reared under treatment 2S → 3F laid down more circuli per unit of body increase than those reared under the other two regimes. In all the comparisons the slopes of the regression lines did not differ significantly (Table 13).

(b) Scale radius (A-N)—body length relationship

The scale radius-body length relationship appeared to be influenced more by the feeding treatments than was the circulus-body length relationship (Table 14). Among the same 11 crosses subjected to different

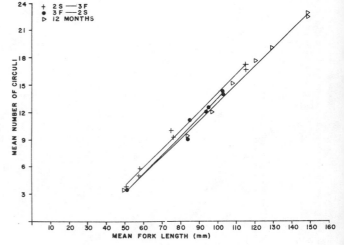

Fig. 3. Circulus-body length relationships of 3 populations of 1 cross of Stellako River sockeye, reared under three treatment regimes.

feeding treatments there was a significant difference in the relationship in 3 comparisons. The intercepts of the regression lines of populations from the first Pitt River sockeye cross (1.3, 576 × 1.2, 454), the first Stellako River sockeye cross (1.2, 443 × 1.3, 509), and the Scully Creek sockeye cross differed significantly between treatments. Among the Pitt sockeye populations those fed for 12 months increased more in scale radius per unit of body increase than those reared under the two other regimes. For the Stellako populations those reared under treatment 3F → 2S increased the least in scale radius per unit of body increase. Among the Scully populations those fed for 12 months increased the most in scale radius, whereas for those fed throughout, the scale radius increased the least per unit of body increase (Fig. 4). In all cases the slopes of the regression lines did not differ significantly (Table 14).

Table 13. Results of analysis of variance comparing the relationships between mean increments in circuli on mean increments in fish length for population sampled up to 6 times originating from the same crosses but reared under different treatment regimes. Differences in slopes and intercepts of the regression lines are indicated at the 5% level.

Species	Race	Cross ♂	Cross ♀	Between treatments	F ratio b = 0	df	b's equal	df	a's equal	df	Can be pooled	Mean of Y	Mean of X	a	b
Sockeye	Pitt R.	1.3 576	1.2 454	2S → 3F	1108.07	1, 15	No 2.368	2, 15	Yes 1.811	2, 17	Yes Yes	7.38	62.34	−6.963	0.230
				3F → 2S								10.65	77.11	−9.927	0.267
				Fed 12 months								14.01	94.25	−7.096	0.224
		1.3 615	1.3 540	2S → 3F	1048.619	1, 15	No 2.791	2, 15	Yes 2.413	2, 17	Yes Yes	7.79	65.26	−5.613	0.205
				3F → 2S								11.46	82.76	−9.641	0.255
				Fed 12 months								14.43	99.68	−7.161	0.217
		1.3 615	1.2 499	2S → 3F	2352.194	1, 15	No 1.060	2, 15	Yes 0.764	2, 17	Yes Yes	7.39	64.86	−6.681	0.217
				3F → 2S								11.12	80.90	−8.065	0.237
				Fed 12 months								13.82	94.22	−7.345	0.225
	Stellako R.	1.2 443	1.3 509	2S → 3F	796.53	1, 15	No 1.758	2, 15	Yes 1.252	2, 17	Yes Yes	7.79	71.34	−5.706	0.189
				3F → 2S								10.94	84.22	8.097	0.226
				Fed 12 months								12.75	95.58	−5.674	0.193
		1.2 443	1.2 476	2S → 3F	1358.747	1, 15	No 0.249	2, 15	Yes 3.761	2, 17	No No	7.70	69.33	−6.524	0.205
				3F → 2S								11.00	88.19	−7.503	0.210
				Fed 12 months								14.23	106.23	−6.995	0.199
	L. Babine R.	1.2 467	1.3 521	2S → 3F	1132.104	1, 14	No 0.187	2, 14	Yes 2.420	2, 16	Yes Yes	6.44	59.84	−9.291	0.263
				3F → 2S								9.45	72.14	−8.523	0.249
				Fed 12 months								11.95	83.75	−9.785	0.259
	Scully Cr.	1.2 440	1.2 436	2S → 3F	273.150	1, 15	No 0.811	2, 15	Yes 0.915	2, 17	Yes Yes	6.52	63.99	−6.135	0.198
				3F → 2S								10.17	79.33	−8.387	0.234
				Fed 12 months								11.05	86.98	−6.078	0.197
Kokanee	Meadow Cr.	— 185	— 260	2S → 3F	171.195	1, 9	No 1.321	1, 9	Yes 4.745	1, 10	Yes Yes	5.91	51.92	−7.411	0.256
				3F → 2S								8.18	65.47	−11.848	0.306
		— 185	— 176	2S → 3F	56.773	1, 10	No 0.800	1, 10	Yes 3.756	1, 11	Yes Yes	5.57	46.64	−6.828	0.266
				3F → 2S								7.11	58.28	−12.541	0.337
Coho	B. Qualicum	1.1 461	1.1 452	2S → 3F	0.328	1, 10	Yes 0.013	1, 10	Yes 0.087	1, 11	Yes Yes	6.70	63.87	3.995	0.042
				3F → 2S								7.97	75.34	3.206	0.063
Chinook	B. Qualicum	— 675	— 675	2S → 3F	31.081	1, 15	No 1.957	2, 15	Yes 0.513	2, 17	Yes Yes	8.88	70.51	−5.039	0.197
				3F → 2S								11.79	86.20	−6.401	0.211
				Fed 12 months								13.06	105.94	2.321	0.101

Table 14. Results of analysis of variance comparing the relationships between mean increments in scale radius on mean increments in fish length for populations sampled up to 6 times originating from the same crosses but reared under different treatment regimes. Difference in slopes and intercepts of the regression lines are indicated at the 5% level.

Species	Race	Cross ♂	Cross ♀	Between treatments	b = 0	df	(sig)	b's equal	df	(sig)	a's equal	df	(sig)	Can be pooled	Mean Y	Mean X	Mean a	Mean b
Sockeye	Pitt R.	1.3 576	1.2 454	2S → 3F	2920.582	1, 15	No	1.442	2, 15	Yes	4.805	2, 17	No	No	38.66	62.34	−53.805	1.483
				3F → 2S											64.76	77.11	−57.347	1.584
				Fed 12 months											87.21	94.25	−49.609	1.452
		1.3 615	1.3 540	2S → 3F	1698.386	1, 15	No	0.382	2, 15	Yes	0.057	2, 17	Yes	Yes	41.316	65.26	−47.217	1.356
				3F → 2S											66.304	82.76	−46.343	1.361
				Fed 12 months											89.58	99.68	−51.819	1.418
		1.3 615	1.2 499	2S → 3F	1658.593	1, 15	No	0.894	2, 15	Yes	2.086	2, 17	Yes	Yes	38.157	64.86	−47.686	1.323
				3F → 2S											63.92	80.90	−54.008	1.458
				Fed 12 months											80.13	94.22	−51.616	1.398
	Stellako R.	1.2 443	1.3 509	2S → 3F	732.884	1, 15	No	0.617	2, 15	Yes	4.705	2, 17	No	No	42.01	71.34	−47.730	1.258
				3F → 2S											66.36	84.22	−53.240	1.420
				Fed 12 months											81.06	95.59	−45.445	1.323
		1.2 443	1.2 476	2S → 3F	1995.967	1, 15	No	1.031	2, 15	Yes	1.171	2, 17	Yes	Yes	44.03	69.33	−64.161	1.560
				3F → 2S											72.13	88.19	−60.934	1.509
				Fed 12 months											96.21	106.23	−57.911	1.451
	L. Babine R.	1.2 467	1.3 521	2S → 3F	1215.933	1, 14	No	0.352	2, 14	Yes	0.653	2, 16	Yes	Yes	27.83	59.84	−49.335	1.289
				3F → 2S											45.99	72.14	−50.324	1.335
				Fed 12 months											60.67	83.75	−53.725	1.366
	Scully Cr.	1.2 440	1.2 436	2S → 3F	383.116	1, 15	No.	1.356	2, 15	Yes	7.815	2, 17	No	No	30.39	63.99	−44.940	1.177
				3F → 2S											53.95	79.33	−43.276	1.225
				Fed 12 months											52.75	86.98	−34.933	1.008
Kokanee	Meadow Cr.	— 185	— 260	2S → 3F	630.422	1, 9	No	2.873	1, 9	Yes	0.000	1, 10	Yes	Yes	23.87	51.92	−45.395	1.334
				3F → 2S											42.99	65.47	−57.046	1.528
		— 185	— 176	2S → 3F	39.178	1, 10	No	0.364	1, 10	Yes	1.008	1, 11	Yes	Yes	22.85	46.64	−38.194	1.309
				3F → 2S											33.82	58.28	−58.747	1.588
Coho	B. Qualicum	1.1 461	1.1 452	2S → 3F	0.307	1, 10	Yes	0.011	1, 10	Yes	0.233	1, 11	Yes	Yes	34.66	63.87	21.442	0.207
				3F → 2S											43.10	75.34	20.149	0.305
Chinook	B. Qualicum	— 675	— 675	2S → 3F	35.813	1, 15	No	1.489	2, 15	Yes	0.337	2, 17	Yes	Yes	50.05	70.51	−26.732	1.089
				3F → 2S											66.00	86.20	−22.776	1.029
				Fed 12 months											75.43	105.94	11.583	0.603

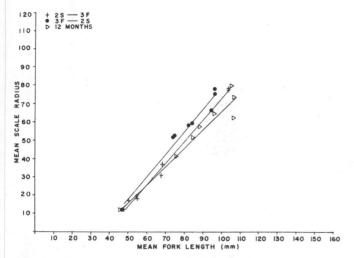

Fig. 4. Scale radius-body length relationships of 3 populations of 1 cross of Scully Creek sockeye, reared under three treatment regimes.

F. Comparison of the body-scale relationship between populations from different crosses of the same species and race subjected to the same treatments

(a) *Circulus-body length relationship*

Among 8 comparisons where populations originating from different crosses of the same species and race were reared under the same treatments there was a significant difference in the relationship in 3 comparisons (Table 15). The intercepts of the regression lines of populations from 3 crosses of Pitt River sockeye fed for 12 months, the 2 crosses of Stellako sockeye reared under treatment 3F → 2S, and the 2 crosses of kokanee reared under treatment 3F → 2S differed significantly. Among the Pitt River sockeye crosses, progeny from the cross having the smallest male and female parents (♂1.3 576 × ♀1.2 454) formed more circuli per unit of body increase than did either of the other crosses. This was also the case for the Stellako sockeye crosses. Progeny from the smaller female parent and the same male parent formed more circuli per unit of body increase than did those from the other cross originating from the larger female. The opposite was indicated for the kokanee where progeny from the smaller female parent and the same male parent formed fewer circuli per unit of body increase. The slopes of the lines were the same in all cases.

(b) *Scale radius (A-N)—body length relationship*

Among the 8 comparisons where populations originating from different crosses were reared under the same treatments there was a significant difference in the relationship in 4 comparisons (Table 16). The intercepts of the regression lines of populations from 3 crosses of Pitt River sockeye reared under treatments 2S → 3F, 3F → 2S, and fed for 12 months differed significantly (Fig. 5 shows the regressions for 3 crosses of Pitt River sockeye fed daily for 12 months). Both the intercepts and the slopes of the regression lines of populations from 2 crosses of Stellako River sockeye reared under treatment 2S → 3F differed significantly.

Among the Pitt River sockeye reared under treatments 2S → 3F and 3F → 2S the progeny from the cross

having the smallest male and female parents increased less in scale radius per unit increase of body length than did the other crosses which originated from larger parents. Among those fed for 12 months the opposite was true; the progeny from the cross having the smallest parents increased more in scale radius per unit increase of body length. The opposite was the case between progeny from 2 crosses of Stellako sockeye. In addition, the slope of the line for progeny from the cross having the smaller female was significantly steeper.

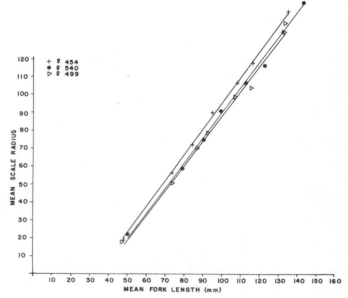

Fig. 5. Scale radius-body length relationships of 3 populations each originating from a different cross and reared for 12 months on daily feeding.

DISCUSSION

Regardless of species, race, or cross, changes in length and weight of the fish and in the scale characters in response to periods of feeding and starvation were generally similar. The present findings for several species and races support the earlier results which involved the study of scales from only 1 race of sockeye salmon (Bilton and Robins 1971a, b, c). Significant increases in mean lengths of fish associated with feeding periods were indicated in most cases. During periods of starvation there was no change in length with the exception of 1 population (Babine River sockeye), where the length increased significantly. Repeated sampling had some effect in a number of cases but not in all. Among 20 pairs of comparisons the mean lengths of 8 populations sampled six times were significantly less than those sampled only once at the end. For 11 of the other comparisons there was no difference in length.

For fish reared under the regime 2S → 3F the mean weight did not change significantly until the end of 2 months of feeding which followed two periods of 2 months of starvation and 1 month of feeding. The mean weight of fish increased significantly again by the end of 3 months of feeding. There were no increases in weight during periods of starvation. For fish reared under the regime 3F → 2S there were significant increases in weight that were associated with feeding and generally none during starvation. (How-

Table 15. Results of analysis of variance comparing the relationships between mean increments in circuli on mean increments in fish length for populations sampled up to 6 times reared under the same treatment regimes but originating from different crosses of male and female parents. Differences in slopes and intercepts of the regression lines are indicated at the 5% level.

Species	Race	Treatment	Between crosses ♂	Between crosses ♀	F ratio b = 0	df	b's equal	df	a's equal	df	Can be pooled
Sockeye	Pitt R.	2S → 3F	1.3 576 1.3 615 1.3 615	1.2 454 1.3 540 1.2 499	842.146	1, 15	No 0.897	2, 15	Yes 1.392	2, 17	Yes Yes
		3F → 2S	1.3 576 1.3 615 1.3 615	1.2 454 1.3 540 1.2 499	790.651	1, 15	No 0.939	2, 15	Yes 1,994	2, 17	Yes Yes
		Fed 12 months	1.3 576 1.3 615 1.3 615	1.2 454 1.3 540 1.2 499	2566.36	1, 15	No 0.354	2, 15	Yes 4,283	2, 17	No No
	Stellako R.	2S → 3F	1.2 443 1.2 443	1.3 509 1.2 476	433.507	1, 10	No 0.712	1, 10	Yes 0.603	1, 11	Yes Yes
		3F → 2S	1.2 443 1.2 443	1.3 509 1.2 476	433.035	1, 10	No 0.596	1, 10	Yes 5.838	1, 11	No No
		Fed 12 months	1.2 443 1.2 443	1.3 509 1.2 476	1528.702	1, 10	No 0.482	1, 10	Yes 4.756	1, 11	Yes Yes
Kokanee	Meadow Cr.	2S → 3F	185 — 185 —	260 176	43.770	1, 9	No 0.013	1, 9	Yes 0.934	1, 10	Yes Yes
		3F → 2S	185 — 185 —	260 176	1550.488	1, 10	No 3,565	1, 10	Yes 32.865	1, 11	No No

Table 16. Results of analysis of variance comparing the relationships between mean increments in scale radius on mean increments of fish length for populations sampled up to 6 times reared under the same treatment regimes but originating from different crosses of male and female parents. Differences in slopes and intercepts of the regression lines are indicated at the 5% level.

Species	Race	Treatment	Between crosses ♂	Between crosses ♀	F ratio b = 0	df		b's equal	df		a's equal	df		Can be pooled
Sockeye	Pitt R.	2S → 3F	1.3 576	1.2 454	2291.607	1, 15	No	2.775	2, 15	Yes	4.233	2, 17	No	No
			1.3 615	1.3 540										
			1.3 615	1.2 499										
		3F → 2S	1.3 576	1.2 454	939.937	1, 15	No	1.701	2, 15	Yes	8.731	2, 17	No	No
			1.3 615	1.3 540										
			1.3 615	1.2 499										
		Fed 12 months	1.3 576	1.2 454	2760.704	1, 15	No	0.318	2, 15	Yes	9.148	2, 17	No	No
			1.3 615	1.3 540										
			1.3 615	1.2 499										
	Stellako R.	2S → 3F	1.2 443	1.3 509	1001.195	1, 10	No	11.560	1, 10	No	6.666	1, 10	No	No
			1.2 443	1.2 476										
		3F → 2S	1.2 443	1.3 509	323.424	1, 10	No	0.294	1, 10	Yes	0.000	1, 11	Yes	Yes
			1.2 443	1.2 476										
		Fed 12 months	1.2 443	1.3 509	1223.625	1, 10	No	2.528	1, 10	Yes	0.015	1, 11	Yes	Yes
			1.2 443	1.2 476										
Kokanee	Meadow Cr.	2S → 3F	— 185	260 —	43.638	1, 9	No	0.003	1, 9	Yes	1.192	1, 10	Yes	Yes
			— 185	176 —										
		3F → 2S	— 185	260 —	1114.323	1, 10	No	0.403	1, 10	Yes	3.471	1, 11	Yes	Yes
			— 185	176 —										

ever, a loss in weight was indicated in many instances.) Repeated sampling had an effect on the weight of a number of populations of fish, particularly those reared under the regime 3F → 2S. Among 10 pairs of comparisons, 6 which had been sampled six times were significantly lighter than those sampled only once. As would be expected, circuli formed during periods of feeding. However, in most populations, circuli did not form during periods of starvation. In several instances (the chinook and coho) there were significant decreases in mean number of circuli suggesting resorption of the scale material. In most of the fish, circuli formed when the length increased. This was not always the case for the scale radius. At the end of 1 month of feeding in both regimes (2S → 3F, 3F → 2S), where mean lengths of most populations increased (9 out of 11 in each case), the mean circuli increased in 6 and 7 of the populations, respectively, but the scale radius increased in only 1 and 3 populations, respectively.

Repeated sampling not only affected the length and weight of the fish but this was also reflected in the increment in number of circuli and the scale radius in almost half the comparisons. In these populations, increments in circuli and the scale radius were less among populations sampled six times.

In most populations the nucleus radius was found to decrease significantly over the 12-month period. For those reared under the regime 2S → 3F most of the decrease had occurred by the end of 1 month of feeding. For those populations reared under the other regime (3F → 2S) there was an overall decline in size to the point where the nucleus radius of 6 of the 11 populations was smaller at the end than at the beginning of the experiment. A decrease in the size of the nucleus was unexpected. It was thought that this portion of the scale, because it was the first to form, would not change. However, this does not appear to be the case. Like the edge of the scale, which does change (resorption, increase, etc.), the centre of the scale, too, appears to change for some unknown reason. In the present study, changes in size were not associated with the periods of starvation and feeding. In most cases, differences between individual periods were not significant. It might be argued that the repeated sampling may have caused a reduction in nucleus radius. This is not the case. A similar reduction in size was indicated for those populations sampled only once at the end of the experiment. In 20 comparisons there was no difference in the decrease at the end of the experiment between 16 pairs of populations. Of the remaining 4 pairs of populations 3 of those sampled only once had a greater decrease in size of the nucleus. A differential mortality of fish in the populations could also have accounted for the decrease in the average nucleus size if fish having the larger nucleus radius were the ones to have suffered the mortality. However, examination of the data does not support this hypothesis. The average mortality among all the populations was 7% and ranged from 1% for the Babine sockeye to 13% for the Big Qualicum coho. For the Babine sockeye sampled six times there was a mean decrease of 5.6 mm and the coho a mean decrease of 1.6 mm.

Of what significance is the decrease in size of the scale nucleus? Some speculation is warranted. It has generally been thought that the position of each circulus, once it was laid down on the scale, was fixed. Present results suggest this may not be the case. The scale nucleus appeared to vary in size over a period of a year, and generally became significantly smaller. Thus the position of the first circulus that was formed changed with time. If the first circulus which delineates the nucleus changes its position, then it is also possible that circuli laid down subsequent to this also change their position. Perhaps the position of each new circulus after it is first laid down at the scale periphery changes for a period of time before stablizing and becomes fixed. Such changes could have a significant effect on the method of estimating the growth of fish at earlier ages from their scales. For example, a decrease in the size of the nucleus as was indicated here might result in underestimating the length of the fish during its first year of life. Such changes in the scale may be a contributing factor to the error often encountered in estimating growth from scales, particularly to that type of error that is referred to as Lee's phenomenon.

In most populations the mean number of checks increased during periods of feeding rather than starvation. These results support our earlier findings from a study of only 1 race of sockeye (Bilton and Robins 1971a, b, c). However, there was some difference in check formation between fish reared under the two regimes. Under the regime 2S → 3F there was a significant increase in checks in most populations at the end of each feeding period. Under the regime 3F → 2S, which began with 3 months of feeding, checks did not form on scales of fish from any of the populations at the end of the 3-month feeding period. An increase in checks was not observed until the end of 2 months of feeding which followed 2 months of starvation.

For populations fed daily for 12 months an average of one check was indicated on the scales by the end of the experiment of both those sampled up to six times (Table A V) and those sampled only once. Among those sampled six times the check was indicated on the scales of 2 populations (Scully and Stellako sockeye) in mid-July when sampled for the first time after approximately 3 months of daily feeding. Formation of the check did not coincide with the winter period when the annulus is usually thought to form. Thus it would appear that the check formed not long after the fish were placed on an *ad libitum* diet and was probably associated with an increase in growth rather than the opposite.

It is generally accepted that checks such as so-called 'fry checks,' 'estuarine checks,' and 'supplementary checks' form during periods of low abundance of food. Annuli are also thought to form during periods of slow growth as a result of low abundance of food and/or low temperatures. This may not be the case. In the present study, we have examined a number of species and races and the results in all instances indicate checks form during increased feeding rather than the opposite. If these results can be applied to wild populations, then it would appear that the various checks and the annuli are a result of improved conditions for growth rather than the opposite. The so-called annulus or 'winter band' may not form in the winter at a time of poor growing conditions but rather at a time such as in the spring when conditions for growth improve. This may also be true for the estuarine checks and supplementary checks, etc. In most instances, sampling the fish up to six times did not induce the formation of checks. Among 20 pairs of comparisons 7 of those sampled six times had significantly fewer checks than those sampled only once. For 10 comparisons there was no difference in the number of checks and for 3 comparisons those sampled six times had a higher mean number of checks.

Changes in circulus spacing between individual starvation and feeding periods were insignificant in most cases. There did not appear to be a strong relationship between circulus spacing and periods of starvation or feeding. However, at the end of the 12-month period of the experiment, under both regimes there was a significant decrease in the spacing in 14 of the 22 comparisons. Of the remaining 8 there were 3 in which the spacing increased and 5 where it did not change from that at the beginning. Repeated sampling had little effect on circulus spacing; in most instances (17 of 20 comparisons) the spacing did not differ from populations sampled only once.

Although it had been hypothesized that there was a correlation between the nucleus radius and the size of the eggs from which the fish originated, the present results were inconclusive. Because larger eggs are known to produce larger fry (Bilton 1970) and that the larger fry may lay down their first circulus at a larger size it had been expected that the nucleus would be larger, reflecting the size of the fry at the time the first circulus was formed. Thus, in the present study the chinook and coho which originated from the largest eggs should have had the largest nucleus, and the kokanee, because they originated from the smallest eggs, should have had the smallest nucleus. This was not completely the case. The kokanee did have the smallest nucleus and their eggs also produced the smallest fry. However, for the chinook and coho, even though they had the largest eggs and did produce the largest fry, they did not have the largest nucleus. Thus the results were inconclusive. However, this does not mean that the hypothesis should be rejected. A comparison between species may not be valid. Such a relationship may occur within species which could not be determined from the present data.

In a number of instances there were significant positive correlations between the nucleus radius on scales of fish and the length of the fish at the end of the experiment. Some speculation may be warranted. Bilton (1970) reported a positive correlation between size of female parent, size of egg, and size of resultant fry. As egg size influences growth of the fry it is possible that it effects the size of the scale nucleus (despite the fact that it could not be demonstrated in the present paper) and the subsequent growth of the fish. Thus there may be a potential for growth that is correlated with egg size which is reflected in the size of the scale nucleus. It may be that it is possible from examination of the scale nucleus of scales from wild fry to predict whether or not the fish is likely to grow more rapidly. Also, it may be possible to examine the scales from adult wild fish and estimate whether or not fish had originated from smaller or larger fry and perhaps from smaller eggs. Treatment regimes appeared to have little effect upon the relationship between nucleus radius and fish length, but the fact that there were fewer significant correlations for populations sampled six times suggests repeated sampling may have affected the relationship. In an earlier study (Bilton and Robins 1971a) where only 1 race of sockeye was studied there were significant positive correlations between nucleus radius and number of circuli. None were indicated in the present study, although there were positive trends indicated in all comparisons.

The three treatment regimes ($2S \rightarrow 3F$, $3F \rightarrow 2S$, fed 12 months) had no effect on either the circulus-body length or scale radius-body length relationships in nearly all comparisons. For most, the slopes and intercepts of the regression lines were not significantly different. Among the comparisons of the circulus-body length relationship there was only one exception where fish fed under the regime $2S \rightarrow 3F$ laid down more circuli per unit of body increase than those reared under the other two regimes. Among the comparisons of scale radius-body length relationships there were three exceptions where the intercepts of the lines differed significantly.

The age and/or length of the male and female parents appeared to have more effect on both the circulus- and scale radius-body length relationships than did the treatment regimes. Among the 8 comparisons of the circulus-body length relationship the intercepts of regression lines differed significantly in 3 comparisons. For the Pitt sockeye crosses that had been fed for 12 months, progeny from the smallest male and female formed more circuli per unit of body increase. This was also the case for the kokanee that had been reared under feeding regime $3F \rightarrow 2S$. However, for the Stellako sockeye the opposite was indicated. The progeny from the larger female that had been reared under feeding regime $3F \rightarrow 2S$ formed more circuli per unit of body increase. Among the 8 comparisons of the scale radius-body length relationship the intercepts of regression lines differed significantly in 4 comparisons and in 1 the slopes differed significantly. For the Pitt River sockeye the size of the parents may have influenced the relationship. Progeny from the smallest parents in each of the crosses had greater increases in scale radius per unit increase of body length than did those which originated from the larger females. This was also indicated between the Stellako crosses. However, in addition, the slope of the regression line for progeny from the smaller Stellako female was also significantly steeper. Such differences in the relationships indicate differences in growth which are probably both of genetic and/or maternal origin. Thus it would appear that these factors probably do influence the rate at which both the circuli form and the scale radius increases.

Fish appeared to grow more in length and weight when fed either for 1 or 3 months near the end of the 12-month period than when they were fed for the same periods of time near the beginning of the period. However, this was not always reflected in the increments in circuli and scale radius. Quite often there was no difference between the mean increments for the same feeding periods at the beginning and the end.

For fish reared under treatment regime $2S \rightarrow 3F$ the increment per month in both length and weight was highest during the 3-month feeding period at the end. This was not always reflected in the rate that the scale radius increased or in the number of circuli. For sockeye the monthly rate of circulus formation was highest during the 3 months of feeding (2.0 circuli per month) but for the other species this occurred during the 2-month feeding period (from 1.2 to 3.0 circuli per month). The rate of increase of scale radius was highest during the 2- and 3-month feeding periods and lowest during the 1-month feeding period near the beginning of the experiment.

For fish reared under treatment regime $3F \rightarrow 2S$ the increment per month in length was highest during the 3-month feeding period at the beginning. How-ever, this was not the case for the rate of increase in weight. Weight increased most rapidly during the 1-month feeding period near the end of the experi-ment. In general, both the rate of increase in circuli and scale radius tend to reflect more the rate of in-crease in length than in weight.

ACKNOWLEDGMENTS

The author would like to thank Mr. F. Nash of the Computer Services for his valuable assistance in the statistical analyses, and Mr. D. W. Jenkinson for his technical assistance.

REFERENCES

Bilton, H. T. 1970. Maternal influences on the age at maturity of Skeena River sockeye salmon *(Oncorhynchus nerka)*. Tech. Rep. Fish. Res. Bd Can. 167: 20 pp.

Bilton, H. T., and G. L. Robins, 1971a. Effects of feeding level on circulus formation on scales of young sockeye salmon *(Oncorhynchus nerka)*. J. Fish. Res. Bd Can. 28: 861-868.

—— 1971b. Effects of starvation, feeding, and light period on circulus formation on scales of young sockeye salmon *(Oncorhynchus nerka)*. J. Fish. Res. Bd Can. 28: 1749-1755.

—— 1971c. Response of young sockeye salmon *(Oncorhynchus nerka)* to prolonged periods of starvation. J. Fish. Res. Bd Can. 28: 1757-1761.

Clutter, R. I., and L. E. Whitesel. 1956. Collection and interpretation of sockeye salmon scales. Bull. int. Pac. Salm. Fish. Com. 9: 159 pp.

International North Pacific Fisheries Commission. 1957. Proceedings of the Annual Meeting 1957. 70-73.

Koo, T. S. Y. 1962. Age designation in salmon. Studies of Alaska red salmon. University of Washington Press, Seatle. Wash., pp. 37-48.

Li, J. C. R. 1964. Statistical inference. Edward Brothers Inc., Ann Arbor, Michigan. 658 pp.

APPENDIX TABLES

Appendix Tables A I to A VII. The actual values of mean increments in body and scale measurements are given at the end of each feeding and starvation period for each species, race, and cross. The total increment for the 12-month period for those sampled six times and for those sampled only once at the end are also shown.

Table A I. Mean increments in length (mm) at end of each feeding and starvation period.

Species	Race	Cross age ♂	Cross age ♀	Start point	Feeding regime 2S	1F	2S	2F	2S	3F	Sampled 6 times	Sampled Once	Fed 12 months sampled 6 times	Fed 12 months sampled Once
Sockeye	Babine R.	1.2 ×	1.3	47.7	+1.2	+4.4	−0.4	+13.3	Missing	+23.1	+41.8	+44.1	+65.8	+62.2
	Scully Cr.	1.2 ×	1.2	47.7	+2.8	+4.4	−0.2	+13.1	+0.6	+35.5	+56.2	+63.6	+59.6	+89.1
	Pitt R.	1.3 ×	1.2	47.8	+0.4	+3.5	+0.7	+14.6	+1.7	+31.8	+52.7	+53.2	+87.2	+81.7
	Pitt R.	1.3 ×	1.3	50.2	+1.0	+3.6	+0.9	+13.7	+1.0	+34.8	+55.0	+55.2	+93.1	+92.2
	Pitt R.	1.3 ×	1.2	48.2	+2.2	+3.6	+1.3	+15.5	+0.03	+32.4	+55.5	+57.6	+85.1	+84.9
	Stellako R.	1.2 ×	1.3	50.3	+2.3	+7.1	+1.3	+17.0	+1.7	+36.8	+66.2	+65.1	+88.8	+98.4
	Stellako R.	1.2 ×	1.2	51.8	−0.4	+6.1	+0.6	+16.1	−1.2	+40.4	+63.6	+58.5	+97.3	+99.2
Kokanee	Meadow Cr.	—	—	37.8	−1.1	+8.5	Missing	+8.6	−0.2	+29.5	+46.3	+47.0		
	Meadow Cr.	—	—	36.5	−0.3	+3.2	+0.2	+11.9	−1.0	+22.4	+36.4	+36.2		
Chinook	B. Qualicum	—	—	53.9	+0.5	+6.4	+0.2	+15.2	−1.0	+30.9	+53.2	+67.0	+94.8	+91.6
Coho	B. Qualicum	1.1 ×	1.1	50.5	+0.9	+6.0	−1.1	+15.8	−3.7	+22.6	+40.5	None		+55.2

Species	Race	Cross age ♂	Cross age ♀	Start point	Feeding regime 3F	2S	2F	1F	2S	2S
Sockeye	Babine R.	1.2 ×	1.3	47.7	+20.2	+1.0	+7.9	+4.1	+1.2	+1.4
	Scully Cr.	1.2 ×	1.2	47.7	+27.0	−0.3	+8.3	+10.7	+1.5	+1.8
	Pitt R.	1.3 ×	1.2	47.8	+24.4	+0.8	+9.0	+7.5	+0.8	+1.3
	Pitt R.	1.3 ×	1.3	50.2	+29.1	+0.9	+7.7	+7.7	+0.4	+1.4
	Pitt R.	1.3 ×	1.2	48.2	+26.4	+1.3	+10.2	+7.2	+2.5	+1.2
	Stellako R.	1.2 ×	1.3	50.3	+29.3	+1.0	+10.4	+7.5	+0.5	+1.0
	Stellako R.	1.2 ×	1.2	51.8	+32.7	+0.9	+9.1	+7.3	+1.5	−0.4
Kokanee	Meadow Cr.	—	—	37.8	+25.2	+0.3	+7.3	+6.7	−0.3	−0.6
	Meadow Cr.	—	—	36.5	+18.9	+0.5	+6.8	+5.0	−0.2	+0.1
Chinook	B. Qualicum	—	—	53.9	+27.2	0.0	+12.6	+8.6	−1.6	+0.1
Coho	B. Qualicum	1.1 ×	1.1	50.5	+22.1	−0.9	+11.4	+2.9	−1.8	−0.5

Table A II. Mean increments in weight (g) at end of each feeding and starvation period.

Species	Race	Cross age ♂	Cross age ♀	Start point	Feeding regime 2S	1F	2S	2F	2S	3F	Sampled 6 times	Once	Fed 12 months sampled 6 times	Once
Sockeye	Babine R.	1.2 ×	1.3	1.09	−0.27	+0.57	−0.35	+1.85	Missing	+3.89	+5.69	+6.09	+12.36	+11.11
	Scully Cr.	1.2 ×	1.2	1.17	−0.25	+0.73	−0.41	+1.98	−0.67	+8.13	+9.51	+12.91	+8.40	+24.39
	Pitt R.	1.3 ×	1.2	1.21	−0.38	+0.60	−0.38	+2.41	−0.69	+8.23	+9.79	+9.89	+25.42	+21.19
	Pitt R.	1.3 ×	1.3	1.26	−0.32	+0.69	−0.47	+2.39	−0.69	+9.79	+11.39	+11.58	+30.61	+29.79
	Pitt R.	1.3 ×	1.2	1.09	−0.18	+0.61	−0.35	+2.38	−0.67	+8.56	+10.35	+10.73	+23.68	+23.08
	Stellako R.	1.2 ×	1.3	1.32	−0.31	+1.15	−0.69	+3.86	−1.42	+13.43	+16.02	+15.95	+29.34	+35.48
	Stellako R.	1.2 ×	1.2	1.27	−0.38	+0.90	−0.53	+3.39	−1.12	+14.06	+16.32	+14.23	+33.08	+35.87
Kokanee	Meadow Cr.	— ×	—	0.44	−0.09	+0.32	Missing	+0.88	−0.38	+4.60	+5.33	+5.63	None	
	Meadow Cr.	— ×	—	0.39	−0.10	+0.24	−0.16	+0.92	−0.33	+2.96	+3.53	+3.43	None	
Chinook	B. Qualicum	— ×	—	1.60	−0.25	+1.12	−0.58	+3.12	−0.81	+10.86	+13.46	+20.09	+33.08	+35.87
Coho	B. Qualicum	1.1 ×	1.1	1.60	−0.27	+0.92	−0.55	+3.14	−1.54	+6.68	+8.38	None		+14.30

Species	Race	Cross age ♂	Cross age ♀	Start point	Feeding regime 3F	2S	2F	1F	2S	2S
Sockeye	Babine R.	1.2 ×	1.3	1.09	+1.79	−0.48	+2.02	+1.37	−0.77	−0.99
	Scully Cr.	1.2 ×	1.2	1.17	+2.85	−0.48	+2.23	+3.22	−0.74	−1.37
	Pitt R.	1.3 ×	1.2	1.21	+2.77	−0.68	+2.60	+2.41	−0.83	−1.23
	Pitt R.	1.3 ×	1.3	1.26	+4.04	−0.83	+2.72	+2.43	−1.29	−1.59
	Pitt R.	1.3 ×	1.2	1.09	+3.05	−0.60	+3.07	+2.74	−0.65	−1.85
	Stellako R.	1.2 ×	1.3	1.32	+3.61	−0.88	+3.44	+3.70	−1.73	−2.25
	Stellako R.	1.2 ×	1.2	1.27	+4.57	−0.90	+3.32	+3.52	−1.43	−2.48
Kokanee	Meadow Cr.	— ×	—	0.44	+1.76	−0.32	+1.26	+1.43	−0.46	−0.54
	Meadow Cr.	— ×	—	0.39	+1.11	−0.23	+1.32	+0.90	−0.76	−0.30
Chinook	B. Qualicum	— ×	—	1.60	+4.01	−0.87	+3.51	+3.45	−1.18	−1.53
Coho	B. Qualicum	1.1 ×	1.1	1.60	+2.81	−0.75	+3.05	+1.56	−1.43	−0.68

Table A III.   Mean increments in total number of circuli at end of each feeding and starvation period.

Species	Race	Cross age ♂	Cross age ♀	Start point	Feeding regime 2S	1F	2S	2F	2S	3F	Sampled 6 times	Once	Fed 12 months sampled 6 times	Once
Sockeye	Babine R.	1.2 × 1.3		2.9	+0.6	+0.9	+1.3	+2.1	Missing	+6.5	+11.4	+13.0	+16.8	+16.2
	Scully Cr.	1.2 × 1.2		2.7	+0.7	+0.9	+1.0	+2.0	+1.3	+5.4	+11.3	+14.9	+13.0	+19.8
	Pitt R.	1.3 × 1.2		3.4	+0.4	+1.4	−0.3	+4.1	+0.7	+5.9	+12.2	+12.8	+18.8	+18.7
	Pitt R.	1.3 × 1.3		3.7	+0.6	+1.9	+0.1	+2.6	+0.6	+6.1	+11.9	+13.1	+19.5	+20.8
	Pitt R.	1.3 × 1.2		3.5	+0.1	+1.9	0.0	+3.3	+0.5	+6.2	+12.0	+14.2	+18.6	+18.6
	Stellako R.	1.2 × 1.3		3.5	+0.1	+2.0	+0.4	+3.9	+0.5	+5.1	+12.0	+13.3	+16.9	+20.4
	Stellako R.	1.2 × 1.2		3.5	+0.3	+1.1	+0.8	+3.6	+0.7	+6.5	+13.0	+11.3	+19.1	+20.1
Kokanee	Meadow Cr.	—	—	None	+2.5	+1.5	Missing	+3.5	+0.7	+5.0	+13.2	+14.9	None	
	Meadow Cr.	—	—	None	+2.1	+1.1	−0.9	+4.6	−0.1	+5.3	+12.1	+12.0	None	
Chinook	B. Qualicum	—	—	4.7	+1.2	+0.7	+1.1	+2.5	+1.4	+3.8	+10.7	+11.3	+17.7	+16.1
Coho	B. Qualicum	1.1 × 1.1		4.8	+0.6	+1.3	−1.6	+6.1	−1.8	+3.5	+8.0	None		+10.39

Species	Race	Cross age ♂	Cross age ♀	Start point	Feeding regime 3F	2S	2F	2S	1F	2S	Sampled 6 times	Once
Sockeye	Babine R.	1.2 × 1.3		2.9	+5.6	+1.3	+1.1	+0.5	+1.4	+0.1	+9.0	+10.8
	Scully Cr.	1.2 × 1.2		2.7	+6.2	+0.7	+1.1	+0.5	+1.7	+2.3	+12.5	+15.3
	Pitt R.	1.3 × 1.2		3.4	+5.1	+0.6	+3.1	−0.4	+2.4	+1.2	+12.0	+13.2
	Pitt R.	1.3 × 1.3		3.7	+6.1	+0.4	+2.5	−0.1	+3.3	−0.6	+11.6	+13.0
	Pitt R.	1.3 × 1.2		3.5	+6.5	−0.8	+3.2	+0.6	+1.6	+0.5	+11.6	+12.4
	Stellako R.	1.2 × 1.3		3.5	+5.3	+1.6	+1.9	+0.8	+1.2	0.0	+10.8	+15.1
	Stellako R.	1.2 × 1.2		3.5	+5.7	+2.0	+0.9	+0.5	+1.5	+0.3	+10.9	+13.0
Kokanee	Meadow Cr.	—	—	None	+7.1	+2.0	+2.0	+0.2	+2.7	−0.3	+11.9	+13.0
	Meadow Cr.	—	—	None	+6.0	−0.1	+2.6	0.0	+1.9	+0.1	+10.5	+11.8
Chinook	B. Qualicum	—	—	4.7	+5.9	+0.3	+2.6	+0.6	+1.2	−1.9	+8.7	+14.0
Coho	B. Qualicum	1.1 × 1.1		4.8	+4.5	−0.3	+2.9	+2.6	+0.7	−2.2	+8.2	None

Table A IV. Mean increments in nucleus radius (in mm × 254) at end of each feeding and starvation period.

Upper panel

Species	Race	Cross age (♂ × ♀)	Start point	Feeding regime 2S	1F	2S	2F	2S	3F	Sampled 6 times	Sampled Once	Fed 12 months sampled 6 times	Fed 12 months sampled Once
Sockeye	Babine R.	1.2 × 1.3	26.1	+2.7	−2.9	−2.0	+2.2	Missing	−3.6	−5.6	−3.6	−3.4	−4.1
	Scully Cr.	1.2 × 1.2	24.9	+0.8	−0.9	−1.2	−1.0	+0.2	−1.8	−4.3	−2.0	−2.7	−3.4
	Pitt R.	1.3 × 1.2	24.4	+3.8	−5.2	+0.6	+0.9	−2.8	+1.5	−5.0	−4.7	−0.9	−1.6
	Pitt R.	1.3 × 1.3	22.6	+4.5	−5.5	+1.0	+0.9	0.0	−0.6	0.0	−0.3	−0.7	−0.6
	Pitt R.	1.3 × 1.2	21.5	+5.6	−6.4	+0.8	+1.1	−2.5	−0.5	−1.5	−1.7	−1.1	0.0
	Stellako R.	1.2 × 1.3	24.0	+4.2	−4.4	−3.4	+2.7	+0.7	−2.8	−3.0	−3.6	−2.1	−3.3
	Stellako R.	1.2 × 1.2	26.4	0.0	−2.7	−2.5	+2.3	−1.5	−0.8	−5.2	−10.0	−5.4	−4.8
Kokanee	Meadow Cr.	—	None	18.0	−2.5	Missing	−0.5	−0.6	−0.1	−4.1*	−4.0*	None	None
	Meadow Cr.	—	None	17.1	−3.5	+7.7	−7.6	−0.4	+0.9	−2.9*	−5.8*	None	None
Chinook	B. Qualicum	—	24.0	−0.6	−0.7	−1.1	−2.2	+1.1	−0.7	−3.8	−7.5	−4.0	−0.7
Coho	B. Qualicum	1.1 × 1.1	23.6	+0.6	+1.7	−0.8	−3.9	−1.3	+2.7	−1.6	None		+4.2

Lower panel

Species	Race	Cross age (♂ × ♀)	Start point	Feeding regime 3F	2S	1F	2S	2F	2S	Sampled 6 times	Sampled Once
Sockeye	Babine R.	1.2 × 1.3	26.1	−2.5	+0.9	−0.7	+0.7	−2.2	−1.5	−5.3	−4.7
	Scully Cr.	1.2 × 1.2	24.9	+0.3	−1.9	+0.6	−2.9	+0.2	+2.0	−1.7	−2.9
	Pitt R.	1.3 × 1.2	24.4	+1.5	−1.4	−0.8	+0.5	+0.5	−2.0	−1.7	−0.4
	Pitt R.	1.3 × 1.3	22.6	+3.4	−2.7	−0.4	−0.9	−2.4	−0.7	−3.7	+1.2
	Pitt R.	1.3 × 1.2	21.5	−0.1	+0.9	+1.0	0.0	−0.6	−1.1	+0.1	+0.5
	Stellako R.	1.2 × 1.3	24.0	+4.3	−6.1	+1.1	+0.9	−0.4	−3.8	−4.0	−1.5
	Stellako R.	1.2 × 1.2	26.4	+1.3	−3.3	−1.2	+0.5	−0.1	−2.8	−5.6	−4.7
Kokanee	Meadow Cr.	—	None	19.8	+0.7	−1.8	+0.9	0.0	+0.6	+0.4†	−2.1†
	Meadow Cr.	—	None	18.8	+3.0	−2.2	−1.7	−0.3	+0.3	−0.9†	−1.4†
Chinook	B. Qualicum	—	24.0	−1.9	+0.5	−2.3	+0.8	−2.0	−3.9	−8.8	−6.1
Coho	B. Qualicum	1.1 × 1.1	23.6	+0.9	−2.1	−2.9	−4.5	+4.1	+3.6	−0.9	None

* Difference in nucleus radius between end of 2S and at end of 3F.
† Difference in nucleus radius between end of 3F and at end of 2S.

Table A V. Mean increments in number of checks at end of each feeding and starvation period.

Species	Race	Cross age ♂	Cross age ♀	Start point	Feeding regime 2S	1F	2S	2F	2S	3F	Sampled 6 times	Sampled Once	Fed 12 months sampled 6 times	Fed 12 months sampled Once
Sockeye	Babine R.	1.2 × 1.3		0.0	0.0	0.0	+1.0	0.0	Missing	+1.2	+2.2	+2.7	+1.2	+1.2
	Scully Cr.	1.2 × 1.2		0.0	0.0	0.0	+0.8	+0.2	+0.1	+0.9	+2.0	+2.9	+1.0	+1.1
	Pitt R.	1.3 × 1.2		0.0	0.0	+0.7	−0.5	+1.1	−0.1	+1.0	+2.2	+2.5	+1.0	0.0
	Pitt R.	1.3 × 1.3		0.0	0.0	+1.0	−0.4	+0.5	0.0	+0.9	+2.0	+2.2	+1.0	+1.0
	Pitt R.	1.3 × 1.2		0.0	0.0	+1.0	−0.1	+0.5	−0.5	+1.0	+2.0	+3.0	+1.1	+1.0
	Stellako R.	1.2 × 1.3		0.0	0.0	+0.8	0.0	+0.8	+0.2	+1.0	+2.8	+2.6	+1.2	+1.0
	Stellako R.	1.2 × 1.2		0.0	0.0	+0.7	+0.2	+0.7	−0.4	+1.4	+2.6	+1.7	+1.0	+1.0
Kokanee	Meadow Cr.	——	——	None	0.0	+0.7	Missing	+0.5	0.0	+0.8	+2.0	+2.4	None	
	Meadow Cr.	——	——	None	0.0	+0.4	−0.3	+0.8	−0.1	+1.1	+1.9	+1.9	None	
Chinook	B. Qualicum	——		0.0	0.0	+0.1	−0.7	+0.8	+0.1	+1.0	+2.1	+1.8	+1.0	+1.1
Coho	B. Qualicum	1.1 × 1.1		0.0	0.0	+0.5	−0.1	+1.5	−1.3	+0.1	+0.7	None		+2.1

Species	Race	Cross age ♂	Cross age ♀	Start point	Feeding regime 3F	2S	2F	1F	2S	2S	Sampled 6 times	Sampled Once
Sockeye	Babine R.	1.2 × 1.3		0.0	+0.1	0.0	+0.7	+0.3	−0.3	0.0	+0.8	+1.4
	Scully Cr.	1.2 × 1.2		0.0	0.0	0.0	+0.7	+0.1	+0.3	+0.5	+1.6	+1.7
	Pitt R.	1.3 × 1.2		0.0	0.0	0.0	+1.0	+0.4	0.0	+0.5	+1.9	+1.8
	Pitt R.	1.3 × 1.3		0.0	+0.2	−0.2	+0.9	+0.7	+0.1	−0.2	+1.5	+1.7
	Pitt R.	1.3 × 1.2		0.0	+0.1	0.0	+1.0	+0.2	0.0	0.0	+1.2	+1.8
	Stellako R.	1.2 × 1.3		0.0	0.0	0.0	+1.0	+0.6	0.0	−0.3	+1.3	+0.8
	Stellako R.	1.2 × 1.2		0.0	0.0	+0.2	+0.6	+0.1	+0.2	0.0	+1.1	+2.0
Kokanee	Meadow Cr.	——	——	None	0.0	0.0	+0.5	+1.0	0.0	−0.2	+1.3	+1.3
	Meadow Cr.	——	——	None	0.0	+0.1	+0.5	0.0	+0.1	+0.6	+1.3	+1.1
Chinook	B. Qualicum	——		0.0	0.0	+0.2	+1.1	−0.1	+0.1	+0.4	+1.7	+1.5
Coho	B. Qualicum	1.1 × 1.1		0.0	+0.4	−0.3	+0.7	+1.0	−0.5	−1.0	+0.3	None

Table A VI. Mean increments in circulus spacing (A-N/C-1) (in mm × 254) at end of each feeding and starvation period.

Upper section

Species	Race	Cross age ♂	Cross age ♀	Start point	Feeding regime 2S	1F	2S	2F	2S	3F	Sampled 6 times	Sampled Once	Fed 12 months sampled 6 times	Fed 12 months sampled Once
Sockeye	Babine R.	1.2 ×	1.3	6.0	−0.3	−0.4	−0.2	−0.2	Missing	+0.2	−0.9	−0.9	−0.4	−0.8
	Scully Cr.	1.2 ×	1.2	7.2	−0.1	−1.7	−0.9	+0.4	−0.1	+0.3	−2.1	−1.5	−1.9	−1.4
	Pitt R.	1.3 ×	1.2	7.9	−0.8	−1.3	−0.7	+0.4	+0.2	+0.8	−1.4	−1.4	−1.1	−1.0
	Pitt R.	1.3 ×	1.3	6.3	0.0	−0.5	−0.3	−0.1	+0.2	+1.0	+0.3	+0.1	−1.1	−1.4
	Pitt R.	1.3 ×	1.2	7.3	−0.2	−1.7	+0.4	−0.5	+0.4	+0.5	−1.1	−1.4	−0.7	−1.2
	Stellako R.	1.2 ×	1.3	7.0	−0.4	−1.3	+0.3	+0.5	0.0	+0.1	−0.8	+0.1	0.0	+0.1
	Stellako R.	1.2 ×	1.2	6.4	+0.6	−1.5	+0.6	−0.1	+0.1	+1.2	+1.0	+1.0	+1.0	+1.0
Kokanee	Meadow Cr.	— ×	—	None	4.4	−0.8	Missing	+0.8	+0.1	+0.8	+0.9*	+1.1*	None	
	Meadow Cr.	— ×	—	None	4.3	−1.4	+2.9	−1.7	+0.6	+0.5	+0.9*	+0.7*	None	
Chinook	B. Qualicum	— ×	—	7.5	−0.6	−0.1	−0.2	−0.4	−0.3	−0.2	−1.8	−2.3	−0.1	−1.2
Coho	B. Qualicum	1.1 ×	1.1	6.9	−0.4	−0.6	+1.1	−2.0	+0.9	+0.1	−0.9	None	−1.0	

Lower section

Species	Race	Cross age ♂	Cross age ♀	Start point	Feeding regime 3F	2S	1F	2S	2F	2S	Sampled 6 times	Sampled Once
Sockeye	Babine R.	1.2 ×	1.3	6.0	−0.5	−0.1	−0.5	+0.4	−0.2	−0.3	−1.0	−0.7
	Scully Cr.	1.2 ×	1.2	7.2	−0.2	+0.5	−0.5	−0.1	−0.6	−0.3	−0.9	−1.0
	Pitt R.	1.3 ×	1.2	7.9	−0.2	+0.5	−0.5	−0.1	−0.6	−0.3	−0.9	−1.0
	Pitt R.	1.3 ×	1.3	6.3	−1.1	+0.1	−0.5	−0.7	−0.1	+0.3	−2.0	−1.7
	Pitt R.	1.3 ×	1.2	7.3	−1.3	+0.5	−0.3	+0.3	−0.3	+0.1	−1.0	−1.3
	Stellako R.	1.2 ×	1.3	7.0	−0.1	+0.1	−0.1	0.0	−0.2	−0.4	−0.7	−0.8
	Stellako R.	1.2 ×	1.2	6.4	+1.6	−0.9	−0.6	+0.1	+0.2	+0.4	+0.8	+0.5
Kokanee	Meadow Cr.	— ×	—	None	6.4	+0.3	−0.5	+0.2	−0.9	0.0	−0.9†	−0.6†
	Meadow Cr.	— ×	—	None	6.0	−0.4	−0.8	+0.4	−0.3	+0.3	−0.8†	−0.5†
Chinook	B. Qualicum	— ×	—	7.5	−0.9	+0.3	−0.1	−0.9	−0.3	−0.8	2.7	−1.6
Coho	B. Qualicum	1.1 ×	1.1	6.9	−1.0	+0.4	0.0	+0.2	−0.9	+1.0	−0.5	None

* Difference in circulus spacing between end of 2S and at end of 3F.
† Difference in circulus spacing between end of 3F and at end of 2S.

Table A VII. Mean increments in scale radius (A–N) (mm × 254) at end of each feeding and starvation period.

Species	Race	Cross age ♂	Cross age ♀	Start point	Feeding regime 2S	1F	2S	2F	2S	3F	Sampled 6 times	Once	Fed 12 months sampled 6 times	Once
Sockeye	Babine R.	1.2 ×	1.3	11.0	+3.5	+2.7	+6.6	+9.2	Missing	+33.8	+56.1	+64.6	+92.6	+83.1
	Scully Cr.	1.2 ×	1.2	12.1	+4.8	+1.1	+1.6	+11.3	+6.1	+41.3	+66.2	+83.9	+65.9	+113.8
	Pitt R.	1.3 ×	1.2	19.2	−2.4	+7.9	−4.2	+23.5	+10.0	+45.2	+76.0	+78.3	+127.2	+126.3
	Pitt R.	1.3 ×	1.3	22.2	−1.0	+9.8	−1.7	+14.8	+3.5	+49.2	+74.6	+79.3	+134.4	+136.1
	Pitt R.	1.3 ×	1.2	18.2	+0.2	+6.3	+1.0	+15.7	+6.2	+43.4	+72.8	+80.3	+122.0	+111.7
	Stellako R.	1.2 ×	1.3	17.7	−0.5	+7.3	+4.7	+25.1	+3.3	+37.9	+77.8	+95.0	+120.6	+147.3
	Stellako R.	1.2 ×	1.2	15.8	+3.2	+3.5	+5.8	+21.4	+6.4	+60.6	+100.9	+67.7	+145.5	+153.3
Kokanee	Meadow Cr.	—	—	None	7.0	+4.0	Missing	+16.6	+5.0	+32.4	+65.0	+73.5	None	
	Meadow Cr.	—	—	None	4.7	+1.7	−15.7	+33.4	+3.0	+30.8	+57.9	+54.4	None	
Chinook	B. Qualicum			27.7	+5.7	+4.8	+6.0	+12.9	+5.7	+24.3	+59.4	+64.1	+112.6	+98.2
Coho	B. Qualicum	1.1 ×	1.1	26.5	+2.0	+4.2	−5.0	+24.7	−5.1	+23.6	+44.4	None		+57.4

Species	Race	Cross age ♂	Cross age ♀	Start point	Feeding regime 3F	2S	2F	2S	1F	2S
Sockeye	Babine R.	1.2 ×	1.3	11.0	+30.1	+4.9	+7.8	−0.3	+5.3	−1.2
	Scully Cr.	1.2 ×	1.2	12.1	+40.2	−0.7	+6.7	+0.9	+7.0	+11.7
	Pitt R.	1.3 ×	1.2	19.2	+32.6	+8.4	+16.6	−4.2	+10.8	+5.8
	Pitt R.	1.3 ×	1.3	22.2	+37.1	+3.3	+17.0	−7.9	+12.4	+1.0
	Pitt R.	1.3 ×	1.2	18.2	+35.0	+0.1	+17.0	+8.2	+5.3	+6.4
	Stellako R.	1.2 ×	1.3	17.7	+36.2	+11.4	+11.5	+6.1	−2.6	+8.1
	Stellako R.	1.2 ×	1.2	15.8	+50.0	+5.7	+9.3	+5.6	+1.3	+9.3
Kokanee	Meadow Cr.	—	—	None	+39.6	+2.6	+5.9	+3.1	+9.3	−1.0
	Meadow Cr.	—	—	None	+30.2	−4.1	+14.4	+2.1	+5.0	+2.2
Chinook	B. Qualicum			27.7	+35.5	+6.2	+4.5	+0.5	+4.7	−4.8
Coho	B. Qualicum	1.1 ×	1.1	26.5	+22.7	+1.4	+12.9	+10.4	+5.4	−2.6

Age determination in *Tilapia melanotheron* (Ruppell) in the Lagos Lagoon, Lagos, Nigeria

with a discussion of the environmental and physiological basis of growth markings in the Tropics

by S. O. FAGADE

School of Biological Sciences, University of Lagos, Lagos, Nigeria

SUMMARY

1. Specimens of *Tilapia melanotheron* (Ruppell) collected in the Lagos Lagoon between June 1968 and December 1972, were analysed for age and growth. Age determination was based on growth rings found on the opercular bones. The growth rings showed that *T. melanotheron* rarely attain more than 4 years of age in the lagoon. It is suggested that the growth rings are formed during the period June to October when the salinity of the lagoon is drastically altered from brackish to a fresh water condition due to the effects of the rains. During this period the species usually migrate into the flooded area on the edges of the lagoon.

2. The problems involved in using the growth rings on the opercular bones for age determination are shown to include the determination of the time the rings are formed; whether one or more rings are formed during the year and whether the rings are formed as a result of spawning activities which from available evidence spreads throughout the greater part of the year. These problems are discussed in as far as it affects other fish species caught in the Lagos lagoon and other areas close to the tropics.

INTRODUCTION

A knowledge of growth rate of fish species is important in any fishery development programme. Growth rate can only be known from a knowledge of increase in length with time. It is important therefore that growth rate studies must of necessity involve age determination. Growth is influenced by many physical factors like temperature, food, length of day light, salinity, pH etc. The effect of temperature and food on growth is pronounced among fish species present in temperate regions of the world—producing rapid growth during the summer months and reduction or cessation of growth during the winter months. This reduction in growth during particular period results in formation of growth marks on hard parts of the fish species (But see Bilton 1974, this volume page 60; Ed.). These hard parts include scales, opercular bones, otoliths, vertebrae and spines. The growth marks so formed have been used by many investigators to determine accurately the age of temperate fish species.

In the tropics, the temperature varies only slightly during the year—for example the surface water temperature in the Lagos lagoon varies from 24°C to 31°C during the year. The day light hours extend for about twelve hours each day all the year round making primary production possible all the year round. The rather uniform temperature coupled with availability of food makes for uninterrupted growth during the year. This uniform growth can however be interrupted by physiological factors like breeding and salt tolerance. Commonly, annual growth rings are therefore not formed in most tropical fishes as in temperate fishes, and consequently the age of the fish species cannot easily be determined.

It is therefore, desirable to find other methods in determining the age of tropical fishes. Attempts to solve this problem have been few. Garrod (1959) correlated the spawning of *Tilapia esculenta* (Graham) with the formation of annual growth rings. The Petersen's method of age determination has also been used to determine the age of *Ethmalosa fimbriata* (Bowdich) by Salzen (1958), Fagade and Olaniyan (1972) and Scheffers (1973). Attempts to determine the age of *Tilapia melanotheron* in the Lagos lagoon is reported in this paper.

MATERIALS AND METHODS

During the period June 1966 to June 1968 inclusive, 508 specimens of *T. melanotheron* were obtained from cast net operations in the Lagos lagoon, Fig. 1. There was no collection of specimens throughout 1969. Although cast net was being used occasionally during the period Jan. 1970 to Dec. 1972, most of the 862 specimens obtained during this period were from enclosed areas of the lagoon where traps are set, Fagade (1969). These enclosed areas are similar in construction to Acadja fishing practised in Dahomey and described by Welcomme (1972).

In the laboratory, specimens were examined fresh; the total and standard lengths of each specimen were measured, the body weight was taken, the sex was determined and stage of development of gonad was classified on the scale given by Kesteven (1960); scales on the flanks posterior to the insertion of the pectoral fins were removed; opercular bones on both sides of the head were also removed; scales on these opercular bones were removed and kept in the envelopes containing the opercular bones. The opercular bones were boiled in water to remove surrounding tissues. The radius of each opercular bones was measured. The number of rings on each was noted and the radius of each ring was also noted. The position of the last ring on each of the opercular bones was recorded.

The radius of each opercular bone was plotted against the total length and the data obtained from measuring the radius of each ring on the opercular bone was used in making an estimate of annual growth.

Growth Rings in *T. melanotheron*

The specimens examined had total length varying from 70.0 to 24.5 cm. The result of a plot of the radius of the opercular bone against total length is shown in Fig. 2. It is seen from the figure that a linear relationship exist between the radius of the opercular bone and body length. From this relation-

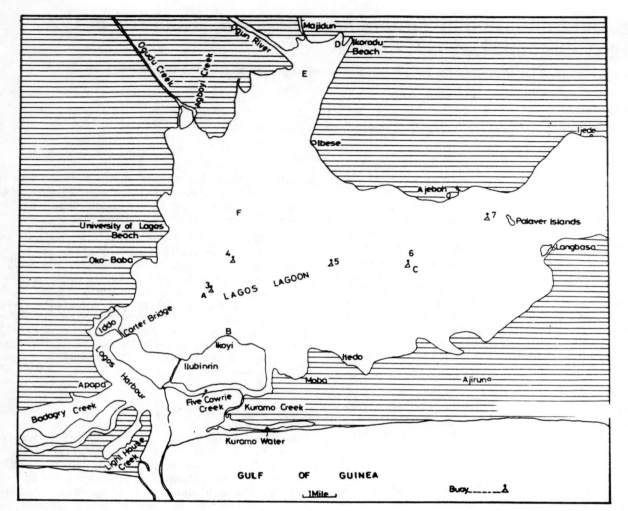

Fig. 1. Map of Lagos Lagoon

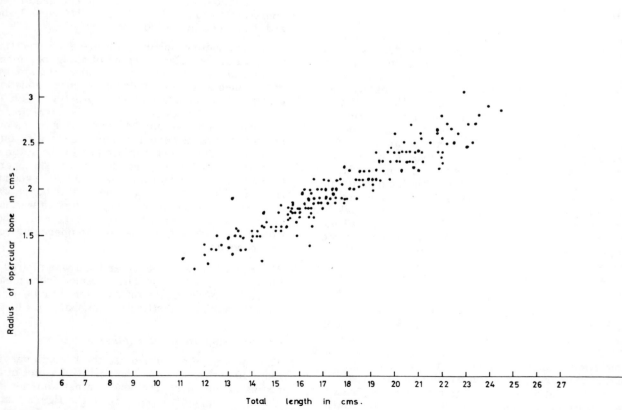

Fig. 2. Relationship between radius of opercular bone and length of *Tilapia melanotheron*

ship a back calculation of growth for the various rings could be made.

The specimens had two types of rings; the first type is an incomplete type extending from one edge of an opercular bone to about half way, while the second type is complete extending from one edge of the opercular bone to the other, see Fig. 3.

Specimens whose total length reach 14.0 cm had a single complete ring with two or more incomplete rings before this. Specimen whose total length was below 11.0 cm had no complete ring on the opercular bone.

Factors in formation of growth rings

Observation of the position of the last complete ring on the opercular bone shows that most of the fishes caught during the period July to October of each year had the complete ring close to the edge while only a very small fraction of the fishes caught outside this period had the last ring close to the edge, as shown below.

Fig. 3

(a) Opercular bone of male *Tilapia melanotheron*
(b) Opercular bone of a female *Tilapia melanotheron*

	No. of Specimens	No. of Specimens with ring close to edge.	Percentage of Specimens having rings close to edge.
Jan	31	2	12.8
Feb	15	1	6.7
March	12	1	8.3
April	59	2	3.3
May	60	2	3.3
June	18	10	55.6
July	27	25	92.6
Aug.	38	37	97.4
Sept.	16	15	93.8
Oct.	21	20	95.2
Nov.	18	8	44.4
Dec.	50	4	18.8

The data above is for specimens obtained in 1970

The observations above show that in *T. melanotheron* growth rings laid down between July and October could be used in age determination, although this raises other problems.

The growth rings found on the opercular bone are probably due to the spawning activity of this species. The male *T. melanotheron* is a mouth brooder and it is possible that the female stays close by during this period. This breeding habit would prevent feeding and thus lead to growth ring formation. Garrod (1959) has shown that in the mouth breeding *T. esculenta* (Graham) caught in L. Victoria the growth rings are formed on the scales as a result of spawning.

If the growth rings are formed in *T. melanotheron* as a result of spawning the presence of two types of growth rings suggests differences in spawning activities during the year. One explanation which could be offered is that during the dry season (Nov.-May) breeding is confined to short periods and many may take place during this period. This is because during the dry season the lagoon is characterised by

transparent water, having high temperatures and high salinity which favours high productivity (see figs. 4a, b and c). The presence of adequate food would make for quick recovery after spawning. The effect of spawning in arresting growth would be slight, hence the formation of incomplete growth rings.

The complete growth rings are possibly formed during the height of the rainy season when the lagoon is characterised by lower salinity, turbid water and reduced temperature leading to reduction in productivity. The reduction in salt content of the lagoon water and an increase in its silt content will also influence the physiology of the fish in one way or another. Although, many of the specimens examined during this period had food in their stomachs, the quantity (and possibly quality) was considerably less than the food found in the stomachs of specimens caught during the dry season. Thus the recovery rate after spawning would be slower, hence the formation of complete growth rings on the opercular bones.

If complete growth rings are formed during the rainy season this markings could possibly be used for ageing the fish. However, the number of spawning and therefore the number of growth rings formed during this period is unknown. It would be reasonable to assume that with the reduced rate of feeding the spawning will not occur more than once, therefore one growth check will be formed, although, it is also possible that there may be no spawning during this period and therefore no growth check will be formed. If spawning occurs during this period throughout the life history, the growth checks could be used in estimating the age and hence the growth of the species. On this basis, 7. 9% of the specimens examined were one year old, 36. 0% were two years old, 40. 3% were three years old, 14. 6% were four years old, while 1. 2% were five years.

T. melanotheron spawns all the year round (Fagade 1969). We are thus faced with the rather difficult problem of determining the age of the various broods. This is almost impossible. Specimens spawned during the rainy season of one year would have grown and spawned before the rainy season of the following year when a complete growth ring would be formed, and by which time these specimens will be one year old. Specimens spawned at the beginning of the dry season of the same year will also have grown and spawn before the next rainy season when they will also form complete growth checks. These specimens will be less than one year old. Specimens spawned

late in the dry season may still be immature before the rainy season, and their first complete growth ring will not be formed until the following rainy season, by which time they are more than one year old.

Thus the first complete growth ring may indicate one of three possibilities: (i) that the fish is one year old, (ii) more than one year old, and (iii) less than one year old. The subsequent complete growth rings may also not be annual if spawning does not occur during the rainy season.

The number of incomplete growth checks formed before a complete one varies from one to four, with an average of three. This suggests that *T. melano theron* spawns three times before the rains and once during the rainy season making a total of four spawns in the first year of sexual maturity. The number of incomplete growth rings after the first complete ring was observed to decrease to an average of two before the second complete growth check is formed. Similar frequency was observed for third and fourth complete growth checks. This shows that the spawning frequency decreases as the fish grow older.

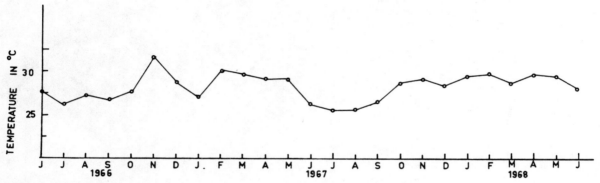

Fig. 4a.   Monthly variation in surface water temperature at station F (from Fagade and Olaniyan (1972))

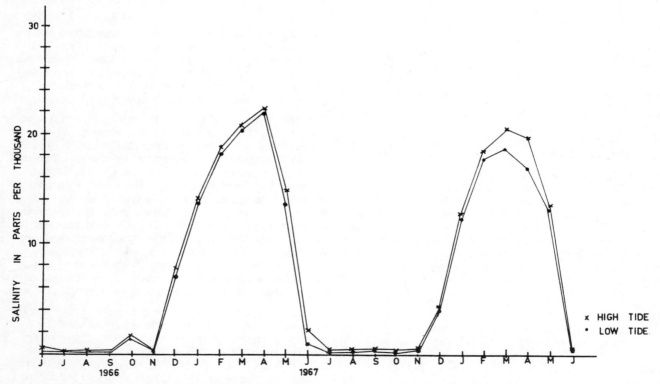

Fig. 4b.   Monthly tidal variation in salinities of surface water at station F

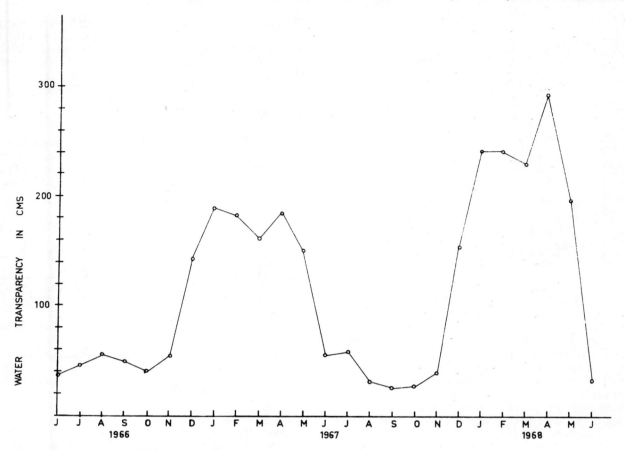

Fig. 4c.   Monthly variation in transparency of water at station F

Growth in *T. melanotheron*.

In estimating the growth rate the first complete growth ring found on the opercular bone is taken as representing one year although the limitation indicated above was borne in mind.

The body length at each given complete growth ring is as shown below:

No. of complete ring	Length range in cm	Mean
1	11.1 to 14.7	13.9
2	14.0 to 17.0	16.7
3	16.8 to 20.3	19.1
4	20.2 to 22.4	21.2
5	22.1 to 24.4	22.9

The data also provide information on the average growth between successive growth rings. The result shows a growth of 13.9 cm, in the first year, 2.8 cm in the second year, 2.4 cm in the third year, 2.1 cm in the fourth year and 1.7 cm in the fifth year. This growth rate compares favourably with growth rate given for *T. esculenta* by Garrod (1959) although the year class lengths given for *T. esculenta* are much higher than those observed in *T. melanotheron*. The low growth rate can be attributed to the several spawnings which occur in the year giving room for only a small increase in body length and weight.

AGE DETERMINATION IN OTHER TROPICAL FISHES

The record of tropical fishes whose age has been determined by one of the several methods is very few. In West Africa, a few commercial species, *Ethmalosa fimbriata* (Bowdich), *Pseudotlithus typus* (Bleeker), *P. elongatus* (Bowdich), *P. senegalensis* (Valenciennes), and *Drepane africana* (Osorio) have had their ages mentioned in the literature, Salzen (1958), Longhurst (1963 and 1964) Bayagbona (1965), Fagade and Olaniyan (1972), and Scheffers (1973).

Ethmalosa fimbriata

This pelagie clupeid supports important drift net and cast net fisheries along the West African coast and has received the attention of a good number of investigators including Cadenat (1950 and 1954), Postel (1950), Poll (1953), Bainbridge (1957, 1961 and 1963), Watts (1957 and 1963), Salzen (1958) Boely and Elwertowski (1970), Scheffers and Correa (1971), Scheffers (1971), Scheffers, Conand and Reizer (1972), Fagade and Olaniyan (1972) and Scheffers (1973). In spite of the long list of investigators, age determination was reported only by Salzen (1958), Fagade and Olaniyan (1972) and Scheffers (1973). These authors used the length frequency distribution to estimate age in this species, see Fig. 5. This species rarely attain 4 years of age in the Sierra Leone river estuary (Salzen, 1958), in the Lagos lagoon specimens reaching 3 years of age are rare (Fagade and Olaniyan, 1972). Specimens caught in the St. Louis region attain only 3 years of age (Scheffers, 1973). Since this species rarely exceeds 4 years of age, possible overlap in the length distribution is not present and the length frequency

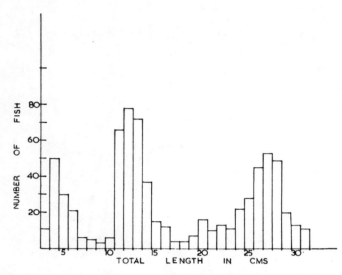

Fig. 5. Total length distribution in *Ethmalosa fimbriata* (from Fagade and Olaniyan (1972)).

distribution may thus be a suitable method for age determination in this species. The use of length frequency distribution should normally serve as a supplement to other methods of age determination but in this species other methods of age determination could not be used since growth markings are absent on various structures like scales, opercular bone, vertebrae and otolith. The length frequency method assumes that spawning is annual and confined to only a short period.

Observations in the Lagos lagoon by Fagade and Olaniyan (1972) on the spawning habit of *E. fimbriata* showed that the eggs and larvae of this species occur in the plankton samples from November to May, with highest numbers in February and March. This indicates that the length distribution may be suitable in age determination for this species.

Pseudotolithus typus, Pseudotolithus senegalensis and *Pseudotolithus elongatus*

P. typus, P. senegalensis and *P. elongatus* are demersal croakers common in the trawling grounds of the continental shelf of the West African Coast. The importance of the species in the commercial landing along the West African Coast has been emphasized by Poll (1954), Watts (1959 and 1962), Bayagbona (1963 and 1965), Longhurst (1957 and 1964). Longhurst (1963) used the length frequency distribution to estimate the age of these species. Bayagbona (1965) also made reference to age of this species.

The author has examined a few otoliths of *P. typus* prepared in the Department of Federal Fisheries in Lagos. These show growth markings but enough data has not been collected to enable accurate interpretation.

The length frequency distribution has also been used to estimate the age of *Drepane africana*.

Other tropical fishes

It is not possible to determine the age of many other commercially important tropical fish species. These species include *Tilapia guineensis* (Dumeril) which are caught in many rivers, lagoons and estuaries along the West African Coast; *Arius latiscutatus* (Pellegrin), a mouth brooding marine cat fish which is important in the trawl landings; and *Cynoglossus senegalensis*

(Kaup) caught both in the sea and in the estuaries and lagoons. The problem of age determination in these species may require an entirely different approach from the conventional methods of growth rings and or Petersen's method.

ACKNOWLEDGEMENT

I am grateful to the following for varied assistance. Mr. M. Okuomo for collection of specimens, Messrs. J. O. Akinniran and E. O. Fagade for assistance in measurements, computations and checking of data.

REFERENCES

Bainbridge, V. (1957). Food of *Ethmalosa dorsalis* Nature, Lond., **179**, 874-875.

Bainbridge, V. (1961). The early life history of the Bonga, *Ethmalosa dorsalis* (Cuvier and Valenciennes). J. Cons. perm. int. Explor. Mer. (26), (3), 347-353.

Bainbridge, V. (1963). The food and feeding habits and distribution of the Bonga, *Ethmalosa dorsalis* (Cuvier and Valenciennes). J. Cons. perm. int. Explor. Mer. **28**, (2), 270-283.

Bayagbona, E. O. (1963). Biometric study of two species of *Pseudotolithus* from Lagos trawling ground. Bull. Inst. fr. Afr. noire, ser. A, **25**, No. 1, 238-264.

Bayagbona, E. O. (1965). The effect of fishing effort on croakers in the Lagos fishing ground. Bull. Inst. fr. Afr. noire, Ser. A, **27**, No. 1, 334-338.

Bilton, H. T. (1974). Effects of starvation and feeding on circulus formation of young sockeye salmon of four racial origins and one race of kokanee, coho and chinook salmon. In this volume, Bagenal, T. B. (Ed), Ageing of Fish, Unwin Brothers, 40-70.

Boely, T. and Elwertowski, J. (1970). Observations prelimnaires sur la peche de l'*Ethmalosa fimbriata* (Bowdich) des eaux senegalensis et son aspect biologique. Cons. Internat. Explor. Mer. Rapp. et Proc. Verb., **159**, 182-188.

Cadenat, J. (1950). Poissons de mer du Senegal. Inst. fr. Afr. noire. Initiations Africaines; **3**, 345 pp.

Cadenat, J. (1954). Note d'Ichthyologie Quest. Africaine. VII-Biologie. Regime alimentaire. Bull. Inst. fr. Afr. noire, ser. A., **19**, (1), 274-294.

Fagade, S. O. (1969). The biology of some fishes and the fisheries of the Lagos lagoon. PhD thesis, Univ. of Lagos, Lagos, Nigeria.

Fagade, S. O. and Olaniyan, C.I.O. (1972). The biology of the West African Shad, *Ethmalosa fimbriata* (Bowdich) in the Lagos lagoon, Nigeria. J. Fish. Biol., **4**, 519-533.

Garrod, D. J. (1959). The growth of *Tilapia esculenta* Graham in Lake Victoria. Hydrobiologia. **12**, (4), 268-298.

Kesteven, G. L. (1960). Manual of field methods in fisheries biology. F.A.O. Man. Fish. Scien. No. 1., 152 pp.

Longhurst, A. R. (1957). The food of the demersal fish of a West African Estuary. J. Ani. Ecol. **26**, 369-387.

Longhurst, A. R. (1963). The bionomics of the Fisheries resources of the eastern tropical Atlantic. Col. Off. Fishery Publ. No. 20, 66 pp.

Longhurst, A. R. (1964). Bionomics of the Sciandae of tropical West Africa. J. Cons. perm. int. Explor. Mer. **29**, (1), 93-114.

Poll, M. (1953). *Ethmalosa dorsalis* (C. and V.) Res. Sci. Exped. Oceanogr. Belge. Eaux cot. Afr. Atlan. Sud (1948-49), **4**, fasc. 2, Poissons, 3 Teleosteens M Malacopterygiens, 29-32.

Poll, M. (1954). Poissons IV. Teleosteen Acanthopterygiens. Res. Sci. d'Exp. oceanogr. belg. eaux Cot. afr. Atl. sad., **4**, 1—390.

Postel, E. (1950). - Note sur *Ethmalosa fimbriata* (Bowdich). Bucl. Etev. Indust. Anim. Afr. Occ. Fr. **3**, (1), 45-59.

Salzen, E. A. (1958). Observations on the Biology of the West African Shad, *Ethmalosa fimbriata* (Bowdich). Bull. Inst. Fr. Afr. noire. **20**, ser A, (4), 1388-1426.

Scheffers, W. J. (1971). Note preliminaire sur quelques aspects de la biologie de *Ethmalosa fimbriata* (Bowdich) dans les eaux Senegambiennes. Project 264 SEN 8. 'Etude et Mise en Valeur des Ressources en poissons Pelagiques'. C.R.O. Dakar, Senegal, Rapport No. 9.

Scheffers, W. J. (1973). Etude de *Ethmalosa fimbriata* (Bowdich) dans la region Senegambienne. 2 me note: La pêche et le stock des ethmaloses dans le fleuve Senegal et al région de Saint-Louis. Project SEN 66/508. Etude et mise en valeur des resources en poissons pélagique. C.R.O. Dakar-Thiaroye, D.S.P. No. 45, 19 pp.

Scheffers, W. J., Conand, F. and Reizer, C. (1972). Etude de *Ethmalosa fimbriata* (Bowdich) dans la region senegambienne. l'ere note; Reproduction et lieux de ponte dans le fleure Senegal et la region de St. Louis. C.R.O. Dakar-Thiavoye, D.S. P. 44, 17 pp.

Scheffers, W. J. and Correa, J. B. (1971). Investigations on the biology and fisheries of Bonga (*Ethmalosa fimbriata* Bowdich) in the Senegambia. Project 264 Sen 8. 'Etude et Mise en Valeur des Ressources en Poissons Pelagiques' C.R.O. Dakar, Senegal. Rapports No. 5 and 10.

Watts, J. C. D. (1957). The chemical composition of West African Fish. 1. The West African Shad *Ethmalosa dorsalis* (C. and V.) from the Sierra Leone River Estuary. Bull. Inst. Fr. Afr. noire, **19**, ser A, No. 2, 539-547.

Watts, J. C. D. (1959). Some observations on the marking of demersal fish in the Sierra Leone. River Estuary. Bull. Inst. fr. Afr. noire Der. ser. A, **21**, 1236-1252.

Watts, J. C. D. (1962). Evidence of over-fishing in the Sierra Leone trawl fishery. Bull. Inst. fr. Afr. noire, ser. A, **24**, 909-911.

Watts, J. C. D. (1963). A note on *Ethmalosa fimbriata* (Bowdich) from Sierra Leone. Bull. Inst. fr. Afr. noire, ser. A. **25**, 1, 235-236.

Welcomme, R. L. (1972). An evaluation of the acadja method of fishing as practised in the coastal lagoons of Dahomey (West Africa). J. Fish Biol. **4**, 39-55.

The sources of errors in ageing fish and considerations of the proofs of reliability

by ROMAN SYCH

The Inland Fisheries Institute, Poland

Editors Note: This paper has been rather drastically edited and it is possible that in some cases the author's meaning has been inadvertently altered. In case this has occurred, all detailed comments on the text and the concepts should be based on Sych (1971) which is written in the author's native language. This will avoid the possibility that while trying to avoid semantic difficulties I have misrepresented the author.

INTRODUCTION

This paper reconsiders the cybernetics approach to the processes of age determination in fish (dealt with in an earlier paper, Sych 1970) in relation to the problems considered in this Symposium volume. This approach, which uses the methods of communication analysis, is designed to identify the sources of errors, and to eliminate them, during age determination of fish.

It is necessary from the start to put forward some general propositions which will introduce my specific approach to the subject and its development in this paper.

The First Proposition

The first proposition is that the age determination of fish is not a unique process without an equivalent elsewhere which would therefore need completely separate treatment. On the contrary it belongs to the family of effects related to communication which are common phenomena in nature and the life of a civilized man.

Let us consider the analogy of telecommunications practice. Thought, spoken or recorded information passes through a communications channel and is received by the addressee.

At the same time the information changes its form in the communications channel—thoughts are transformed into sound, sound into electric signals, etc. Similarly the age of a fish, as a piece of 'real information' travels a certain distance before it is recognised by the investigator, and the information about the fishes age undergoes transformations on the path of communication with the investigator, at first these are natural transformations, and subsequently others are connected with the investigation process.

Continuing with the analogy of telecommunications, telephone information sometimes becomes distorted and it is then necessary to adjust the communications channel and the functioning of its individual elements. Similarly, thinking of the process of ageing a fish as a differentiated communications channel should lead to identifying the sources of probable error. Since we ascribe determined information to certain marks in the structure of scale and bones, it requires little imagination to identify these marks with some records of language—a language of nature, and these special means of communications, consisting of human languages and their use, may provide us with useful analogies. Strictly speaking, we are dealing with a set of languages because the information on the scales and bones assumes different forms depending on the fish population and the conditions.

Therefore the first proposition puts the age determination of fish on an equal footing with other communications phenomena and leads to new ideas for our method.

The Second Proposition

Let us look for a moment at the history of ageing fish, and in particular at the history of ageing salmon and sea trout. The creator of the method was Johnston (1905) (Cited by Masterman, 1913) who not only set out the basic hypotheses, but also justified them empirically. This however, did not remove the doubts, and soon afterwards Nall (1930), using different material gave numerous examples. In America the age determination of *Oncorhynchus* spp. was started by McMurrich (1912, Cited by Gilbert, 1913). A year later Gilbert (1912) using the same material, criticised his interpretation of the scales and otoliths. And so the history of age determination has continued until the present day.

These controversies are hardly surprising. In telecommunications the languages and the principles of the systems of communication do not vary and are not haphazardly diverse. But the communications channels in the study of fish age are without any exaggeration extremely diverse. In this case the variability of the language and its transformations are related to the undetermined variability of the scale and bone structures and to the variability of the investigation process, which includes, among other things, the variability of the investigator's personality. Hence we come to need the second proposition which refers to what has been described in the title as 'considerations of the proofs of reliability'.

[*Editors Note:* There may be semantic confusion here. The author uses 'Reliability' here in the telecommunications sense, and 'Reproducibility' might be a better word. A radio is reliable if it always works when it is switched on. It is also reliable if the wave form of the output is exactly that of the input. Whether the content of the spoken messages are always reliable or not, uses the word in quite a different sense.]

The problem of reliability [or reproducibility in this telecommunication sense] is the finding of methods and criteria for the individual control of each process in the investigation and so of the result. It is in this direction that I will attempt to analyse the possibility of reaching the proof of reliability [that is the possibility of absolute reproducibility. Ed].

In the traditional nomenclature found in the literature there are two common terms: 'Scale reading' and 'Scale interpretation'. Although in practice these terms are often loosely used synonomously, in conception their difference is obvious and corresponds to two approaches to the scale method.

Scale interpretation implies an explanation of the details of scale structure and the connection of these structures with the detailed life of the fish. Scale reading on the other hand is the learned identification of certain marks by comparison with a master alphabet or key. In the case of fish scales and bones the master alphabet and 'spelling books' are provided by scales and bones from fish of known age. I think it is only by such a literally conceived reading of scale and bone structures can the reliable age determination of fish be guaranteed. I have always associated the other traditional interpretation of scales with sooth saying in which probable realities intermingle with phantasy, or like the ancient science of celestial bodies, where the same facts—stellar systems—have led both to the achievements of astronomy and to misguided astrology.

THE BLACK BOX PRINCIPLE

My approach to the method of ageing fish can be considered as that in which the results of age determination are dependent on the knowledge of the natural physiological processes of scale and bone formation. To illustrate this I shall use the cybernetical 'black box' principal as a figurative comparison (Fig. 1).

Let us imagine first that A is a glass box with an electrical system where t_n, x_n, z_n are switches and $(S)_n$ are bulbs. In order to find which of the switches must be turned on to light a given bulb it is only necessary to trace the pathways of the wires, and if they are coloured the solution is found immediately. However, if the electrical system is mounted in a black box such as B in Fig. 1, the connection between the switches and the bulbs can only be found by trying different combinations of the t_n, x_n and z_n switches and watching the lighting of the bulbs $(S)_n$.

Let us now give the symbols a different meaning as in the legend to Fig. 1. Now the 'network' of physiological processes in the glass box A lead to the formation of certain scale or bone structures $(S)_n$ which are a function of the time t_n, specific population characteristics x_n and of the environmental conditions z_n. However, it would probably be hopeless to try to determine the relation between the features of a bone or scale structure $(S)_n$ and the time (i.e. the age of the fish) t_n through a knowledge of the physiological processes owing to the multitude of different x_n and z_n.

Next let us turn to the 'black box' B. Now we are only able to abstract from the interior (that is discover the physiological processes) and determine the relationship of bone and scale structures $(S)_n$ and the age t_n if we have some fish samples of known age from tagging from population x_1, x_2, x_3 etc. in environment z_1, z_2, z_3, etc.

Earlier I said that the information coded in the scale and bone structures is a certain form of language and human languages can continue to provide useful analogies. For example, the process with B is analogous to acquiring the practical ability to understand and be understood. The process with A is analogous to the principles of linguistics. The learning of languages does not require knowledge of linguistics though it may be helpful. Historically the practical knowledge of languages (on the principle of B) led to the theory of language formation (on the principle of A). In our case with fish, the path from B to A can be understood as follows; firstly one should

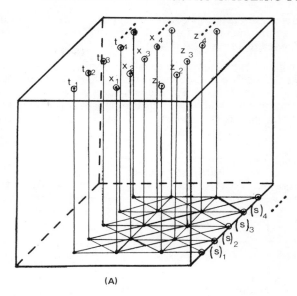

(A)

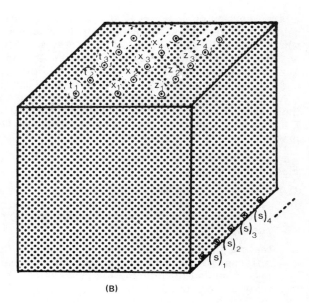

(B)

Fig. 1. An explanation of the 'black box' principle with reference to the ageing of fish. Each box represents a physiological process in which $(S)_n = f [t_n, x_n, z_n]$. The ageing of fish $t_n = f[(S)_n, x_n, z_n]$.

t_n = period of time (age of fish)
x_n = genetic characteristic (species, population)
z_n = environmental conditions
$(S)_n$ = structure of scales and bones

gather information on the variable correspondence between fish age t_n and their scale or bone structures $(S)_n$, and subsequently, against this background, cases could be chosen which would give insight to the box interior, i.e. into the natural processes and conditionings. However, for practical reasons we will now assume that the whole system of ageing fish as presented in the rest of this paper, is contained in a 'black box' whose interior is unknown to us.

AGEING AS A COMMUNICATIONS SYSTEM

I have said earlier that the principles of communication apply to the age determination of fish. The communication is between sent and received information and our case is illustrated in Fig. 2. The sent message is the age of the fish.

This information is naturally coded in the structure of the scales and bones. During the investigation of the scale or bone, the investigator receives the coded information and with suitable processes decodes it. As a result of the decoding he determines the fish age.

identification. Information processing consists among other things of supplementing its deficiencies and confronting the supplemented information with the date of fish catch and with the hatching season in order to obtain the age as measured as the number of years since 'birth'. Thus defects in information processing can result from assuming the wrong principles and from the wrong application of these principles.

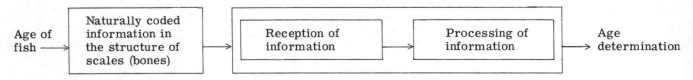

Fig. 2.   Age determination of fish as a communications system

Of course, from the philosophical point of view, such a concept of the ageing system as in Fig. 2 contains a large portion of 'naive realism'. In the scheme the natural processes and the investigation processes, which have a different dynamic character and occur at different times, are represented as one system. Moreover, the origin of the scheme is the fish age, understood as a certain period of time, whereas this concept of time is a product of the human mind and thus stems already from the investigation process. But then why should we give up naive ideas and re-presentations if they are useful?

The usefulness of this scheme in Fig. 2 consists of a clear illustration of:

1. that on the input and on the output must be the same information (the same age of the fish) which is a condition for the reliability of the determined result.

2. that the communications channel comprises three different links (a) natural coding (b) information receiving and (c) information processing. Accordingly defects in the coding, receiving and processing of information form three separate sources of possible errors in ageing fish.

The first part of the communications system illustrated in the scheme in Fig. 2 is a natural process which is beyond our interference. On the other hand it is possible to interfere with the second part of the system by changing the principles of receiving the information and the principles of its processing. This second part of the system can be isolated and represented as a system with two inputs (Fig. 3). At input 'a' we have the set of natural information contained in the investigated object. At input 'b' we now have the reception and processing rules for this information and the output is the determined fish age.

Let us take as an example the traditional method of investigating the scale or bone structure with the use of a microscope. Starting with image perception, psychological processes are involved that will be a sequence of consecutively made decisions. We must decide which fractions of the scale or bone structure are rings, which rings are annual rings, whether any of the annual rings are missing, etc. The general principle of such decision making in the investigation process can be illustrated in a scheme as in Fig. 4. The decision here is identified with the result of the investigation 'c'. It arises from associating the decision information 'a' with the decision rule 'b'.

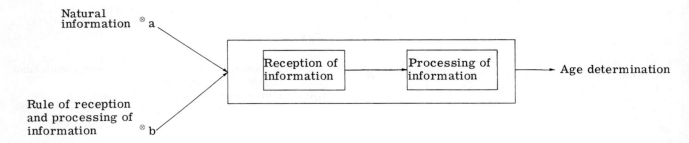

Fig. 3.   Isolated part of the system in Figure 2. The input 'b' enables our interference with the functioning of the system.

Defects in the coding of information in the scales or bone structure may be indistinct differentiation of the growth zones, lack of rings or their excess. The receiving of information consists of observing the physical image and its identification by comparison with certain master images fixed in the memory of the investigator. Accordingly faults in this reception may be either due to bad image perception or wrong

This scheme has a general applicability and can be used to illustrate any investigation, giving the individual, elements 'a', 'b' and 'c' specific detailed contents.

The detailed contents adequate for ageing fish is presented in Table 1. The Decision information is the information contained in the scale or bone structure,

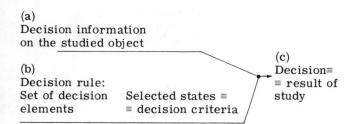

(a)
Decision information
on the studied object

(b)
Decision rule:
Set of decision   Selected states ≡
elements   ≡ decision criteria

(c)
Decision≡
≡ result of
study

Fig. 4. Formal decision scheme illustrating an
arbitrary study in a general way.

Table 1. Detailed contents of the decision scheme in
Fig. 4 adequate for ageing fish

(a) Decision information:

information contained in the scale (bone) structure, date of catching the fish,
the length of fish

(b) Decision rule:

(1) concept of ring,

(2) concept of annual ring as distinguished from
non-annual,

(3. 1) alternative of the absence of some annuli.

(3. 2) alternative of the absence of this year's annulus,

(4) season of hatching of fish

(c) Result of study:

age of fish ⟶ distribution of age in the sample

(c) = f [(a), (b)].

the date of the fish catch and the fish dimensions.
The composition of the Decision Rules includes the
concept of annual rings as distinguished from non-
annual rings, the alternative of non-formation of
certain rings, the alternative of periodical lack of this
year's ring and the conventionally assumed hatching
season. The result of the investigation is the determined age of the fish and the age distribution of the
sample.

The investigation result 'c' is a function of the set of
decision information 'a' and decision rules 'b'. To
measure the reliability of the result 'c', we may give
this function a quantitative sense by introducing some
measure of the errors committed during age determination of a sample of fish, so depending on the
adopted rule 'b', the investigation result for a given
set of information 'a' will have a determined error
'er'.

The full exact defining of rule 'b' consists of relating
its elementary concepts to a complex of characteristic
properties which are useful for the unambiguous
identification and transformation of the information.
This is equivalent to the establishing of decision
criteria. For example an annual ring can be rather
vaguely understood as the limit of the yearly increment of a scale (or bone), or as a certain incremental
zone, e.g. the belt of condensed circuli. Depending
only on how this apparently simple criterion is made
up, the perception and identification of the image will
differ. The concept of an annual ring and of an
accessory ring is always connected with a complex of

appearance characteristics with separate definitions.
The criterion for detecting the lack of this year's
ring may follow from an estimation of the size of the
scale (or bone) increment behind the last annual ring,
etc.

HOW TO ESTABLISH AND VERIFY THE RULE

One of the methods of establishing the rule in sufficient detail would be to set up hypotheses and to test
them. A sample of scales or bones from fish of known
age (i.e. whose ages were definitely known by other
means) would provide the means for verifying the
hypotheses. Here is an example of such a procedure.

Professor Svärdson was kind enough to make available scale samples of roach *Rutilus rutilus,* various
coregonids *Coregonus* sp. and pike *Esox lucius* with
information on the independently known age of these
fish. A group of skilled Polish investigators determined the age of these fish using different sets of
criteria. Subsequently the determined age was compared with the known age of the fish. The results of
this comparison for four selected fish samples are
given in Table 2, where a_2, a_6, a_9 and a_{13} are different
information sets (i.e. fish samples), and b_1, b_2, b_3 etc.
are the successive sets of rules. The Table gives the
errors 'er' expressed as the percentage of fish which
had incorrectly determined age.

Table 2. An example of seeking a rule for ageing
fish by setting forth hypotheses and their
verification. b_i-hypothetical rules, a_j-fish
scale samples of known age. The table
gives the errors er_{ij} expressed as the
percentage of fish which had been incorrectly aged.

	Rutilus rutilus	Coregonus sp.		Esox lucius
	a_2	a_6	a_9	a_{13}
b_1	0, 0	10, 8	32, 2	56, 6
b_2	—	—	28, 9	56, 6
b_3	—	—	31, 1	51, 9
b_4	—	—	32, 2	72, 4
b_5	—	—	32, 2	60, 5
b_6	—	—	32, 2	56, 6
b_7	—	—	32, 2	57, 9
b_8	—	—	32, 2	57, 9
b_9	—	—	32, 2	48, 7

$$\begin{cases} er_{ij} = f\,[(a_j),\,(b_i)] \text{ (minimum)}, \\ er_{ij} \leqslant 25\%. \end{cases}$$

It can be seen in the Table that for the first two
samples, the first rule immediately gave a satisfactory result. For sample a_9 the best rule was b_2
while for sample a_{13} the best rule was b_9.

The procedure can now be stated shortly: to a given
rule b_i against a given information set a_j corresponds
one and only one error er_{ij}, and we seek such a rule
b_i for which the error er_{ij} will be the least. The
search for this minimum function er_{ij} is carried
out empirically—by trial and error.

Next we can determine some limits of admissible
solutions. For example let us assume that the error

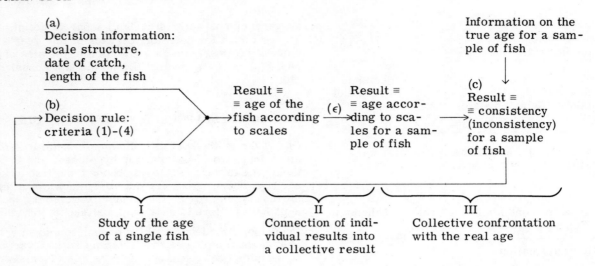

Fig. 5. Confrontation of the age of fish according to scales with their true age. Procedure 1—information on true age of fish is utilized only after establishing age on scales for the whole sample.

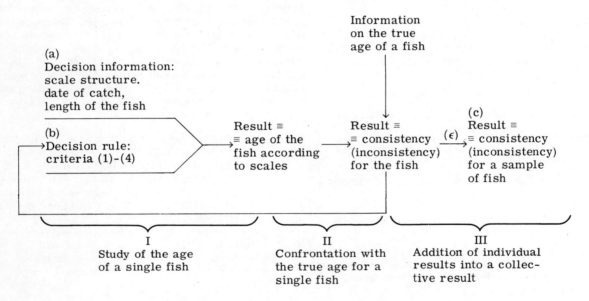

Fig. 6. Confrontation of the age of fish according to scales with their true age. Procedure 2—information on true age is utilized after establishing the age of fish on scales.

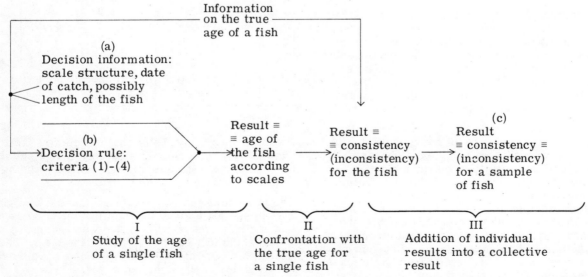

Fig. 7. Confrontation of the age of fish according to scales with their true age. Procedure 3—information on true age is utilized already during the study of scales of individual fish.

er$_{ij}$ must be equal to or less than 25%. This problem was easily solved for samples a$_2$ and a$_6$ (Table 2) while for samples a$_9$ and a$_{13}$ one would further change, the rule b$_i$. Of course this could turn out to be hopeless and then one must give up determining the ages of populations such as a$_9$ and a$_{13}$. Indeed, in population a$_9$ the fish (and also their scales) stopped growing after a certain age, while with population a$_{13}$ there were numerous accessory rings similar to annual rings. This caused deficiencies of information or disturbed information which were impossible to identify by means of the traditional methods of analysing the scale structures.

The correct procedure to verify a set of proposed rules is illustrated in Fig. 5. The decision scheme, which we already know from Fig. 4, leads to age determination of individuals whose set (ϵ) comprises the age determination of the whole sample. Only at this stage, after determining the age of the whole sample can information on the known real age of the fish be made available to the investigator, and depending on the comparison, the rule b$_i$ that was employed will either be accepted or changed.

Another procedure is illustrated in Fig. 6. Here the data on the known age are made available to the investigator earlier, directly after the ageing of each fish. This procedure would not be correct since the coupling of the rule b with the results would take place during the process of verification.

It would be even more incorrect to provide the information on the true age during the age determination from the scales (or bones) as is shown in Fig. 7. However, such a direct comparison of information with its coding would provide a good empirical method for establishing the rule. Later, however, the rule would have to be taught and the ability to use it verified and this would have to proceed in the manner already illustrated in Fig. 5.

APPLYING THE RULE TO ROUTINE SAMPLES

Finding and confirming the rules is only a partial decoding of the language. Certain limits have already been accepted (e.g. er$_{ij}$ $\leqslant$ 25% as in Table 2). Now the routine samples may differ from the control samples with respect both to the set of information and to the manner of coding them.

With routine samples the method of approach is in a way the reverse from that when seeking a rule suitable for the control sample. Now the fixed rule b$_i$ is given and there may be some variability in the information a$_j$ as well as its relationship with the errors (er$_{ij}$).

During the actual age determination the set of rings on the scales or bones can be divided into three subsets (Fig. 8): S$^{(1)}$ are weak rings which are always accessory; s$^{(3)}$ are distinct rings which are always annual; and s$^{(2)}$ are intermediate rings of indeterminate appearance among which can be annual and accessory rings. The arrows in the shaded areas 'A' and 'B' in Fig. 8 illustrate the assumption that with increasing number of S$^{(2)}$ type rings the inaccuracy of age determination also increases. This relationship is illustrated in Fig. 9, based on an example of 12 samples of coregonids of known age. Here each sample is represented by one dot and 'er' is, as before the percentage error while ageing fish according to some rule and 'di' is the measure of doubts

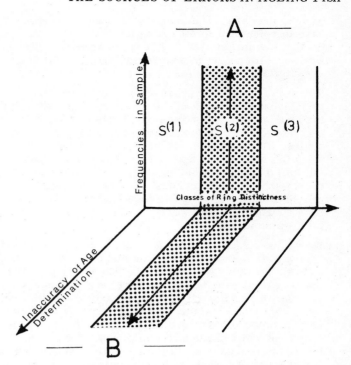

Fig. 8. Scheme illustrating an elementary idea of 'doubt indices method'. Arrows in the shaded area indicated sample relationship between the number of S$^{(2)}$ type rings (in plane A) and the errors committed in ageing (in plane B).

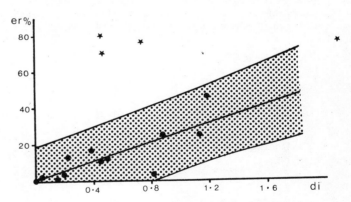

Fig. 9. Dependence of Errors (er) on the Doubt Indices (di) during determination of age of *Coregonus* sp. The mean function is given by:-

êr = 26. 264. di − 0. 102 and the limiting functions by:-

er = 26. 264. di − 0. 102 ± 18. 069 ×

$\sqrt{1.0833 + di^2/4.8407}$

for the material denoted by the points. Stars correspond to omitted material in which the errors were committed due to lack of rings. (See Sych, 1970 for further details)

during age determination expressed as the number of S$^{(2)}$ type rings in the sample divided by the number of fish in the sample (N)

$$di = \frac{\sum S^{(2)}}{N}$$

In accordance with the limiting function (0. 10) in Fig. 9, when 'di' is equal to or less than 0. 22, 'er' is equal or less than 25%. The investigator would therefore have to reject the routine samples of scales with a doubt index larger than 0.22 to gain proof that he is working with an error not greater than 25% (strictly speaking $P_{er \leqslant 25\%} = 0.95$).

The set of samples marked with asterisks in Fig. 9 lies beyond the region of the function. The reason for the lack of correlation between doubts (di) and errors (er) was the frequent absence of annual rings on the scales. This lack of correlation will always apply when the established ageing rule is not consistently (skilfully) applied by the investigator. In this way, the 'method of doubt indices' provides important proofs of the reliability of ageing and at the same time corroborates very strictly the principles and their employment by the investigator.

We can now demonstrate the whole process of routine ageing of fish, including the 'method of doubt indices', and this is illustrated in Fig. 10. The upper part of the scheme illustrates the normal course of age determination. Here the information contained in the scale (or bone) structure and in the data on the fish is associated with the established rule and the result is the determined age of the individual fish and then the age in the sample. At the same time signals about every doubt are conducted and recorded by the lower path so that in due course the doubt index (di) and its corresponding error (er) are calculated. When the error is large, the age determination is not accepted and the sample is rejected, or if possible a new rule will be sought. For this process to be established and for the rule to be verified it is essential to have control fish samples of known age. This is also necessary in order to study and estimate the relation between the doubt indices (di) and the errors (er).

Obviously this detailed arrangement and the solution of the reliability problem will need some modification if the set of rings 'S' is divided into more numerous subsets $S^{(1)}, S^{(2)}, S^{(3)}, S^{(4)}, S^{(5)}$, etc. with which are associated different error probabilities.

AGEING WITH MULTI-VALUED LOGIC

From the theoretical point of view the elementary principle of logic adopted in traditional fish ageing could be questioned. The investigator must make an unambiguous decision 'Yes' or 'No'—the given ring either is or is not an annual ring. It would be more correct to replace this two-valued logic with multi-valued probabilistic logic. The problem now has the following form. There exist natural subsets of rings $(S^{(1)}, S^{(2)}, S^{(3)}, S^{(4)},$ etc.) which are unconnected in appearance. Using control fish samples of known age it would be necessary to determine the probability P of the occurrence of annual rings, and the probability $1-P$ of the occurrence of accessory rings in each of these subsets.

Table 3 shows an hypothetical example of the further calculations. In this absurd example the uniformity of the environment and reaction of the fish to it, has led to the formation of only one type of ring which we will call $S^{(2)}$. Also in this particular case it is given that ring $S^{(2)}$ is an accessory ring with a probability of 0.40 and an annual ring with a probability of 0.60. There is a sample of 20 fish of which 10 have one ring $(1 S^{(2)})$ on the scales and 10 fish have two rings $(2 S^{(2)})$ on the scales. Therefore a scale with one ring has the probability of 0.40 of age 0^+ and probability of 0.60 of age 1^+. When there are two rings on the scale the age can equal 0^+, 1^+ or 2^+ with the

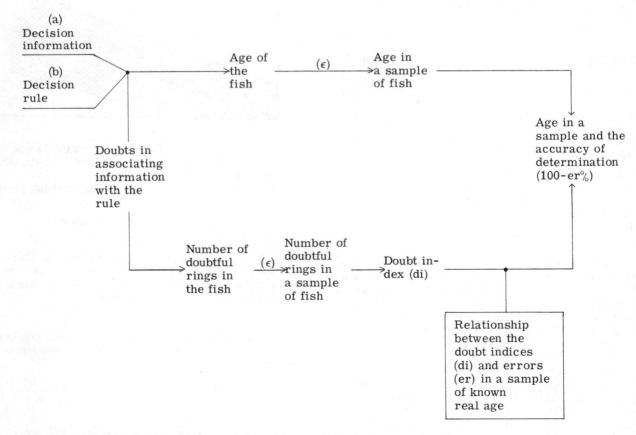

Fig. 10. Scheme of routine study of fish age with consideration of the reliability of result.

Table 3. An hypothetical example of using the probabilistic principle to determine fish age

	accessory ring $1 - P = 0.40$	annual ring $P = 0.60$	Distribution of age
	$1s^{(2)} +$	$2s^{(2)} +$	
	$N_1 = 10$	$N_2 = 10$	$N = 20.0$
0^+	$0.40 . 10 = 4$	0.16 $(0.40 . 0.40) . 10 = 1.6$	5.6
1^+	$0.60 . 10 = 6$	0.48 $(0.60 . 0.40 + 0.40 . 0.60) . 10 = 4.8$	10.8
2^+	$0.00 . 10 = 0$	0.36 $(0.60 . 0.60) . 10 = 3.6$	3.6

(At top of table: $s^{(2)}$)

corresponding probability of 0.16, 0.48 and 0.36. Multiplying the probabilities by the numbers of fish and summing the products in rows we obtain the age distribution in the sample. When in a real situation the number of ring types and the number of their combinations increases, the calculations illustrated in Table 3 can be realized by a digital computer.

The probabilistic decision rule could be related to other age indicators. Early in the history of fish ageing Malloch (1911, Cited by Masterman, 1913) tried to use the number of circuli as an age indicator. This idea was strongly criticized since the scales of fish with the same age can differ in the number of circuli. However it has not been considered what the probability is of a given number of circuli occurring in the scales of fish in a given age class.

CONCLUSIONS

In this paper I have tried to present age investigations as a system of communications between the sent and received information. Referring to the traditional methods of age determination, I indicate the need and possibility to control the functioning of this system. Consistently I have employed the 'black box principle', assuming that the processes are unknown to us. However, there is an exact relationship between the input and output of the system which could be investigated and established empirically.

The information set (a) in Fig. 3 need not necessarily contain scale or bone structures but could be something quite different requiring a completely different rule (b). For example if we analysed the number of circuli instead of rings on the scales we would maintain the traditional information set (a) but would need a new rule (b) for their reception and processing. To take as another example there is the novel work of van Utrecht (van Utrecht and Schenkkam, 1972; van Utrecht, 1973) in which scale structures are automatically recorded by a densitometer on a graph. With scales of Polish sea trout I have been determin-

ing the age with the probability of a correct result approaching 0.95, using a traditional projector and my verified criteria. With the densitometer the scales appear to have been unsuitable for age determination whereas the analysis of bone structure with this method was found to be almost reliable. In this case the rule for reception and processing of information (b) was changed and the information set (a) had to be adapted to this change since the scale structures had to be substituted by bone structures.

Thus irrespective of what innovations we introduce to the age investigation of fish, the relationship between the result (c), the set of investigated phenomena (a) and the rule (b) will always be valid, and it will always be necessary to control the mutual correspondence of these three elements. In this paper I have presented examples of some solutions for what are mainly traditional situations. However, I hope that the approach to the problem has also been illustrated, and this approach can be useful in seeking solutions in different situations.

REFERENCES

Gilbert, C. H. 1913. Age at maturity of the Pacific coast salmon of the genus *Oncorhynchus*. Bull. Fish., Wash., **32**, 3-22.

Johnston, H. W. 1905. The scales of Tay salmon as indicative of age, growth, and spawning habit. Rep. Fishery Bd. Scotl., **23**, 63-79.

Malloch, P. D. 1910. Life History and habits of the salmon, sea trout and other fresh-water fish. London. 239 pp.

McMurrich, J. P. 1912. On the life cycles of the Pacific coast salmon belonging to the genus *Oncorhynchus*, as revealed by their scale and otolith markings. Trans. R. Soc. Can., 3, Ser. **6**, 9-28.

Nall, G. H. 1930. The life of the sea trout. London 335 pp.

Sych, R. 1970. Elements of the theory of age determination of fish according to scales. The problem
of validity. E.I.F.A.C. Technical Paper 70/SC
1-3.

Sych, R., 1971. Elementy Teorii oznaczania wieku
ryb wedlug lusek. Problem wiarygodnosci.
Roczn. Nauk. roln. Ser. H., **93,** (1), 7-73.

van Utrecht, W. L. 1973. Some adventures with scales.
Proc. 6th Br Coarse Fish Conf., 203-205.

van Utrecht, W. L. and Schenkkan, E. J. 1972. On the
analysis of the periodicity in the growth of scales,
vertebrae and other hard structures in a teleost.
Aquacult, **1,** (3), 293-316.

A semi-automatic machine for counting and measuring circuli on fish scales

by JAMES E. MASON

Northwest Fisheries Center, National Marine Fisheries Service,
National Oceanic and Atmospheric Administration,
2725 Montlake Boulevard East, Seattle, Washington 98112, U.S.A.

ABSTRACT

1. A computer controlled optical scanner made from a microscope, an image dissector tube to sense transmitted light, an interface to the computer, and a teletypewriter was used to make counts and measurements of circuli in part of the ocean growth zone shown on plastic impressions of scales of sockeye, *Oncorhynchus nerka*, and chinook, *O. tshawytscha*, salmon.

2. There were no significant differences in results between preliminary reader versus reader tests, nor between final reader versus machine tests. Scales from 60 sockeye and 20 chinook were used.

3. A slight tendency for the human to count more circuli and to measure greater distances than the machine was observed for sockeye. Human counts were slightly less than the machine for chinook. No measurements were available for chinook. The effect of these types of bias on the results of growth or racial studies based on scale data remains to be determined.

4. Most of the processing time was taken by required operator procedures. Complete processing of a scale averaged less than 4 minutes. This time could be reduced to about $2\frac{1}{2}$ minutes per scale for some applications and to a lesser time with a more sophisticated machine.

INTRODUCTION

One of the responsibilities of the Northwest Fisheries Center of the U.S. National Marine Fisheries Service is to provide data for management of many species of marine and anadromous fishes of the northeastern Pacific Ocean. Many studies require knowledge of age, some require knowledge of place of origin, some require information on maturity schedules, and some on growth. For many species of fish, at least some of this information may be obtained by interpretation of scale features including the use of circulus counts and measurements. In the Pacific salmon (genus *Oncorhynch*), scales are commonly used to determine age, or length of residence, in both fresh and salt water. Sockeye, *O. nerka*, chinook, *O. tshawytscha*, pink, *O. gorbuscha*, and chum, *O. keta*, salmon scales have been used to determine continent of origin of fish caught in the North Pacific Ocean. Some efforts have allowed classification by specific river system within a continent (sockeye, chinook); in other cases fish have been classified by broad geographical area within a continent (pink and chum). Major, Mosher and Mason (1972) described the techniques and application analyses in studies of Pacific salmon.

Preliminary studies indicate that scales of sockeye taken at sea may contain information of possible use in prediction of sexual maturity. If this informa-

tion can be obtained for sockeye, it may aid in predicting the size of a returning run and might lead to techniques that can be used on other species.

The number of species of marine fish of economic importance is increasing, and as the number increases it is necessary to collect and process more data in less time. The task might be accomplished through employment of more people or through instrumentation. It would be virtually impossible, however, to employ enough people to completely process the annual collections of salmon scales, let alone the scales and otoliths of the many other important species. There is little choice but to try to automate, or at least semiautomate the process. If this is to be done, the objective will be to read a scale once, obtaining a complete record of the counts and measurements obtainable from the scale. The data should be of a high enough quality that they can be used for all purposes. The quantity of data produced must be at such a level that it will be economically practical for a machine at least to supplement, perhaps ultimately supplant, the human operator.

This report summarizes progress to date on the development of a semiautomatic scale reading machine and has five objectives: (1) to evaluate the accuracy of counts of circuli made by the machine, (2) to evaluate the accuracy of measurements made by the machine, (3) to report on attempts to determine ocean age, (4) to estimate the time required to process a scale, and (5) to describe certain limitations encountered. The evaluations are based principally on results obtained from circuli found in the first and part of the second year of ocean growth of scales taken from sockeye salmon. Some supplementing data from chinook salmon are included.

MATERIALS AND METHODS

Description of the Machine

The machine included a microscope (Unitron model N), an S-11 image dissector tube (camera) and its control circuits (DRC-150) which were interfaced with a small computer (PDP 8/S), and a teletypewriter for information transfer by keyboard or perforated tape. Fig. 1 shows the machine and Fig. 2 its schematic diagram.

The microscope was an inverted type. The transmitted light source had a rheostat to control the amount of direct current reaching the tungsten filament of a light bulb. A stage micrometer was installed so that the image viewed by the operator could be rotated and moved in X and Y dimensions in addition to the usual focusing adjustments. The operator viewed an enlarged image of the scale on a Fresnel screen. A horizontal line (X-axis) was etched into the frosted glass near the bottom of the viewing screen and a second line (Y-axis) was etched at the midpoint of and perpendicular to the horizontal line. The point of intersection was called the target. An 'end of scan' point was marked on the Y-axis near the top of the screen.

A prism and reduction lens in the microscope presented the image seen by the operator to the light

Fig. 1 Semiautomatic fish scale reading machine

sensitive surface of the camera. The usable area on the surface of the camera was square, measuring 12.7 mm on a side (0.5 inch). The light sensitive aperture within the tube was .0254 mm (0.001 inch) in diameter. The image seen by the operator at 41 X on the Fresnel screen appeared on the camera face at a smaller magnification, about 8.7 X.

The DRC-150 camera control unit could be operated in either manual or computer mode. Manual operation used to align and calibrate is described in Appendix I. In either mode, the operator had to select the scan rate and use the power on-standby-off switch to open and close the camera shutter. In the manual mode the operator did the work done by the computer when in the computer mode.

The PDP 8/S computer was a one address, fixed word length, serial computer using a word length of 12-bits and two's complement arithmetic. It had a 4,096 word random access magnetic core memory. Programming was done in assembly language.

Programs read into the computer did three things: (1) they provided for transfer of data into and out of the computer, (2) they controlled the DRC-150, and (3) they processed data obtained by the DRC-150.

The operator, through the computer and DRC-150, commanded the camera to examine the light level at selected X, Y coordinates. After the interrogation, a report was received back at the computer as to which one of 64 different shades of gray was recorded at the point X, Y. This information was stored in the computer memory.

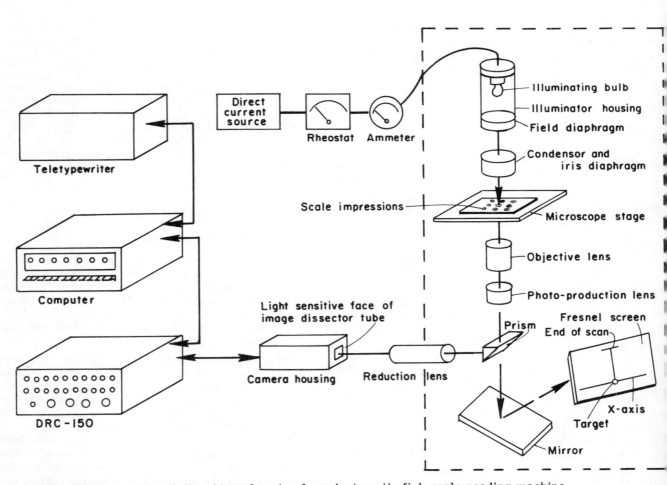

Fig. 2. Diagrammatic relationships of parts of semiautomatic fish scale reading machine.

Four thousand and ninety-six points on the X-axis and 4,096 points on the Y-axis could be interrogated in any desired sequence at a rate of 1, 10, or 100 points per second. For the purpose of this study, 512 slightly overlapping points were interrogated along the Y-axis—in effect, a single scan line.

The computer programs and data were transferred into and out of the machine by teletypewriter at a fixed rate of 10 characters per second by either keyboard or perforated tape. Data could be presented in the form of graphs or tables via the keyboard. The perforated tape output could be in a variety of formats acceptable to other data processing devices or for conversion to cards or to disks for storage.

Operating Procedures

The scale reading machine was a semiautomatic device that required operator control, data contributions by the operator, and operator-generated commands at certain times.

Before proceeding with a series of scale readings, the operator checked to insure that the X, Y coordinates seen on the Fresnel screen coincided with their digital equivalents on the camera (see Appendix I). In addition, the light source was adjusted for effects of ageing of the filament through extended use and was recalibrated after a changing of the illumination bulb.

Perforated Tape Output

The procedures used in producing a perforated tape required operator commands, operator intervention, and machine procedures.

OPERATOR PROCEDURES

The operator readied the machine, then selected a scale card containing a number of plastic impressions of sockeye scales. The card was mounted on the microscope stage and a particular impression brought into focus on the Fresnel screen. If the scale was regenerated, excessively dirty or deformed, or if excessively resorbed, it was rejected. If the scale was judged readable, the operator selected the axis used for reading by the operator and scanning by the machine (see Appendix III) and through the use of the stage micrometer, moved the impression until the reading (scanning) axis coincided with the Y-axis on the Fresnel screen. The operator identified the last circulus before the first circulus of the first year of ocean growth and moved the impression until the last circulus lay on the target. It was thus known that the data to be stored in the computer memory started on a 'black' (circulus) area.

The last circulus in the first year of ocean growth was identified by the operator and the number of circuli in the first year of ocean growth counted as well as the total number of circuli visible on the Fresnel screen between the target and the end of scan point. The operator also aged the fish by counting the number of winter growth zones in the freshwater and ocean zones of the scale.

The following information was stored in sequence in the computer via the teletypewriter by the operator:

a. two digits for the year in which the scale sample was collected
b. one digit to identify the species
c. three digits to identify the scale card number
d. two digits to identify the particular impression on the card
e. one digit for the number of freshwater winter growth zones
f. one digit for the number of saltwater winter growth zones
g. two digits for the number of circuli in the first year of ocean growth
h. two digits for the total number of circuli

The operator used the focussing controls freely up to this point to identify scale features and to obtain the best possible circulus counts available to the human eye at 41 X. After this was done, the operator tried to select a compromise position where all circuli were in equal focus. This was a subjective decision that had to be made since the focus could not be changed during scanning.

MACHINE PROCEDURES

After selection of the focus, the operator started the computer, 512 points on the Y-axis were scanned, and the resulting gray scale values stored in the computer. The average light level was computed and displayed to the operator on the computer console lights. If the average light level was acceptable; i.e. 24, 25, or 26 on the 64 point gray scale, the operator gave a continue command to the computer.

On some occasions the average light level was not acceptable. This occurred when some scale impressions were light and required less illumination or when some were dark and required more illumination. The operator adjusted the rheostat on the light source and repeated the scanning operations until an acceptable average light level was obtained, then issued a continue command.

The data were processed by a series of algorithms until the total number of circuli defined by the algorithms (see Appendix II) was compared with the number counted by the operator (see item h above). If the difference was greater than four, an arbitrarily chosen number, the machine stopped. The operator then made one or more of the three following adjustments: (1) refocused the scale impression, (2) changed the light level, or (3) reset the start to scan point on the target. The scanning process was repeated until the adjustments resulted in counts that differed by four or less. At this time the machine produced a perforated tape without operator intervention.

Graphical Data Output

Four types of graphs shown in Fig. 3 could be printed at the operator's command. While the graphs were time consuming to print, they were of considerable value in developing algorithms and in finding repeatable errors. The 'A' output displayed gray scale values as ordinates and 512 abscissa values corresponding to the number of points interrogated. These were the 'basic data' from which decisions were to be made. The 'B' output used the same ordinate and abscissa elements but the data had been processed by the algorithm SLOPE (see Appendix II). The 'C' output was available in a high and a low form. At the time of printing either of the C outputs, the data had been discriminated into circuli and intercirculus spaces. The circuli were printed with $Y = 0$ and with $Y = 3$ for intercirculus values in the

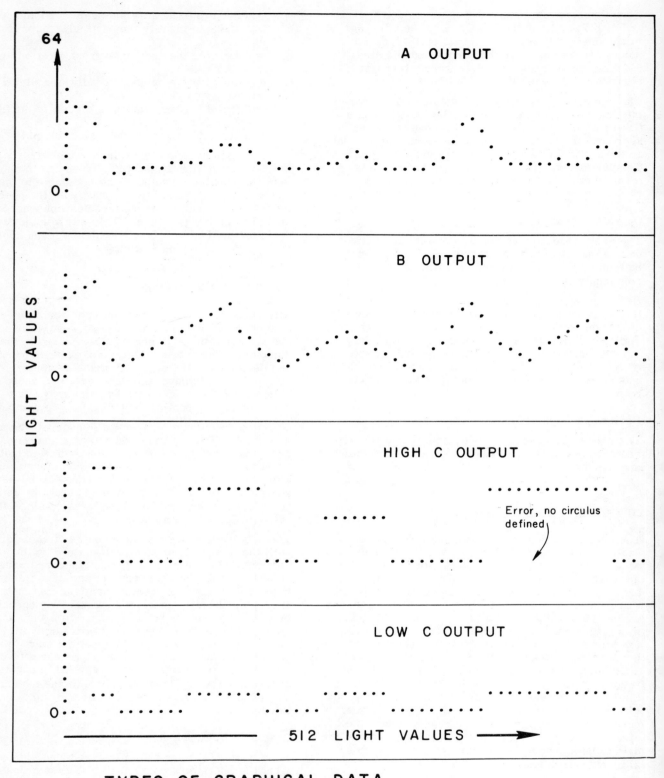

TYPES OF GRAPHICAL DATA

Fig. 3

low C output. In the high C output, circuli were printed with Y = 0 and intercirculus spaces with a Y value
equal to the maximum light value found in the intercirculus space.

Output Analysis

Some additional processing of data from graphs and
perforated tape was necessary since there was
insufficient space in the computer memory for all
desired algorithms. For both graphs and tape, the
first six points were discarded for reasons given
in Appendix I. The inner edge of the first ocean circulus was identified visually on the graphs and by a
suitable algorithm for tape. The last six data points
were also discarded and enough additional points to
terminate the data at the outer edge of the last
complete circulus. The maximum usable number of
points was 500. The usual number ranged between
about 480 and 500.

Data Output Time

If the operator chose one or more graphical outputs, certain instructions to the computer were changed and the processes of scale selection, axis alignment, etc. described above carried out. The data concerning scale card number, year of capture of the fish, etc. were not typed into memory unless the final output was to be in the form of perforated tape.

The following approximate times for data output were measured.

Graphs:

'A' output	25.5 minutes
'B' output	25.5 minutes
'C' high output	22.3 minutes
'C' low output	4.0 minutes
Perforated tape	1.25 milutes

The time of output for different scales varied from the above values depending on the number of circuli and relative transparency of different scales.

TEST PROCEDURES

Preliminary work had indicated there were no significant differences in circulus counts in reader versus reader tests using 30 sockeye samples and 20 chinook scales. The details of machine versus reader tests are given below. The procedures followed were slightly different from those described above to allow maximum control in the least amount of time.

Sample Selection

Plastic impressions of 30 scales from sexually maturing sockeye salmon collected within rivers of Bristol Bay, Alaska, were selected. An additional 30 impressions were chosen from fish collected in the North Pacific Ocean at a time and place when it was believed that only maturing sockeye of Kamchatkan origin were present. The samples represented a variety of ages of sockeye and were judged to be of 'average' reading difficulty for a human.

Operator Recorded Data

Each of the selected impressions was manually projected at 100 X onto a horizontal surface using a monocular microscope with an attached prism and separate mirror as described by Mosher (1950). The reading axis was identified as described by Lyons (see Appendix III). A scalpel was used to mark the plastic at the edge of the impression at a point that coincided with the reading axis.

The operator then used a different lens in the microscope turret to project the image at 41 X. Tissue paper was placed over the projected image and a pencil used to mark on the paper the reading axis, the start to read (scan) point, the end of read (scan) point and, as accurately as possible with a pencil, the centre of each circulus where it crossed the reading axis. The last circulus in the first year of ocean growth was identified and the number of circuli in that zone and the total number of circuli to the end of scan point were counted and written on the tissue paper. In addition, the tissue paper tracings were used to determine the distances between centres of successive circuli and to determine the number of circuli within each quarter of the total distance scanned. These procedures gave the human (HU) counts and measurements used in the analyses.

Machine Recorded Data

Each of the 60 scale impressions manually processed by the operator was mounted in turn on the stage of the scale reading machine microscope. The scale was oriented on the Fresnel screen using the centre of the focus of the scale and the scalpel mark at the edge of the scale to select the scanning axis and to align it with the Y-axis. The tissue paper tracing was placed on the screen to aid in orienting the scale and placing the start to scan point on the target.

The machine was manually started and automatically stopped after 512 points had been scanned and an average gray scale value computed. If the light value was not acceptable, the scale was rescanned. When the average light value was acceptable, a perforated tape was generated which contained the 512 basic data points. The data were then processed by the algorithms until the comparison between human and machine counts was made. If the difference between counts exceeded four, the basic data tape was destroyed and adjustments made in focus, start to scan point, or illumination. The scale was rescanned and a new basic data tape made. The process was repeated until average gray scale values and count differences were acceptable; then the next scale was processed.

Processing Machine Produced Basic Data

After basic data tapes for all 60 impressions were obtained, the data for each scale were loaded back into the computer and a low-C output printed after processing by the combination of algorithms identified as HP (see Appendix II). The operator manually eliminated the first six and the last six data points from each low—C output and identified the inner edge of the first ocean type circulus and the outer edge of the last complete ocean type circulus. The number of circuli were counted by the operator and calculations made of the distances between the centres of successive circuli. The total distance scanned was divided into quarters and the number of circuli within each quarter was determined. These were the machine counts and measurements for the UP algorithms that were compared with the human (HU) counts and measurements described above.

RESULTS

Circulus counts for the machine method were compared with those of the human reader in two ways: first, by comparing total circuli counted and second, by comparing counts within quarter sections of the scales. Following these comparisons, measurements between circuli were examined.

Circulus Counts for Sockeye

Table 1 lists the scales by origin, identification number, and number of circuli counted by the operator (HU) and by the machine (HP). Average HU counts exceeded average HP counts by +0.67 circuli for those from Bristol Bay and +0.43 for those from Kamchatka. The significance of these small differences was examined by use of the t-test. The calculated t-value for the HU versus HP data for Bristol Bay was 1.02 and 0.46 for Kamchatka. The t-value at the 5% point for 29 d.f. is 2.048. It was concluded that there was no statistical difference in mean total circulus counts between those made by the operator and those made by machine.

Table 1. Circulus counts by human (HU) and machine (HP) for sockeye samples from Bristol Bay and Kamchatka.

Origin and identification no. of scale	HU count	HP count	Difference	Origin and identification no. of scale	HU count	HP count	Difference
Bristol Bay				Kamchatka			
400-1	35	37	−2	817-3	40	38	+2
2	36	37	−1	4	41	41	0
4	36	35	+1	5	36	37	−1
6	34	32	+2	11	34	31	+3
7	37	39	−2	12	35	34	+1
411-1	33	32	+1	14	38	39	−1
2	30	28	+2	838-2	37	37	0
3	34	33	+1	4	35	35	0
4	27	27	0	15	35	39	−4
7	33	34	−1	18	39	38	+1
422-1	33	31	+2	852-3	35	33	+2
2	34	30	+4	4	38	35	+3
3	34	33	+1	9	32	31	+1
4	37	35	+2	11	36	37	−1
5	35	34	+1	22	31	31	0
435-1	31	32	−1	Q64-4	35	34	+1
2	35	34	+1	6	29	29	0
3	32	33	−1	7	37	38	−1
4	35	33	+2	11	36	36	0
5	32	34	−2	13	34	34	0
450-1	30	28	+2	21	37	39	−2
3	33	30	+3	24	32	34	−2
4	31	30	+1	30	44	44	0
5	35	33	+2	L82-4	33	31	+2
7	33	31	+2	5	33	32	+1
459-1	33	30	+3	6	39	37	+2
2	30	32	−2	13	33	30	+3
3	33	37	−4	15	33	31	+2
4	35	33	+2	23	27	28	−1
6	33	32	+1	24	36	34	+2
$\overline{X}$	33.30	32.63	+0.67		35.33	34.90	+0.43
s^2	5.11	7.83			12.30	14.37	

Table 2. Sample computer output from 60 Chi-square analyses.

Origin	Identification number	Type of value	Counting method	Circuli by quarter sections				Total circuli
				1	2	3	4	
KA	817-3	Observed	HU	9	8	12	11	40
			HP	10	9	11	8	38
			Total	19	17	23	19	78
		Expected	HU	9.74	8.71	11.79	9.74	40.00
			HP	9.25	8.28	11.20	9.25	38.00
			Total	19.00	17.00	23.00	19.00	78.00

Chi-square value is 0.577 for three degrees of freedom. P(0.05) value is 7.815.

The Y-axis on the Fresnel screen was divided into four sections and the number of circuli in each section counted. Similar counts for equivalent distances on the C outputs were made. Separate Chi-square values were calculated for all 60 scales. A typical computer listing is shown in Table 2.

None of the 60 Chi-square values were significant.

measurements for each scale was then computed as listed in Table 3. If the HU circulus count exceeded the HP count, only the number of circuli in the HP count was used and visa versa.

The hypothesis that there was no difference between means was tested. The value of t- at 29 d.f. is 2.048 at the 5% level. Since the computed value of t- was

Table 3. Mean differences (HU minus HP) in millimeters between successive circuli common to both HU and HP measurements by origin and scale number.

Origin and identification no. of scale	Number of circuli	Mean difference (mm)	Origin and identification no. of scale	Number of circuli	Mean difference (mm)
Bristol Bay			Kamchatka		
400-1	34	2.41	817-3	37	1.78
2	35	2.34	4	40	0.12
4	34	0.50	5	35	1.67
6	31	−1.79	11	30	0.56
7	36	4.94	12	33	0.53
411-1	31	0.72	14	37	4.27
2	27	−0.81	838-2	36	2.00
3	32	0.18	4	34	1.75
4	26	0.38	15	34	6.04
7	32	3.60	18	37	0.39
422-1	30	−0.43	852-3	32	−0.75
2	29	−2.10	4	34	0.75
3	32	1.81	9	30	−0.35
4	34	0.60	11	35	1.07
5	33	−1.30	22	30	2.16
435-11	30	3.21	Q64-4	33	0.72
12	33	0.46	6	28	1.64
13	31	1.61	7	36	0.66
14	32	−0.79	11	35	0.57
15	31	5.06	13	33	3.42
450-1	27	0.25	21	36	2.43
3	29	−0.60	24	31	3.85
4	29	0.37	30	43	0.39
5	32	−0.42	L82-4	30	−0.65
7	30	0.55	5	31	0.12
459-1	29	−1.05	6	36	−1.01
2	29	4.12	13	29	−1.55
3	32	6.17	15	30	0.60
4	32	−0.01	23	26	2.48
6	31	2.19	24	33	−0.15
Mean		+1.072			+1.184

The conclusion was that differences in circulus counts between those made by a human and those made by the machine were not significantly different either by total counts or by counts by quarter sections.

Circulus Measurements for Sockeye

The differences in millimeters (at 41 X) between the centre of the first circulus and the centre of the second circulus (to the nearest half millimeter), between the centre of the second and the centre of the third, etc., were computed for each of the 60 scales, first from HU data then from HP data. The mean difference (HU minus HP) between circuli

0.505 for Bristol Bay and 0.715 for Kamchatka data, it was concluded that there was no difference between mean human and machine measurements.

Data for HU and HP measurements were plotted for all 60 scales. Four scales were selected as examples for presentation in Fig. 4. BB 459-3 was selected as an example where HU almost always exceeded HP measurements (23 of 60 cases), BB 422-2 where HU measurements were greater than HP at the start and then became less (11 of 60 cases), L82-5 as an example where HU and HP were essentially equal (23 of 60 cases), and Q64-11 as an example where the data crossed at two places (3 of 60 cases).

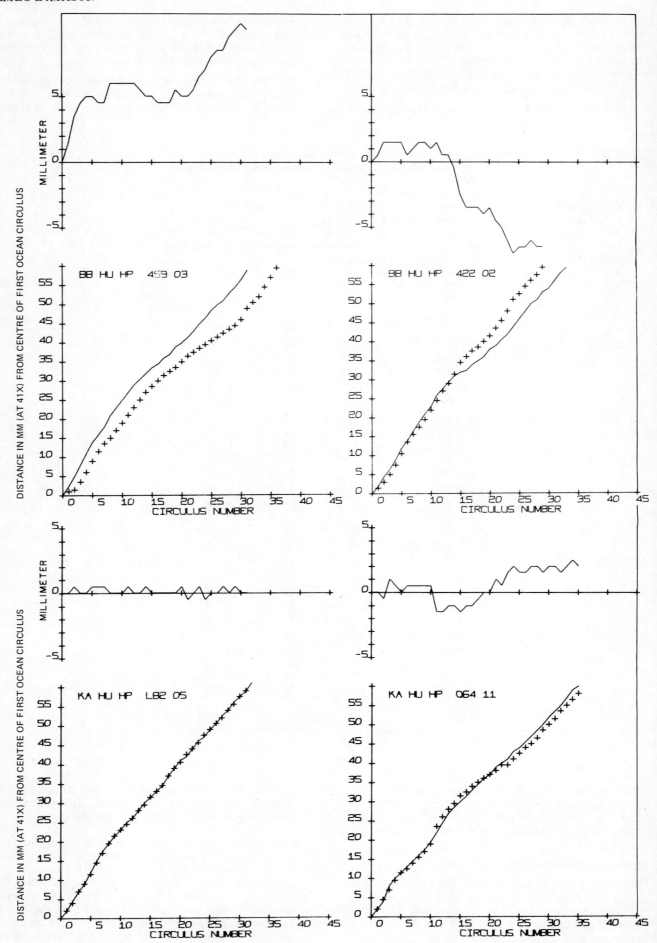

Fig. 4. Cumulative distances from circulus centre to circulus center as determined by HU (solid line) and HP (crosses)

Circulus Counts for Chinook

The algorithms collectively defined as HP were developed for use on sockeye salmon scales. A preliminary evaluation of the utility of HP for scales of chinook salmon was made with the help of Kenneth Mosher[1] who randomly selected a plastic card of scale impressions of chinook salmon from the files. He mounted the card on the stage of the microscope, determined if impressions were readable, selected a reading axis and oriented it on the target of the Fresnel screen and counted the total number of circuli. I then counted the number and proceeded to get a low-C output from the computer from which the machine count of circuli was determined. The process was repeated with results listed in Table 4.

Table 4. Circulus counts by human (HU) and machine (HP) for chinook samples from the Yukon River, Alaska.

Scale number	HU count	HP count	Difference
440-1	36	37	−1
2	31	30	+1
3	29	29	0
4	31	29	+2
5	31	31	0
6	34	34	0
7	38	41	−3
8	37	37	0
10	33	34	−1
11	32	34	−2
12	30	30	0
14	30	30	0
15	33	34	−1
16	31	32	−1
18	31	33	−2
19	31	32	−1
20	27	27	0
21	35	34	+1
22	32	33	−1
23	29	30	−1
Sum X	641	651	−10
N	20	20	20
$\overline{X}$	32.05	32.55	−0.50
Sum X^2	20693	21397	
s^2	7.84	10.89	

The machine counts were slightly higher than human counts but again, as with the sockeye, there was no statistical difference between human and machine counts, nor between the two readers.

Attempts to Determine Age

Koo (1962) described a graphical method of determining the ocean age (i.e. the number of years that the salmon had lived in salt water) of sockeye salmon collected in the Nushagak River area of Bristol Bay, Alaska. His method was based on the width and spacing of the ocean growth circuli—on average, the circuli of the winter growth zone were narrower and closer together than the circuli of the summer growth zone. Koo's procedure resulted in a graph with ordinate values expressing the average width of circuli and abscissa values, ranging from zero to 100%, representing the length of the scale on the reading axis. Low or minimum values on the graphs were interpreted as showing a slow growth portion of the scale and were designated as winter growth zones.

Encouraged by the success of Dr. Koo's procedure, I read several hundred sockeye scales using a reading axis defined by Anas and Murai (1969) which differed from Dr. Koo's but not greatly. Each scale was projected at 100 X onto a card. Pencil marks were made on the card to indicate each circulus and its width. Data showing circulus and intercirculus widths were then transferred to punched cards. A large number of analyses were made using graphical methods which could be programmed in FORTRAN and processed in a large card reading computer. None of the methods exactly duplicated Dr. Koo's.

Scale samples from fish taken within rivers tributary to Bristol Bay were used as well as samples from fish collected on the high seas and from fish believed to be of Asian origin. Some success in determining age was achieved with scales from sockeye taken in Bristol Bay rivers. Generally, however, there was an unacceptable degree of error in identifying age of fish taken on the high seas and fish more than four years in total age. After trying a great number of analytical procedures, I came to the conclusion that the data on a single reading axis were insufficient to allow the use of a particular graphical procedure for determination of saltwater ages for all sockeye from all areas.

When the present scale reading machine became available, Robert Lander[2] suggested that plotting of accumulated light values, which could be quantified by the machine but not the eye, might result in points of inflection on a curve that could be related to the presence of annuli. Several scales from fish of the Naknek River in Bristol Bay were scanned and the results plotted as suggested by Lander. Results were so unpromising that further attempts were abandoned.

Since efforts to determine saltwater ages of sockeye salmon from a single reading axis were unsuccessful, no effort was made to find a machine method for determining freshwater ages which are more difficult for a human to interpret.

Estimation of Production Reading Rate

A stop watch was used to time the individual machine and operator operations. Average time for the individual procedures were computed and are shown in Fig. 5. It was assumed that scale cards would be conveniently available to the operator so timing started when a card was lifted from a nearby table and ended when the machine was available for mounting of another scale. Since the computer required only 2-3 seconds to process the data through the algorithms, the time is not shown in Fig. 5.

The data indicate that on an average it would take 3 minutes 55 seconds to process a scale since mounting of a new scale could be started while the punch was operating.

[1] Formerly, Fishery Research Biologist, Northwest Fisheries Center, Seattle.

[2] Biometrician, Northwest Fisheries Center, Seattle.

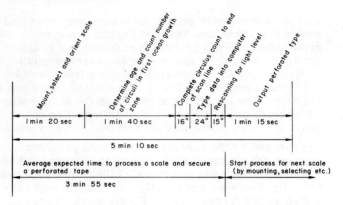

Fig. 5. Average times (by stop watch) to execute required operations in producing a perforated tape by machine scanning a scale.

The 3 minute 55 second estimate could be reduced if certain processes were to be shortened or eliminated. A probable minimum time include the following:

	Min.	Sec.	
1. Mount, select and orient	1	20	timed
2. Determine age	0	30	estimated
3. Type data into computer	0	15	estimated
4. Rescanning for light level	0	15	timed
Total	2	20	

Again, the process of mounting a new scale could start during the 1 minute 15 seconds required to punch a tape.

The time could be shortened if it were possible to (1) eliminate the time required for the operator to identify the last circulus in the first year of ocean growth and (2) count the number of circuli from the first year of ocean growth to the end of scan line, (3) reduce the time required to type data into the computer and (4) acquire a more sophisticated machine.

Part (1) could be done if there were no need for the operator to identify a particular circulus. Part (2) could be accomplished if the risks of acquiring spurious data (see section on computer capacity and software) could be accepted or circumvented.

Obviously a more sophisticated machine requiring less time to accept, scan, and transmit data would hasten processing. However, unless a machine and software are found that can perform more of the operator's tasks, the human will continue to be the principal production bottleneck.

MACHINE ADVANTAGES

The advantages, known at present, of machine reading compared to human reading include: (1) a once-only scale reading by which the operator determines the fresh- and saltwater ages and the machine counts and measures circuli in and beyond the first ocean growth zone, in about 4 minutes. (2) Results are immediately available for processing through a large computer. Any definable scale character can be programmed and results obtained without referring to the scale again. (3) Machine results should be the same from day to day and not vary with time as a human's results might.

Our conventional scale reading process may require two or more scale handling steps, the first to deter-

mine ages and on some occasions a second to take three measurements to determine origin. Any additional information requires a rehandling of the scale. Each handling requires an operator's hand transcription of data followed by a key punch operation and key punch verification. Each step increases the likelihood of introducing errors. The conventional reading process can take as long as 45 minutes to read, record, transcribe, keypunch, and verify the results for 2 single scales as compared to less than 4 minutes for present machine processing.

Possible future advantages lie in results that may be obtained in maturity prediction and growth studies without rereading of scales that have been previously processed by machine.

LIMITATIONS

Experimental use of the machine revealed a number of limitations involving mechanics, optics, electronics, and computer capacity and software—as well as limitations with regard to use of the system on scales from other species of fish. Collectively, these limitations restricted machine accuracy, speed of operations, and utilization of results; they also caused greater operator involvement than was anticipated. These restrictions and the complexity of the problems of interpreting scales did one other thing—they caused an underestimate of the time required to develop software.

The problems and deficiencies deserve some elaboration since they might be encountered by anyone planning or using a fish scale reading machine.

Mechanics

The scale reading machine was designed to be used as a laboratory instrument. It required meticulous alignment and extreme care to avoid physical shocks. It could not be used aboard a vessel unless redesigned or unless the vessel was stable.

The use of an inverted microscope had certain advantages but it forced the operator to either stand or to half-sit on a high stool while mounting and orienting scales. This was endurable for the tests described but would present a problem in continuous scale processing.

The scale scanning process required that the operator be in close contact with the microscope, the computer, the teletypewriter, and the various controls and switches. The equipment was awkward to use, which contributed to operator errors and waste of time.

The teletypewriter transmitted information at a fixed rate of 10 characters per second. While this rate was acceptable in some situations, it resulted in great time losses while developing and debugging algorithms (about 25 minutes for a single B output).

Most of the problems could be largely overcome by adequate engineering. However, a thorough time and motion study of human and machine operations should be made before designing any new machine.

Optics

Only a part of most scales could be projected and scanned in one operation. When magnification was reduced to a point where the whole scale appeared on the Fresnel screen and on the window (12.7 by

12. 7 mm) of the image dissector tube, it was impossible to discriminate resulting data into circuli. There were three contributing factors: (1) the size of the window, (2) the resolution capabilities of the tube, and (3) space limitations in the computer. The only practical solution was to scan a part of the scale so magnifications of 41 X at the Fresnel screen and 8. 7 X at the tube were used.[3] This was acceptable at the time since work priorities were concerned with studies of circuli in the first year of ocean growth which could be covered in one scanning operation.

Problems encountered in alignment, illumination, and calibration are described in Appendix I. It is apparent that no good solution was found for providing a uniformly illuminated field or for standardizing the level of illumination.

The depth of focus of the lens system was insufficient to accommodate variations in scale thickness and allow sharp focussing of all circuli at a single microscope setting. The operator could vary the focus while working at the Fresnel screen but had to make a visual and subjective selection of a focus level before scanning started. Unless this was done with some skill, results were sometimes spurious.

Electronics

Two electronic deficiencies were found. The first was discussed in Appendix I and concerned apparent differences in slope of data resulting from scanning from a black to a white area as compared to scanning from a white to a black area. The second deficiency involved the rate of scanning. The machine was supposed to scan at rates of 1, 10, 100, and 1, 000 points per second. Results from using 1, 10, and 100 were almost identical while results at 1, 000 were useless. No satisfactory explanation was found.

Computer Capacity and Software

The 4, 096 word capacity of the computer memory was too small to deal with the basic programming problem and all the problems. The programmer had to continually concern himself with developing algorithms which would stay within available memory space. If more core capacity had been available, there would have been a greater opportunity to address the real problem—that of finding the most effective algorithms. While the assembly language required to program the computer was tedious and time consuming to use, it allowed the development of more effective algorithms than would have been possible with FORTRAN or one of the more conversational languages which by themselves occupy a large amount of memory space.

The limited core space prevented complete data processing and required that it be completed elsewhere. The space limitation also prevented program redundancy which could have been used to detect errors made by the computer, e.g., jumping to a wrong subroutine or discriminating data into a circulus of infinite width. Only one error check could be used, a comparison of the number of circuli counted by the operator with the number counted by the machine as described in Appendix I.

---

[3] A program to process a whole scale by sections was developed but it was too large for the computer.

Scale Characteristics

The algorithms collectively identified as HP were developed to count and measure circuli in part of the ocean growth phase of the life history of sockeye salmon. How effectively these data may be used is beyond the scope of this report and remains to be determined. The limited work with chinook suggests that HP might be applied satisfactorily to some problems involving that species. Perhaps HP might have some utility with other salmon species or even other species having cycloid type scales. It is improbable that HP as it is or unless extensively modified, would work with species having other types of scales.

SUMMARY AND CONCLUSIONS

More effective management of fishery resources could be accomplished if the process of determining various vital statistics, obtainable from scales, could be automated. If this could be accomplished, it would be possible to produce data virtually as fast as samples are collected and results could be used almost immediately—a far different situation from that which generally exists today.

The machine and algorithms described were tested with selected samples of impressions of sockeye and chinook salmon scales of various ages and origins. Because of limitations, only the first ocean growth zone and part of the second were scanned. There were no significant differences in circulus counts and measurements between a human and the machine. There was a tendency for the machine to make higher counts and to measure greater distances for sockeye and to make lower counts (no measurements were made) for chinook. Whether these differences indicate fixed or random biases is not known nor is their effect known on the results of growth or racial studies based on scale data.

Results indicate that the machine might be used on salmon scales in situations where data adequate for racial, maturity, and growth studies may be obtained from a single reading axis. These studies require careful measurement of the widths of circuli and their numbers and require a great deal of time when made by a human—a situation ideal for automation.

Age analysis comprised a relatively minor part of the total work done with the machine. Attempts to determine ocean age of sockeye salmon resulted in a high degree of error and were generally unsuccessful. Assuming that the machine could be programmed to determine the ocean age of a salmon it would probably be impossible to program to determine freshwater age—which is on the average more difficult to determine than the ocean age. It might be possible to determine the age of certain marine species by scanning a series of lines radiating from the focus of the scale or by using the machine as a basic data (gray scale values) source and processing the data in a large computer. For some species, it seems rather probable that sophisticated image analysis will be required.

The rate of data production, about 4 minutes per scale, is acceptable when compared to the time required for the same work by a human. The operator's manipulations account for most of the 4 minutes. Until the machine does a greater part of the work, the operator will be the principal bottleneck to increasing the amount of data produced in a given time period

ACKNOWLEDGMENTS

Much of the material presented in this report resulted from ideas and help given by R. Lander, J. Lyons, R. Major, K. Mosher, S. Murai, F. Ossiander, and D. Worlund. Their contributions are gratefully acknowledged and notice given that the responsibility for any remaining errors is mine.

REFERENCES

Anas, R. E., and Murai, S. 1969. Use of scale characters and a discriminant function for classifying sockeye salmon (*Oncorhynchus nerka*) by continent of origin. Bull. int. N. Pacif. Fish. Commn, **26**, 157-192.

Koo, T.S.Y. 1962. Age and growth studies of red salmon scales by graphical means. In Ted S. Y. Koo (editor), Studies of Alaska red salmon, Univ. Wash. Publs Fish., N.S. **1**, 49-121.

Major, R.L., Mosher K.H., and Mason, J.E. 1972 Identification of stocks of Pacific salmon. In Raymond C. Simon and Peter A. Larkin (editors). The stock concept in Pacific salmon. MacMillan Lect. Br. Columb. Univ. 1970 209-231.

Mosher, K.H. 1950. Description of a projection device for use in age determination from fish scales. Fishery Bull. Fish Wildl. Serv. U.S., **51**, 405-407.

APPENDIX I

ALIGNMENT, ILLUMINATION CALIBRATION, FIELD UNIFORMITY AND CONVERSION CONSTANTS

Alignment

Alignment of the target on the Fresnel screen with the image dissector tube was done with the use of an opaque metal disk having an aperture of 10 microns in diameter. The disk was mounted on the microscope stage and was moved on the stage until the aperture (magnified to about 410 microns) appeared as a light point that coincided with the Fresnel screen target.

A piece of white opaque plastic was placed over the light-sensitive part of the image dissector tube and the reduction lens adjusted until a clear sharp image of the light point appeared on the plastic. The plastic was then removed.

The DRC-150 was switched to manual mode control and binary numbers entered into the DRC-150 which identified the light sensitive point X = 0 and Y = 6. The horizontal and vertical positions of the camera were then changed until the light spot and the target coincided with these coordinates. This was indicated by a high gray scale value appearing on the display lights of the DRC-150.

The binary coordinates were then changed to identify Y = 506 at the 'end of scan' point, about 62 mm from the target. The camera was moved horizontally, vertically, and rotated as required until all specified

points on the Fresnel screen coincided with their binary equivalents on the window of the image dissector tube.

Illumination Calibration

The tungsten filament of the light (for illuminating the plastic scale impression) was heated by rheostat-controlled, direct current. An ammeter indicated the amount of current flowing at various rheostat settings. The direct current eliminated some of the complications that came from the original power source which used 60-cycle alternating current.

A modified type of Kohler illumination was developed that was concerned with the quality of the light that reached the image dissector tube—not what the operator saw on the Fresnel screen. After aligning the optics, the face of the tube was again covered with the white opaque plastic. The iris and field diaphragms of the microscope were fully opened and the height of the light bulb changed and rotated until the filament of the bulb appeared as follows in relation to the scan line.

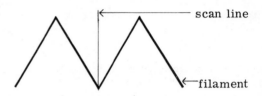

When this orientation was obtained, the bulb was fixed so that no further rotation was possible.

Two additional adjustments were made—the height of the condensor above the microscope stage and the distance between the bulb and the condensor. These were trial and error adjustments and were continued until the illumination on the white plastic appeared uniform. The field diaphragm was left open and the iris diaphragm closed until the light reaching the plastic resulted in a darkened but uniform-appearing light field. It was sometimes necessary to readjust the distances between bulb, condensor, and stage to maintain a uniform field under reduced light conditions. When the light appeared uniform to the eye, the objective lens was removed and a General Electric Model 8DW58Y4[4] photographic exposure meter was placed in the space occupied by the lens. The rheostat control was changed until desired current flows were indicated on the ammeter and the light level indicated on the meter in foot candles was noted. Diaphragm adjustments were made as needed and the process repeated. The desired light levels were as follows:

Ammeter reading	Foot candles
2.0	3
2.2	7
2.4	13
2.6	21
2.8	38
3.0	53
3.1	64

---

[4] Trade names referred to in this publication do not imply endorsement of commercial products by the National Marine Fisheries Service.

When adjustments resulted in foot candle readings close to those shown, the position of the iris diaphragm was fixed and a sockeye scale (1966, Naknek River #401-20), used as a standard, was placed on the microscope stage and oriented on a reading axis where the operator counted 45 circuli. The scale was scanned at an average light level of 23 and a C output obtained. If the machine identified 43 circuli, the illumination was accepted as being satisfactory. If some other number of circuli was counted, the alignment and the illumination calibration process was repeated. Light level was extremely important and small variations, undetectable to the eye, could have a great effect on results.

Field Uniformity

After all aligning and calibration work was done, a number of scans was made at various light levels without anything on the microscope stage. It was noted that light levels at the centre of the field tended to be less than at the edges and that some light levels tended to be irregular

For reasons unknown, the first six and the last six points tended to vary considerably even on successive repeated scans. The solution adopted was to scan 512 points then discard the data obtained for the first six and the last six points scanned. This is the reason for using the coordinates X = 0, Y = 6 and X = 0, Y = 506 while aligning the optics. Discarding of the points was done after the data had been discriminated into circuli as described in Appendix II.

With an uninterrupted light beam and the rheostat set to give an ammeter reading of 2.8, the light values near the centre of the scan were about 12 values less than at the edges. The changes from edge to centre to edge were fairly uniform except between points 138 and 159 where the values varied rather abruptly with a range of about four. The effects of the variations in uniformity superimposed upon light values obtained from scanning a scale are not known but are believed to be negligible.

Scanning of the ronchii rulings revealed a type of nonlinearity that could not be attributed to illumination. The B outputs showed that the rate (slope) of change from a black to a white area tended to be less than the rate of change from a white to a black area. The difference was small, the effects on results presented in this paper probably were negligible and probably came from characteristics inherent in electronic design and components.

The optical spectral response of the image dissector tube was determined by the spectral sensitivity of the photocathode, in this case described as an S-11. The spectral distribution of the S-11 was between about 3,000 and 6,500 Angstroms with a peak at about 4,500. The response of the human eye lies between about 4,800 and 6,400 Angstroms with a peak at about 5,560 Angstroms. The effect of the differences in sensitivity is not known. Occasionally the light values in the A, B, and C outputs indicated the presence of a circulus that could not be identified by the operator on the Fresnel screen. The differences may have been due to differences in spectral sensitivity or simply to the inability of the eye to detect small changes in levels of illumination that would reveal a circulus.

Conversion Constants

A glass ronchii ruling with 300 lines per 25.4 mm (1.0 inch) was used to determine magnification at the Fresnel screen and at the image dissector tube; it was also used to find conversion constants for calculating width of circuli, etc., in mm or inches.

The ruling was placed on the stage and oriented so the lines were parallel to the X-axis with a white interspace over the target. The number of bars appearing on the Fresnel screen between the target and end of scan point was determined and the magnification calculated as 41 X.

The magnification of the image appearing on the image dissector tube was calculated as a product of the power of the objective lens times the power of the photo projecting lens times the power of the reduction lens, or 2.0 × 20 × 0.218 = 8.7 X. The magnification of the tube was also checked with the ronchii ruling. A precise measurement could not be made because of the relative inaccessibility of the window of the tube; however, comparisons between calculated and measured results were close.

A low-C output was secured from scanning the ronchii ruling and the average number of points per bar was determined. Different conversion factors for different purposes could then be calculated; e.g., if a circulus contained seven points, multiplying by 0.29689 resulted in a product giving the width of the circulus in mm when projected at 100 X.

APPENDIX II

ALGORITHMS

The basic data were processed by a series of algorithms that classified all data points as black (circuli) or white (intercirculus spaces) and either printed a graph or generated a perforated tape at the operator's command. The algorithms used in sequence were identified as SLOPE, UPDN, REJLO, REJHI, OUTPUT, SPLIT, H2DN, H2UP, CCNT, PROG, AND FDP. These algorithms, collectively, were identified by the mnemonic HP. The essentials of each algorithm are described below. All input and output routines and miscellaneous housekeeping routines were omitted as well as the methods of dealing with successive level zero or level 64 gray scale values.

SLOPE

SLOPE smoothed the basic data and started the processes of eliminating two types of anomalies; small light zones in large dark zones, and small dark zones in large light zones.

The algorithm took the first light value from memory, incremented that light value by one, deposited the new value in memory, incremented the new light value by one, deposited the second new value in memory, then incremented again and deposited the third new value in memory. Thus the first three light values always successively increased and were always identified as having a positive or UP slope.

The light values in core location 4, 5, and 6 were drawn from memory and their possible geometric configurations examined. If point 4 were of the same value as point 3; it was defined as an UP-EQUAL geometry; if point 4 were less than point 3, as an UP-DOWN geometry; and if point 4 were greater than point 3, as an UP-UP geometry.

Only the UP-EQUAL geometries will be discussed since the others may be developed along similar lines.

The UP-EQUAL geometric possibilities involving points 4, 5, and 6 are shown in Fig. II-1. The points in the figure are identified with the mnemonics which are used in the algorithm (e.g. 4 = T3, 5 = T4, 6 = T5). The figure shows only the relationships of adjacent points, whether they are equal to, less than, or greater than each other. The magnitude of differences, if any, between adjacent points is not indicated although magnitude is considered in making certain types of decisions to be described.

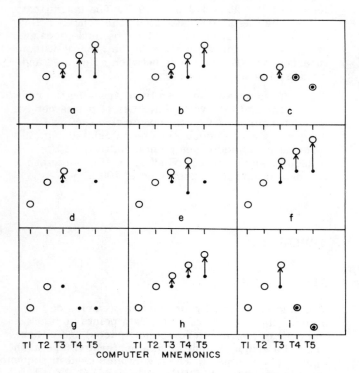

Fig. II-1. UP-EQUAL geometries. Periods indicate new light values, arrows indicate direction of change of light values and circles indicate values deposited in memory. Ordinate values are described in text.

In Fig. II-1a, the value of point T3 was incremented by one and defined as T3, incremented again and defined as T4, then incremented again and defined as T5 as shown by the arrows. The three new values were deposited in memory. Three new points were taken from memory and a decision made as to whether the new geometries were UP-UP, UP-EQUAL or UP-DOWN. The same procedure used for the Fig. II-1a was used for Fig. II-1b, f, and h.

In Fig. II-1c, and 1i, T3 was incremented as shown; then T3, and T4, and T5 were deposited in memory. The next three new points were taken from memory and examined to see if they formed DOWN-DOWN, DOWN-EQUAL or DOWN-UP geometries.

In Fig. II-1d, T3 was incremented. If T3 was then equal to T4, T4 was incremented, T3 and T4 were deposited in memory, T5 was renamed T3, two new points taken from memory, identified as T4 and T5, and a determination made as to what type of geometric pattern existed. If after being incremented, T3 were less than T4 then T3 and T4 were deposited in memory, T5 was renamed T3, two new points acquired,

and the UP geometries examined. If T3 were greater than T4, T3 and T4 were deposited in memory, T5 was renamed T3, two new points acquired and the DOWN geometries examined.

In Fig. II-1e, T3 was incremented, defined as T3, incremented again, and defined as T4, then T3 and T4 were deposited in memory, two new points obtained, and the UP geometries examined.

In Fig. II-1g, the magnitude of the difference between adjacent points was considered in decision making. If T3 were greater than T4 by 3 or more, T3 was decremented by one and defined as T3; T4 was incremented; T3, T4, and T5 were deposited in memory; three new points were acquired and the DOWN geometries examined. If the difference between T3 and T4 were not greater than 3, T3 was incremented and defined as T3, incremented again and defined as T4, incremented again and defined as T5, the three new values deposited in memory, three new points obtained, and the UP geometries examined.

UPDN

The UPDN algorithm determined the number of points that were in each successive positive or negative slope sequence and retained certain light values which were either high points or low points of a sequence. Due to SLOPE, the first slope was always positive and always had at least three points. UPDN counted the number of points in the first positive slope sequence; 100 was then added to the number to indicate the slope was positive by the prefix 1 and the sum deposited in memory. The highest light value in the positive slope segment was deposited in the next memory location. The number of successive points in the following negative slope sequence was counted, 200 added to indicate a negative slope with the prefix 2, and deposited in memory. The lowest light level in the negative slope segment was then deposited in the next memory location. The process was repeated until a total of 512 points had been counted. At that time the data in storage were in the following sequence:

108	plus slope, 8 points
28	highest light value
212	negative slope, 12 points
06	lowest light level
108	
24	

The first 28 points of Fig. II-2 use these same values.

REJLO

REJLO was used to eliminate small white areas in large black areas and is shown in Figure II-2. The following formulas were solved by shifting the binary number in the computer accumulator three times rather than by conventional division by 8:

$$HFPT = \frac{H1 + H2 + H3 + H4}{8}$$

$$DIF = HFPT - H5.$$

If DIF were negative, L4, L5, and H5 were eliminated as shown by the dashed lines to create a new L4 and to change H6 to H5 and L6 to L5. New values for H6 and L6 were taken from memory and the process continued.

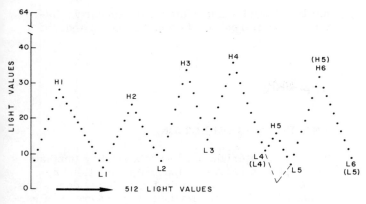

Fig. II-2. Definition of high and low light values used to eliminate small white areas in a large dark area.

If DIF were positive, H5 was accepted, all identities shifted to the right (the first L2 became a new L1, etc.), new values for H6 and L5 taken from memory, and the process continued.

After all data were processed, REJLO was repeated using the following formula:

$$DIF = (HFPT + 2) - H5$$

REJHI

REJHI was used to eliminate small black areas in large white areas as illustrated in Fig. II-3. Division by 2 was accomplished by shifting the binary contents of the accumulator. The algorithm solved the following formula:

$$L3 - \frac{L1 + L2 + L4 + L5}{2}$$

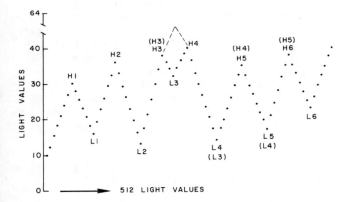

Fig. II-3. Definition of high and low light values used to eliminate small black areas in a large white area.

If the solution were positive, L3 was accepted as being a possible circulus, the values of high and low points were shifted to the right (L2 became the new L1, etc.) and the process repeated. If the solution were negative, L3 was eliminated as indicated by the dashed lines and the identities of H3, H4, H5, L3, L4, and L5 were changed.

OUTPUT

This algorithm provided the means by which the operator could secure either a low- or high-C output and is described to explain how positive and negative slope data were discriminated into circuli and inter-circulus spaces. The first part of each positive slope was made into a circulus and the second part into an intercirculus space. Negative slopes were split first into an intercirculus segment, then into a circulus segment. The data in memory were not changed; they were simply processed to make a graphical output.

Data in storage in the first memory location were recovered (see UPDN). The number of points (always at least three in this location) was divided by two by an accumulator shift. The result was subtracted from the original number, e.g., 6 points resulted in 3 and 3, 10 in 5 and 5; 5 points resulted in 3 and 2, 11 in 6 and 5, etc.

The first value printed on a low-C output was identified as a circulus and was printed with the ordinate equal to zero. If there were six points in a positive slope, three were printed with Y = 0 and three at Y = 3. If there were nine points, five were printed at Y = 0 and four at Y = 3.

Negative slope data were treated the same except the first number was printed at Y = 3 and the second at Y = 0.

If a high-C output were desired, the intercirculus space was printed with Y equal to the high light value.

In order to make the results of the high- and low-C graphical outputs agree with any finally produced perforated tape, the operator had to complete the graphs by hand to accomplish what was to be done in the algorithms to follow. This handwork required the elimination of the first and last six points scanned, defining the inner edge of the first circulus and the outer edge of the last full circulus scanned, and doing the selections done by H2DN and L2UP.

SPLIT

The algorithms used up to this point processed the data so that the first memory storage location contained a number between 103 and 177 as lower and upper limits. If these data were plotted, at least two points were plotted at Y = 0 in a low-C output. No information was available to define an abscissa value if a high-C output were desired. Gray scale value 12 was arbitrarily chosen to be this value and was deposited in the first memory location; SPLIT, thereafter, processed data as described under OUTPUT and stored the results in the following sequence and format:

  12 — low light level
204 — circulus 4 units wide
  28 — high light level
109 — intercirculus 9 units wide
  06 — low light level
210 — circulus 10 units wide
  24 — high light level
etc.

Note that the contents of the memory have changed. The prefix 2 now indicates a circulus (not a negative slope) and the prefix 1 an intercirculus space; 14 and 06 are low light values and 28 and 24 are high.

H2DN

This algorithm examined each intercirculus space for the number of points it contained. If the number were 1 or 2, the intercirculus space was combined

with the two adjacent circuli to make one larger
circulus e.g.,

12	resulted in	12
204	"	216
28	"	30
102	"	105
06	"	08
210		
30		
105		
08		

L2UP

L2UP was similar to H2DN. If a circulus were 1 or
2 units wide, it was combined with the two adjacent
intercirculus spaces to make one large intercirculus
space.

CCNT

CCNT counted the total number of circuli defined
by the algorithms and stored the number in memory.

PROG

After the data were processed by PROG, the computer
either halted or continued and produced a perforated
tape. A halt indicated that the total number of circuli
counted by the human and the number counted by the
machine (CNT) differed by more than four, an
arbitrarily chosen number. The magnitude of the
difference, or which number was larger, was not known
to the operator. On a halt, the operator restarted the
machine as described in the text to produce an acceptable difference between human and machine counts.

FDP

The FDP algorithm resulted in a perforated tape.
The tape could then be converted to punched cards
and further data processing and analyses done in
FORTRAN on a larger and faster computer than the
one used in the scale reading machine. Some further
processing of the data was required in the larger
computer because of the lack of space in the computer of the scale reading machine. This machine
processing accomplished what was done by hand as
described under OUTPUT. In addition, the number of
points in each circulus or intercirculus could be converted to their equivalents in millimeters (or inches)
by use of a suitable conversion factor. (See Appen-

dix I). Thus circulus widths and cumulative distances to different points could be computed, etc.

APPENDIX III[5]

READING AXIS SELECTION

The basic materials used were a reading template
(white plastic rectangle approximately 12 by 8
inches—30 by 20 cm) and draftsman's dividers. The
reading template was marked in the centre by a vertical line. Near the base of the line, approximately
1 inch (2.54 cm) from the bottom of the template,
a small hole was punched. At 165 mm from the
centre of the hole, a line was drawn across the template at right angles to the vertical line.

To make an axis selection, the reading template was
placed upon the projected scale image (100 X) and
the small hole placed at the centre of the scale's
central platelet. One of the pointed ends of the divi-
der was placed in the hole so that the template could
be rotated while retaining the centre of the central
platelet as an orientation point. The template was
then rotated until it was visually determined that
the vertical line passed over the highest point of
that last circulus immediately below, but not touching, the horizontal line. When this was done the template was considered oriented and the vertical line
used as a reading axis.

In case the major axis was not usable due to broken
circuli, etc., two alternate axes were provided. A
second small hole was punched in the template 65
mm above the first on the vertical line. Using the
second hole as a starting point, two lines were drawn,
each at a 10 degree angle, from the vertical line.
The template was first oriented in the manner described above. To retain this orientation, some visual
landmark was found upon a circulus which the vertical line passed directly over. Using this landmark
as a reference point, the template was moved until
the second of the punched holes was in the centre of
the scale's central platelet, while the vertical line
still passed over the circulus landmark. Then either
of the lines drawn at a 10 degree angle could be used
as a reading axis.

---

5 Prepared by Julaine Lyons, Biological Technician,
Northwest Fisheries Center, Seattle, Wash.

The use of image analysis in the ageing of fish

by J. K. FAWELL

Division of Biological Sciences, Inverest Research International, Scotland

SUMMARY

Image analysis systems using television scanners can be used to determine the age of fish by measurement of the number of annual mark intercepts of a single line scan. The necessary contrast between the annual marks and the background in both scales and otoliths can be achieved by using a variety of methods of illumination. The advantages and disadvantages of ageing fish with Image Analysis are discussed.

INTRODUCTION

Assessing the age of fish from scales, otoliths or finrays, like many other essential jobs, is slow and tedious, while it is also a difficult task which requires trained and experienced staff. Consequently, as in similar fields, there is a good deal of current interest in the development of automated techniques which can speed the processing of specimens and reduce the time commitment of skilled personnel.

One of these techniques which has been generally accepted and used by materials scientists, but the wide potential of which is just being recognised by life scientists, is television image analysis. This has been in its current, relatively advanced, form for some four years and is used in medical research and toxicology (Fawell and Newman, 1972; Mawdesley Thomas and Healey, 1969) for measurement of changes in tissue components, particularly where large numbers of specimens are involved.

The aim of this paper is two-fold. Firstly to outline image analysis as a general technique and, secondly, to outline some uses of the technique in fish ageing and stimulate further ideas on the subject.

IMAGE ANALYSIS EQUIPMENT

Image analysis as a concept has been around for some time, from the original flying spot microscope to some of the highly sophisticated, computerised, pattern recognition systems of today. There are now several commercial image analysing computers available which are comparatively straightforward and easy to use, since they are operator oriented and the soft ware is extremely simple. Though there are many similarities between the systems, it is my intention to describe the Quantimet 720 (Fisher, 1971) made by Imanco Ltd, Melbourne Near Royston, Herts., England, as a representative example. The basic layout of this system is shown in Fig. 1.

Specimen handling and imaging are closely linked and can take a variety of forms. Any optical input may be used, including microscopes, epidiascopes and specialised inputs for 35 mm slides or 16 mm

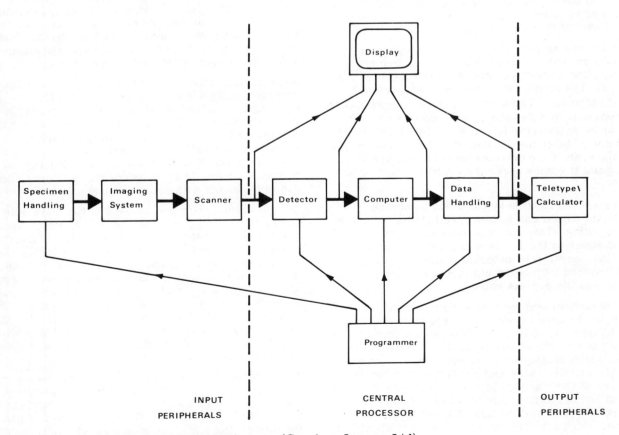

INPUT PERIPHERALS   CENTRAL PROCESSOR   OUTPUT PERIPHERALS

Fig. 1. The Quantimet 720 Block Diagram (Courtesy Imanco Ltd).

film. The criterion for use with the system is an ability to project a sharp, undistorted image on to the scanner. Specimen handling may be by standard slide mounting or by specialised systems such as tape mounting for a rapid throughput. Specimen stages may be either automatic or manual as appropriate.

With the 720 system, there are two television scanner types available, both specialised. These are Vidicon and Plumbicon, operating with a scan speed of 10.5 frames per second over 720 lines to give increased resolution and low noise levels. The Vidicon scanner operates better at medium to high light levels while the Plumbicon operates better at low levels with the resultant capability of resolving low intensity images. The problem of shading errors introduced by both scanner and optics is dealt with by an automatic shading corrector which electronically evens out the signal over the whole frame. The Plumbicon system also has a light integration facility which enables the scan to be stopped while light integrates on the phosphor to give full output at lower light levels than would otherwise be possible. The integration factors are $\times 5$ and $\times 25$.

The system uses digital logic and the signal passes from the scanner to the detector as the image of 631680 square picture points. At the detector each picture point is assessed and allocated to its appropriate grey level in binary form. This grey level is pre-selected by the operator and up to four levels can be selected at any one time to be measured by successive scans which can be recorded as cumulative steps or as the difference between levels. The vidicon scanner can discriminate up to 30 grey levels while the plumbicon can discriminate up to 50. According to the pre-set polarity, the instrument can measure from black to white or vice versa. When presented with a noisy specimen, e.g. one with fading, boundaries, the resolution of the detector may be reduced to 4, 8 or 16 picture points to fill subsequent variation in detection.

The computer is very simple from the operator point of view and can be selected to measure area, intercept (the number of scan lines intercepted by a grey level boundary), perimeter and the number of discrete features. The signal can also be modified electronically by this module, e.g. end count would count an M shape three times, while full feature count would count the same shape once. The computer can, as in the case of the detector be set to automatic at which point it comes under the control of a programmer.

As well as modification by the basic computer module, the signal can be amended between detection and computing. This enables chord sizing to be applied, which is the removal of horizontal chords (scan lines covered by detected feature) or the counting of features with horizontal chords either greater or less than the pre-set value.

The standard measuring frame size is 500,000 picture points to accommodate a surrounding guard region, the function of which is to avoid the repeated counting of re-entrant features. The live frame (the area in which measurement is being made) can be infinitely varied in size and position within the dimensions of the standard frame. This frame can also be modified in effect by use of a light pen module. The operator can use the light pen to select discrete features which can then be measured, thus effectively reducing the live frame to the boundaries of the detected feature.

The data can either be accumulated in the eight-channel store, or be fed out to an external peripheral such as a teletype or an electronic calculator. There is a monitor system which enables the operator to observe the operation if required. This is fully equipped with controls to allow the best possible image for viewing with the appropriate detection and frame clearly visible. Detection is visible as a bright interference signal overlaying the appropriate features. To facilitate automatic operation there is also a programming system which uses diode pins in lines and subsequent sets of instructions are on successive lines. Each programme line requires one scan for it to run, and up to 32 programme steps can be made with one programmer module.

The system described above is a fairly basic one but much more complex systems are available incorporating such features as densitometry and pattern recognition. The most important points to remember are that the system 'sees' in terms of grey level and is incapable of making subjective analyses. It merely makes measurements of features falling into operator selected grey levels.

METHODS

The preparation of scales, otoliths or finrays is fairly well documented (Tesch, 1971) but it is of value to look at some of the available methods of illumination and presentation. The instrument 'sees' in terms of grey level and therefore requires the best contrast possible with each specimen type. The methods available of enhancing the contrast are incident illumination, oblique illumination, transmitted illumination of various types and modification of the specimen. This last includes polishing and grinding of otoliths and finrays and mounting or coating with various refractive media. As with manual methods of ageing, different species often require a different approach to illumination and preparation.

Incident illumination tends to produce a reduction in contrast partly due to the glare and with the low magnifications required the light level is also low. Incident dark ground illumination can give fairly good contrast but since it reduces the light level even further, it is usually of little use even with image intensification. With incident illumination, the use of refractive media to coat the specimen is precluded due to problems with reflection and glare.

Oblique illumination can be used in two ways with good effect. Straightforward oblique illumination on some types of otoliths, especially the flat types, may generate the required contrast and light levels. For the longer type of otoliths such as whiting or haddock the standard technique of breaking the otolith in half and shading the top may give adequate contrast but often the light level is so low that image intensification is required. With both types of oblique illumination, coating with, or mounting in, refractive media may be used to further enhance the contrast between the growth regions.

Transmitted illumination requires a thin specimen and is suitable for scales, small otoliths and thin sections of otoliths and finrays. Straightforward transmitted light will usually be more than adequate for thin sections of otoliths and small otoliths while scales may benefit from modified illumination. Phase contrast at high magnifications and dark ground illumination at low magnifications will often prove suitable in providing the extra contrast which is required.

Specimen preparation will often make a considerable difference to contrast. The simplest and quickest form of preparation is to coat the surface with a refractive liquid such as xylene or creosote. Alternatively a histological mounting medium such as DPX (RI 1.522) or a resinous embedding material may be used with a cover slip to give a permanent preparation. This is of particular importance with smaller specimens. Polishing is very valuable in giving a flat surface which does not have unnecessary interference from specimen highlights and shadows.

Burning of otoliths (Christensen, 1964) can provide superb contrast and in many cases may be the ideal answer but the species must be selected carefully and some problems of specimen noise may be introduced with an unpolished specimen, especially with oblique lighting.

One important point to remember in specimen illumination is to obtain as even an illumination as possible. Whereas the human eye will discriminate light bands separated by dark bands even when a gradation of grey levels occurs (i.e. a light band at one side of the specimen is the same grey level as a dark band on the other side) the image analyser obviously cannot. Similarly, what may be termed specimen noise, extraneous grey particles or features, may cause problems if allowed to intercept the live frame in use. Obviously, the higher the contrast between the features to be measured and their background, i.e. annuli and circuli, the less the problem with specimen noise.

RESULTS

A number of specimens of both otoliths and scales have been examined on the quantimet and though finrays (Deelder and Willense, 1973) have not been assessed the principles are exactly the same. Any particular specimen may require a number of different approaches before the most suitable form of illumination and presentation is found. It may also require the use of novel methods which may not follow some of the classic theories but which give results.

Whiting, plaice and sprat otoliths have been examined by different methods of illumination. With whiting the standard method of oblique illumination of the broken otolith with the top shaded did not provide a high enough light level (Fig. 2). Thick sections embedded through plasticine and illuminated with transmitted light gave good contrast (Fig. 3) while burning the otoliths and using oblique illumination gave an even better contrast which may provide the basis for routine assessment of this species (Fig. 4).

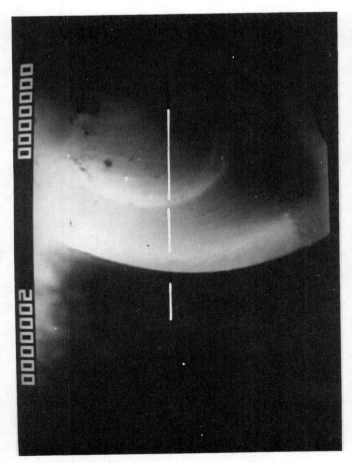

Fig. 2. QTM 720 Monitor Single line live frame with detection of whiting otolith, oblique illumination, top shaded.

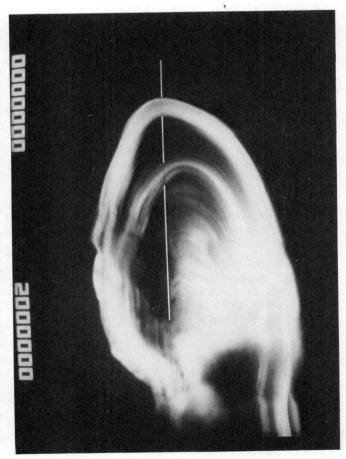

Fig. 3. Detection of annuli in section of whiting otolith embedded in plasticine, transmitted illumination.

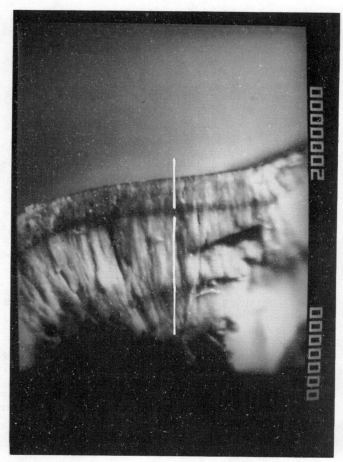

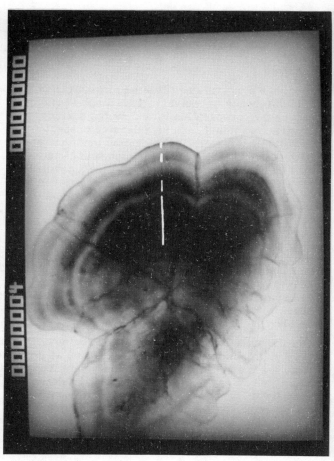

Fig. 4. Whiting otolith burnt, oblique illumination.
The dark line between the annuli is specimen noise
due to a shadow on the uneven surface.

Fig. 5. Sprat otolith, transmitted illumination
mounted in DPX.

Plaice otoliths gave adequate contrast with oblique
illumination of specimens soaked in water for 24
hours but the light level was too low for practical
purposes. However, the use of a modified low power
objective with a reflector to concentrate the light
would probably provide the necessary increase in
available light. Sprat otoliths were tried with a
variety of preparation and illumination methods.
Transmitted illumination gave good light and contrast levels with the dry specimen but mounting in
DPX improved the image immensely (Fig. 5). Incident
lighting proved inadequate but oblique provided good
contrast and brightness particularly with specimens
mounted in DPX or resinous embedding medium.

The best method for scales was found to be low
powered dark ground illumination which gave very
good contrast (Fig. 6). The use of low power objectives with scales makes the problem of illumination
somewhat simpler, since the specimen can be so
easily presented in a variety of ways, and is of a
natural high optical contrast.

DISCUSSION

The preceding paragraphs are not intended as a
manual but as a presentation of one or two problems
with the intention of providing a starting point for
further ideas.

Image analysis can be used for both the ageing of
fish and for various measurements. In most cases a
live frame consisting of a line one picture point

high is best and measurement of intercept will give
the number of annuli or circuli as required and
according to the magnification used assuming contrast is adequate. By measuring area, measurements
such as the average spacing of circuli or various
diameters can be made very accurately and very
quickly. This can be further facilitated by the use
of a polarising stage which enables the specimen
to be rotated on its nucleus and a number of measurements on different axes can be made very quickly.
The ideal situation, with, for example, salmon scales
is to make impressions (Cartright, 1964) on plastic
16 mm tape. By orientating the scales correctly
when the impression is made, the 16 mm cine input
could be used and the system left on automatic so
that close attendance by the operator would become
unnecessary. A number of measurements could be
made and, by using a supervisor module or an interfaced calculator, such as the Hewlett-Packard or one
of the Wang series calculators the data could be
checked against permissible limits. Measurements
could also be made along several axes by the use of
the programmed scanner auto-rotation system. The
use of the auto-focus system would remove difficulties with variation in impression depth and data
could be recorded on a printer or punch tape as
required

The advantages of automated techniques are that
they introduce objectivity and reduce the tedium
while enabling less experienced staff to process
routine materials. At the very best, automated techniques may free a worker almost completely and
speed up specimen evaluation to a very great extent.

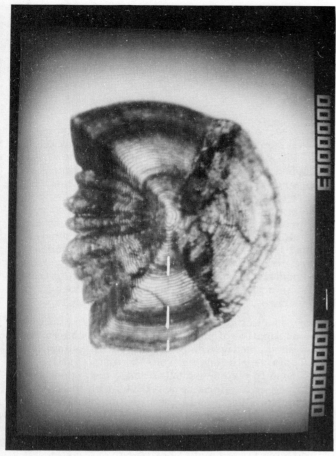

Fig. 6. Grayling scale, transmitted, dark-ground illumination.

methods of ageing, may lie in computer analysis of data which makes use of special knowledge of a particular area. It may lie in a series of zonal measurements or it may lie in ageing by growth periods linked with back ground data on physiological state and maturity.

Many workers will view the discussion of automated and computerised techniques with great scepticism and possibly question the reasons. The reasons are that in a world where social and population changes are occurring at ever increasing speed and where technological advances are enabling more intensive exploitation of resources then utilisation of those resources needs close management. This management in turn requires information, often very quickly, and computers are not only faster than man in operation on routine processes but they are not liable to fatigue and both these features will be necessary to collect data and assess it as part of a multi-parameter model. Image analysis provides a versatile and readily available starting point for the automated collection of data.

With specialised modifications of an instrument, such as the quantimet 720, one could envisage scale reading centres to which samples were sent thus enabling a concentration of expertise and a standardisation of reading and measurement. The versatility of image analysis is also a great asset since a number of different inputs can be used to the same basic computer from the scanner onwards.

The disadvantages of automated techniques are the problems of specimen preparation and the inability of most systems to recognise false checks. This latter point is the most important and in the context of our present lack of basic knowledge on false check formation and check formation in general, is not surprising. The resolution of this problem, which does introduce a great deal of difficulty in manual

REFERENCES

Cartright, R. C. 1964. A method for Making Fish Scale Impressions in the Field or Laboratory. Trans. Am. Fish. Soc., **93**, 201-1.

Christensen, J. M. 1964. Burning of Otoliths, a Technique for Age Determination of Soles and Other Fish. J. Cons. perm. int. Explor. Mer. **29**, 73-81.

Deelder, C. L. and Willense, J. J. 1973. Age Determination in Fresh-Water Teleosts, Based on Annular Structures in Fin-Rays. Aquaculture, **1**, 365-371

Fawell, J. K. and Newman, A. J. 1972. Automated Method of Quantitating Experimental Pulmonary Emphysema. Am. Rev. resp. Dis., **105**, 849-851. 851.

Fisher, C. 1971. The New Quantimet, 720. The Microscope, 1971, **19, 1**, 1-20.

Mawdesley-Thomas, L. E. and Healey, P. 1969. Some Uses of Automated Image Analysing Systems in Toxicological Pathology. Excerpta Medica. International Congress Series, no. 198. Proceedings of the European Society for the Study of Drug Toxicity, vol. XI.

Tesch, F. W. 1971. Age and Growth. In 'Methods for the Assessment of Fish Production in Fresh Water'. IBP Handbook No. 3, Ed. W. E. Ricker., pp. 98-130, 2nd Ed., Blackwell Scientific.

The ICNAF cod otolith photograph exchange scheme

by R.W. BLACKER

Fisheries Laboratory, Ministry of Agriculture, Fisheries and Food, Lowestoft, England

INTRODUCTION

Early in the history of the International Commission for Northwest Atlantic Fisheries (ICNAF) an *ad hoc* committee was set up to examine the problems associated with age-determination of cod and other species. The assessment of natural fluctuations in fish populations and the effects of fishing on them requires a knowledge of the age of the fish, and the accuracy of assessments depends to a considerable extent on the accuracy of the age-determinations. Inconsistencies in the age data used for the assessment of the cod populations in the north-west Atlantic indicated that age readers in different countries might have been using different techniques for reading cod otoliths and, perhaps, different criteria for interpreting the growth zones. An exchange of cod otoliths amongst these readers was started in 1958 in an attempt to determine the extent and cause of variations in the age data. A number of sets of cod otoliths from different areas were circulated amongst the otolith readers of the interested countries. The results showed that, although there was a considerable measure of agreement amongst the readers, there were also many significant discrepancies. The cause of these discrepancies could not be determined from this initial exchange, so a detailed survey was made of the techniques used by all the otolith readers who took part. This survey (Keir 1960) highlighted the need for closer co-operation between otolith readers, so in 1962 a workshop of otolith readers was convened by ICNAF. The workshop met at Bergen in November 1962, and the experts were able to compare and discuss their techniques in detail. This meeting showed the value of the use of photographs in discussions of the interpretation of otoliths, which ensures that the readers are discussing the same structures. The report on the workshop (ICNAF 1963b) was submitted at the 1963 annual meeting of ICNAF and the Working Group on Ageing Techniques agreed that there was little value in continuing the cod otolith exchange by sending out sets of otoliths for age-reading without any means of recording the interpretation of the zonation. The Working Group recommended: 'that future co-ordination of age-reading techniques take the form of exchange of sets of photographs (transparencies and prints) marked by each country in the way that they would read them. The photos should be accompanied by corresponding otoliths' (ICNAF 1963a).

This form of exchange was made possible by the author's development of a simple apparatus for photographing cod otoliths (Blacker 1964), which facilitated the production of negatives and transparencies from considerable numbers of otoliths.

METHOD

The aim of the subsequent exchanges was to delineate the problems of age-determination in all the cod stocks of the north-west Atlantic. Samples of selected otoliths, usually numbering 15 to 20, but occasionally

more, were sent to the author for photographing, and seven samples from an exchange which took place in 1962 were used again. The otoliths were photographed in black and white, and sets of prints were prepared for sending with relevant data sheets to the participating countries. For the first two series, photographs only were sent, because fourteen countries were taking part, and it was felt that circulating the otoliths themselves would take an inordinately long time. For subsequent series the otoliths themselves were circulated with the photographs, and the number of countries reading each set was reduced to those with an active interest in sampling the stock concerned.

The reduction in the number of participants allowed the duplication of photographs and data sheets, so that each country was sent two sets of photographs and data sheets: one set could be annotated and returned to the co-ordinator while the second was retained as a reference set. Even with the number of participants reduced to eight or nine each series of otoliths involved the production of at least 300 prints. The circulation of colour transparencies of each series was impossible because of the cost involved in producing large numbers of colour duplicates, but a master set of colour transparencies was made for the ICNAF archives.

Altogether twelve series totalling 233 otoliths were circulated in the period 1963-1967. Each series took six months or more to complete its circulation. In practice it was often convenient to send out two or three series of photographs at the same time, with the otoliths following slightly different courses around the participants, so that hold-ups caused by the absence of otolith readers at sea or on leave were minimized.

RESULTS

A typical table of results is given in Table 1 for a sample from ICNAF Subarea 2H (Labrador). The otoliths were selected from a Canadian research vessel sample and included undersized as well as commercial-size fish. Table 2 gives a comparison of the readings of the five countries which read the otoliths in 1962 as well as in the later exchange.

For the purposes of analysis, each otolith was given a 'best age' which was decided after consideration of the otolith itself and all the interpretations given by other readers. The best age is not necessarily the majority reading, nor is it the mean of the exchange readings, because these ages could be definitely wrong for a variety of reasons. Table 3 and Fig. 1 summarized for all samples the comparison of all readings with the best age. The differences from the best age are given in two ways: firstly for all fish of all ages (233 fish) and secondly, for those fish younger than 10 years (187 fish). For the first group the percentage of readings agreeing with the best age varied from 35.2 to 91.3 per cent, while for the younger fish the variation was from 50.4 to 90.9 per cent. Fig. 2

Table 1. 1966 results of ICNAF cod otolith exchange series 8 (Nos. H1-26)

No.	1962 Exch. No.	Length	Otolith Reading								
			Canada St. Andrews	Canada St. Johns	Germany	Iceland	Norway	Portugal	Spain	U.S.S.R.	Best reading
H 1	1 — 1	42	5	5	5	5	7	5 ?6	6	4	?5
H 2	1 — 3	47	5	6	6	6	5	6	6	6	6
H 3	1 — 5	54	7	7	8	8	8	8	8	8	8
H 4	1 — 6	54	8	8	8	8	8	9	9	8	8
H 5	1 — 7	55	14	14	14	14	14	14	13	10, 11 ?	14
H 6	1 — 8	61	11	10, 11	12	12	13	12	12	11	12
H 7	1 — 9	60	6	8	?8	?8	7	?7	11	7	?
H 8	1 —10	60	6	7	8	8	7	8	8	7	8
H 9	1 —11	61	12	14	13	14	14	14	14 ?15	12	14
H10	1 —12	63	10	11	13	9	10	11 ?10	12	9	?11
H11	1 —13	65	8	9	9	9	8	8	9	9	9
H12	1 —14	66	15	16	15	15	15	15 ?14	16	15	16
H13	1 —15	70	9	10	9	9	9	?9	9	8	?9
H14	1 —16	70	12	13	14	14	15	14	15	11	15
H15	1 —19	80	12	12	12	11	11	?11	17	?13	?13
H16	1 —20	89	13	13	13	13	13	12 ?11	12	11	13
H17	1s— 1	22	2	3	4	4	3	4	4	2	4
H18	1s— 2	22	3	3	4	3	3	4 ?5	4	2	?3
H19	1s— 3	24	3	3	3	3	3	3	3	3	3
H20	1s— 4	25	3	3	4	3	3	4	4	3	?3
H21	1s— 5	26	3	3	3	3	3	3 ?4	3 ?4	3	3
H22	1s— 6	28	3	3	4	3	4	5	5	3	4
H23	1s— 7	33	3	4	4	4	4	4	4	4	4
H24	1s— 8	33	4	4	5	4	5	5 ?6	6	4	?6
H25	1s— 9	37	5	5	5	4	5	5	5	4	?5
H26	1s—10	39	5	5	5	5	6	6 ?5	5	5	5

shows the percentage agreement with the best age for the nine main participants, with a comparison of results from the 1962 and 1967 exchanges where appropriate.

The figures in Tables 1 and 2 merely give the age readings for individual otoliths and the figures for percentage agreement or disagreement with best age in Table 3 are based on these readings. However, the use of photographs for recording the interpretations of each otolith reader allows for the first time a detailed comparison of readings, and it is possible to find the actual causes of some of the differences between readers. The average number of different interpretations of the otoliths in each series is shown in Table 3. In only 24 out of the 233 otoliths did all readers agree on both the age and the interpretation, and for one otolith there were twelve different interpretations giving five different ages. On eleven occasions nobody gave the best interpretation. The analysis of the interpretations was made by tracing a 'map' of the zonation from each photograph and marking on this map all the readings (Fig. 3A and B).

These maps show that the best age was sometimes arrived at by two, three, or even four different interpretations, some of which indicate that the arrival at the best age was a chance occurrence and not a logical deduction from the otolith zonation.

VALUE OF THE EXCHANGES

The photograph exchange results show that there were several important causes of error or of disagreements amongst otolith readers. One of the simplest causes, and one of the easiest to cure, was *incorrect cutting of the otoliths*. The cod otolith at the end of its first year may be very small in late-spawning fish, so that if the otolith is not broken or cut through the correct place (through the centre of the interruption in the *sulcus acusticus*) the cut will miss the first year's growth zones and an error of one year will be made. Several of the otoliths in the 1962 exchange samples were incorrectly cut but few readers commented on these mistakes.

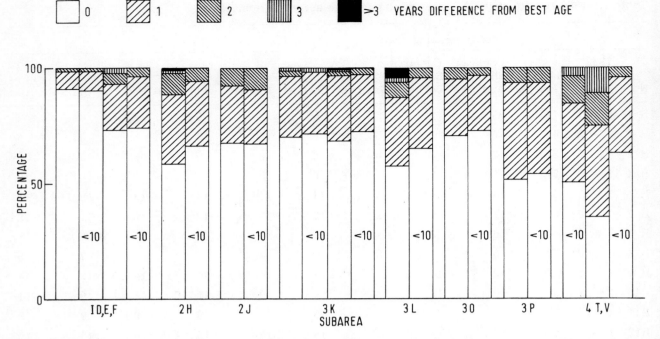

Fig. 1. Percentage agreement of the 1963-67 exchange results with the best ages, plotted for each subarea represented in the samples. The values for fish of all ages and those for fish nine years old or less are given. Illustration of data in Table 3.

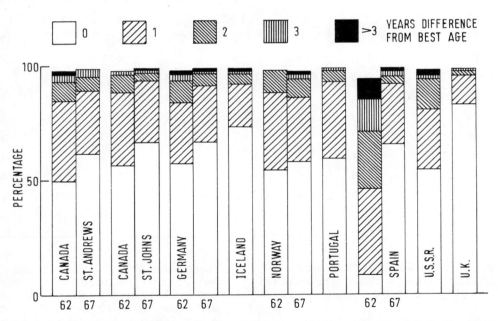

Fig. 2. Percentage agreement of the 1963-67 exchange results with the best age for the nine main participants. The comparison with the 1962 exchange results is given where appropriate.

The second cause of error was the *interpretation of the otolith edge*. For assessment data the cod's birthday is taken as 1 January, and the zonation at the edge has to be interpreted according to the date of capture relative to the birthday. Counting the current year's growth introduces an error of one year. Admittedly it is often very difficult to decide whether a hyaline edge is the current or previous year's growth in mature fish, when the hyaline zone may be a single narrow ring laid down very late in the year and not completed until the following spawning season. As a general rule the opaque zone is laid down earlier in young fish than in older ones.

Related to this error was the failure to count spawning zones in otoliths where these zones are not laid down all around the otolith (Fig. 3). There can be no doubt that these are valid zones, and failure to count them was the cause of most of the readings which differed by three or more years from the best age. This error stems from the practice of some readers of always reading otoliths along the same line towards the wider end of the otolith section.

Another important source of disagreement was in the interpretation of the central zones, and the situation was aggravated by incorrect cutting. There were

Table 2. Series 8: Comparison of results of the 1962 and 1966 exchanges

No.	1962 Exch. No.	Length	Canada St. Andrews 1962	1966	Canada St. Johns 1962	1966	Germany 1962	1966	Norway 1962	1966	Spain 1962	1966	Best reading
H 1	1 — 1	42	5	5	5	5	5	5	6	7	3	6	?5
H 2	1 — 3	47	5	5	6	6	6	6	6	5	4	6	6
H 3	1 — 5	54	7	7	7	7	8	8	8	8	5	8	8
H 4	1 — 6	54	7	8	8	8	8	8	9	8	6	9	8
H 5	1 — 7	55	13	14	14	14	14	14	15, 14	14	12	13	14
H 6	1 — 8	61	10	11	11	10, 11	12	12	13	13	10	12	12
H 7	1 — 9	60	6	6	7	8	8	?8	10	7	?	11	?
H 8	1 —10	60	6	6	7	7	8	8	8	7	5, 6	8	8
H 9	1 —11	61	12	12	13	14	14	13	14	14	11	14 ?15	14
H10	1 —12	63	10	10	11	11	10, 11	13	10	10	9	12	?11
H11	1 —13	65	8	8	9	9	9	9	9	8	7	9	9
H12	1 —14	66	14	15	16	16	16	15	16	15	12, 13	16	16
H13	1 —15	70	9	9	9	10	9	9	10(9)	9	7	9	9
H14	1 —16	70	12	12	13	13	14	14	14	15	10	15	15
H15	1 —19	80	12	12	12	12	11	12	15	11	?16	17	?13
H16	1 —20	89	13	13	13	13	13	13	13, 14	13	?12	12	13
H17	1s— 1	22	2	3	2	3	4	4	2	3	? 0	4	4
H18	1s— 2	22	3	3	2	3	4	4	2, 3	3	0	4	?3
H19	1s— 3	24	3	3	3	3	3	3	3, 4	3	2	3	3
H20	1s— 4	25	3	3	3	3	4	4	3	3	?0	4	?3
H21	1s— 5	26	3	3	3	3	3	3	3	3	?1	3 ?4	3
H22	1s— 6	28	3	3	3	3	3	4	4	4	?1	5	4
H23	1s— 7	33	3	3	3	4	3	4	4	4	?1, 2	4	4
H24	1s— 8	33	4	4	4	4	5	5	5	5	1	6	?6
H25	1s— 9	37	5	5	4	5	5	5	5, 6	5	1	5	?5
H26	1s—10	39	5	5	5	5	5	5	5	6	1	5	5

Fig. 3. (A) Cod otolith from Labrador (2H; 70 cm long, caught in August 1960). The best age is 15 years. Note how the outermost spawning zones do not extend around the broad end of the section.

Fig. 3. (B) 'Map' of the same otolith, showing the various interpretations received in the exchange.

obviously widely differing opinions on what should be counted as the first annual hyaline zone. For example, the otolith in Fig. 4 has a single well-marked but narrow hyaline zone in the centre which all readers except one counted as the first annual zone in a sample of otoliths from young fish. Yet in a sample of older fish from the same area the identical zone was counted as the first year by that reader. Such inconsistencies were the cause of many discrepancies and it cannot be stressed too strongly that the same

Table 3. Comparison of the 1963-67 exchange results with the best age, for divisions of subareas 1, 2 and 3.

	1DEF				2H		2J		3K			
Series Number	.2		3		8		5		4		6 & 9	
Number of readers	15		8		8		7		6		9	
	All ages	<10	All ages	<10	All ages	<10	All ages	<10	All ages	<10	All ages	<10
Number of otoliths	29	25	20	18	26	18	23	17	15	10	25	22
% readings differing from best age by — 0 yrs	91.3	90.9	73.1	74.2	58.5	66.2	67.7	67.3	70.0	71.7	68.2	72.2
1 yr	7.6	8.0	20.4	22.1	30.5	27.9	24.8	23.5	26.7	26.6	28.5	25.0
2 yrs	1.1	1.1	4.6	3.7	9.0	5.9	7.5	9.2	2.2	—	1.9	2.2
3 yrs	—	—	2.0	—	1.0	—	—	—	1.1	1.7	0.5	—
>3 yrs	—	—	—	—	1.0	—	—	—	—	—	0.5	—
Age range (yrs)	3-10	3-9	4-10	4-9	3-16	3-9	2-16	2-9	1-20	1-9	2-13	2-9
Average number of interpretations per otolith	2.0		3.0		3.6		2.6		2.0		3.4	
No. of otoliths with complete agreement on age and interpretation	4		1		1		1		4		1	
Number with no best interpretation given	0		1		1		0		1		2	

	3L		3O		3P		4TV			
Series Number	10		11		12		1		7	
Number of readers	9		8		7		18		9	
	All ages	<10	All ages	<10	All ages	<10	All ages <10		All ages	<10
Number of otoliths	28	22	25	22	15	13	15		12	5
% readings differing from best age by — 0 yrs	57.1	64.4	70.5	72.7	51.5	53.9	50.4		35.2	63.0
1 yr	29.9	31.4	24.5	23.9	41.9	39.5	34.4		39.8	32.6
2 yrs	6.7	4.3	5.0	3.4	6.7	6.6	11.5		13.9	4.4
3 yrs	1.8	—	—	—	—	—	3.7		11.1	—
>3 yrs	4.0	—	—	—	—	—	—		—	—
Age range (yrs)	1-21	1-9	2-16	2-9	4-11	4-9	4-9		6-15	6-9
Average number of interpretations per otolith	3.8		2.9		3.8		5.5		5.5	
No. of otoliths with complete agreement on age and interpretation	5		5		1		0		1	
Number with no best interpretation given	1		1		1		1		2	

criteria should be used for reading all otoliths. It is possible that this narrow zone is the so-called larval check ring that is supposed to be laid down when the young cod change from being pelagic to demersal fish, but there is little published evidence to support this theory. Until evidence supporting or disproving this theory is obtained, greatest consistency in age-readings will be obtained if all readers count such structures as annual zones.

The interpretation of the other central zones also caused difficulty. For example, in Fig. 3 the three

Fig. 4.   Cod otolith from north Newfoundland (3K; 17 cm long, caught July 1961), showing a characteristic narrow but complete innermost hyaline zone, which all readers except one counted as the first annual zone.

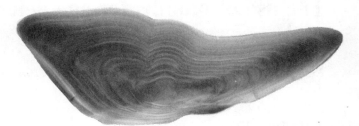

Fig. 6.   Cod otolith from Labrador (2H; 60 cm. caught August 1960). Ages from 6 to 11 years were given. Any age is a guess, and the best interpretation is 'unreadable'.

innermost hyaline zones have exactly the same double ring structure, yet some readers discounted the second of these zones for no apparent reason. A variation on this is illustrated in Fig. 5, in which the second hyaline zone is a very broad one, much wider than both the preceding hyaline zones and the subsequent ones. This zone was sometimes interpreted as a check ring, presumably because it differs in character from the other hyaline zones. Yet if the zonation is related to the growth of the fish, such zones must be laid down over a period of many months, and unless there is evidence that they are laid down in the summer or autumn and are followed by another hyaline zone in the same year they should be counted as annual zones.

Fig. 5.   Cod otolith from Grand Bank (30; 59 cm, caught June 1961), showing the type of broad second hyaline zone which some readers counted as a check ring.

The majority of cod otoliths show a pattern of hyaline and opaque zones which can be reasonably interpreted by an experienced otolith reader, but some show what can only be described as a conglomeration of rings which do not fall into any recognizable pattern at all (Fig. 6). The best interpretation of these is 'unreadable' and it is surprising that in all the exchange series few readers described any of the otoliths as unreadable. In Jensen's notation (ICNAF 1963b) such otoliths are described as 'poor', and the definition includes the phrase'... or where the age is merely estimated'. Often these estimations must have no basis other than the length of the fish, *but length is not a valid criterion of age,* and the inclusion of such 'ages' in data for age/length keys may cause considerable errors.

CONCLUSIONS

The cod otolith photograph exchange showed for the first time the variation in the interpretations of a number of otolith readers. Some of these differences were of no statistical significance because often the best age was arrived at by several different interpretations. Other differences were important because they showed up inadequacies in the technique of some readers or even greater inadequacies in our knowledge of the biology of the cod and of the physiology of otolith growth.

One of the main problems for the cod stocks of the north-west Atlantic is the interpretation of the zones laid down in the early years of the life of the fish. This problem, which can only be solved by the examination of large numbers of otoliths from small fish collected at all seasons of the year, with the relevant data on feeding, is a fundamental one for all fish stocks. It is essential that such validation data are collected whenever age-determination programmes are started. The assumption that, because a fish from one area has been reliably aged by a particular method, the same species from elsewhere can be aged equally easily and reliably by the same method, is a dangerous one. For this reason it is essential that age-validation studies should be illustrated with annotated photographs of the otoliths or whatever other structures are used for age-determination.

REFERENCES

Blacker, R. W. 1964.   Electronic flash photography of gadoid otoliths. Res. Bull. int. Commn. NW. Atlan. Fish., 1: 36-38.

ICNAF 1963a.   Appendix II—Working group on Ageing Techniques. Redbook int. Commn. NW. Atlant. Fish., 1963 (1): 47-48.

ICNAF 1963b.   Report of Workshop on Ageing Techniques in Bergen 1962. Redbook int. Commn. NW. Atlant. Fish. 1963 (3): 127-134.

Keir, R. S. 1960.   Answers to the questionnaire on age reading. ICNAF Annual Meeting 1960. Doc. 4. (Ser. No. 714—D.C.2, 17 pp. (Appendices 1-19).

The use of otoliths for age determination

by T. WILLIAMS AND B. C. BEDFORD

Fisheries Laboratory, Ministry of Agriculture, Fisheries and Food, Lowestoft, Suffolk, England.

INTRODUCTION

Part of the work of the demersal fish section of the Fisheries Laboratory at Lowestoft is to monitor continuously the state of those stocks of marine fish that are important to the British fishing industry. For this purpose it is necessary to obtain the age structure of the fish populations being monitored. Experimental work (Gulland 1958; Saetersdal 1958) indicated that otoliths would, in most cases, be more suitable for this work than scales, finrays or other bones, and for all demersal teleost species these are now used. The programme dates from 1946 when North Sea plaice was the only species studied. At present 40 separate stocks of plaice, sole, lemon sole, cod, haddock, coalfish and whiting are monitored, involving the collection and reading of 35,000 pairs of otoliths each year. The experience that has been gained at the Lowestoft Laboratory during this period, when training both local staff and numerous visitors, together with a similar programme at the FAO Training Centre in Methodology in Fishery Science (Frederikshavn, 1972), underlined the need for a statement of the basic problems that confront any worker attempting to age fish by otoliths. References to techniques are scattered throughout the literature, and are sometimes contradictory (Blacker 1969), but nowhere to our knowledge are they brought together under one heading and described in detail as they are here.

BASIC PRINCIPLES

If the otoliths of any species of fish are to be used for age determination it is necessary to establish that:

(1) a recognizable pattern can be seen in the otolith, either by viewing it directly by ordinary light or after some method of preparation, e.g. burning or staining;

(2) a regular time scale can be allocated to the visible pattern; this time scale is not necessarily annual although it is usually so, particularly in cold and temperate areas (all the North Atlantic commercial species being investigated in the UK have annual otolith rings).

THE GROWTH OF OTOLITHS

Otoliths are composed mainly of needle-shaped crystals of calcium carbonate radiating outwards in three dimensions from a nucleus and passing through a network of organic material. The size and shape of the crystals may vary within an otolith, and the angle at which they lie in relation to one another and to the otolith as a whole may not be constant. A further complication in their structure is that the organic network is not uniformly distributed either throughout the whole otolith or within similar zones.

The otolith grows as more material in the form of new crystals is deposited on the outer surfaces. In fish living in temperate waters this new material takes two forms, usually of different appearance, which are deposited in an alternating sequence, resulting in the growth of a series of concentric shells of irregular shape about the central nucleus. When the otolith is viewed with an appropriate technique, these shells are seen as a series of rings or zones radiating outwards from the nucleus.

Because the larval fish must be able to orientate itself relative to its environment immediately upon hatching, it is probable that the beginning of the otolith is already present in the fish at this time. Well formed otoliths are observable in post-larval fish of 15-20 mm total length, and the formation of what will eventually be seen as the nucleus of the otolith is well under way at this stage. In most winter- or spring-spawning marine teleosts of the northern hemisphere the nucleus is usually composed of opaque material. Opaque material continues to be deposited throughout the first months of the life of the fish, usually until the onset of late autumn or early winter, when the hyaline zone begins to form. Hyaline material is deposited during the next few months, deposition of opaque material beginning again in the late winter or early spring. This rough pattern of seasonality in the growth of the two different types of zone continues each year throughout the life of the fish, although some slight changes may occur in the timing of zone formation as the fish grows older. The pattern of otolith growth for North Sea cod is shown schematically in Fig. 2.

In the early years of the life of the fish the opaque zone, laid down during the period of the year when the fish's growth is rapid, is usually much wider than the corresponding hyaline zone which is laid down at the time when there is little or no growth. As the fish grows older the opaque zones become progressively narrower but the hyaline zones remain approximately the same width. This process continues until the outermost rings (both opaque and hyaline) become extremely narrow, regular and of about equal width.

There are considerable differences in the size and shape of otoliths between species. Those from flatfish, such as plaice, sole, etc., are generally oval, thin and saucer-like for much of the life of the fish, thickening only when the fish is very old. Otoliths from roundfish, such as cod, haddock and coalfish, are elongated, narrow and thick, and in cross-section at right angles to the longitudinal axis are roughly pear-shaped. Some other roundfish, such as hake and whiting, also have long narrow otoliths but these do not thicken to the same extent.

The basic shape of the otolith is determined at the time of the formation of the nucleus. The deposition of new material is not uniform and the concentric shells vary in thickness in different parts of the otolith. In the length of the otolith growth is usually greater at one end than the other; similarly, in width one side often grows more rapidly. In thickness more material is often deposited on one face than on the other. As a result the nucleus is usually eccentrically positioned in each plane within the whole otolith.

Often the very narrow regular rings observed at the edge of the otolith in older fish appear to grow only on one face of the otolith. This is particularly noticeable in many species of flatfish, in which the otoliths appear to grow to a maximum size (different for each individual fish) in length and width, after which the new growth that is deposited has the effect only of thickening the otolith. A similar pattern is sometimes observed in the otoliths of some very old gadoid fish such as cod, haddock and coalfish, and Macer (1970) has also shown it in horse mackerel otoliths in which it is very marked.

METHODS

Collection and storage

The method most commonly used to remove the otoliths from a fish rapidly and in an undamaged condition is to split open the head, exposing the cavities in which they are located; a single cut with a sharp stiff-bladed knife is usually sufficient, although with some larger specimens it may be necessary to use a hacksaw or small bone saw. The large sacculus otoliths are then easily visible and it is a simple matter to lift them out with forceps. Plates 1 and 2 show typical cuts for flatfish (*Pleuronectes platessa*) and roundfish (*Gadus morhua*). Locating the precise position for the cut is simple and is a quickly acquired skill. This method is suitable for most sizes of fish, although those less than 40 mm total length are usually best dissected under a low power microscope.

Although some otoliths are best read immediately at the time of removal from the fish (see below), it is usual to store them until they are required for reading. A simple method of storage, effective for a majority of species, is to keep them in small plastic bags or paper envelopes. The otoliths must first be thoroughly cleaned and dried. An advantage of paper envelopes is that details of the fish (such as species, length, sex, weight, etc.) may be permanently recorded directly on the packet. The envelopes used at Lowestoft are 2 inches square and these are conveniently stored in three rows in rigid card boxes 10 × 7 × 2 inches. Depending on their thickness, between 350 and 550 pairs of otoliths can be stored in a single box.

Small otoliths, such as those of sandeel, herring or mackerel, are best stored by mounting a series in resin on a microscope slide or a specially designed tray. A 2 × 1 inch glass slide conveniently holds 10 pairs of these otoliths.

Occasionally it is possible to improve the visibility of the ring structure by storing the otoliths in a suitable liquid medium such as alcohol, glycerine, alcohol/glycerine mixture or creosote. Care should be taken to ensure that the ring structure is not damaged or rendered unreadable by storage in an unsuitable medium. Formalin or any other acid medium should not be used. In some cases a short-term storage in liquid may make the rings more easily readable, but this can often be followed by a period during which there is a progressive deterioration in the clarity of the ring structure. It is therefore advisable to check otoliths stored in a liquid medium, from time to time, to see whether there has been any change in their appearance. A further disadvantage of holding in a liquid medium is that the otoliths need to be kept in small glass tubes, which require much greater storage space than envelopes.

Preparation and methods of viewing

General Rarely are the otoliths of commercial marine species large enough for their rings to be observed accurately by the naked eye, and it is usual to view them under low power microscope magnification. Either the whole otolith or a section through a suitable plane may be viewed. The whole otolith method is best suited for those that are relatively thin and translucent and is commonly used for many flatfish. The section method is used for those fish that have thick otoliths which are too dense for the innermost zones to be observed in the whole state. For some species, such as whiting, hake and some juvenile flatfish, it is best to view the whole otolith immediately after removal from the fish, when the rings are often most clearly visible.

Lighting Two means may be used to illuminate the surface that is being viewed. Light is either shone directly on to the surface from above (reflected light) or directed through the otolith from below (transmitted light). Either form of lighting may be used for both the whole otolith and the section methods, although it is generally most convenient to use reflected light for the thin translucent type of otolith and transmitted light for the thicker types.

A simple technique to improve viewing by reflected light is to immerse the whole otolith (or section) in a clear liquid (water is commonly used) in a black dish and to shine the light on to it at an angle from above. Against the dark background the opaque zones appear as white or light coloured rings and the hyaline zones as dark rings. Viewing by transmitted light is simply achieved by placing the otolith or section on a ground glass slide and shining the light directly through it from below. Under this type of illumination the opaque zones (which obstruct the passage of light) appear as dark shadowy rings and the hyaline zones (which permit the passage of light) appear as bright light rings. The two alternative forms of lighting are clearly illustrated in Plate 3 which shows the same plaice otolith lit by each method. The fact that the same zones can be described as light or dark, depending upon the form of illumination, can lead to considerable confusion and for this reason the terms opaque and hyaline must always be used and never the terms light and dark.

Sectioning Some otoliths need to be sectioned in order to see the ring structures. This may be done in a number of ways and the section may be made across any regular plane or at any angle through the otolith. However, practical considerations of holding it usually limit the possibilities to two positions, either a lateral section square across the length or a longitudinal section square across the width of the otolith (A-A and B-B in Fig. 1a). The section may be made in the form of a very thin slice (0.5 mm or less in thickness) and an excellent view of the rings is afforded by this method. However, for the mass reading of large numbers of otoliths the time required for the preparation of this type of section would be too great and a simpler, equally effective method is to break the otolith, either with pressure of the thumbs or by a cutting tool. This produces half-otoliths, one of which is mounted in a piece of plasticene with the broken surface uppermost and horizontal. The half-otolith is then illuminated from the side and the surface placed in shadow. The light entering at the side passes upwards through the otolith and lights the surface from below. The effect is the same as direct illumination from below of a thin section, with the opaque zones

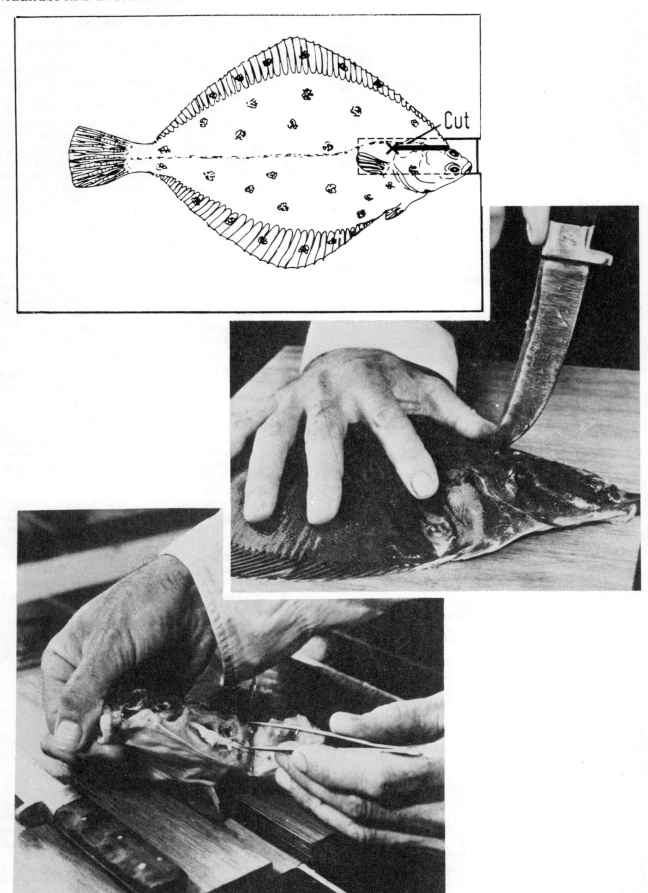

Plate 1. Removal of otoliths from flatfish.

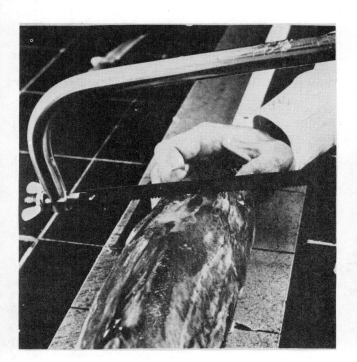
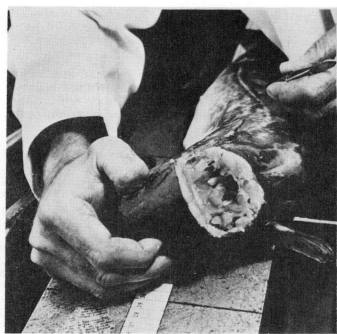

Plate 2.   Removal of otoliths from roundfish.

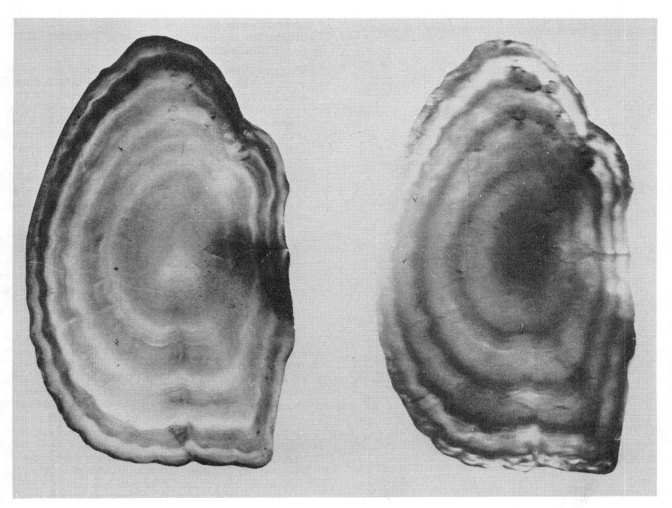

Illuminated from above
viewed against a dark background

(a)

Illuminated from below
by transmitted light

(b)

Plate 3.   A plaice otolith viewed by two different methods.

appearing as dark shadowy rings and the hyaline zones as clear light rings. This method requires only a few seconds and is therefore very suitable for the ageing of large numbers of specimens.

When this method is used, it is essential that the break or section passes through the centre of the nucleus. The eccentricity of the nucleus, already mentioned, is important and its position in each plane within the whole otolith must be established before breaking. Once this is done it is usually a simple matter to determine the centre of the nucleus relative to some external mark or characteristic and to break the otolith at that point. Failure to section across the centre of the nucleus can result in a number of errors in interpretation. If the section fails to pass through the nucleus then the age will be underestimated by at least one year. If the section passes through one of the extreme ends of the nucleus then the whole appearance and spacing of the zones will be different from those seen at a section through the true centre, making them more difficult to interpret (Fig. 1b). Even a slight change in the angle of the cross section (e.g. section C-C in Figure 1a) often reveals a considerable difference in the spacing and appearance of the ring structure. It is therefore important to investigate all the practical possibilities for the position of the section before adopting that which is best suited for routine studies.

For many otoliths the rough surface resulting from breaking is good enough for an accurate interpreta-

tion of the structure to be made. Occasionally, however, it is found that interpretation is helped if the surface is completely smooth and square. Such a surface can be quickly and easily prepared by using a specially designed electric grinding machine (Bedford 1964). The machine is also useful for removing excess material in those cases where breaking the otolith produces a surface that does not pass through the centre of the nucleus. Some slight striations and dust are usually left on the surface after grinding. When the otolith is viewed these marks and the rough surface resulting from breaking can be clarified by brushing the surface with a suitable clearing agent such as xylene, cedar wood oil or creosote.

Burning of otoliths For sole (*Solea solea*) and some other species, the opaque and hyaline rings are usually clearly visible only when the fish is very young (up to 4 years) and these can be seen by the whole otolith method. The zones which are formed afterwards appear to be almost completely translucent, whether viewed by the whole otolith or the section method. If, however, the broken surface of a half-otolith is gently burned in a very low flame of a small Bunsen burner or spirit lamp until it is slightly charred, the appearance is changed and narrow black rings are produced at the boundary between the end of each completed hyaline zone and the beginning of the following opaque zone (Christensen 1964). The amount and rate of burning required to produce the best result varies according to species and the size of the otolith, but the technique required to achieve it can be quickly learned.

Care must be taken to burn the whole of the surface evenly. The centre of the sectioned surface must be held barely touching the side of the flame and removed when it begins to turn dark brown. If, after examination, it is found to require additional burning then it is a simple matter to return it to the flame until the desired result is achieved. If the otolith is burned too much it will crumble into a grey ash. This usually occurs first at the edges and results in the complete disappearance of the ring structure. If insufficient heat is applied then the organic zones will not char.

Each black ring encloses a white area representing the total growth during one year. A large number of extremely fine hair-like concentric black rings can be seen in the white zone but the true, much thicker, annual black rings are clearly distinguishable.

The method can also be used to resolve problems of ageing those fish in which new material appears to be deposited on only one surface of the otolith. In such cases the narrow alternate layers of opaque and hyaline material are often visible when a section is viewed by transmitted light, but their accurate counting is usually difficult. The black rings resulting from burning are much easier to see and accurate ageing is possible. It has been found that the ages of many fish, particularly of very old specimens, have been consistently underestimated when other methods of viewing were employed. One further advantage of burning the otoliths is that this method is sometimes useful for the resolution of problems of nucleus identification or false rings, by clearly marking the true annual ring.

The burning method has been tried experimentally with the otoliths of gadoid species, but it has been found that they do not react in the same way as those of sole, plaice and turbot, and there is no clearly

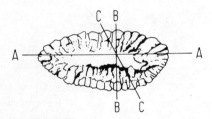

Fig. 1a.   Three possible sections through a cod otolith: A-A longitudinal; B-B lateral; C-C diagonal.

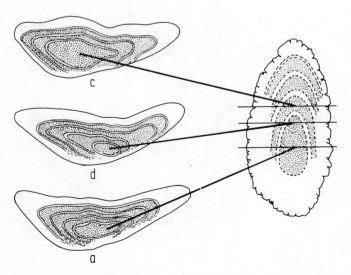

Fig. 1b.   The varying appearance of the ring structure of a cod otolith when broken

(a)   through the centre of the nucleus
(b)   through one end of the nucleus
(c)   missing the nucleus completely

defined thin black line. Some charring of the surface occurs, but generally the method offers no improvement on the usual method of viewing the unburned section by transmitted light.

Often a combination of methods of preparation and viewing, e.g. whole otolith and section, reflected and transmitted light, together with the burning of the otolith, can be used to resolve most problems of interpretation of the ring structures.

Measurement of otolith rings

If ring measurement is being considered for any purpose, e.g. back-calculation of growth rate, then it must be accepted that this cannot be done accurately if a cross section of the otolith is being used. When an otolith is sectioned the relative size of the rings depends on the point at which the break occurs. This was described on page 118. In addition to the difficulty in locating the exact centre of the nucleus, the edge of the otolith is very irregular and this irregularity is also reflected in the structure of the internal zones. A fractional difference in the point at which the section is made may be perfectly acceptable for age determination, but can result in a considerable difference in the size of the rings that are visible for measurement. A series of transverse sections taken through the nucleus of the same otolith will show considerable differences in both the shape of the otolith; and the size of the rings.

INTERPRETATION

Validation of the time scale

If the deposition of alternate opaque and hyaline zones is a regular annual occurrence, then this can be confirmed by examining otoliths from samples taken throughout the year and observing the type of growth present at the extreme outside edge. In this way it is possible to observe fairly precisely at what time each zone begins to grow. However, there can be wide variations in the timing of the formation of the zones from year to year. Some of this variation may be due to differences in climatic conditions between years but in addition it is apparent that the timing also varies with (i) species, (ii) geographical location of the stock and (iii) the age of the fish.

In the North Sea most demersal species begin to grow the opaque zone in the late winter or the spring of the year, but it usually starts much earlier in plaice and cod than in sole.

In general in the northern hemisphere the opaque zone starts to grow earliest in the southern extremes of the species range and becomes progressively later further north. Within each stock the younger fish, in which wide opaque zones are growing, begin to lay down the opaque zone before the older fish. In the North Sea the otoliths of a 2-year-old cod may show the beginning of an opaque zone in **February**, whereas those of an older mature fish (say 7 or 8 years old) may show no sign of it until June. A similar difference in the timing of opaque zone formation also occurs in the otoliths of cod from the north-east Arctic, but the whole process can be delayed by as much as three months compared with those of the North Sea. In consequence the opaque zone of the older fish may still be growing at the edge of the otolith as late as January of the following year (Fig. 2).

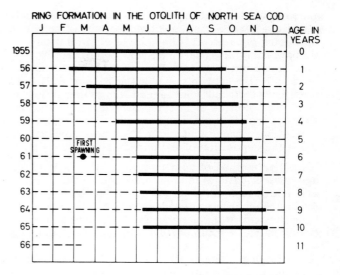

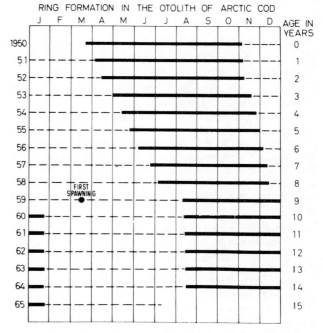

Fig. 2. Timing of the growth of opaque and hyaline zones in the otoliths of cod from two different stocks.

——————— = opaque zone growth
————— = hyaline growth

These factors should be taken into consideration when selecting otoliths for validation studies. A sample taken from fish of one age group all from the same area will usually show a clear seasonal pattern of zone development, if one exists, but if a sample is composed of a wide range of age groups taken from different areas then the seasonal pattern can be obscured by the variations described above.

Injection with tetracycline offers a simple method to determine the seasonality of zone formation. This material is readily absorbed and deposited where active calcification is taking place at the time of assimilation. As it fluoresces yellow in ultra-violet light the areas in which it has been deposited are easily detected. When a fish is injected with a small dose of tetracycline there follows a period of a few weeks during which it is absorbed by the system. The growth that occurs during this period on the bones, scales and otoliths appears under ultra-violet light as a narrow ring marking the type of zone that was being deposited at the time of assimilation (Kobayashi *et al.* 1964; Jones and Bedford 1968; Holden and Vince, 1973). This method has been used with fish kept in tanks at the Fisheries Laboratory, Lowestoft and with tagged fish released in the wild. The otoliths of injected tagged fish recaptured some years after release have shown a regular pattern of one opaque and one hyaline zone for each year since the deposition of the narrow fluorescent ring.

A further method of confirmation of the validity of age determinations is possible when otolith samples are available from a period of consecutive years during which a very abundant known year-class has been present in the population. If the age determinations are valid a number of independent experienced observers, each reading a sample of otoliths from a different year, should all produce an age composition showing the same dominant year-class.

Allocation of a birthday

When a suitable method has been devised to view the rings and it is established that their formation conforms to a definite regular time pattern, then it is possible to age the fish simply by counting the rings.

The terms 'age', 'age-group' and 'year-class' are frequently used. The *age* of a fish at a given time refers to the period of time from birth to that given point of time. When the age of a fish has been determined it can be assigned to the appropriate *age-group*, which is an integral number of years according to a convention based on an arbitrarily adopted birthday. Fish said to be of a given *year-class* are fish born in that particular year.

To simplify ageing, age determinations are usually made in terms of age groups with reference to a designated birthday. For stock assessment purposes, this birthday does not have to coincide with the biological time of birth. There is an internationally accepted convention to use 1 January for most North Atlantic demersal species. This means that there can be no ambiguity about the year-class to which a fish belongs and all data are comparable. The concept of a single birthday for all fish of the same species is important. To express the age as 3 rings, 2+ or in similar vague terms creates confusion.

Using the 1970 year-class, with an official birthday of 1 January, this may be demonstrated as follows:

which kind of ring is counted, but an advantage of counting the opaque zones is that each one is laid down during a calendar year and can therefore be identified and described as the ring of a particular year, e.g. the '1968 ring'. Furthermore, the basic growth pattern of the fish is, for most readers, reflected more in the decreasing width of the opaque zones than in the comparatively regular narrow hyaline zones, and it is the acceptability of each opaque zone as a year's growth that the experienced reader evaluates.

Splits, checks and false rings

The appearance of the opaque zones can be very variable and it is seldom that they are of uniform opacity either within an individual zone or from ring to ring within the whole otolith. Differences in opacity in a single opaque zone can be either gradual, with very dense areas slowly giving way to less dense areas, or abrupt with a narrow band of completely hyaline material being deposited within the overall boundaries of the opaque zone. These narrow hyaline rings are termed 'splits' or 'secondary', 'false' or 'check' rings, and generally speaking their presence in the structure is the main source of difficulty in the interpretation of the otolith as a whole.

If the otolith burns satisfactorily, this method usually clears up any queries, since the true annual ring becomes readily apparent. There is however no way of determining beyond all doubt the validity of any ring. Some hyaline false rings can be of such width and so positioned within an opaque zone that there appear to be two narrow rings instead of one wide one. In such cases the accuracy of the age-determination depends finally upon the training and skill of the reader, whose reasoned decision as to the validity of the rings is based on past experience. This skill is not quickly or easily acquired, and to be reasonably competent it is necessary to look at several thousand otoliths to build up a 'memory bank'. After 6 months' training, readers should be competent to deal with the majority of straightforward otoliths. After 2 years' experience, and having examined at least between 5 000 and 10 000 otoliths, they should be proficient, provided that they have the required aptitude for this type of work.

Variation of age for a given size of fish

It is not at all uncommon for the growth rate of the same species of fish taken from the same area to

	Jan.	Feb.	Mar.	Apr.	May	June	Nov.	Dec.
1970								
Age			Born	1 mth	2 mth	3 mth	8 mth	9 mth
Age group			0	0	0	0	0	0
1971								
Age	10 mth	11 mth	1 yr	1 yr.1mth	1yr.2mth	1yr.3mth	1yr.8mth	1yr.9mth
Age group	1	1	1	1	1	1	1	1
1972								
Age	1yr.10mth	1yr.11mth	2yr	2yr.1mth	2yr.2mth	2yr.3mth	2yr.8mth	2yr.9mth
Age group	2	2	2	2	2	2	2	2

Counting

Most workers at the Fisheries Laboratory, Lowestoft have found it easiest to count the opaque zones when reading otoliths. Individual preference determines

show an extremely wide variation. For example, the ages of small (25 to 29 cm total length) plaice from the North Sea range from 1 to 7 years, the 1-group being most likely to occur in December when their true age is 1 year 9 months. Plaice in the size group 30-34 cm include fish between 2 and 12 years old, and amongst the larger fish (45-49 cm in length) the age may lie between 7 and 20+ years. Similarly, wide variations in growth rates can be observed in other species. It is therefore important to avoid the error of first noting the length of the fish from which the otoliths have been taken, deciding its probable age (possibly on the basis of considerable experience) and then attempting to make the visible ring structure fit that age. This kind of self-deception can easily occur, and open-minded objectivity must be maintained for every otolith being read.

Another similar common error is to define size limits within which either the nucleus or a given number of rings must fall, based on the size of rings found on other otoliths. A slow-growing fish may have three or four rings completely typical of an annual pattern, and recognizable by all accepted criteria as such, and they may occupy the same space on the otolith as one or two rings in a fast-growing fish. In the authors' experience it is not uncommon for some readers, when confronted with rings that are narrow and regular but otherwise identifiable as annual, to contend that some rings must be false or split. A simple basic rule which otolith readers should always bear in mind is that although length is often a useful indicator as to the likely age of a fish it is not necessarily a function of age. Either ring structures that are observed on the otolith conform to a regular recognizable time scale or they do not, and must be so interpreted.

Recognition and use of stock-specific otolith patterns

The otoliths of the same species of fish from different areas usually have very different ring structures, reflecting the different growth patterns of separate stocks. At least ten different stocks of cod are sampled regularly as part of the monitoring programme at the Fisheries Laboratory, Lowestoft and the otoliths of each have a characteristic appearance which, with practice, can usually be identified. This is a valuable facility which has application in reading samples from areas where mixing of stocks occurs. The fishery for spawning cod at northern Norway is based on the adult fish from three stocks, those of the eastern Barents Sea, the Spitsbergen and the western Barents Sea, and local Norwegian coastal area. Each has a distinctive otolith pattern and their identification in the samples permits an assessment of the contribution of each constituent stock to the overall fishery. The same separation of stocks by otolith types is employed in the analysis of the spawning cod fishery off the south-west coast of Iceland, where migrants from south-east Greenland join the resident Icelandic stock.

Recognition and use of particular characteristics

In some years the regular recognizable growth pattern of the otoliths of a given stock may be disrupted so that a particular year may produce an atypical zone. Very occasionally, this may happen in two or more consecutive years. Such zones may be exceptionally wide or narrow, or may have a marked check ring or some other unusual characteristic which is easily recognizable. These atypical rings may not necessarily be present in the otoliths of all fish but may occur in sufficient quantity to constitute a notable phenomenon. Examples were recorded among the

1944 and 1947 year-classes of North Sea plaice. Many of the otoliths of the 1944 year-class fish had an extremely thin 1946 opaque ring which was present in 20 per cent of the fish in some samples. The 1947 year-class fish had a distinctive triple ring nucleus which was first observed in 0- and 1-group fish caught close to the Dutch coast. Similarly, many of the 1954 year-class of Arctic cod laid down very narrow atypical opaque zones, immediately following the nucleus, in 1955 and 1956; the inner zone structure that resulted was easily recognizable as typical of this year-class. In all of these cases the special identifiable characteristics proved to be extremely useful in later years as a means of confirming the age of very old fish, sometimes with difficult outer rings.

These unusual zones often create difficulties in interpretation of the structure at the time that they are being formed, but resolution of the difficulties may be simplified when they can be compared with other subsequent zones. Given that they can be identified confidently, they serve as a valuable check on the validity of age readings many years later by acting as a biological mark on the otolith. However, observers should guard against becoming overfamiliar with such a particular phenomenon and must resist the temptation to recognize the pattern in marginal cases where interpretation is difficult. It is stressed that the presence of such phenomena should be used only to confirm, and not to determine, age.

Spawning zones

Reference has been made earlier to the growth of regular narrow rings on the otolith in older fish. With some species it has been possible to establish that these zones begin (in the context of the total life-span) with the onset of sexual maturity and that the annual occurrence of spawning may be identified with those particular zones. The identification of 'spawning zones' and hence the facility to calculate the year of first spawning has a useful application in stock assessment studies of those special discrete seasonal fisheries where only the adult fish are exploited and where recruitment to the fishery is a function not of age but of sexual maturity, which is not age-specific. Rollefsen (1933) identified spawning zones in the otoliths of Arctic cod and was able to use 'spawning class' data for forecasting future fisheries.

Spawning zones are not easily identified in all adult cod. Some difficulty is usually experienced with first-time spawners, taken at the time of spawning or soon after, when a change in appearance is only just beginning. Particularly difficult are those which spawn for the first time as relatively young and small fish, because the zones laid down subsequent to sexual maturity reflect both spawning and continued growth characteristics. The most easily identifiable spawning zones are those found in fish which have reached maximum size (or nearly so) before first spawning.

There are two diagnostic characteristics that are observed with many—but not all—otoliths where spawning zones are exhibited. These are (i) the presence of an unusually wide and bright hyaline zone laid down immediately before the first opaque spawning zone, and (ii) a very weak hyaline zone between the last two opaque zones before first spawning. This latter phenomenon can sometimes be sufficiently marked to present the appearance of an opaque zone of about double the normal expected width. Plate 4 shows spawning zones in a cod otolith.

Plate 4. Otolith of a 14-year-old Arctic cod, showing five spawning zones

Differences between otoliths from the same fish

Usually the two sacculus otoliths bear identical ring structures, and the matching of pairs of otoliths from a mixture of single otoliths is not difficult for an experienced reader. Occasionally, however, there can be differences in the number of rings present in two otoliths from the same fish. Fortunately such occurrences are extremely rare, but in these cases there are often superficial differences between the otoliths (such as a deformity of shape), which are readily evident.

CONCLUSION

Satisfactory results have been achieved at Lowestoft in the use of otoliths for ageing large numbers of fish from a number of different stocks and species. Consistently similar interpretations of particular individual ring structures by several observers have been achieved by the training methods employed. It is the authors' view, however, that otolith reading remains, for the present at least, as much an art as a science, and that proficiency cannot easily be achieved without examination of very large numbers of otoliths.

Once a routine age determination programme has been established there should be frequent cross-checking of results, both between different readers, and by the same reader repeating the reading of a sample at a later date, to ensure that no wide differences of interpretation occur and that the readings remain consistent.

Methods of scanning otoliths automatically and interpretation of the results by computer analysis have been attempted without notable success, but may hold promise for the future. For any such system to be effective it must be able to result in considerable saving on manpower and an improved accuracy over present methods. The great variation in otolith pattern that occurs, and the widely differing growth rates that are found, could make an automated programme impracticable.

Brown (1946) and Hewett (pers. comm.) have shown that rings on scales and zones on otoliths may still be laid down when fish are kept in uniform unvarying conditions. Graham (1929) postulated that the formation of zones in an otolith was as dependent upon an innate physiological rhythm as upon external factors. If this so, then possibly the resolution of the problems involved in ageing fish by counting these zones will always remain essentially one of judgement, based on the skill and experience of the reader in interpreting what can be seen.

REFERENCES

Bedford, B. C. 1964. Two mechanical aids for otolith reading. Res. Bull. int. Commn NW. Atlant. Fish. (1), 79-81.

Blacker, R. W. 1969. Chemical composition of the zones in cod (*Gadus morhua* L.) otoliths. J. Cons perm. int. Explor. Mer, 33, 107-108.

Brown, M. E. 1946. The growth of Brown Trout (*Salmo trutta* Linn.). 2. The growth of two-year-old trout at a constant temperature of 11.5°C. J. exp. Biol., **22**, 130-144.

Christensen, J. M. 1964. Burning of otoliths, a technique for age determination of soles and other fish. J. Cons. perm. int. Explor. Mer, **29**, 73-81.

Graham, M. 1929. Studies of age determination in fish. Part II. A survey of the literature. Fishery Invest., Lond., Ser. 2, **11**, (3), 50 pp.

Gulland, J. A. 1958. Age determination of cod by fin rays and otoliths. Spec. Publs int. Commn NW. Atlant. Fish., (1), 179-190.

Holden, M. J., and Vince, M. R. (1973). Age validation studies on the centra *Raja clavata* using tetracycline. J. Cons. perm. int. Explor. Mer. **35**, 13-17.

Jones, B. W., and Bedford, B. C., 1968. Tetracycline labelling as an aid to interpretation of otolith structures in age determination—a progress report. ICES C.M. 1968/Gen: 11, 3 pp. (mimeo).

Kobayashi, S., Yuki, R., Furui, T., and Kosugiyama, T. 1964. Calcification in fish and shellfish. I. Tetracycline labelling patterns on scale, centrum and otolith in young goldfish. Bull. Jap. Soc. scient. Fish., **30**, 6-13.

Macer, C. T. 1970. Age determination in the horse-mackerel (*Trachurus trachurus* L.). ICES C.M. 1968/J: 4, 3 pp. (mimeo).

Rollefsen, G. 1933. The otoliths of the cod. Preliminary report. FiskDir. Skr., (Ser. Havunders.), **4**, (3), 14 pp., plates.

Saetersdal, G. 1958. Use of otoliths and scales of the Arctic haddock. Spec. Publs int. Commn NW. Atlant. Fish. (1), 201-206.

Age determination of American eels based on the structure of their otoliths

by PETER K. L. LIEW

Biology Department, Ottawa University, Ottawa, Canada

SUMMARY

1.   Otoliths of elvers of American eel *Anguilla rostrata* transplanted from Digdeguash River, New Brunswick into White Lake Hatchery Pond, Sharbot Lake, Ontario during 1967-1970 were used to establish the validity of age determination of this species. The structure and time of formation of different otolith zones were determined by means of acetate impressions, scanning electron microscopy and grinding methods.

2.   Under reflected light, the American eel otolith consists of a nucleus, which is translucent centre formed in the sea and successive broad opaque summer zones and narrow translucent winter zones. Under transmitted light, the appearance of these zones is reversed. In acetate replicas and scanning electron micrographs, the broad summer zone was seen to consist of concentric, thin, organic lamellae intersected by well-defined inorganic calcium carbonate crystals. The narrow winter zone consisted of relatively fewer crystals and concentric lamellae and appeared as a wide deep groove. In age determination, the winter zone was counted as an annual zone.

3.   In addition to translucent winter and opaque summer zones, translucent supplementary zones or checks were quite often observed in otoliths. The check usually appeared as an isolated narrow zone and could be differentiated from the true winter zone. All elvers transplanted into the pond formed a distinct check on their otoliths before freshwater growth started. The formation of checks in eel otoliths was also found to be correlated with periods of starvation induced either by low temperatures, sudden temperature changes, handling or starvation under laboratory conditions.

4.   The validity of age determination from otoliths of eels was demonstrated by the annual formation of the winter translucent zone for the fish kept in the pond and by comparing the back-calculated lengths with the empirical lengths for the samples taken from the pond. Therefore, the otolith of American eel is reliable for age determination.

INTRODUCTION

The American eel *Anguilla rostrata* is widely distributed in the fresh waters and marine littoral areas of Eastern Canada. Recently, interest in this species has increased considerably. This is probably due to their abundance, annual removal of considerable amounts of organic matter from the environment, their status as predators and competitors to salmonids and their increasing economic importance. This interest had heightened the need for a better understanding of the biology of this species, especially of aspects bearing on population studies including sex, age and size composition.

Age determination is of great importance to investigations of growth rates, maturity, longevity, mortality rates and yields of eel populations. The age and growth of the American eel have been studied by Smith and Saunders (1955), Vladykov 1967), Boetius and Boetius (1967), Ogden (1970), Gray and Andrews (1971) and Hurtley (1972). With the exception of Smith and Saunders and Boetius *et al*, otoliths have been used for age determination. Smith and Saunders used scales for ageing eels, while Boetius and Boetius used otoliths together with scales to determine the age of Bermuda eels. As with the European eel the time of appearance of the scales of the American eels seems to vary with locality and growth rates (Smith and Saunders, Boetius and Boetius). Furthermore, a series of scales from any one fish may not show the same number of annual zones; the number of annual zones varying from place to place on the body. Due to these disadvantages, scales of American eels are seldom used for age determination. Since otoliths are formed in eels at a very early age, they have been employed by most investigators for age determination.

Vladykov, Boetius and Boetius, Ogden (1970), Gray and Andrews and Hurtley (1972) determined the age of American eel from otoliths, but only Vladykov, and Gray and Andrews gave a description and an illustration of their ageing method. Although there is no information on the validation of this ageing method, their works stimulated the use of American eel otoliths for age determination.

During a study of the environmental factors influencing the sexual development of the American eel, the opportunity arose to test the validity of the otolith method of ageing these fish. Firstly, it was possible to compare otolith structures against the known age of these fish. Secondly, observations on the morphology and fine structures of the otoliths under light and scanning electron microscope were made and thirdly, a modified acetate peel method was developed to examine the otoliths. In addition, young eels were kept in the laboratory under different conditions. This permitted the examination of different environmental factors on the otolith zones formation.

MATERIALS AND METHODS

This study was conducted at White Lake Hatchery Pond, Sharbot Lake, Ontario. The pond has a mud bottom over a rock formation and a maximum depth of 7 feet, mean depth of 3.6 feet. The surface area is one acre. The pond is fed by a valve-controlled pipe which is fitted with a fine mesh copper screen. Water flows by gravity from a large oligotrophic lake, White Lake, above the pond. The water flow was maintained at about 300 gallons per minute during the experiment. The excess pond water flows over a sluice gate which has a fine mesh copper screen to prevent the escape of elvers. The pond was stocked only with eel but minnows and young sunfish were found at a later date.

In order to stock the hatchery pond with known age fish, elvers of the Américan eel were collected with a hand seine from Digdeguash River, New Brunswick, between July 22 to 25 of 1967. There were about 10,000 elvers, ranged in length from 46 to 67 mm with an average of 56.6 mm. These fish were kept in a 25-gallon galvanized metal tank and transported by automobile from the collecting site to the White Lake Hatchery Pond. The water in the tank, up to 14 inches in depth, was oxygenated with pure oxygen from a clyinder and kept cool (15°C) by dripping melting ice held in a net above the tank. Upon arrival, the elvers were acclimated from 15°C in the tank to 23°C in the pond over a period of three hours. After removing about 200 elvers for otolith as well as other studies, the rest were released into the pond.

To supplement natural food such as insect larvae, crustaceans and other aquatic invertebrates, the eels in the pond were fed with a mixture of ground beef heart and liver once a week for the first two years. In the third year they were fed every two to four weeks.

The fish in the pond were regularly sampled and otoliths were removed for examination thereafter until the termination of the experiment on May 18, 1970.

Collection and measurement of specimens

During the first twenty-six months of experiment, with the exception of winter months, the eels in the pond were collected every two weeks with an 18-inch dip net, 6-foot hand seine and traps made of fine mesh nylon net baited with beef heart. On October 11 1969, and May 18 1970, an electric shocker was used.

The eels collected were either measured in fresh or frozen condition within a few days of capture. Measurements were taken to the nearest millimeter and specimens were weighed to the nearest gram.

Extraction and preparation of otoliths for examination

Only the sagitta, the largest of the three otoliths was extracted for age determination. To remove the otoliths, a transverse incision was made through the ventral wall of the head region and a cut was made along the midline to the lower jaw to expose the roof of the mouth. A transverse cut was then made on the lower side of the cranium with a pair of bone scissors at a point where the auditory capsules are situated. The cranium was broken open at the incision to expose the brain and the auditory labyrinth. The sacculus and enclosed otoliths lodged in the auditory capsules were removed with a pair of forceps. The sacculus was rubbed off gently by hand, and the otoliths were mounted on black depression plates with 1-2 dichloro-ethane. The plastic plates were 6 cm × 12 cm with fifty 3 mm × 8 mm vacuum-formed depressions. The otoliths can be removed from the plates for examination by dissolving the plastic plate with 1-2-dichloro-ethane.

Otoliths from elvers or small eels less than 200 mm are thin and transparent, and require no grinding or polishing prior to examination. These otoliths were treated with dilute HCl before being mounted in Permount. The acid treatment has the effect of showing up the otolith zones more clearly.

The sagittae of large eels are thick and opaque and need grinding and polishing before the alternating opaque and translucent zones can be clearly seen.

The following methods were used to prepare otoliths of large eels for study.

(a) *Preparation of otoliths for light microscopy*

Vladykov (1967) prepared American eel otoliths for age determination by grinding them with a steel burr rotated by a small portable dentist drill. The ground otolith was then heated to a dark brown colour and the otolith was examined immersed in creosote. In the present study, some of the otoliths were processed with this method. The method is complicated and takes considerable time, so an acetate peel technique was adopted. The otolith was placed in distilled water and cut into two through the nucleus. The posterior part of the otolith was ground by holding down the convex surface of the otolith with one finger on a fine carborundum powder (3 micron equiv.). The ground otolith was etched with one per cent aqueous solution of HCl, for times ranging from one to three minutes in a depression slide. Etched otoliths were immersed in acetone and placed on a piece of 0.05 mm thick acetate sheet. After the acetone had evaporated the peel was removed from the otolith and mounted between a glass slide and a cover glass for age determination under the microscope.

The ground otolith was then stained with dilute aqueous toluidine blue and mounted on the plastic depression plates for comparison. The translucent zones were stained in blue and can easily be distinguished from the opaque white zone.

(b) *Preparation of otoliths for scanning electron microscopy*

To prepare the sagittae for scanning electron microscopy the otolith was immersed in water in a depression slide. The sagitta was cut into two through the nucleus. They were either etched with one per cent HCl solution for five minutes or not treated. The cut otolith was mounted on specimen stubs with conductive paint, and shadowed in vacuum, with gold and studied with a Cambridge Stereoscan MKII.

Measurements of the sagittae

The acetate replica and whole mount of otoliths were carefully examined under a microscope for annuli or false annuli. For each otolith, measurements were made from the focus to the posterior edge for the radius of the otolith and from the focus to each annulus. The measurements were made through a microscope equipped with a micrometer eyepiece. The large otoliths were measured in millimeters directly from a vernier microscope.

AGE INTERPRETATION FROM THE AMERICAN EEL OTOLITH

Description of the otolith

The eel sagitta is a laterally compressed, oval structure which has a concave and a convex surface, the latter having a ridge down the centre. Anteriorly it is cleft into a long central rostrum and a short dorsal antirostrum. The posterior edge is blunt and rounded while the margins of the otolith are irregularly indented.

The eel otoliths, when seen by reflected light against a dark background showed alternating opaque (light) and translucent (dark) zones. Under transmitted light the opaque zone became dark while the translucent zone became light. In European eels the opaque zones are laid down in summer and the translucent zones are formed in winter (Ehrenbaum and Marukawa, 1913). This interpretation of zones has also been applied to the American eels by various investigators (Vladykov, 1967; Gray and Andrews, 1971).

In the present study, the regular collection of eel otoliths during different periods of the year showed that the opaque zones were formed during the summer while the translucent zones were formed during the winter.

Structure of otoliths

Fish sagittae are made of an inorganic material, generally calcium cabonate in the form of aragonite crystals and an organic matrix. As early as 1908, Immerman studied the microscopic structure of the otoliths of plaice and showed that the otolith comprised of inorganic crystalline constituent and an organic fibrous constituent. Degens *et al.* (1969) studied the otoliths of twenty-five different fishes and found that all otoliths are composed of aragonite and organic matter. The organic matter is otolin, a protein (MW > 150,000), which is characterized by a high abundance of acidic amino acids. The amino acid composition is biochemically unique and apparently is not affected by phylogenetic or environmental events.

Hickling (1931) found that in a transverse section, the otoliths of hake *Merluccius merluccius* consisted of organic 'concentric lamellae' and inorganic needle-like crystals. The 'concentric lamellae' which were thick when formed in the summer and thin when formed in the winter, were probably fibrous in nature. They were bound together by comparatively stout radial fibres. These structures were also observed in the partially decalcified otolith of American eels (Fig. 1). The concentric and radial organic fibres are interwoven to form a complex matrix in which the inorganic crystals are laid. Due to the formation of bubbles in the process of decalcification, the fibres

were not intact. With the exception at the lower part of the photograph, the concentric lamellae are not clearly seen.

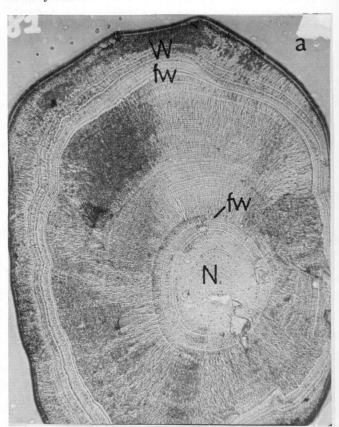

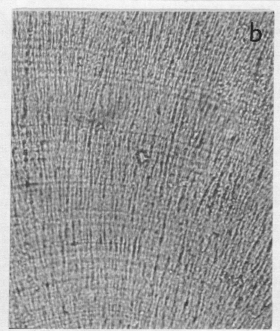

Fig. 2. The acetate replica of otolith of a 213 mm eel which had spent two summers in the pond. (a) The summer zone is wide and consisted of concentric lamellae and needle-like aragonite crystals. The winter zone consists of a light concentric ring and preceded by two false annuli. The needle-like aragonites are faintly-defined in it. Fw is false annuli, N is nucleus and w is winter zone. × 115

(b) High magnification of (a) showing the arrangement of concentric lamellae and needle-like aragonites. × 460

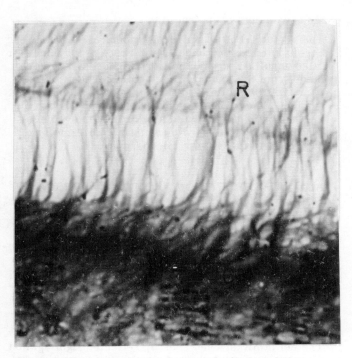

Fig. 1. The photograph of a decalcified otolith showing the arrangement of concentric lamellae (C) and radial fibres (R). × 365

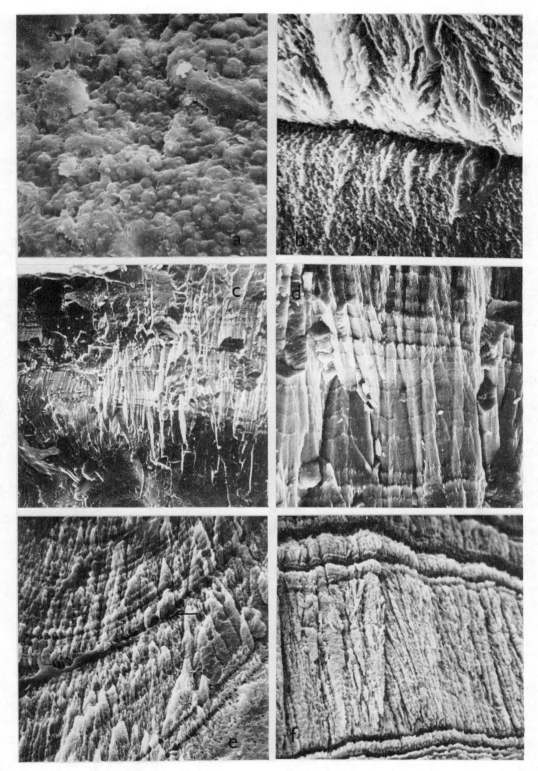

Fig. 3. Scanning electron micrographs of the cross section of American eel otoliths.

(a) The dorsal surface of an unetched otolith showing the tubercle-like protuberance. × 490

(b) The scanning electron micrograph of an etched
otolith showing a winter and two bordering
summer zones. × 8, 800

(c) The cross-section of an unetched otolith showing
the structures of aragonite crystals and concentric bands representing true or false winter
zones. × 192

(d) High magnification of (c) showing the arrangement of aragonite crystals. The crystals are
generally parallel to each other but some over-
grew the others while some showed the signs

of twisting. × 970.

(e) The cross-section showing the concentric lamellae of summer zone of an etched otolith. Each
lamella consists of a wide grey and a narrow
dark secondary rings. Arrow shows the winter
zone which consists of a few narrow concentric
lamellae. × 1, 560

(f) Photograph showing another example of the
summer and winter zones of an etched otolith.
In the summer zone, the aragonite crystals are
most distinct and concentric lamellae can not be
seen. The winter zone lacks of aragonite crystals and appears as a deep groove. × 1, 988

Recently, the acetate replica method has been applied to study the daily growth patterns of marine gadids by Pannella (1971). He found that the zone of fast growth (summer zone) has a light colour and thick, well-defined growth bands that intersect the needle-shaped structural elements at right angles. The zone of slow growth (winter zone) has a dark colour, very thin layer, and faintly defined acicular structural elements. In the present study, the acetate replica of American eel otoliths showed a similar structure (Fig. 2) The summer growth zone consisted of thick, well-defined concentric lamellae and needle-shaped elements. The concentric lamellae which again consisted of alternating dark and light rings intersected the needle-shaped elements at right angles and ran parallel to the outer surface of the otoliths. The slow growth winter zone consisted of a few concentric lamellae but with faintly-defined needle-shaped elements. The concentric lamellae examined under an electron microscope have been described by Degens *et al.* (1969) as 'oriented in a kind of corrugated pattern with well-defined lineages and the individual chains are organized in helical fashion. At certain intervals the chain are twisted to such an extent that lumps or knots of apparently tangled fibres appear about 0.1 to 0.3 micron apart'.

The needle-shaped elements as found by previous investigators are the aragonite crystals, arranged with their long axes roughly perpendicular to the outer margin of the otoliths. They run from the centre to the margin of the otolith without being interrupted.

By using decalcified sections and the acetate peel method, the structure of the otoliths has been partly elucidated. The organic matter appears in the forms of concentric and radially arranged fibres which are interwoven to form a complex organic network. The inorganic needle-shaped aragonite crystals which run parallel to the radial fibres were laid in this organic matrix and interlocked with it to form a solid structure.

In order to examine the external structure of the sagittae of American eels further, the otoliths were studied by scanning electron microscopy. Fig. 3a shows the dorsal surface of an unetched otolith. It contains only tubercle-shaped protuberances which vary in size as well as in height. The base of these tubercle-shaped structures were fused to form a solid, non-porous surface. By accretion and fusion the otolith increases in size as the fish grows.

The transverse section of an unetched otolith revealed well-spaced grey coloured bands that run approximately parallel to the outer surface of the otolith. These bands appear as grey dots at high magnification, probably representing the organic lamellae of false or true winter zones. The aragonite crystals were scarce or not defined in the areas of each band and gave rise to a shallow groove. The aragonite crystals were abundant in the whole section and perpendicular to these concentric bands or their projected surface. In general, individual crystals were arranged parallel to each other and ran from the centre to the margin of the otolith without being physically interrupted by the bands pattern. However, some crystals intergrew and gave a zig-zag pattern while some showed signs of twisting.

The cross section of an otolith of a known age eel, after etching with dilute HCl provides valuable information on the pattern of the zones and the structure of their consituents. Fig. 4 shows the arrangement of the alternating wide summer and narrow winter zones.

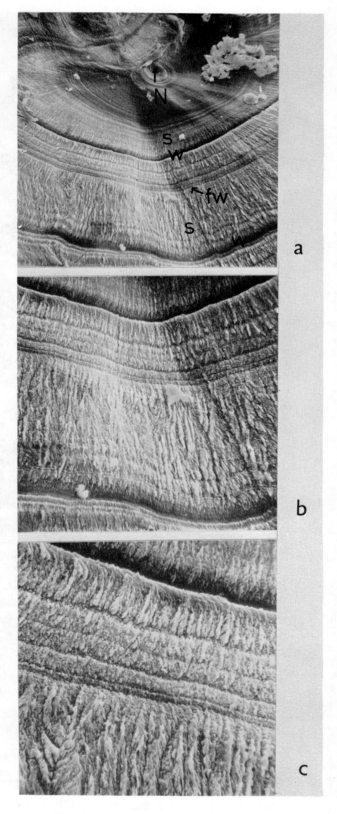

Fig. 4. Scanning electron micrographs of an etched cross-section of the otolith of a known age White Lake Hatchery Pond eel collected on May 18, 1970.

(a) Photograph shows the summer, winter and false winter zones of the otolith. F is focus, fw is false winter zone, N is nucleus, s is summer zone and w is winter zone. × 175

(b) High magnification of (a). × 437

(c) High magnification of (a) showing the true and false winter zones. × 873

The grey well-defined aragonite crystals protruding from the otolith surface were observed mainly in the summer zone. In the winter zone which appeared as a deep groove the aragonite crystals were either absent or much smaller than that in the summer zone. The pattern of the concentric lamellae could vaguely be seen in some of these photographs but can be clearly seen in Fig. 3e. The secondary alternating light and dark rings of concentric lamellae were found in the summer zone. The light rings varied from 2 to 3.5 μ and the dark rings varied from 0.5 to 1.5 μ in width. The aragonite crystals were found on top of both of these rings. The cause of the formation of these secondary rings is unknown. Although Pannella (1971) found the daily formation of these secondary rings in the otoliths of marine gadids, the number of these light and dark rings of eel otoliths did not correspond to the number of days spent by the eels in fresh water. In the middle of the summer zone, the shallow grooves representing the false winter zone were ocasionally found. Regardless of the appearance of the summer zone, the winter zone always appeared as a deep groove and had no or very few aragonite crystals in them. Therefore, the summer and winter zones correspond to two different production rates of organic fibres and aragonite crystals. During the fast growing period, the production of organic fibres and calcification rate are high, so that a wide summer zone with large aragonite crystals is formed. During the slow growing period, fewer organic fibres are produced and the calcification rate is low or almost nil, so a narrow winter zone with no or few small aragonite crystals is formed.

However, the structure of the nucleus of the American eel otolith is different from that of the summer and winter zones formed at a later date. In the nucleus, the aragonite crystals are not defined and only the concentric lamellae can be seen. It appeared as a dark centre in the scanning electron micrograph (Fig. 4a).

Under microscopic examination, the light or dark alternating zones were observed in the otoliths. Through the above studies on the structures, it is clear that the zones of the otoliths of American eels were produced by their structures and the character of the illumination. A translucent zone appeared dark under reflected light because it had fewer aragonite crystals and reflected much less light than the surrounding opaque zone. It appeared light under transmitted light largely from its less dense and poor light-scattering quality. An opaque zone appeared white under reflected light because of its strong reflecting and refracting properties as a result of the high abundance of the aragonite crystals. Under transmitted light, its thickness and its excellent light scattering qualities rendered it dark.

Age determination from the sagittae

Elver otoliths

The leptocephalus and 'glass eel' stages of the American eel are spent in the sea. This part of the eel's life is represented by the tightly packed zones found in the centre of an eel otolith. The alternating broad and narrow zones which surrounded the centre 'sea rings' are formed during the successive stages of the life of the eel in fresh water. In age determination, the interpretation of the number and position of 'sea rings' of American eel otoliths by different investigators were inconsistent. The 'sea rings' determined by Gray and Andrews had one more

opaque and one more translucent zones than those determined by Vladykov (1967). In order to obtain a more accurate interpretation of the centre of the adult otolith, the otoliths of non- or slightly pigmented elvers which had just arrived in fresh water were examined. Under reflected light on a dark background, these otoliths showed a translucent centre. The translucent centre, hereinafter referred to as the nucleus, was bound by an opaque zone which again was bound by a clearly marked translucent zone. Outside this translucent zone was an opaque edge (Fig. 5a and 7b). The width of the last opaque zone varied with the time when the elvers were collected. During the summer, the last opaque zone of elver otoliths widened and no distinct translucent zone was observed between the last elver opaque zone and the first freshwater opaque zone. However, the otoliths of elvers transplanted to White Lake Hatchery Pond all formed a new translucent and an opaque zones in the summer of transplantation. Therefore the zones inside the first translucent zone formed in fresh water are elver zones. Since the last sea and the first freshwater opaque zones represent the growth of the same year, for back-calculation, the first year of freshwater growth included this part of the marine growth.

Under transmitted light, the acetate replicas of large White Lake Hatchery Pond eel otoliths revealed the detailed structure of the nucleus. It showed a focus, a light spot in the centre, surrounded by a wide dark zone which again was surrounded by a narrow light zone. The structure of the nucleus was also clearly shown in the scanning electron micrograph (Fig. 4). Ehrenbaum and Marukawa (1931) and Frost (1945) interpreted the central dark area of European eel elver otoliths as the first year of leptocephali in the sea. The elver otoliths and acetate replica of the European adult eels showed that their leptocephali and elvers probably spent three years in the sea (Fig. 5). The nucleus of the American eel otolith, showing the pattern of a summer and a winter growth should also represent their first year of life spent in the sea. In other words, the American leptocephali and elvers could possibly spend two years in the sea before they entered freshwater streams and rivers. However, Schmidt (1922, 1925) postulated that the American eel leptocephali spent only one year in the sea while the young of European eels spent three years to reach European waters. Further information on the age of the American eel leptocephali collected in the sea will certainly help to prove the validity of the present interpretation on the elver's age. At present, there is no such information available and no definite conclusion on the age of American eel elvers can be reached yet.

Adult otoliths

In the otoliths of American eels collected from White Lake Hatchery Pond, it was found that generally the opaque zone was formed during the summer growing period while the translucent zone was formed during the winter period. In normal conditions, only one opaque (summer) and one translucent (winter) zones are formed during a single year. However, there are cases where one or more supplementary translucent zones or false annuli have been laid down between normal opaque and translucent zones. The presence of false annuli in otoliths adds to the difficulty of interpretation of age from the eel otoliths.

The acetate replicas of White Lake Hatchery Pond eel otoliths showed that the dark summer zone was wide

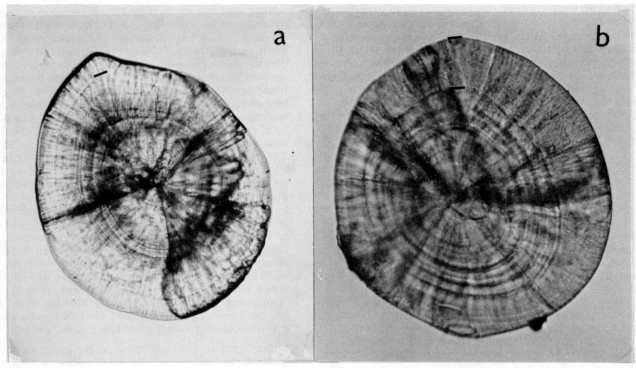

Fig. 5. The otoliths of elvers of American (a) and European (b) eels showing the structural differences between the 'elver's rings' of these two species. The American eel elver is 59 mm in length and collected on July 25, 1967. The European eel elver is 70 mm in length and collected on March 21, 1970. × 125

and consisted of well defined concentric growth 'lamellae' and needle-shaped aragonite crystals which have previously been described. With the exception of the summer zones in the nucleus, the needle-shaped elements were most abundant in summer zones but faintly defined in winter zones. The zone of winter growth was comparatively narrow and generally consisted of one to five or more closely arranged light rings which sometimes were separated by a few concentric lamellae. This structure indicates that the fish probably did not stop growth completely in the winter period. The low temperature of early winter or the end of autumn might affect the physiology of the fish and stop the fish from feeding and growth for a certain period of time. After being acclimatized to the low temperature, they might have resumed feeding and growth at a lower rate until the lower temperature completely inhibited their activity and growth. However, there were cases where the winter zone was preceded by two marked rings which were separated by multiple concentric lamellae. These were often found in the annuli of fast growing fish. By tracing the monthly collection of otoliths in different years, it was found that the first deep ring was formed between September 20 and October 20 of the year. Therefore it must represent a false annulus. The other ring was not formed in the sample collected on October 20 and should be formed at a much later date. In the laboratory, the eel fed very little or did not feed at all at 5°C and ceased feeding completely at a temperature below 5°C. It is assumed that the American eel did not grow after the end of November when the pond water temperature is always below 5°C. Although the appearances of false annuli might affect the accuracy of age determined from otoliths, the false annulus formed in the fall gives a definite pattern to the winter zone and renders it recognizable from false annuli formed at other periods of the growing season. The winter zone formed in the sea did

not always follow the same pattern of lamella arrangement as those found in fresh water. It sometimes appeared as single wide light zone. Under the stereo dissecting microscope, the boundary between summer and winter zones can hardly be defined, and measurement of winter zones depends on what the investigators judges to be a valid winter zone. This difficulty is not encountered in the acetate peel method.

Fig. 4 shows the scanning micrograph of part of the otolith of a 322 mm eel collected from the White Lake Hatchery Pond. The summer zone, which is wide and pale grey in colour, mainly consisted of aragonite crystals. The winter zone appeared as a wide, deep groove accompanied inside and outside by two to four narrow grooves placed closely together. There were few aragonite crystals found in the winter zone. The false winter zones however, were grey in colour, usually appeared as an isolated groove consisting of one to a few well spaced narrow grooves and can be distinguished from the true winter zone by their width and depth and the amount of aragonite crystals present in them.

The summer zones of young eels may be as much as ten to fifteen times wider than the following winter zone. As the eel becomes larger the differences between the width of the alternating summer and winter zones gradually decreases, but the summer zones continue to be more distinct.

Occurrence of false annulus

False annuli were apparent and occasionally observed in the otoliths of eels collected from the White Lake Hatchery Pond and the natural waters. The sagittae collected on August 15, 1967, three weeks after the transplantation to the pond, showed a translucent edge. An opaque margin was noted in sagittae of those fish collected in September and October of the same year.

By comparing these otoliths with those of elvers collected on July 26, this translucent zone was found to
be formed between the period July 26 and August 15.
Since this translucent zone did not represent the true
winter growth it was a false winter zone or false
annulus. All 1,400 samples collected in successive
years exhibited this translucent zone in the relative
position and true annuli were formed at the expected
times and in their normal position in spite of previous
development of a false annulus. The formation of this
false annulus was probably related to the transport-
ation and sudden change of their environment. In the
acetate replicas, this zone appeared as a single light
ring and could be distinguished from the true annulus
which is a relatively wide, light ring preceded and
followed by one to five narrow rings (Fig. 6).

As mentioned previously, there were one to two distinct false annuli formed in the fall on the otoliths of
some fast growing fish. Formation of these checks
began at the end of September or at the beginning of
October and was completed by the end of October.

Another example of false annuli was found in fish
collected in the summer of 1968. Forty per cent of
the otoliths from 41 eels collected after July 28 1968,
showed an opaque margin preceded by a marked translucent zone. This translucent zone was not observed
in the samples collected on June 28 and should be

formed in July. The occurrence of this false annulus
was accompanied by the rise in water temperature up
to 30°C for a week in the second week of July. A similar type of false annulus was occasionally found in
the middle of the 1969 summer. Since supplementary
food and the natural food items such as crustaceans,
some insect larvae and minnows were abundant during
July, it is unlikely that the short of food supply was the
primary factor responsible for the formation of this
check. The high temperature probably have affected
the physiology and feeding of these fish and responsible for the formation of this false annulus.

Time of annulus formation

The annulus as stated above is a narrow light zone. It
is not apparent at the edge of the otoliths until the
summer growth has begun. To get the range in time
of annulus formation, therefore, knowledge is required
of the period when new otolith summer growth starts
on fish collected during the spring and summer
months. An examination was made of the margins of
sagittae from the White Lake Hatchery Pond eels
caught during the springs and summers from 1968 to
1970 (Table 1). An opaque margin was noted on sagittae of 29 per cent of fish caught on May 18 and a distinct narrow opaque margin was formed in most of
the otoliths collected after June 20.

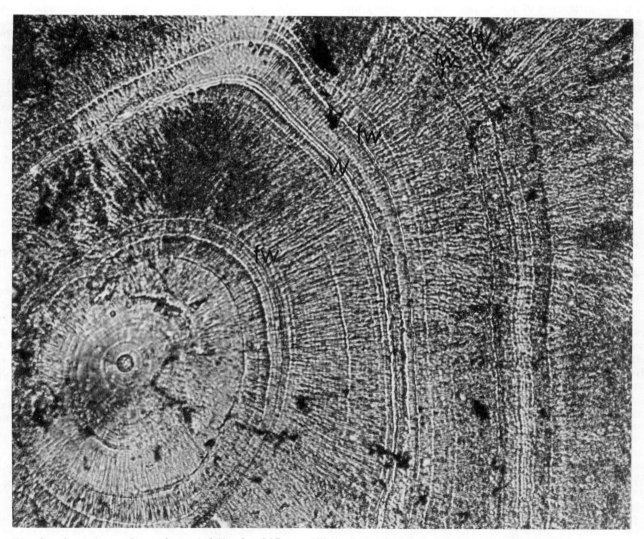

Fig. 6. Acetate replica of an otolith of a 315 mm White Lake Hatchery Pond eel collected on
May 18 1970, showing the structures of winter (W) and false winter zones (fw). × 106

Table 1. The earliest spring dates when the translucent zone, corresponding to the previous winter period, became visible on otoliths of the American eels from Digdeguash River, N.B., kept in White Lake Pond during the period July 16 1967-May 18 1970.

Date		No. of fish examined	With translucent winter zone					Without translucent winter zone			
			N	%	Length (mm)		N	%	Length (mm)	
					Average	Range			Average	Range
May 18,	1970	93	27	29.0	306.6	257.355	66	71.0	311.0	220-582
May 19,	1969	2	1	50.0	164.0	164	1	50.0	210.0	210
May 20,	1968	2	—	—	—	—	2	100.0	116.0	107-124
May 27,	1969	10	1	10.0	310.0	310	9	90.0	188.8	174-212
June 2,	1970	15	15	100.0	341.0	313-396	—	—	—	—
June 16,	1968	29	27	93.1	111.3	94.145	2	6.9	127.0	123-131
July 26,	1968	21	21	100.0	102.5	74.120	—	—	—	—
Aug. 4,	1969	39	39	100.0	279.4	164.491	—	—	—	—
Oct. 11,	1969	89	89	100.0	304.3	219-360	—	—	—	—

Although the end of the growing season for the sagittae is difficult to determine from sagittae themselves under low magnification, the translucent margins of some otoliths collected on October 28 could be seen at a magnification of 400 times. As previously mentioned, some fast growing fish formed false annuli in September and October. However, the slow growing fish did not form false annuli during this period and showed a translucent margin on their otoliths at the end of October or November. Fish collected in March and April did not show any new growth on their otoliths. Therefore, the period for the summer growth of American eel in White Lake Hatchery Pond extended from May to November depending on water temperature and growth of the fish. The annulus was generally formed between November to May.

VALIDITY OF AGE DETERMINATION FROM THE OTOLITH

The validity of the assumption that recognizable annuli appear annually on eel sagittae can be tested by following the otolith development of fish of known age. In this manner any false or indistinct annuli on otoliths of individuals of each age group are identified and the knowledge applied in the interpretation of otoliths from adults.

In the present study, approximately 10,000 elvers were collected on July 26 1967, from Didgeguash River, New Brunswick, and brought to the White Lake Hatchery Pond. A random sample of 50 pairs of otoliths were obtained from these fish. All of these fish were assumed not to have spent any time in fresh water and their sagittae were taken as the initial condition of these fish. Any new zone found on the otoliths of the recaptured fish represented their freshwater growth in the pond. At periodic intervals subsequent to their release, samples of these fish were obtained, their lengths were measured and their otoliths were removed for detailed study. With the exception of the formation of false annuli, these fish formed an opaque zone in the summer and a narrow translucent zone in the winter (Fig. 7). The periodic samples collected throughout 1967 to May 18 1970, showed that translucent zones began forming at the end of October

in some fish and virtually all otoliths exhibited translucent zones by the following May. The opaque zones were formed in the summer between May and the end of October or even later. Therefore, the translucent winter zones of sagittae were formed annually and represent the true year mark. If the false annuli can be properly distinguished from the true annuli, the age of American eels can be determined from the otolith accordingly.

An indirect evidence of the validity of the otolith method was obtained by comparing the back-calculated lengths with known lengths which eels attained in the preceding year. The body-otolith length relationship for the American eel can be described by a straight line, thus a direct proportion method was used to back calculate the lengths attained at end of each annulus.

Length was back-calculated from the formula:

$$L_n = L_t \frac{O_n}{O_t}$$

where L_n equals length of fish at annulus n, L_t equals fish length at time of otolith removed, O_t equals the otolith radius and O_n equals the otolith length at annulus n. The calculated length for the fish of known age at annulus n agreed very closely with the measured length of fish collected at the end of preceding year. Therefore the number of annuli on each fish corresponded to its age. The resulting data were summarized in the form of growth curves as in Fig. 8.

The annual formation of an annulus in the sagittae and the agreement between the actual age and age readings of otoliths demonstrated that the sagittae can be used with confidence for age determination of the American eel.

FACTORS AFFECTING THE TRANSLUCENT ZONE FORMATION IN THE SAGITTAE OF AMERICAN EEL

As previously indicated, false annuli occasionally occurred in the sagittae of American eel. The accuracy of the age determined from otoliths depends on how well the false annulus could be distinguished

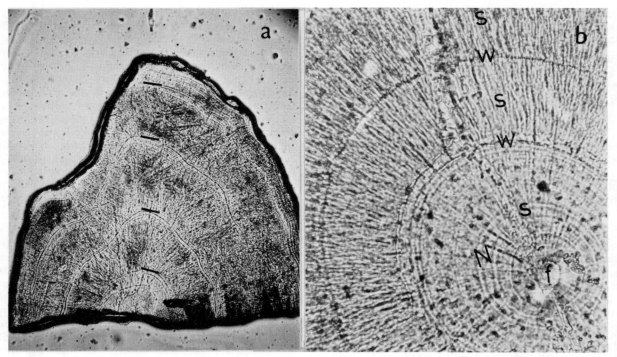

Fig. 7. (a) The acetate replica of otolith of White Lake Hatchery Pond eel (295 mm) collected on May 18 1970 and kept in aquarium till January 16 1971. It shows four clearly defined annuli correspond to the four winters spent by the fish in the pond. × 106
(b) An acetate replica of the 'elver's rings' of American eel. It consists of a nucleus, two summer and one winter zones. The nucleus again comprise of a central focus followed by a summer and a winter zone. F is focus, n, is nucleus, s is summer zone and w is winter zone. × 425

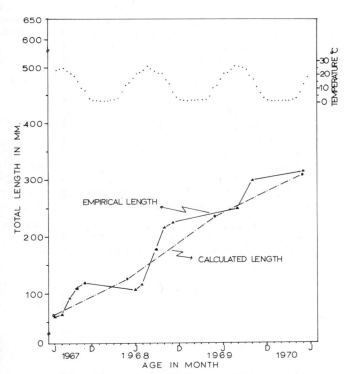

Fig. 8 Empirical and calculated length of American eel and water temperature (dotted line) in White Lake Hatchery Pond.

been suggested by various workers to be responsible for the temporary decrease in growth rate of fish, mainly salmonids. Such decreases in growth rate appear as false annuli or checks on the scales. Although fish otoliths have been used for age determination of many fishes, there is very little information available on factors that might cause the formation of checks in the otoliths. A better understanding of the effects of various factors on otolith zonation can certainly provide a more reliable basis for ageing eels, and other fishes by means of the otoliths.

Young eels collected from Mactaquac Dam on the St. John's River, New Brunswick, were kept in the laboratory of Ottawa University at 20 °C. After spending three months in the laboratory, they were subjected to different treatments to determine the effects of temperature, food and handling on the zones formation of the otoliths of American eel. In these experiments fish of equal size were grouped together and kept in 15-gallon aquaria. Photo-period was automatically controlled to provide 12 hours of light in each 24-hour period. The fish were measured and weighed at the beginning and at the end of each experiment after they had been anaesthetized with 0.05 per cent MS 222 (Tricaine methane sulphonate) solution.

The otoliths of fish collected at the beginning of the experiments were used as the 'starting point' against which subsequent growth of otoliths was compared. As with the eels transplanted to the White Lake Hatchery Pond, a distinct false annulus was formed in sagittae of all eels collected from the Mactaquac Dam. It provides a convenient way to separate the growth of otoliths in the laboratory from their growth

from the true one. Various factors such as low temperatures, midsummer rise of temperature near the upper lethal limit, change of environment, starvation, cessation of feeding caused by handling or tagging, change of feeding levels, or the onset of maturity have

in natural waters. These fish ranged from 80 to 140 mm in length, and had spent one to four years in fresh water.

All otoliths of these fish were mounted in Permount and examined under the microscope with transmitted light. Any narrow false winter zone formed under the laboratory condition was referred as check.

(a) Effects of temperature on check formation

In most species of fishes the annuli on scales and otoliths are laid down during winter when metabolic activity and growth were at a minimum. The false annuli resemble the true annuli, and must, therefore, represent a change in growth rate. As the temperature affects the metabolic rate of a fish, it also would have considerable effects on the growth of its otoliths.

Four groups of 40 fish each were acclimated and kept at 5, 10, 20 and 30°C for five weeks and offered an *ad libitum* diet. One half of these fish reared under each temperature regime was removed for examination at the end of five weeks. The remaining fish were acclimated and kept at 20°C for another ten weeks.

Fish kept at 5°C seldom fed, but did not grow, while the fish reared at 10°C fed very little and increased slightly in length. All fish kept at 5°C formed a marked check in their otoliths. With the exception of seven, 40 fish kept at 10°C also showed the presence of a check corresponding to their stay at this temperature. At 30°C, besides the acclimation period, experimental fish consumed about 25 per cent more food than those kept at 20°C. They grew slower than fish kept at 20°C. Seventeen per cent of the fish kept at 20°C formed checks on their otoliths (Table 2). It has been found in the laboratory that some aquarium-cultured fish responded to anaesthesia and measurement by forming a check in their otoliths (Liew, unpublished). Therefore, the formation of check in fish kept at 20° could be caused by handling. At 30°C, most of the experimental fish formed a wide dark zone while a total of 27 per cent of them formed a check which was followed by a wide dark zone. The occurrences of checks in these fish could not be completely explained by the handling. Since the check was formed at the beginning of the treatment, it could have been induced by the 'stress' caused by handling accompanied by the high temperature treatment.

In another experiment on the effects of temperature on the check formation, each 16-fish group was acclimated from 20°C to 10 and 30°C in two days and kept at the respective temperatures for one week. They were then acclimated back to 20°C in two days and kept at this temperature for another ten weeks. A group of 16 fish was kept at 20°C without being subjected to any temperature changes as control. Fish subjected to 10°C treatment fed sparingly or not at all for a week while those fish kept at 30°C which stopped feeding for at least three days all formed a check in their otoliths. Twenty-five per cent of the control group showed the presence of a check in their otoliths. Fish held at the high temperature, because they had stopped feeding and because of their high metabolic rate, probably have to expend their stored energy for maintenance therefore have no excess energy for the growth process. A check is thus formed. Low temperature decreased the apetite and metabolism of these fish, and had the same effect. The food intake therefore, seems to influence the growth and check formation of the otolith.

(b) Effects of food on the check formation

The amount of food available is one of the primary factors determining growth of fishes. In order to determine the effects of food on the check formation in eel's otoliths, beginning on January 25, 1972, groups of ten fish were subjected to 5, 10, 15 and 30 days of starvation and then offered an *ad libitum* diet for at least ten weeks. Fish starved as short as five days produced a weak check in their otoliths. Fish starved for 10 to 30 days all formed a marked check.

This experiment was repeated in January 18 1973 and the same result was obtained.

The abundance or scarcity of food has been considered as the main factor responsible for the check formation in the scales of fish (Gray and Setna, 1931; Bhatia, 1931; Blair, 1938; and Major and Craddock 1962). Fish fed with abundant food formed abnormally wide rings even though during the winter periods when the temperature was kept unchanged and fish fed with limited diet developed abnormally narrow rings.

Food has the same effect on the formation of zones in otolith. Fish fed with abundant food formed a dark zone and fish starved for more than five days formed a light zone. The formation of calcium carbonate under laboratory conditions is closely related to the food supply. When fish fed actively, there were large amounts of aragonite formed in the otolith and the zone appeared dark. When the fish stopped feeding, the calcification process of the otoliths was apparently reduced and very little calcium carbonate was formed, thus the zone appeared light.

Bilton and Robins (1971) reported that young sockeye salmon *Oncorhynchusnerka* starved 20 weeks had shown no indication of starvation on their scales. This

Table 2. Increment in length (mm) and percentage occurrence of checks on the otoliths of eels kept at 5°, 10°, 20°, and 30°C for five weeks then at 20°C for another ten weeks during Jan 25 to May 18, 1972. The number of fish is indicated in brackets.

Temperature °C	Jan. 25-Mar. 10			Mar. 11-May 18		
	Mean length, mm	Length increment	Check presence	Mean length, mm	Length increment	Check presence
5	116.0 (40)	0.2	100	112.7 (20)	3.7	100
10	107.5 (40)	0.5	85	108.5 (20)	2.6	80
20	101.6 (40)	5.0	15	105.5 (20)	4.5	20
30	102.4 (40)	2.5	15	104.5 (20)	7.4	40

situation is not found in the otoliths of American eel. Fish starved for more than three months showed a light margin in their otoliths.

(c) *Handling*

The elvers transplanted from Digdeguash River to White Lake Hatchery Pond and young eels transplant- ed from Mactaquac Dam to the laboratory all formed a marked check in their otoliths corresponding to this handling. Blair (1938) found that transference of fish from one place to another induced the formation of a marked check in the scales of Atlantic salmon. He considered that such a check was produced by the weakening of the fish during transit and the slow recovery thereafter.

Young eels which had been kept in wet astyro-foam cooler for eight hours in the laboratory stopped feed- ing for about five days. A check was observed in the otoliths of these fish corresponding to this treatment. The eels from Mactaquac Dam also did not feed for at least one week in the laboratory. This indicates that the handling probably disturbed the physiology of the fish and caused stress in these fish. The stress prevented them from feeding and the subsequent star- vation induced the formation of a check in the otoliths of American eel.

The above experiments showed that feeding played a prominent role in the formation of checks in otoliths. Eels which had been subjected to starvation, tem- perature and handling treatments ceased feeding and showed a check in their otoliths. Therefore, when fish are living in a favourable environment and taking plentiful food, they grow fast and form a dark growth zone; when they are living in an unfavourable en- vironment and taking insufficient food, they either decrease or cease growing and form a check in their otoliths.

ACKNOWLEDGMENTS

This study was conducted under the guidance of Dr. V. D. Vladykov. The author extends his thanks to Messrs. D. James and R. W. Gray for their helps in collecting elvers and young eels, to Mrs. E. Ford for her help in Scanning Electron Microscopy and to Mr. G. Ben for his technical assistance in preparing the photographs. The author also wishes to thank Messrs. C. Gruchy and B. Coad for their helpful criticisms of the manuscript.

REFERENCES

Belanger, L. F. 1960. Development, structure and composition of the otolithic organs of the rat pp. 151-162. In Reidal F. Sognnaes (ed.), Calci- fication in biological systems. Am. Ass. Advanc. Sci., Washington D.C., publ. 64.

Bertin, L. 1956. Eels. A biological study. Clearer- Hume Press, London 192 pp.

Bhatia, D. 1931. On the production of annual zones in the scales of the rainbow trout (*salmo irideus*). J. exp. Zool., **59**: 45-49.

Bilton, H. T., and G. L. Robins. 1971a. Effects of feeding level on circulus formation on scales of young sockeye salmon (*Oncorhynclus nerka*). J. Fish. Res. Bd. Can., **28**: 861-868.

Bilton, H. T., and G. L. Robins. 1971b. Effects of starvation, feeding and light period on circulus formation on scales of young sockeye salmon. J. Fish. Res. Bd. Can., **28**: 1749-1755.

Bilton, H. T., and G. L. Robins. 1971c. Response of young sockeye salmon to prolonged periods of starvation. J. Fish. Res. Bd. Can., **28**: 1757- 1761.

Blacker, R. W. 1969. Chemical composition of the zones in cod otoliths. J. Cons. perm. int. Explor. Mer., **33** (1): 107-108

Blair, A. A. 1938. Factors affecting growth of the scales of salmon (*Salmo salar*) Ph.D. Thesis, Univ. Toront. 227 pp.

Boetius I., and J. Boetius. 1967. Eels, *Anguilla rostrata* LeSueur, in Bermuda. Vidensk. Meddr. dansk naturh. Foren. **130**: 63-84.

Cooper, E. L. 1951. Validation of the use of scales of brook trout, *Salvelinus fontinales*, for age determination. Copeia No. 2, pp. 141-148.

Dannevig, A. 1956. The influence of temperature on the formation of zones in scales and otoliths of young cod. Rep. Norw. Fishery mar. Invests., II, no. 7: pp. 1-16.

Dannevig, E. H. 1956. Chemical composition of the zones in cod otoliths. J. Cons. perm. intern. Exp. Mer, **21** (2) 156-159.

Degens, E. T., W. G. Deuser and R. L. Haedrich, 1969. Molecular structure and compositions of fish otoliths. Mar. Biol., **2** (2): pp. 105-113.

Ehrenbaum, E., and H. Marukawa. 1913. Ueber Altersbestimmung und Wachstum beim Aal. Z. Fisch., **14**: 89-127.

Frost, W. E. 1945. The age and growth of eels (*Anguilla anguilla*) from the Windermere catch- ment area. Part I. J. Anim. Ecol. **14** (1): 26-36.

Graham, M. 1956. Sea fisheries. Their investiga- tion in the United Kingdom. Edward Arnold Ltd., London. 487 pp.

Gray, J., and S. B. Setna. 1931. The growth of fish. IV. The effect of food supply on the scales of *Salmo irideus*. J. exp. Biol., **8**: 55-62.

Gray, R., and C. W. Andrews, 1971. Age and growth of the American eel in Newfoundland waters. Can. J. Zool., **49**: 121-128.

Hatch, R. W. 1960. Regular occurrence of false annuli in four brook trout populations. Trans. Am. Fish. Soc., **89**: 6-12.

Hickling, C. F. 1931. The structure of the otolith of the hake. Q. J. microsc. Sci., **74**: 547-562.

Hogman, W. J. 1968. Annulus formation on scales of four species of coregonids reared under artifi- cial conditions. J. Fish. Res. Bd. Can., **25** (10): 2111-2122.

Hurley, D. A. 1972. The American eel in Eastern Lake Ontario. J. Fish. Res. Bd. Can., **29**: 535-543.

Immerman, F. 1908. Die innere struktur der schol- len-otolithon komm. Untersuch. Deut. Meere. Abt. Helgoland, N.F. **8** (2): 129-176.

Irie, T. 1955. The crystal texture of the otolith of a marine teleost Pseudosciaena. J. Fac. Fish. Anim. Husb. Hiroshima Univ. **1** (1): 1-8.

Irie, T. 1957. On the forming season of annual rings in the otoliths of several marine teleosts. J. Fac. Fish. Anim. Husb., Hiroshima Univ. **3** (1): 311-317.

Irie, T. 1960. The growth of the fish otolith. J. Fac. Fish. Anim. Husb., Hiroshima Univ. **3** (1): 203- 221.

Jensen, A. C. 1965. A standard terminology and notation for otolith reader. ICNAF Res. Bull. **2**: 5-7.

Johnson, L. D. 1971. Growth of known-age muskel- lunge in Wisconsin and validation of age and growth determination methods. Tech. Bull No 49. Dept. Natural Resources, Madison, Wisconsin.

Ketchen, K. S. 1970. An examination of criteria for determining the age of Pacific cod (*Gadus macrocephalus*) from otoliths. Tech. Rep. Fish. Res. Bd. Can. No. 171, 41 pp.

Major, R. L., and D. R. Craddock. 1962. Marking sockeye salmon scales by short periods of starvation. U.S. Fish and Wildlife Service special scientific report—Fish. No. 416, 12 p.

May, A. W. 1965. The validity of otolith ages of southern Grand Bank cod. ICNAF Res. Bull. No. 2: 19-24.

Mugiya, Y. 1964. Calcification of fish and shell-fish III. Seasonal occurence of a prealbumin fraction in the otolith fluid of some fish, corresponding to the period of opaque zone formation in the otolith. Bull. Jap. Soc. scient. Fish., **30**, (12): 955-961.

Mugiya, Y. 1965. Calcification in fish and shell-fish IV. The differences in nitrogen content between the translucent and opaque zones of otolith in some fish. Bull. Jap. Soc. of scient. Fish., **31**, (11) 896-901.

Ogden, J. C. 1970. Relative abundance, food habits and age of the American eel in certain New Jersey streams. Trans. Am. Fish. Soc., **99**, (1): 54-59.

Pannella, G. 1971. Fish otoliths: Daily layers and periodical patterns. Science, **173**: 1124-1127.

Regier, H. A. 1962. Validation of the scale method for estimating age and growth of bluegills. Trans. Am. Fish. Soc., **91** (4): 362-374.

Schmidt, J. 1922. The breeding places of the eel. Phil. Trans. Ser. B. 211: 179-208.

Schmidt, J. 1922. The breeding places of the eel. Smithsonian Rep. for 1924, 279-316.

Sinha, V. R. P., and T. W. Jones. 1967 On the age and growth of the freshwater eel (*A. anguilla*) J. zool., **153**: 99-117.

Smith, M. W. 1966. Amount of organic matter lost to a lake by migration of eels. J. Fish. Res. Bd. Can., **23** (1): 1799-1801.

Smith, M. W., and Saunders, J. W. 1955. The American eel in certain fresh waters of the maritime provinces of Canada. J. Fish. Res. Bd. Can. **12** (2): 238-269.

Vladykov, V. D. 1967. Age determination and age of the American eel from New Brunswick waters. In Can. Dept. Fish. and Forest. Progr. Rep. No. 3, 22 pp.

Watson, J. E. 1964. Determining the age of young herring from their otoliths. Trans. Am. Fish. Soc., **94**: 11-20.

Studies on growth, ageing and back-calculation of roach *Rutilus rutilus* (L.), and dace *Leuciscus leuciscus* (L.)*

by A. E. HOFSTEDE
Oosterbeek, The Netherlands

SUMMARY

1.   During the years 1958 to 1963 ageing and growth of roach *Rutilus rutilus* (L.), and dace *Leuciscus leuciscus* (L.) as additional stock in carp growing ponds were studied.

2.   The rapid growth which manifested itself under these conditions was hitherto not known in The Netherlands' inland waters. It amounted to the following (in cm.):

roach	maximum	11 — 22 — 26 — 30
	average	10 — 20 — 25 — 28 — 30 — 31
dace	average	12 — 21 — 24 — 26 — 27 — 28

3.   In addition to data on growth in length and weight scale samples were taken at the end of each growing period. In the beginning the scales served to separate the various generations (restocked roach and new invasions of almost exclusively roach which apparently enter the ponds every year). Later on this scale collection from fish of known age was used to verify the ageing method and also a study was made of scale measurements and back-calculation.

4.   Ageing by means of scale reading of these rapidly growing roach proved to be 100% reliable. Dace, on the contrary, presented a problem by the formation of a false ring in the second year. This happened in the long, dry and hot summer of 1959. This river fish, apparently, came into difficulties in these ponds perhaps due to high temperatures or water shortage. Therefore, ageing of fish not originating from its normal habitat should be executed with great caution. Retardation of growth after the second year may also indicate a less suitable milieu.

5.   Scales were measured in different directions and the back-calculated average lengths of the stock were compared with the actual lengths found in previous years. Corrections were expressed in percentages either to be added to or to be subtracted from the back-calculated data.

6.   By expressing the correction percentages in centimetres it became evident that in the case of measurement in the caudal direction the back-calculated never differed more than plus or minus one centimetre from the actual lengths measured in previous years. In view of practical evaluation of a fish stock this is considered sufficiently accurate.

---

* This article is an abridged form of two reports (Hofstede, 1963 and 1970) which gave detailed information. The second one was submitted in a preliminary version to EIFAC Sc I for the programme 'Study of ageing methods in coarse fish'.

1.   INTRODUCTION

When draining a carp pond in the spring of 1959, 54 roach *Rutilus rutilus* (L.) of 8-11 cm (average 9.6 cm) and 38 dace *Leuciscus leuciscus* (L.) of 10-13 cm (average 12.3 cm) were found. Ageing by means of the scales proved these fish to be one summer old. Because the length of roach of this age was not known in The Netherlands it was decided to restock these fish for a further study of growth and ageing under these conditions. This could be done for a period of another 5 years, so that the observations covered the years 1958 to 1963.

It soon became evident that such invasions which almost always concern roach and perch *Perca fluviatilis* L., take place with the water supply every year in late spring or early summer.

Because all roach were restocked the population finally consisted of several year classes which overlapped each other in the larger sizes; see Table A (Tables labelled with letters are at the end of this paper).

All roach and dace were measured and weighed after each growing period at which time scale samples were also taken. In the beginning this scale sampling was done with the purpose of collecting demonstration material of fast growing fish. Later the roach scales were used to separate the different year classes. Furthermore, since the growth history of both species and their age were known the material collected was used to check the reliability of ageing by means of scales and the exactness of back-calculation.

In the present paper the roach year classes 1958 and 1959 and the dace year class 1958 are discussed.

All these observations were carried out in ponds of the Fish breeding Station at Valkenswaard of the Organization for Improvement of Inland Fisheries. I should like to thank Mr. C. M. Bungenberg de Jong and his staff for the assistance given, and also my former assistant Mr. A. Vetter for scale reading and the execution of numerous calculations.

2.   THE MATERIAL

The roach material originating from the 1958 year class was selected as the main source for the present report. Of this generation 54 fish were collected as one-year-old fish, since growth of roach, and also of other cyprinids, takes place approximately from June until September, it can be stated that such fish caught in late autumn, winter or early spring have already reached the length of a complete year cycle. The ages of the fishes are therefore given in complete years, 1, 2, 3, etc, and not as 1+, 2+, etc., which only indicates that the fish were caught before their next birthday. The development of the 54 roach could be followed in adequate numbers for a total of 6 years. The 1959 year class consisted of only 3 fish but they could be followed during 5 years without losses. They may serve as a check. Tables B and C give the length frequencies with the number from which scales were sampled in brackets and the average lengths and weights at the end of each growing period.

Table D gives similar information for the generation of dace born in 1958. During the whole period of these observations there never again occurred an invasion of dace in noticeable numbers.

Heavy losses were suffered in 1960. Unfortunately, the dace left were overlooked at the end of 1960 and 1962. They may have been mixed with the roach treated at those times. Careful scrutiny of the roach scale samples did not however reveal any dace scales in this collection.

In most cases the length measurements were carried out in millimetres total length. The length frequencies given in this report are rounded off in full centimetres (0.6 upwards; 0.5 downwards). Average lengths of age groups are calculated from the original measurements.

Scale samples were taken preferably from the left side of the body, above and close to the lateral line, slightly in advance of the first ray of the dorsal fin. In later years on account of the small numbers of fish available samples had to be collected from other parts of the body, e.g. on the right side and further backwards. Each sample consists of 5 to 10 scales. After superficial manual cleaning the scales were compressed between colourslide glasses, numbered and stored. They remain available for future consultation.

3. ROACH

3.1 Growth of roach

The data on the growth of roach in Tables 1 and 2 are summarized from the Tables B and C.

These data on average growth in length and weight are shown in Fig. 1. The curves are fairly regular

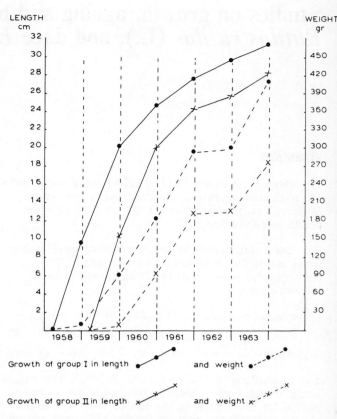

Fig. 1. The growth of roach in length and weight. The 1958 year class (Group I) is shown with dots and the 1959 year class (Group II) with crosses. The continuous line illustrates length and the dashes indicate weight.

with the exception of the weight curves at the end of the 1962 growing season. Before the day of measuring the roach had been kept in storage tanks for about three weeks. As the increase in length does not deviate from the usual curve it can be assumed that

Table 1. Roach-1958 year class; average growth in 6 years

year of growth	1958	1959	1960	1961	1962	1963
age	1	2	3	4	5	6
length (cm)	9.6	20.1	24.6	27.6	29.6	31.4
weight (gr)	9.0	91.6	183.0	293.4	300.0	411.5
increase in weight	9.0	82.6	91.4	110.4	6.6	111.5

Table 2. Roach-1959 year class; average growth in 5 years.

year of growth	1959	1960	1961	1962	1963
age	1	2	3	4	5
length (cm)	10.3	20.0	24.3	25.7	28.2
weight (gr)	10*	93.3	193.3	196.7	276.7
increase in weight	10	83.3	100.0	3.3	80.0

* calculated.

the fish lost a considerable amount of weight during this storage. In consequence the increase of weight in 1963 cannot be considered normal.

The conclusion is justified that the growth of roach under the conditions existing in the carp ponds concerned (e.g. a light stock of roach in intensively managed carp culture) was extremely fast compared to data on the growth of roach found in literature.

3.2 Ageing, scale measurement and back-calculation

Under the above mentioned conditions the scales developed very clearly and had easily readable annuli in all directions. The photographs (Figs. 2-4) give a few samples of roach scales of different age. The

Fig. 2.   A scale of a two year old roach 20.2 cm long.

Fig. 4.   A scale of a six year old roach 31.8 cm long.

Fig. 3.   A scale of a four year old roach 25.7 cm long.

Table 3.   The back-calculated lengths at the end of the first growth period for 8 two-year-old roach of the 1968 year class calculated from measurements made in four different directions.

Scale	Sample	Calculated length			
No	length	A	B	C	D
1	20.1	8.9	7.6	6.0	6.4
2	20.1	9.8	8.9	7.8	7.6
3	20.1	8.8	7.7	6.4	6.4
4	20.1	9.9	9.2	7.9	7.9
5	20.2	10.0	8.6	7.2	7.4
6	20.3	9.7	8.8	7.9	7.8
7	20.6	9.8	9.1	8.2	8.1
8	21.6	10.7	10.5	8.1	8.8
average length		9.7	8.8	7.4	7.5
correction in %		— 1.0	+ 9.1	+ 29.7	+ 28.0

chances of misinterpretation of age determined by scale reading proved to be nil.

Scale measurements were carried out to determine the average length in previous years and in order to compare the calculated data with the actual figures recorded in those years.

The distance between the focus and the subsequent annuli was measured in four directions in order to check on the accuracy of back-calculation and the necessity of corrections. The directions were caudal (indicated by A in Table 3), oral (D), vertical or dorso-ventral (B) and diagonal between B and D (indicated by C).

Measurements were taken by means of an ocular-micrometer on a stereo microscope with a magnification of 50. A combination of transmitted and

reflected light was used. The intensity of light was influenced by screening with the hands.

Back-calculations were carried out on the assumption that direct proportionality exists between the growth of body length and of the scales.

From each scale sample containing 5 to 10 scales from one fish, three scales of normal shape were selected and measured as described above. The average value of the three back-calculations thus obtained per annulus in each direction is taken as the back-calculated length.

It stands to reason that if one hopes to find reliable figures the scale samples should be representative for the length frequency. Judging by the figures given in Tables D and C this seems to be the case.

Table 3 may serve as an example of the results of a back-calculation of 8 samples of 2-years old roach. For instance the average length of the A-measurement amounts to 9.7 cm. Because the actual length measured in the field one year before amounted to 9.6 cm a correction of minus 1.0 per cent has to be applied to the back-calculated figure of 9.7 cm.

The conclusions of all back-calculations are gathered in Table 4.

centages of measurement A, year class 1958, are expressed in centimetres.

It can be said in conclusion that all lengths measured in the field lie between the limits of the 'back-calculation figure plus and minus 0.9 cm'. Worked out in the same way the 1959 year class gives the limits of minus 0.7 and plus 0.8 cm.

To put it as a general conclusion and in rounded-off figures, it can be said that when measuring in caudal

Table 4.   Roach—Yearclass 1958—Summary of corrections (in %)

age of fish measured	A					B					D				
	1	2	3	4	5	1	2	3	4	5	1	2	3	4	5
2	− 1.0					+ 9.1					+ 28.0				
3	+ 9.1	0				+ 23.1	+ 7.5				+ 54.8	+ 11.0			
4	+ 7.9	+ 4.1	+ 1.2			+ 26.3	+ 10.4	+ 4.7			+ 57.3	+ 16.9	+ 2.9		
5	− 6.8	− 2.0	− 3.5	− 2.5		+ 15.7	+ 6.9	+ 0.8	− 2.1		+ 47.7	+ 12.9	+ 15.5	− 2.1	
6	+ 7.9	+ 2.6	− 0.8	− 1.4	+ 1.4	+ 26.3	+ 10.4	+ 3.8	+ 1.1	+ 2.8	+ 60.0	+ 19.6	+ 6.0	+ 2.2	+ 3.5

This gives the percentages to be either added to, or subtracted from the back-calculated average lengths. Measurement C has been omitted because it was very similar to the results of measurements in direction D.

The data collected from year class 1959 were worked out in the same way. The correction percentages can be summarized as follows:

1958 year class	1959 year class
measurements A minus 6.8 to plus 9.1%	minus 6.4 to plus 3.6%
measurements B minus 2.1 to plus 26.3%	zero to plus 8.4%
measurements D minus 2.1 to plus 60.0	minus 0.8 to plus 32.1%

It is evident that the smallest differences found are those of measurement A, i.e. the caudal direction.

In Table 5 (which is derived from Table 4) the per-

Table 5.   Yearclass 1958; measured in caudal direction; Variation around the back-calculated figure (cm)

1st growing period: −7 to +9%
   For a length of 10 cm this means a
   variation of   −0.7 to +0.9 cm.

2nd growing period: −2 to +4%
   For a length of 20 cm this means a
   variation of   −0.4 to +0.8 cm.

3rd growing period: −3.5 to +1.0%
   For a length of 24.6 cm this means a
   variation of   −0.9 to +0.2 cm.

4th growing period: −1.4 to −2.5%
   For a length of 27.5 cm the maximum
   difference amounts to   −0.7 cm.

5th growing period: +1.4%
   For a length of 30 cm the difference
   amounts to   +0.4 cm.

Table 6.   Dace—1958 yearclass; average growth in 6 years.

year in growth	1958	1959	1960	1961	1962	1963
age	1	2	3	4	5	6
length (cm)	12.3	20.9	24.0*	25.7	27.0*	27.8
weight (gr)	17.1	86.4	140†	185	222†	250
increase in weight	17.1	69.3	54	45	37	28

* derived from Figure 5.
† calculated from the length-weight relation given in Hofstede (1970).

direction the actual length measured in the field lies between the limits of the back-calculated length plus and minus one cm.

For the practical appraisal of fish stocks this is sufficiently accurate and therefore, when measuring in caudal direction no correction is needed.

4. DACE

4.1 Growth of dace

Growth in length and weight are shown in Table D and Fig. 5. The missing data at the end of the 3rd and 5th year can easily be reconstructed. This leads us to the summary in Table 6.

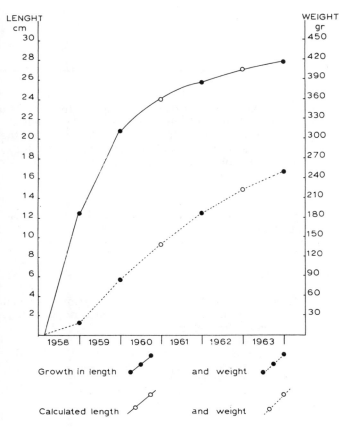

Fig. 5. The growth of dace in length (continuous line) and weight (dashed line). The open circles are calculated figures.

Fig. 6. Scale of a two year old dace 18.9 cm long.

Fig. 7. Scale of a two year old dace 20.6 cm long.

4.2 Ageing, scale measurement and back-calculation

The scales of the one-year-old dace show a clear picture of well growing fish. The regular and transparent layout of the striae do not show any effects of retardation in growth.

Scale samples of the 2-years-old dace (Figs. 6 and 7) show two 'yearmarks', a correct and a false annulus. Because none of the first-year scales have a false annulus, it can be concluded that (when counting from the focus to the margin) the first mark should be the correct annulus

When studying the false ring it was evident that the two 4-years and the one 6-years-old dace (Fig. 8) showed the location of the false ring but without much

danger from misinterpretation. Out of six 2-years-old dace there are two samples which could, and probably would, have caused mistakes in ageing. Attention is drawn to the fact that in addition to various characteristics indicating a false ring, such as 'absence of cut-off striae', 'a non complete ring', 'a ring not clearly present in all scales taken from the same fish', etc. there may be another method for recognizing a false ring.

Fig. 9 shows (1) in a straight line the actual growth according to the measurements in the field, and (2) in an interrupted line the growth if the false ring is considered to be an annulus. Back-calculation of three 2-years-old dace showed the formation at a length of 13.9 cm and the back-calculation of the 6-years-old dace at 14.0 cm. When the habitat is normal it can be assumed that the growth follows a certain regular pattern. The growth may be fast, slow or intermediate. But in any case one can expect

Fig. 8. Scale of a six year old dace 27. 8 cm long.

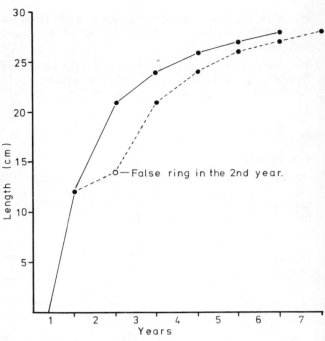

Fig. 9. The growth of dace showing the location of a false ring. The points indicate the average lengths measured in the field. The open circle indicates the location of a false ring calculated from the scales of 3 two year old and one six year old fish.

the growth curve to be a regular line. This is not the case in Fig. 9. Therefore, this irregular curve may indicate the presence of a false ring. It would be worthwhile to investigate this matter more thoroughly.

It is remarked that the false ring in the scales of dace was formed in a pond which was also stocked with roach. However, the roach scales did not show such a false ring. The only explanation which could be suggested is that this happened to dace in the long, hot and dry summer of 1959. Apparently, this river fish came into difficulties in this milieu of stagnant water with high temperatures and water shortage to which roach is better adapted. From this point of view a general conclusion may point to the fact that ageing of fish not originating from its normal habitat should be executed with great caution.

Finally, it can be concluded from Table E that in dace measurements in caudal direction also closely

approach the actual-lengths measured at the end of each growing period.

REFERENCES

Hofstede, A. E. 1963. Growth observations of roach and dace in carp ponds. Documtie Rapp, Afd. Sportvisserij en Beroepsbinnenvisserij. No. 2. 40 pp.

Hofstede, A. E. 1970. Scale reading and back-calculation (Roach and Dace of known age). Documtie Rapp. Afd. Sportvisserij en Beroepsbinnenvisserij, No. 11, 15 pp.

Table A.   The growth observations of roach.

total length cm	Years of growth									
	1958		1959		1960		1961			
	No	a.w.	No	a.w.	No	a.w.	No	a.w.	No	a.w.
7								1 summer		
8	4	6·0							2	–
9	17	7·6			1	(7·6)			2	–
10	30	10·1	1	–	17	9·6	1	(11)		
11	3	10·0	1	–	19	11·5				
12	1 summer		1 summer		1	(11·6)	2	–	2 summers	
13					1 summer		1	–	Stray invasion	
14										
15										
16										
17									1	–
18					2-summers				2	–
19			8	–	1	(90)			3	–
20			29	–	1	(90)	4	100		
21			12	–	1	(100)	2- summers			
22			2	–	2	150				
23			2 summers		4	151	3 summers			
24					7	160	2	185		
25					11	200	1 1	205		
26					4	225	3	230		
27					3 summers		4	260	1	(210)
28							3	300		
29							4	361	4	265
30							1	(420)		
							4 summers		4 summers	

Table B. The length frequencies of the 1958 year class of roach. Under each year is given the number of fish measured with, in brackets, the number in the subsample from which scales were taken. The average weight (a.w) for each length group is also given.

length cm	1958 no.	a.w.	1959 no.	a.w.	1960 no.	a.w.	1961 no.	a.w.	1962 no.	a.w.	1963 no.	a.w.
8	4(1)	6.0										
9	17(1)	7.6										
10	30(2)	10.1										
11	3(1)	10.0										
12												
13												
14												
15												
16												
17												
18												
19			8	—								
20			29(6)	—								
21			12(1)	—								
22			2(1)	—	2	150						
23					4	151						
24					7(1)	160						
25					11(1)	200	1(1)	200				
26					4(2)	225	3(3)	230				
27							4(2)	260	3(2)	220		
28							3(2)	300	1(1)	250		
29							4(3)	361	2(2)	270	2(2)	305
30							1(1)	420	2	310	2(2)	355
31									7(4)	347	1(1)	370
32											5(5)	408
33											3(3)	540
Total number	54(5)	—	51(8)	—	28(4)	—	16(12)	—	15(9)	—	13(13)	—
Average length	9.6 (9.6)	—	20.1 (20.4)	—	24.6 (25.2)	—	27.6 (27.5)	—	29.6 (29.3)	—	31.4 (31.4)	—
Average weight	9.0	(—)	91.6	(—)	183.0	(210)	293.4	(293.4)	300	(298.9)	411.5	(411.5)

Table C. The length frequencies of the 1959 year-class of roach. The layout is the same as in Table B.

Length cm	1959 no.	a.w.	1960 no.	a.w.	1961 no.	a.w.	1962 no.	a.w.	1963 no.	a.w.
8										
9										
10	1(1)	—								
11	1(1)	—								
12										
13										
14										
15										
16										
17										
18										
19			1(1)	90						
20			1(1)	90						
21			1(1)	100						
22										
23										
24					2(2)	185				
25					1(1)	210	1	170		
26							2(2)	210		
27										
28									3(3)	276.6
Total number	2(2)	—	3(3)	—	3(3)	—	3(2)	—	3(3)	—
Average length	10.3 (10.3)	—	20.0 (20.0)	—	24.3 (24.3)	—	25.7 (26.0)	—	28.2 (28.2)	—
Average weight			93.3	(93.3)	193.3	(193.3)	196.7	(210)	276.7	(276.7)

Table.D. The length frequencies of the 1958 year class of dace. The layout is the same as in Table B.

Length cm	1958		1959		1960		1961		1962		1963	
	no.	a.w.	no.	a.w.	no.	a.w.	no.	a.w.	no.	a.w.	no.	a.w.
10	1(1)											
11	5(2)	14.0										
12	15(2)	16.0										
13	17(2)	19.4										
14												
15												
16												
17												
18												
19			1(1)									
20			7(1)									
21			11(1)									
22			9(3)									
23												
24												
25							1(1)	180				
26							1(1)	190				
27												
28											1(1)	250
29												
30												
Total number	38(7)	—	28(6)	—	—	—	2(2)	—	—	—	1(1)	—
Average length	12.3 (11.7)	— —	20.9 (20.9)	—	—	—	25.7 (25.7)	—	—	—	27.8 (27.8)	—
Average weight	17.1		86.4				185	(185)				

Table E. Back calculated lengths derived measurements made in different directions on the scales of the 1958 year class of date.

Caudal direction

Scales measured	Back-calculated lengths				
	1	2	3	4	5
2-year old dace	12.2				
4-year old dace	11.3	20.3	24.0		
6-year old dace	12.5	21.8	23.9	25.6	26.8
actual growthrate	12.3	20.9	24	25.7	27

Dorso-ventral direction

Scales measured	Back-calculated lengths				
	1	2	3	4	5
2-year old dace	11.1				
4-year old dace	9.4	19.2	22.4		
6-year old dace	10.5	19.2	22.8	25.7	26.6
actual growthrate	12.3	20.9	24	25.7	27

Oral direction

Scales measured	Back-calculated lengths				
	1	2	3	4	5
2-year old dace	9.2				
4-year old dace	7.1	18.3	22.5		
6-year old dace	9.4	19.8	23.2	25.9	26.7
actual growthrate	12.3	20.9	24	25.7	27

Scale reading and back-calculation of bream *Abramis brama* (L.) and rudd *Scardinius erythrophthalmus* (L.)

by B. STEINMETZ

The Ministry of Agriculture and Fisheries, The Netherlands

SUMMARY

1.   During the years 1967 to 1972 growth of bream was studied in ponds of the Experimental Pond Station at Beesd. The growth appeared to be faster than the growth standard used for this species in The Netherlands. It amounted to:

Maximum (cm total length)
    8   18   (28-29)*   33   38   42

Average (cm total length)
    7.4 17.0 (26.1-27.2)* 30.0 35.1 38.7

*Growth in two different ponds

2.   Scale samples were taken at the end of each growing period (late autumn or early spring) to verify the ageing method with scales and also to study the reliability of back-calculation. In 1970 and in the spring of 1973 at the end of the experiment fin rays were taken of which only a small number could be studied.

3.   Ageing by means of scale reading and back-calculation in caudal direction proved to be reliable. The actual total lengths measured in previous years and the back-calculated did not in general differ more than minus or plus one centimetre.

4.   Interruption of the growth caused by drainage of the pond in the summer of 1969 could also be checked with the back-calculation. In about 70% of the scale samples the false ring could be discerned by using six criteria mentioned in the paper. The slow growth in the fourth growing period (2.9 cm), resulted in annuli lying very close to each other which sometimes made ageing difficult.

5.   During the years 1968 to 1972 growth of rudd could also be studied in ponds of the same station. The growth amounted to:

Maximum (cm total length)
    8   17   23   25   26

Average (cm total length)
    6.8   16.2 20.1 22.4 23.0

6.   Ageing was done by means of scale reading and this proved to be reliable. The problem of annuli lying very close to each other was also encountered and, consequently, back-calculation was less easy. An experiment in which rudd were stored in concrete tanks for a week with the purpose of inducing the formation of a false ring failed to give clear results. A false ring could not be discerned because of the slow growth that year.

1.   INTRODUCTION

In The Netherlands Hofstede (1963, 1970) started his research on ageing of roach and dace of known age in the late fifties. The results of his studies were of great importance with regard to the development of a method for a rapid and practical 'appraisal of fishing waters and their fish populations'. For various reasons his programme had to be discontinued in 1963. Fortunately the present author could resume this research in 1967 when the Organization for Improvement of Inland Fisheries offered facilities in the newly built experimental station at Beesd.

The experiments reported in this paper were started with bream *Abramis brama* (L.) which is one of the most common and also one of the most problematic fish species in The Netherlands' inland waters.

The rudd *Scardinius erythrophthalmus* (L.) which is also appreciated by sport fishermen could be included in the programme in 1968.

In the spring of 1967 bream fry were produced in a spawning pond of the 'Hofer' type. They were collected in July and a certain number was released into a growing pond. The one-summer old bream were fished at the end of 1967 and a sample was measured in length and weight at which time scale samples were also taken. Once again a certain number was stocked into a growing pond to study the growth in the second year. This procedure was continued during a total period of 6 years.

Rudd fry became available in July 1968 and a programme similar to that of bream was started, and terminated 5 years after.

It is remarked that because the measurements were carried out and the ageing material collected beyond the growing period (appr. June-September) these Cyprinids had already reached the lenghts of a full year when sampled in the cold season (appr. November-March). Therefore, the ages are given in complete years. In addition to the annual collection of scales, fin rays were taken on two occasions, namely in April 1970 and at the termination of the experiment in the spring of 1973.

Scale samples were taken on the left side of the body just above the lateral line and slightly in advance of the dorsal fin. After superficial cleaning the scales were pressed between glass slides. For the determination of the lengths in previous years by means of back-calculation the mean value is taken from three well-readable scales per fish. Fin ray samples were taken from the dorsal fin. In most cases the total lengths of the fish were measured in millimetres The length frequencies are given in full centimetres (0.6 upwards and 0.5 downwards). The average lengths of the age groups, however, have been calculated from the measurements in millimetres.

Because the actual ages of the two species are known the reliability of both methods of ageing can be studied. Unfortunately, the whole collection of fin rays could not be analysed yet. In some cases, however, when scales were difficult to read the fin rays were tried. They did not prove more reliable than the scales. Furthermore, scale measurements were carried out to compare the known growth rates with the back-calculated lengths.

Weatherly's interesting statement (1972) is worth-while remembering in this respect: 'With such a re-search tool (a valid method of age determination from permanent marks laid down in the hard bony parts of the body) interpretation of populations can assume new dimensions. It sometimes becomes possible to discern and evaluate key events in the lives of animals which, though they occurred many years ago, are reflected in their pattern of growth'.

I should like to thank Mr. Hofstede for his stimulating aid to this study and also the staff of the Experi-mental Pond Station at Beesd for the invaluable assist-ance given during the execution of the experiments.

2. BREAM

2.1 Growth of bream

Table one shows the numbers stocked and cropped and the areas of the ponds concerned.

Table 1. Bream—Information on Stocking and cropping

Growing period	number stocked	number cropped	area of pond (sq. m.)
1967	500	331	1000
1968	100	88	1000
1969	50	29	1000; later on trans-planted to 2 other ponds of 1000 each
1970	20	16	1000
1971	16	12	2 ponds of 250 sq. m.
1972	12	11	500

Table 2 summarizes the average growth in length and weight, the weight increase per year and the growth standard. This is shown in figure 1.

It can be concluded that, on the average, growth was faster than the standard used in The Netherlands. However, the curve indicating the growth in the sub-sequent years is not a regular line. In particular, the growth in the 4th year was poor: about 3 cm increase in length from 27 to 30 cm. When reading the scales the following remarks on the development of the environment in the ponds may give a better under-standing.

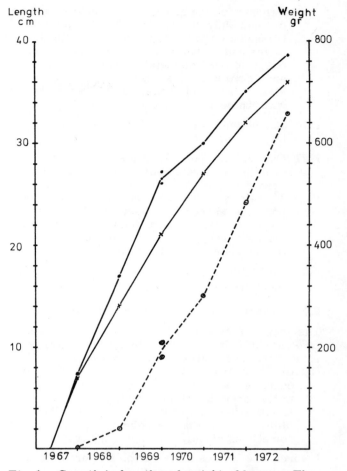

Fig. 1. Growth in length and weight of bream. The upper line represents the growth in length; the middle line shows the growth in length according to the stan-dard and the lower (dotted line) represents the growth in weight.

Growing periods

1967 At the time of cropping the one-summer old bream, 25% of the pond bottom was covered with *Elodea* sp. and *Chara* sp.

1968 The fish were stocked in December 1967. The pond had to be drained on May 24, 1968 by which time the bream were concentrated before the outlet. Because losses turned out to be lower than expected the pond was refilled. The dense vegetation of *Elodea* and *Chara* was raked up at that time.

1969 On account of a heavy growth of *Cladophora* which was assumed to exercise an unfavourable

Table 2. Bream—average growth in 6 years

Growing period in	1967	1968	1969	1970	1971	1972
age in years	1	2	3	4	5	6
average total length (cm)	7.4	17.0	26.1-27.2	30.0	35.1	38.7
average weight (gr)	3	40*	181-209	302	484	659
increase in weight per year	3	37	144-172	121 93	182	175
growth standard (cm)	7	14	21	27	32	36

*Weight calculated.

influence on the growth of bream, the pond was drained (July 2nd, 8 p.m.). The bream were transplanted to 2 other ponds (July 4th, 6 p.m.). At the end of the growing period the bottom of one pond was completely covered with *Elodea* and *Chara* while the other pond was almost clean. Growth of bream was slower in the pond with the dense vegetation.

1970 During the growing period the pond bottom was largely covered with *Elodea*.

1971 Only 2 small ponds of 250 sq. m. each were available this year. After the cropping the difference in growth turned out to be only 0.8 cm. Therefore, both crops could be mixed. In one pond bream fry were observed. The average length and weight amounted to 8.5 cm. and 5 grams at cropping time. Spawning took place in the beginning of the 5th year.

1972 Herbicides and manure were used to prevent plant growth.

2.2 Bream: ageing and back-calculation

The ageing of the one and two year old bream did not give any difficulty. However, there could have been some misinterpretations in later years due

(1) to a slow growth so that the annuli of 2 subsequent years were not easily discerned, and

(2) to the formation of a false ring in the 3rd year (see the remarks made with regard to the milieu of the ponds in the preceding paragraph), which sometimes closely resembles the true annuli.

Figures 2 to 7 gives a few samples of bream scales and fin rays of different ages.

Fig. 2. Scale of a two year old bream 16.9 cm long. The position of the first annulus is marked.

Scale measurements based on the distances between the focus and the subsequent annuli were carried out in caudal direction. In agreement with Hofstede (1970) with regard to roach and dace this is the most accurate method. In the back-calculation direct proportionality was assumed between the growth in length of the fish and the growth in caudal direction of the scales.

Reading and measuring of the scales was done with the help of a Zoom Stereo-microscope provided with

Fig. 3. Scale of a three year old bream 23.0 cm long Two annuli and one false ring are marked. (The false ring with a black spot).

Fig. 4. A dorsal fin spine cross section of a three year old bream 23.0 cm long, from the same fish as the scale in Figure 3.

an ocular micrometer. The scales were mostly read with transmitted light. All scales of one fish and usually also those of the whole group were measured by using the same number of ocular micrometer units. This means that the magnification was different. Table 3 shows the length frequencies of every age group and in brackets the number of fish from which scale samples were taken. At the bottom of this table the average lengths are compared.

The back-calculated lengths are given in Table 4 and the differences expressed in percentages to be added or to be subtracted from the calculated figure to arrive at the actual lengths measured in the field are given in brackets.

Expressed in cm. these differences amount to:

+0.9 to +1.1 for the first annulus
−0.7 to 0.0 for the second annulus
−1.7 to −0.7 for the false ring
−0.4 to +0.2 for the third annulus
−0.8 to −0.3 for the fourth annulus
+0.2 for the fifth annulus

Table 3. Bream—length frequencies 1967-1973

Length cm	1967 no.	1968 no.	1969 no.			1970 no.		1971 no.	1972 no.
6	1*								
7	15 (4)								
8	8 (3)								
9									
10									
11									
12									
13									
14									
15									
16		24 (9)							
17		48 (6)		4-7-'69†					
18		16		1					
19				4					
20				3					
21				2					
22									
23									
24			1						
25			3						
26			4		2 (2)	5‡			
27			4		9 (4)	10	1 (1)		
28			1		4 (3)	5	3 (3)		
29					1 (1)		4 (3)		
30							1 (1)		
31							4 (4)		
32							2 (2)		
33							1 (1)	3 (3)	
34								2 (2)	
35								3 (3)	
36								2 (1)	
37								1 (1)	3 (3)
38								1 (1)	2 (2)
39									2 (2)
40									2 (2)
41									3 (3)
42									1 (1)
Total no.	331	88	13		16	20	16	12	11
Average length	7.4 (7.3)	17.0 (16.5)	26.1		27.2 (27.2)	27.1	30.0 (30.0)	35.1 (35.0)	38.7 (38.7)

*Length frequency of sample. Between brackets: number of scale sample and average lengths.

†The pond was drained in the beginning of July and 32 bream were collected, 10 of which were measured: average length 19.9 cm; average weight 78 gr. The fish were restocked in two other ponds.

‡ Length frequency of the mixed bream population originating from the two ponds of 1969 measured at the beginning of the fourth growing period.

Table 4. Bream—back-calculated lengths in caudal direction and correction in percentage between brackets for five years

Age	Back-calculated length at the end of						
	1967	1968	False ring	1969	1970	1971	1972
2	6.3 (+17.5)						
3	6.3 (+17.5)	17.1 (—0.6)	20.6 (—3.4)				
4	6.3 (+17.5)	17.0 (0)	21.1 (—5.7)	26.9 (+0.7)			
5	6.5 (+16.9)	17.7 (—4.0)	21.6 (—7.9)	27.4 (—1.1)	30.3 (—1.0)		
6	6.3 (+17.5)	17.6 (—3.4)	21.6 (—7.9)	27.5 (—1.5)	30.8 (—2.7)	34.9 (+0.6)	
Actual length	7.4	17.0	19.9	27.1*	30.0	35.1	38.7

*For average length at the beginning of 1970, see Table 3.

Some complications with regard to the ageing of this bream generation were mentioned in the beginning of this paragraph. They were studied thoroughly.

Table 5 demonstrates the conclusions and the experience gained for the six year old bream. It was noted that, in particular, the growth in the 4th year was poor (Figs. 5 and 6). The average increase in length measured in the field amounted to 2.9 cm while the average of the back-calculation is 3.3 cm. When reading the scale samples of these 6-year old bream there appeared to be 3 samples in which the 3rd and the 4th year rings could not clearly be distinguished (marked with asterisks in Table 5). In these fish the back-calculated increase in length amounted to 2.5, 0.8 and 1.8 cm respectively with such a small increase in length the year rings are formed so close to each other that they cannot be safely discerned. In the present case these made up 3 out of the 11 samples. The corresponding fin rays did not give the exact age either.

The last column of Table 5 gives the back-calculated location of the false ring formed in the 3rd year

(1969). When applying the following 6 criteria which are well-known (Chugunova, 1963; Tesch, 1968) in 8 of

Fig. 6. Scale of a six year old bream 36.7 cm long. Five annuli and one false ring are marked.

Fig. 5. Scale of a four year old bream 27.8 cm long. Three annuli with a false ring between them are marked.

Fig. 7. A dorsal fin spine cross section of a six year old bream 38.6 cm long.

Table 5. Bream—6 years old

| Scale sample no | length | Calculated length at the end of | | | | | False ring 1969 |
		1st group	2nd group	3rd group	4th group	5th group	
21024	36.7 ♂	6.1	17.1	27.5	29.4	32.7	(21.1)
21025	37.0 "	6.2	17.6	26.8	29.3*	33.0	(21.3)
21026	37.4 "	6.2	17.5	26.2	29.0	33.3	(21.5)
21027	38.1 "	6.3	18.8	27.9	30.5	34.0	22.6
21028	38.2 "	6.1	17.1	26.5	30.8	34.9	(21.1)
21029	38.6 "	6.7	18.8	29.6	30.4*	34.7	(23.5)
21030	38.7 "	6.2	17.5	27.9	29.7*	34.6	21.4
21031	39.8 ♀	7.2	18.6	28.9	32.9	37.1	(22.8)
21032	39.8 "	5.8	16.7	26.8	32.1	36.6	(20.7)
21033	39.9 "	5.9	17.3	27.4	31.9	36.2	21.3
21034	41.3 "	6.1	16.5	27.0	32.8	36.9	(20.6)
Average length 38.7		6.3	17.6	27.5	30.8	34.9	(21.6)
Correction in %—		+17.5	—3.4	—1.5	—2.7	+0.6	—7.9
Actual length 38.7		7.4	17.0	27.1	30.0	35.1	19.9

Between brackets: false ring which could be distinguished from real annuli or were hardly discernible

*Difficult, annuli are very close to each other.

the 11 samples the false ring could be recognized. For all the scale samples of bream of three to six years this was about 70%.

— Using three scales per fish for back-calculation, each annulus has to be found on each of the three selected scales.
— The annulus must clearly be visible on all parts (oral, caudal, dorso-ventral) of the scale.
— On the dorso-ventral part of the scale cut-off circuli characterize the annuli.
— On the oral part of the scale the circuli of the annulus is/are more or less dotted/interrupted.
— On the scales of older fish the annuli of later years are sometimes formed as ledges. By changing light they become black on the caudal part of the scale.
— The true annuli of a scale have about the same light-intensity while a false ring is mostly less clear.

In addition to these six criteria there is another one which has been already mentioned: it may be assumed that the growth of a yearclass in a sound habitat will be regular. Therefore a growth of 7.4 — 17.0 — 19.9 — 27.1 — 30.0 needs further consideration. It has to be doubted whether such a growth with an increase in length of only 2.9 centimetres in a certain 'Year' could occur in a normal habitat.

3. RUDD

3.1 Growth of rudd

The research was started with 500 fry which became available in July 1968 after an angling experiment on rudd.

Table 6 shows the numbers stocked and cropped and the areas of the ponds.

Table 6 Rudd—information on stocking and cropping

growing period	number stocked	number cropped	area of pond (sq.m.)
1968	500	406	1000
1969	50	48	1000
	100	96	1000
1970	38	33	1000
1971	18	15	250
	15	15	250
1972	15	15	500

In Table 7 the average growth in length and weight and the weight increase per year are presented.

Table 7. Rudd—average growth in 5 years

growing period in	1968	1969	1970	1971	1972
Age in years	1	2	3	4	5
average total length (cm)	6.8	16.2	20.3	21.2-22.4	23.0
average weight (gr)	3	48	94	127-152	153
increase in weight per year	3	45	46	33-58	26-1

In Figure 8 the data on average growth in length and weight are given. The growth of the rudd was good during the first three years though later on it slowed down. Some information regarding the environment in the ponds is given below.

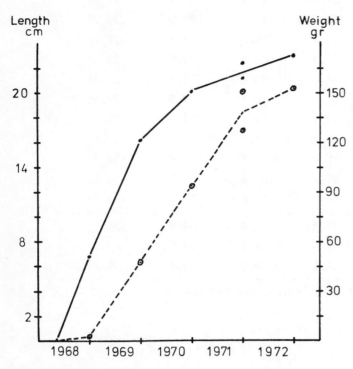

Fig. 8. Graph of growth rate of rudd. The continuous upper line represents the growth in length and the lower line of dashes represents the weight.

1968 During the summer rather heavy vegetation developed, mainly of *Chara* sp., *Utricularia vulgaris* L., *Polygonum amphibium* L., *Glyceria maxima* Holmb. This vegetation was mown in the middle of August.

1969 At the end of June the bottom of the pond with the low stocking density was completely covered with *Chara* sp. and *Elodea* sp. The second pond was almost clear. The experiment was continued with rudd of the low stocking density, which showed an average growth of 6.8 to 16.0 instead of 6.8 to 15.0.

1970 During this year a heavy plant growth of *Elodea* sp. developed.

1971 In 1971 three ponds of 250 sq. m. each were available. One pond was stocked with 18 rudd (average length 19.8 cm) of which 15 (average length 21.2) were cropped in October 1971. Another pond was stocked with 15 rudd (average length 20.5 cm). This pond was drained on 6 August and 7 rudd were immediately stocked in a pond of 250 sq. m., while the other 8 got a fin mark.(average length of these 15 rudd—22.0 cm). These latter 8 fish were kept in a storage tank for one week to induce a false ring in the scales. After that storage the 8 rudd were put into the same pond with the other seven. In October 15 rudd (average length 22.4 cm) were collected.

1972 Herbicides and manure were used to prevent plant growth.

3.2 Rudd: ageing and back-calculation

Table 8 shows the total length frequency of every age group and within brackets the number of fish from which scale samples were taken. At the bottom of this table the average lengths are compared. Figures 9 and 10 gives a few samples of rudd scales of different ages. Scale reading of rudd was done similarly to the bream. The results are presented in Table 9.

Fig. 9. A scale of a three year old rudd 21.2 cm in length. Two annuli are marked.

Fig. 10. A scale of a five year old rudd 24.4 cm in length. Four annuli are marked.

The difference between the actual length measured in the field in previous years and the back-calculated lengths correspond very well. Expressed in centimetres these differences amount to:

0 to +0.5 for the first annulus
—1.1 to —0.7 for the second annulus
—0.7 to —0.4 for the third annulus
—0.4 for the fourth annulus

In Table 10 the back-calculated lengths of the 15 rudd that were left at the end of the experiment are presented. All scales could be read, but when the growth

Table 8. Rudd—yearclass 1968—length frequencies of total length, 1968-1973

Length cm	1968 no.	1969 no.	1970 no.	1971 no.	no.	1972 no.
6	17 (4)					
7	35 (6)					
8	1					
9						
10						
11						
12		1				
13		-				
14		1 (2)				
15		10 (2)				
16		20 (1)				
17		16 (3)				
18			2			
19			10 (3)			
20			9 (3)	3 (3)		
21			8 (2)	7 (6)	6 (4)	1 (1)
22			2	5 (5)	2 (2)	7 (7)
23			2 (1)		4 (3)	3 (3)
24					2 (3)	1 (1)
25					1	2 (2)
26						1 (1)
Total no.	406	48	33	15	15	15
Average length	6.8	16.2	20.1	21.2*	22.4*	23.0†
	(6.6)	(15.7)	(20.3)	(21.3)	(22.4)	(23.0)

*Average length at the beginning of the growing period 1971: 19.8 cm and 20.5 cm instead of 20.1 cm

†Id. 1972: —21.6 cm (mixed population originating from the two ponds of 1971).

diminished it became less easy to measure the scales in caudal direction.

Therefore the scales sampled in the years 1971 and 1972 were back-calculated in dorso-ventral direction, where the annuli are better discernible when the growth slows down. The differences between the actual lengths and the back-calculated ones for both directions are small, except for the first year. It should be possible, using the zoom microscope, to measure the first annulus in caudal direction and the other annuli in dorso-ventral direction. But in that case the total number of micrometre units has to be kept constant.

4. DISCUSSION

Hofstede (1970) stated that the scales of roach and dace, which grow fast, were very transparant and were easily read in all directions. He proved that the back-calculated lengths, based on measurements in the caudal direction, correspond closely to the actual lengths determined in previous years. The differences found amounted to the limits of minus or plus one centimetre.

In our study the scales of the younger bream, one- to three-year old, and the scales of the five age groups of rudd, were clear. The older bream scales were darker. Two problems however, presented themselves namely

(1) the formation of a false ring in the scales of bream, which sometimes closely resembled a true annulus and
(2) periods of slow growth resulting into the formation of annuli so close to each other that in a number of scale samples the annuli were difficult to discern.

The false ring in the bream scales in about 30 percent of the scale samples was not different in appearance from the true second annulus. In general the first and the second annulus are somewhat less pronounced than the following annuli, which made the problem of this false ring in the third growing period more complex. To prevent an error in ageing the special event of the pond drainage in 1969 had to be known. The ageing problem caused by the annuli laying very close to each other could not be solved completely in bream. Some doubts (Table 5) have to be taken into account, especially in the cases with regard to the back-calculation. Normally the growth

Table 9. Rudd—back-calculated length in caudal direction and correction in percentage between brackets for four years

Age	Back-calculated length at the end of				
	1968	1969	1970	1971	1972
2	6.3 (+7.9)				
3	6.7 (+1.5)	16.9 (—4.1)			
4	6.6 (+3.0)	16.9 (—4.1)	20.2 (—2.0)		
4	6.6 (+3.0)	17.3 (—6.4)	21.2 (—3.3)		
5	6.8 (0)	17.2 (—5.8)	20.8 (—3.4)	22.0 (—1.8)	
Actual Length	6.8	16.2	*	21.6[†]	23.0

*The actual length at the end of the third growing period (1970) versus the calculated lengths were respectively 19.8 — 20.2; 20.5 — 21.2 and 20.1 — 20.8 (See table 8).

†Average length at the beginning of the growing period 1972- 21.6 cm.

Table 10. Rudd—5 years old

Scale no	sample length	Calculated length at the end of			
		1st group	2nd group	3rd group	4th group
21061	21.5 ♂(mature)	7.0	16.7	19.3	21.0
21062	21.7 " (")	5.9	16.6	20.1	21.0
21063	21.9 " (")	6.9	16.8	19.2	20.6
21064	22.1 " (")	6.8	15.9	19.7	20.9
21065	22.4 " (")	6.1	16.3	20.5	21.4
21066	22.4 " (")	6.7	17.6	20.9	22.0
21067	22.4 " (")	7.2	18.2	20.6	21.5
21068	22.4 " (")	7.1	16.8	19.6	21.3
21069	22.7 " (")	7.3	17.7	20.9	21.8
21070	22.9 " (")	6.3	17.1	21.4	22.4
21071	23.0 " (")	6.6	17.9	21.0	22.1
21072	24.4 (")	7.3	17.7	22.3	23.4
21073	24.6 " (")	5.7	16.7	21.6	22.8
21074	24.6 " (")	7.2	17.5	22.1	23.6
21075	25.6 " (")	7.5	18.3	23.4	24.4
Average length 23.0		6.8 (5.4)	17.2 (14.9)	20.8 (19.1)	22.0 (21.4)
Correction in % —		0 (+25.9)	—5.8 (+8.7)	—3.4 (+5.2)	—1.8 (+0.9)
Actual length		6.8	16.2	20.1	21.6

Within brackets: The back-calculated length and the corresponding correction in % when the scales are measured in dorso-ventral direction.

conditions will be less variable from smaller and larger ponds, plant growth etc., resulting in a more regular growth.

There were no doubts when ageing the rudd, only the measurement of these annuli lying close to each other was difficult. This could be improved by better cleaning of the scales (more than superficially) or by measuring the scales in two directions as indicated in paragraph 3.2. The conclusion of Hofstede that the variation of all back-calculated data (in caudal direction) of the average lengths of the year-classes in previous years lies between minus and plus one centimetre, is also applicable to bream and rudd. Thus it can be concluded that Weatherly's wish mentioned in the introduction of this paper is already fulfilled for the most important cyprinids of the bream zone, namely bream, roach and rudd. Besides that it holds true for another cyprinid, the dace. Therefore it seems reasonable to expect that the ageing of other cyprinids as for example white bream, can be tackled in the same way.

However, great attention should be paid to the environment because a river fish in a pond (Hofstede 1970) or a bream in a small pond which had to be drained during the summer can have false rings or crowded annuli in their scales.

As was mentioned before an attempt was made to induce a false ring in the scales of rudd by storing them for a period of seven days in a concrete tank. The false ring however, could not be discerned in the scales at the end of the year, because the growth after the storage appeared to be poor (0.4 cm).

Some fin rays (Fig.4 and 7) were used to study the problem of the false ring in bream. They were read by three persons aquainted with the procedure, but the fin rays did not give the exact age.

REFERENCES

Chuganova, N. I. 1963. Age and growth studies in fish. Jerusalem. 132 pp.
Translation of Chuganova N. 1.1959. Rukovodstvo po izucheniya vozrasta i rosta ryb. Moscow.

Deelder, C.L. and Willemse, J.J. 1973. Age determination of freshwater teleosts based on annular structures in fin rays. Aquaculture. 1 (4), 4 365-371.

Hofstede, A.E. 1963. Groeiwaarnemingen van blankvoorn en serpeling in karpervijvers. Documtie Rapp. Afdeling Sportvisserij en Beroepsbinnenvisserij, No. 2.

Hofstede, A.E. 1970. Scale reading and back-calculation (Roach and dace of known age). Documtie Rapp. Afdeling Sportvisserij en Beroepsbinnenvisserij, No. 11, 15 pp.

Hofstede, A.E. 1971. De Beoordeling van de Brasemstand. Documtie Rapp. Afdeling Sportvisserij en Beroepsbinnenvisserij, No. 12, 36 pp.

Tesch, F.W. 1968. Age and growth. In 'Methods for assessment of fish production in fresh water', Ed. W. E. Ricker. I.B.P. Handbook No 3. Blackwell, Oxford. pp. 93-123.

Weatherly, A.H. 1972. Growth and Ecology of Fish Populations. Academic Press, London. 293 pp.

An account of some methods of overcoming errors in ageing tropical and subtropical fish populations when the hard tissue growth markings are unreliable and the data sparse*

by C. P. MATHEWS†

Programa Mexico/F.A.O., Instituto Nacional de Pesca, Apartado Postal M-10778, Mexico (1)

INTRODUCTION

The methods of ageing fish from markings on scales, otoliths and bones, which was the primary subject of the Symposium, have been developed mainly for temperate species. These are often impossible to apply to tropical freshwater or marine fish, even though Fagade (1974, this volume pages 71 to 77) has shown that in some circumstances markings are laid down in tropical fish which can be used for ageing.

It is the object of this paper to present some results obtained when using other methods of age determination of populations (as opposed to individuals) and to discuss the various advantages and disadvantages of these methods both with respect to difficulties arising from the poor quality of the available material and from less than ideal quantities of data.

During the year March 1971—March 1972 the Instituto Nacional de Pesca's Research Vessel Alejandro de Humboldt carried out a series of exploratory and prospective fishing cruises in the Gulf of California. Some results of this work are given by Mathews, Granados and Arvizu (1974), and Mathews (in press). The areas fished lie between latitude 20° and 32° N., at depths from 10 to 1000 m. It was necessary to obtain growth rate estimates of several species of fish and in several instances difficulties were experienced in determining the ages from otoliths and other hard structures. It was also desirable to make age determinations from sparse material. As a result several different methods of age determination were tried.

METHODS

Attention will be confined to four species: *Merluccius angustimanus*, a small hake found in the south eastern Gulf of California; *Merluccius* sp, found in the northern Gulf of California; *Nezumia steglipedlis*, the California rat tail (sometimes called 'boca chica' in Mexico), and an unknown species of ling-like fish, possibly a brotulid, called 'lengua dorada' or golden ling because of its distinctive coppery golden colour. The first two species are usually captured scaleless because their scales, which are only loosely attached to the skin, are usually removed by friction in the cod end of the otter trawl used as a sampling tool (Mathews, Granados and Arvizu, 1973). The rat tail has only very small scales while the golden ling is naturally scaleless. Otoliths were taken where possible, but those of the golden ling were difficult to obtain and did not seem promising.

---

* This paper does not necessarily represent the views of F.A.O.
† Present address: Department of Fisheries, E.S.C.M., University of Baja California, B.C., Mexico.

The graphical method of separating age groups devised by Cassie (1954) was applied when suitable data were obtained, and NORMSEP, a computer programme written by Tomlinson (Abramson, 1971) for separating normal distributions from size frequency distributions was used in an attempt to separate the various age groups in one of the populations.

Otoliths were read according to the procedures developed at the Fishery Laboratory, Lowestoft and presented by Williams and Bedford (1974) in this Symposium volume.

RESULTS

Pairs of otoliths from 88 *Merluccius angustimanus*, the small Gulf of California hake, were obtained, and ages were awarded to 84 of these hake while 4 pairs of otoliths had to be discarded. For work on this species two otolith readers were available and carried out their work independently. The otoliths were difficult to read, multiple annuli were often present and the differences between opaque and hyaline zones were sometimes difficult to determine. In spite of these difficulties, exact agreement was obtained in 90% of good and very good otoliths and 70% of bad and very bad ones. However, the growth curve obtained was highly irregular, and the size frequency distributions of 2 and 3 year olds were bimodal. A revision of the age determinations was carried out as it seemed likely that some of the two and three year olds, and three and four year olds had been confused. The final readings placed the larger 2 annulus fish with the smaller three annulus group, and the larger three annulus fish with the four annulus group. Mathews (in press) has shown the resulting size frequency distributions for each age group and Fig. 1 shows the fitted von Bertalanffy curve and the growth curve based on the otoliths. The fit obtained was acceptable. It is tempting to assume that a fairly close fit of this type justifies the procedure leading up to it. However, the necessity for reviewing and frequently adjusting the age data in the light of a hypothesis the author finds intellectually acceptable throws doubt on the objectivity of the final age determinations, so the method of Cassie (1954) was applied to the size frequency distribution of a sample of 1105 *M. angustimanus*. Fig. 2 shows the results. Table 1 shows the results of age determinations from Cassie's technique and from otoliths. Both methods show that there are five year classes for fish from 5 to 29 cm long. One disadvantage of Cassie's method is that, because the older fish grow more slowly, they tend to be crowded into the upper part of the percentage cumulative frequency curve; therefore a larger number of size classes is necessary. For *M. angustimanus* only 24 size classes, each 1 cm

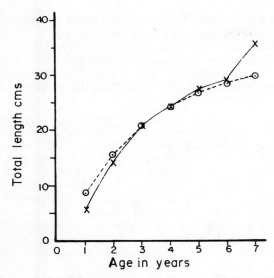

Fig. 1. Growth curves for *Merluccius angustimanus* determined from:-

x——x a sample of 84 pairs of otoliths after revision of ages.

⊙----⊙ fitted von Bertalanffy curve.

Table I. Growth in *M.angustimanus*

| Age-years | Total length (cms) | | | |
	From *otolites mean lengths	From Cassie curve (Fig. 2)	From Cassie curve (Fig. 3)	From NORM-SEP (Fig. 4)
		†		
1	—	8	7.9	7.9
2	12-16	16	19.8	20.1
3	20.5	22.5	22.2	24.5
4	25.0	25.0	23.7	29.5
5	27.0	28.5	29.3	
6	29.0			
7	35.5			

* Mathews in press.   † Median values.

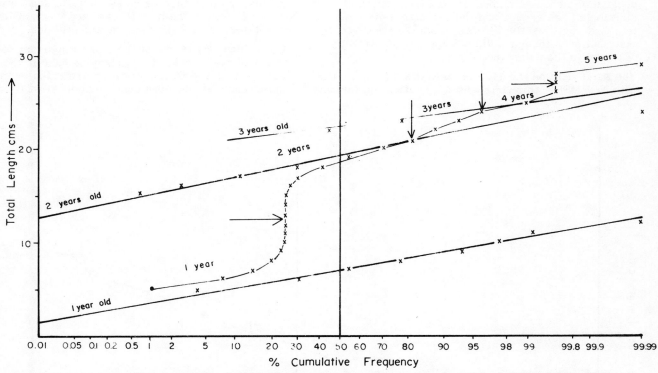

Fig. 2. Cassie curve for a sample of 1105 *Merluccius angustimanus* captured in April and May 1971 The continuous curve represents the percentage cumulative frequency of the whole sample, and the oblique straight lines represent the percentage cumulative frequency in each age group. Arrows (↓) indicate points chosen as dividing the successive age groups. Successive segments of the percentage total frequency curve have been broken into five year classes, each of which has been allocated an age from 1 to 5 years.

wide, were available so that data from 3 to 5 year old fish are crowded into the band covering 22-29 cm fish. Because of this crowding there are too few data points available and mean lengths of the age groups separated by Cassie's method cannot be determined accurately. Therefore median values have been given in Table 1, and they compare quite favourably with means obtained from otolith readings. The fairly close agreement between these two methods of age

determination makes it likely that both give substantially correct results.

During the ageing of fish by means of annuli in otoliths, either a sufficiently large collection of material must be available so that annual laying down of annuli may be demonstrated, or else this must be assumed. For *M.angustimanus* it was assumed that one annulus was laid down each year. This is probably true. However, both the Petersen and Cassie methods demonstrated the existence of an age group (5-12 cm fish, Fig. 2) whose otoliths showed no distinct annulus (Mathews, in press) and both of these methods are useful in showing the omission of the first year class. Data shown in Table 1 have been adjusted so as to compensate for this error.

NORMSEP was also used in distinguishing age groups of *M.angustimanus* and was applied to the size frequency distribution of the same 1105 fish. When NORMSEP is used it is necessary to specify the number of age groups and the expected limits to their standard deviations. The output includes mean length and standard deviation of each age group, the calculated size frequency distribution for the whole sample (1105 fish), and an estimate of χ^2 for the difference between the calculated and the observed size frequency distribution. The computational method is based on maximum likelihood (Abramson, 1971). Fig. 3 shows the Cassie curve obtained from the output when the growth data from otolith readings (Table 1) were used in making the necessary programme specifications. It is very similar to the curve shown in Fig. 2. The mean lengths at each age (Table 1, column 4) are, however, rather distinct and $\chi^2 = 16$ at 7 degrees of freedom with $p \doteq .02$. The programme choose the best fit, for five normally distributed age groups and the calculated distribution was significantly different from the observed distribution, although it did not appear significantly different to the uninstructed eye.

The same data on the 1105 *M.angustimanus* were run with NORMSEP, this time with a specification for only four age groups. The resulting Cassie curve is shown in Fig. 4 and the mean length at each age in Table 1, column 6; $\chi^2 \doteq 15$ at 10 degrees of freedom, and $p = 0.1$, so that the calculated size frequency for four 'age' groups, which is biologically meaningless, is not significantly different from the observed one for five age groups.

The curve shown in Fig. 4, for four groups, is a far better fit to the observed data than the curve calculated for five age groups, which was statistically significantly different from that obtained directly from the sample of 1105 fish. These results encourage scepticism, not only in interpreting the results of NORMSEP, but also those from Cassie's curves. Cassie curves are probably very sensitive to slight changes in the location of the dividing line between age groups and to slight deviations from normality; both of which could cause major differences in interpretation. Where the Cassie curve is smooth—and that shown in Fig. 4 is typical of some observed Cassie curves in this respect—it may also be difficult to distinguish age classes. Perhaps Cassie curves should be used sparingly and where possible independent confirmation should be sought. NORMSEP may be used in distinguishing age groups only if it is possible to specify the number of age groups, and may then be most useful in separating these. However, the best fit obtained from NORMSEP is not necessarily the most meaningful one.

The golden ling is one of the more important constituents of the by catch accompanying hake in the Northern Gulf of California; they are eaten by the hake, reach 50 cms long and provide a first class

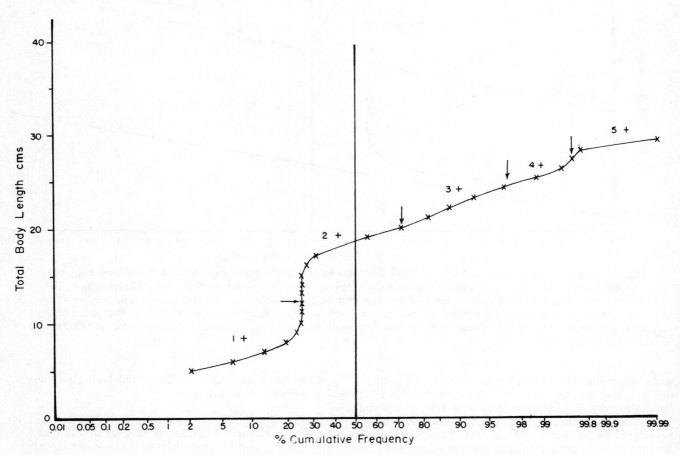

Fig. 3. Cassie curve derived from the computer programme NORMSEP when programme was given the specifications which included 5 age groups from 7 to 29 cm. These specifications were thought to be biologically meaningful. Note the similarity to Fig. 2.

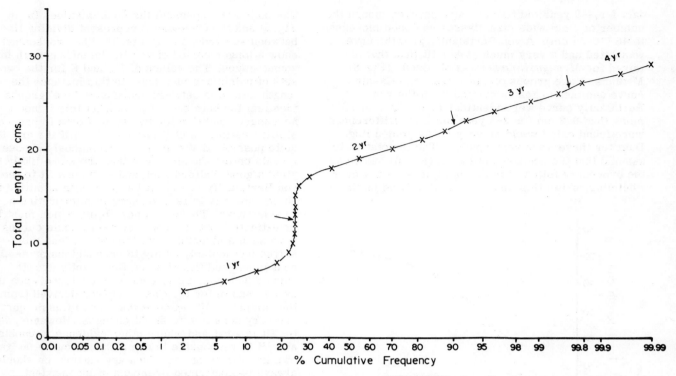

Fig. 4. Cassie curve derived from the computer programme NORMSEP when the programme was given specifications which included 4 age groups from 7 to 29 cm. These specifications were thought to be biologically meaningless.

white flesh eminently suitable for human consumption. Attempts to estimate the age of golden ling were therefore made even though no otoliths or other hard structures were available. Fig. 5 shows the Cassie curve for a sample of 1268 golden ling, with the percentage cumulative frequencies for each age group. The lines for each age group are very nearly rectilinear. Although the data for three year old fish suggest a slightly sigmoidal curve, which would imply some mixing with two and four year old fish, this suggestion is so slight as to be negligible. The medians were used in estimating growth rates, as

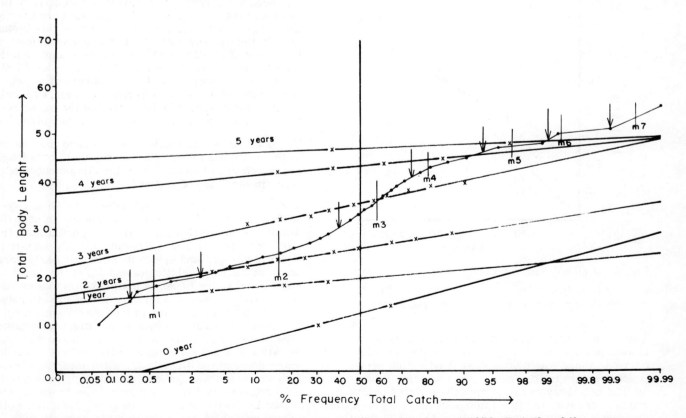

Fig. 5. Cassie curve for a sample of 1268 golden ling collected in August 1972. Details of the curve construction as in Fig. 2. m1 to m7 are the median length for the respective age groups.

data for 4-6 year old fish are sparse, even though the number of 1 cm wide size classes has been increased to 46 (10-56 cm). A von Bertalanffy growth curve was fitted and a very much closer fit than that obtained for *M.angustimanus* was obtained. (Fig. 6). Medians of age groups obtained from the Cassie curve and mean ages calculated from the von Bertalanffy curve were identical, or differed by no more than 0.2 cm for 2-6 year old fish. Differences were found only for old or very young golden ling. Data for these were very sparse. The temptation to assume that the goodness of the fit (Fig. 6) justifies the procedure followed in obtaining it is nearly overwhelming, and in this instance could well be justified.

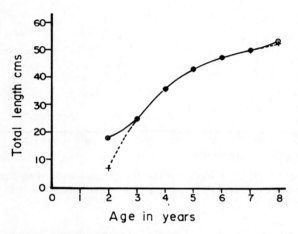

Fig. 6. Growth curves of golden ling.

+----+ derived from the Cassie curve Fig. 5.
o——o filled von Bertalanffy curve.

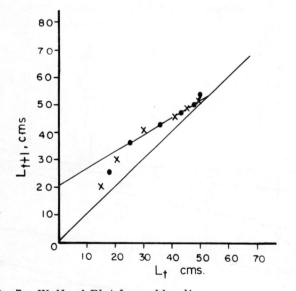

Fig. 7. Walford Plot for golden ling

● = median values from the Cassie curve Fig. 5.
x = dividing points between age groups Fig. 5.

The dividing lines between age groups were all chosen prior to the fitting of the von Bertalanffy curve so there was no question of adjusting inflection points to fit a desired hypothesis. However, as it is not always easy to pick the precise points which represent dividing lines between age groups, an element of subjectivity is involved. Fig.7 shows the Walford Plot for golden ling; the line drawn by eye.

The points (•) represent the median values (m in Fig. 5) and the crosses (x) represent dividing lines between age groups (↓ in Fig. 5). The crosses (x) show a longer period of von Bertalanffy growth in the young stages. The values of $L\infty$ and K for the two sets of points are identical. In this instance the length intervals between successive 'age' groups are identical for both sets of points, but this is not a necessary condition for two sets of data to produce similar estimates of K and $L\infty$. Even if it were, it is quite possible that one may unconsciously choose intervals on the Cassie curve that are more likely to yield a good Walford Plot, and so a good fit to the von Bertalanffy model. It has just been admitted that some subjectivity is necessary in interpreting a Cassie curve. There is a possibility which must be investigated further: could certain Cassie curves have such a structure that they would lend themselves particularly easily to unconscious or semiconscious good fits of a von Bertalanffy growth curve? The possibility cannot be excluded, even if, as was shown for the Cassie curves derived from the sample of *M. angustimanus,* some Cassie curves are very sensitive to slight changes. However, where the fit is good, and where other evidence is unobtainable, it is reasonable to use a Cassie curve on its own in estimating age. Such age estimation should always be confirmed by means of independent methods as soon as possible.

Fig. 8 shows the Cassie curve from the catch curve of of a sample of 11, 964 California rat tail. It is very difficult to break the curve into separate age groups, and in spite of several attempts carried out on different occasions no consistent result could be obtained without reference to the otoliths available. The two sets of arrows in Fig. 8 show results of two different attempts. The arrows with numbers may perhaps be more precise, but it is clear that there has been a considerable element of subjectivity in the choice of these points. The Cassie curve is therefore discarded; Cassie's method in this instance was distinctly less reliable than age determination by means of otoliths, even though the sample available (44 pairs) was very small. A very good fit of the von Bertalanffy model to the observed growth curve derived from otoliths was obtained, with calculated and observed points showing the same extremely close agreement as they did for golden ling.

The poor results from the Cassie curve may be due to the small size of the rat tail (up to 30 cms long) compared to the mesh size of the equipment used (4.5 cm mesh in the cod end).

The large Gulf of California hake is a fish of possible commercial importance; Mathews (in preparation) has shown that there are two populations, the northern one with faster growing, usually mature fish which ripen and spawn in winter or early spring, and a southern population (about 5% of the whole population) which consists mainly of immature and unripe fish. Precise determination of growth rates was more important than in the other species, so that a rather larger sample of otoliths was obtained (704 pairs). Age length keys were constructed and growth rates were determined from these. Growth rates determined directly from the mean lengths of fish whose otoliths (or other hard parts) are available sometimes differ markedly from those determined by means of age length keys. This is a well known source of error. With male hake there is no difference, but the difference for females is very

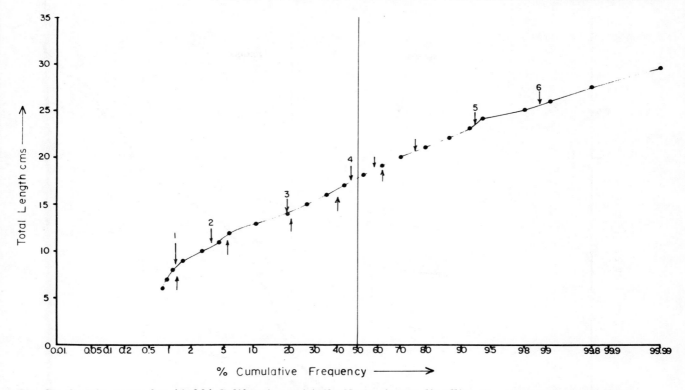

Fig. 8. Cassie curve for 11, 964 Californian rat tails *Nezumia steglipedlis*. Curve construction as in Fig. 2. Arrows with and without numbers denote two separate attempts to distinguish age groups. No consistent interpretation could be obtained without reference to otolith readings.

marked. This is because the length range of the females of known age is very large; while there are about 3×10^6 fish in the 60-70 cm size group, there are only about 200, 000 in the 80-90 cm size group, so that the mean length of fish of a given age in the sample may be very different from the mean length of fish in the population. It seemed appropriate to determine the differences that such errors would lead to, and Fig. 9 shows the graphs $L_{t+1} - L_t$ against L_t for males and females from data derived from age length keys and directly from the lengths of the fish whose ages were determined. Fig. 9a shows that the estimates of L_∞ may vary by over 20 cm.

Fig. 10 shows the Cassie curve for northern female hake; this curve was derived from a sample of 14, 363 fish with a size range from 8 to 107 cm long, so that both the sample and size range should be adequate. In spite of the size of the sample there is some difficulty in determining the dividing lines between different age groups; the cumulative percentage size frequency distributions of each age group are also shown, and there is a suggestion in several of them of mixing of age groups. However, the error is not very large, at least compared to other errors. Table 2 compares the growth rates of northern females obtained in the three different ways discussed.

Close agreement between growth rates determined from age length keys and the Cassie curve exists only for 1 and 2 year old fish. Fish 21-32 cm long may be either 2 or 3 years old; mean lengths of 2 and 3 year old fish are very close (25. 2 and 30 cms long). While 2 year olds vary from 14 to 36 cm long, 3 year olds vary from 24 to 41 cm long. There is a very considerable overlap between 2 and 3 year olds and it was not possible to distinguish clearly between these age groups by means of the Cassie curve, which has yielded a single age group of mean size 26. 0 cm.

This is rather closer to the mean for 2 year olds than that for 3 year olds because of the greater abundance of 2 year olds. A catch curve also showed that 4 year old hake (35 cm long) were under represented.

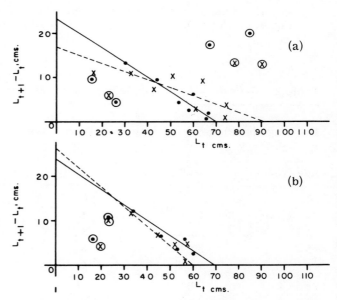

Fig. 9. Graphs of $L_{t+1} - L_t$ for *Merluccius* sp.
   (a) Females   (b) Males

● = age length key data with———least squares regression line.
x = otolith reading age data with - - - least squares regression line.

Data in circles were not used in the calculations because of aberrant growth. Females 12 years and over probably enter a new growth stanza, while juveniles grow more slowly than would be expected.

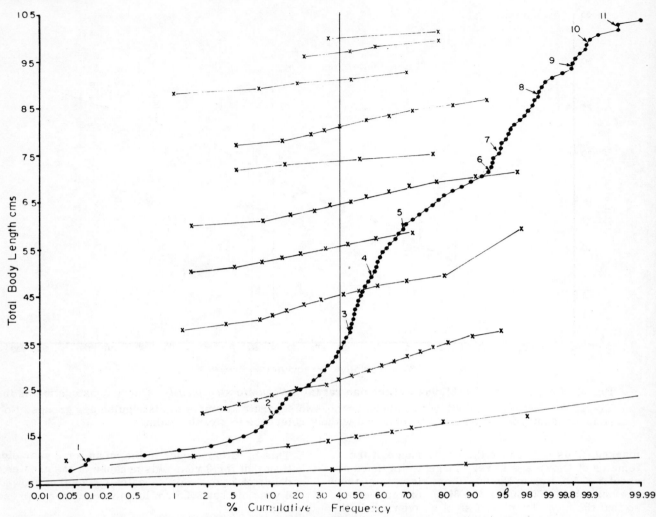

Fig. 10. Cassie curve for female Gulf of California Hake *Merluccius* sp. Construction details as in Fig. 2. Each numbered arrow gives the estimated age of the segment of the curve which lies above it.

Table 2. Growth rates of female hake from the Northern Gulf of California

From age length key		From Cassie curve		From* catch curve and otolith readings	
Age (years)	Length (cm)	Age (years)	Length (cm)	Age (years)	Length (cm) (otoliths only)
0		0	6.5		
1	15.7	1	14.5	1	15.3
2	25.2	2	26.0	2-3	26.3
3	30.3	3	45.0	4	32.2
4	42.9	4	55.5	5, 6, 7	43.3
5	53.0	5	64.5	8, 9, 10	50.6
6	57.7	6	75.0	10, 11, 12	61.1
7	60.0	7	81.0	12	64.2
8	66.0	8	90.5		73.8
9	67.0	9	96.5		74.5
10	68.7	10	101.0		78.3
11	67.7	11			91.9
12	82.6	12			89.8
13	105.0				103.0

* From North and South of Tiburon; data are almost identical to those for Northern females only.

Mathews (in preparation) shows that this is not caused by poor recruitment to this year class, but that it is associated with sexual maturation and a difference in the migratory pattern for fish at this stage in their life cycle. In spite of the under representation of these fish, the Cassie curve has allowed distinction of a year class for fish at 45.0 cm (apparently three year olds), which is close to that for 4 year olds determined from the age length key (42.0 cm). However, there seems to be no relation between the mean lengths for older age groups determined by means of the age length key and from the Cassie curve. Use of the Cassie curve alone would, for female hake, have lead to gross errors in age determination. This underlines the need for using Cassie curves only when other techniques are available for confirming results so obtained. In this particular instance the form of the growth curve obtained from the Cassie curve is highly irregular and this would suggest that errors had been made.

Different growth curves will yield different estimates of L_∞, K, and t_0, different von Bertalanffy growth curves, and different eumetric curves. These differences could lead to rather different fishing strategies. Fig. 11 shows the eumetric curves for males and females, based on mean ages determined from age length keys (the 'true' curve) and also the eumetric curve for females of known ages. The latter curve is rather different from the true (age length key) curve for females, and very markedly different from that for males. The erroneously higher estimates of L_∞ (about 90 cm) for females would suggest a rather higher length at recruitment to the fishery and so a rather larger mesh size for the fishing equipment than would be suitable for males. The best size range at recruitment for females would probably be around 45-55 cm and for males around 40 to 50 cms. Figs. 12a and b show the variation of relative yield per recruit with fishing

effort, using the best available estimates for males and females, and for recruitment lengths of 40 and 55 cm respectively. Total fishing mortalities (F) of 0.5 for females and 1.0 for males are indicated. Using the erroneous estimate of growth rate, F for females would be around 1.0. These values of F correspond to exploitation rates of 0.5, 0.75 and 0.7 respectively. A difference of 0.5 to 0.7 for female hake is a rather marked difference in the exploitation rate, so that the erroneous estimate of L_∞ (about 90 cm) could have lead to a rather different fishing strategy.

The most appropriate fishing strategy for this population of hake would probably require a recruitment

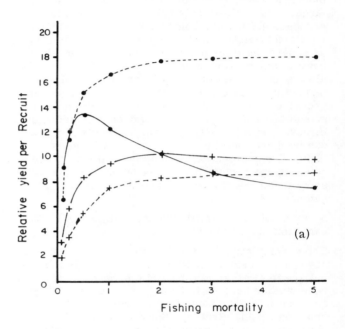

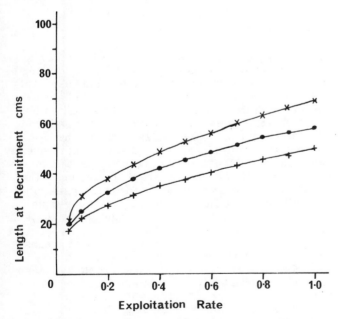

Fig. 11. Eumetric curves for Gulf of California Hake derived from different estimates of L_∞ and K.

+——+ males.

x——x females (from sample of fish of known age).

•——• females (from the age length key).

Values of L_∞ and K estimated from Figs. 9a and b.

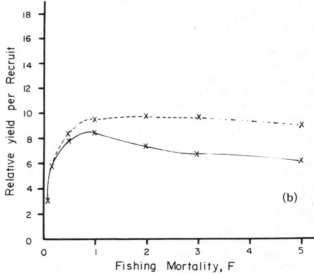

Fig. 12. Relation between relative yield per recruit and fishing mortality for Gulf of California Hake *Merluccius* sp.

(a) from age length keys

• = females   + = males

—— = length at recruitment 40 cm

- - - = length at recruitment 55 cm

(b) from samples of known age, females only

—— = length of recruitment 40 cm

- - - = length of recruitment 55 cm

size of about 50 cms, with an estimated fishing mortality of about 0.75 and an exploitation rate of about 0.6. Fish 50 cm long are about 5 years old, and most are sexually mature.

DISCUSSION

Various methods of age estimation have been contrasted with a view to determining the different results they may give. Cassie's (1954) method may be quite reliable and sometimes gives very good results indeed; however for some populations, such as the larger Gulf of California hake it may give quite erroneus estimates. Some Cassie curves may be very sensitive to slight changes in the points chosen as separating lines between age groups, but other curves may be very much less sensitive. There is always an element of subjectivity involved in interpreting Cassie curves, so that wherever possible growth estimates obtained from Cassie's method should be confirmed by some independent technique. However, with these limitations, Cassie's method can be most useful and can occasionally be used alone. Computer analysis may be useful in distinguishing age groups, but cannot be carried out without some independent previous knowledge of age group number and mean length.

A combination of otolith reading and Cassie curves can often be very fruitful.

The errors introduced by obtaining mean lengths at age from the sample rather than the population studied are too well known to need emphasis. They have been studied here with the object of finding out how great an influence some fairly large errors might exert on fishing strategy. Some errors in size at recruitment and in estimated optimal exploitation rate might have been made, but these do not very greatly affect the most practicable fishing strategy, so for us this can be estimated at this time. It is interesting that the best estimates of L_∞ (70 cm for females, 65 cm for males) are markedly lower than the erroneous estimate for females (90 cm), but that the fishing strategy chosen would probably not have been disastrously wrong with either estimate. The erroneous estimates for female L_∞ includes some rather incorrect growth estimates for 12 and 13 year old fish; the estimates of yield per recruit for the first years of the fishery, when these large fish still remain in the population, might be more accurate than those obtained using the more precise estimates which, however, do not allow for the presence of these large females. However, this will not affect the fishing strategy proposed, as the larger fish will be removed from the population by the same equipment as that used for the smaller. The large fish are also notably cannibalistic, and their removal from the population might increase the number of 50-80 cm fish available to the fishery.

While growth estimates should always be made as precisely as possible, it seems likely that fairly serious errors can often be tolerated from stock assessment purposes, at least where virgin stocks are concerned. Where a fishery exists the greatest possible precision is required because of the economic and political consequences that quite small changes in management strategy may involve e.g. a change of 2 cm in the mesh size, which might be in-volved in the difference between allowing recruitment to the fishery at 40 instead of 50-55 cm.

ACKNOWLEDGEMENTS

I am most grateful to Mr. R. S. Keir, now Project Manager of the FAO/PNUD project in Mexico for much stimulating discussion and help with the computer, Dr. W. Fox for the U.S. National Marine Fisheries Service, La Jolle, California very kindly allowed me to use his new programme, YPER, for estimating yield, based on Beverton and Holt's yield Tables.

REFERENCES

Abramson, N. J. 1971. Computer programmes for fish stock assessment. FAO Fisheries Technical Paper No. 101. FIRD/T. 101.

Cassie, R. M. 1954. Some uses of probability paper in the analysis of size frequency distributions. Aust. J. mar. Freshwat. Res., **5**, 513-522.

Mathews, C. P., Granados, J. L. and Arvizu, J. 1974. Results of the exploratory cruises of the Alejandro de Humboldt in the Gulf of California. California Commission for Oceanic and Fisheries Investigation. Rep. Symposium on Waters around Baja California, held at Yosemite Park, November 1972.

Fagade, S. O. 1974. Age determination in *Tilapia melanotheron* (Rupell) in the Lagos Lagoon, Lagos, Nigeria, with a discussion of the environmental and physiological basis of growth markings in the tropics. In this volume, Bagenal, T. B. (Ed.), Ageing of Fish, Unwin Brothers, 71-77.

Williams, T., and Bedford, B. C. 1974. The use of otoliths for age determination. In this volume, Bagenal, T. B. (Ed.), Ageing of Fish, Unwin Brothers, 114-123.

ADDENDUM[*]

Since this paper was completed it has been possible to carry out some runs with NORMSEP on the length frequency curve of the Gulf of California hake. This allowed the results of the Cassie curve to be contrasted with those of NORMSEP. The specifications for NORMSEP were based on results obtained from the Cassie curve. The two sets of mean lengths were always within one standard error and frequently very close. NORMSEP may always be used in this way to simplify analysis where there are many fish. However, the reconstructed size frequency distribution differed significantly from the real one—both methods failed to distinguish one age group. However, it will be shown elsewhere that even slightly sigmoid cumulative size frequency curves for 'age' groups may conceal two size or age groups. It will also be shown that two age groups inseparable by means of Cassie curve analysis alone can easily be distinguished when the inflection point determined by otolith readings (but indistinguishable by eye) is imposed on the curve. With highly irregular Cassie curves and derived age group data, this cannot be carried out without knowledge of the ages of individual fish.

Care has to be taken that this exercise does not lead to a circular argument.

([*]Shortened by the editor)

The errors likely in ageing roach *Rutilus rutilus* (L.), with special reference to stunted populations

by R. S. J. LINFIELD

Freshwater Fisheries Unit, Department of Zoology, University of Liverpool, England. *

SUMMARY

1.   Features to be found on the scales of roach are briefly described with reference to the work of previous authors.

2.   It is demonstrated that roach in the 1968 year class from Grey Mist Mere (South Lancashire, England) formed two checks on both their scales and opercula in their second year of life. The two checks were separated by a pronounced season of winter growth and both were initially accepted as annuli.

3.   Methods of error detection are briefly reviewed and applied to the scales of fish in the 1968 year class from Grey Mist Mere. None of the commonly used methods are found to be totally satisfactory.

4.   Other sources of error are reviewed. It is concluded that errors are particularly likely to occur with stunted populations but that they will have less effect on the final results of growth studies than similar errors made in ageing 'normal' or fast growing populations.

5.   The difficulty in carrying out adequate proofs of validity in populations which have irregular growth patterns is considered a major problem in ageing roach. The value of long-term studies is stressed.

1.   INTRODUCTION

The scales of roach *Rutilus rutilus* (L.) have been described by Masterman (1923), Segerstrale (1932), Hartley (1947) and Jones (1953). A detailed histochemical study on the features of roach scales used in ageing has been carried out by Wallin (1957). The work of these authors, and others, has led to the general acceptance of scale reading as a useful technique for ageing roach. The validity of the method has been demonstrated many times but it will be shown in this paper that errors can occur in several ways and with sufficient frequency to significantly affect the results of population studies.

2.   BASIC METHODS USED FOR AGEING ROACH

Most workers have found that the growth of roach slows or stops completely during the winter months and that the annual checks ('annuli') are formed at the scale edge of most fish when growth resumes in the summer. Each annulus appears as a number of closely spaced rings (or ridges) in the anterior field and as a single robust ring of thickened material in the posterior field.   From about the third year of life re-absorption of material from the scale edge

---

* Present address: c/o Glamorgan River Authority, Tremains House, Coychurch Road, Bridgend, Glamorgan.

often takes place during the growth stoppage and results in an 'erosion mark' in the position of the annulus. The erosion tends to be most pronounced at the anterolateral corners of the scales, accentuating the phenomenon known as 'cutting-over' of the rings, and is often referred to as a spawning mark.

The opercular bones of the roach also show the annual patterns of growth quite clearly. Banks (1970) preferred the use of opercula to scales in ageing roach from a fast-growing population and they have also been found useful when working with stunted fish (Linfield, 1971). In years when stunting is particularly severe, erosion often obliterates a full season's growth on the scales but has relatively little effect on the opercula. The method of ageing roach from their opercula is basically the same as that described for perch (*Perca fluviatilis* L.) by Le Cren (1947), and the annuli are taken as the leading edge of the opaque summer bands. Throughout this paper the emphasis will be on the use of scales for ageing roach but the remarks made will be equally applicable to the opercular.

It is generally recognised that all species of fish are liable to form 'false checks' on their scales and other bony structures at various times of the year. A true annulus can be followed right around the scale and is a constant feature on all of the scales examined from any one fish. It has therefore become a fairly routine practice in ageing to accept as annuli only those checks which fit this description. When both scales and opercula are used for ageing it is also a helpful procedure to cross-match the checks on the two types of bony structure and to accept as annuli only those checks which can be clearly identified by both methods. The first check (and possibly the second) is excepted from this rule because it is usually obliterated on the opercula of older fish by basal thickening of the bone.

3.   CHECK FORMATION ON THE SCALES OF THE 1968 YEAR CLASS OF ROACH FROM GREY MIST MERE

In Grey Mist Mere, which is an 8½ acre lake in South Lancashire, roach in the 1968 year class are the progeny of a population recovering from a period of severe stunting (Linfield, 1973). A preliminary study on the population was carried out in May 1969 and followed by more detailed work commencing in November of that year.

From November 1969, samples of fish were taken from the lake near the middle of each month over a two year period. All the roach were aged using the combination of scales and opercula with the methods described above. In addition, the number of scale rings outside what was initially accepted as the last annulus (the 'plus growth') was recorded for each fish, using the average value from three scales. The 1968 and 1969 year classes were dominant in the samples, at different times, and each was treated separately from the other age groups. The data were combined into bimonthly samples and the number of scale rings outside the last annulus plotted as a series of frequency histograms. In Fig. 1 it can be seen that the frequency distribution for the 1968 year class in November/December 1969 was markedly bimodal. This resulted from the fact that a large proportion of fish in the year class formed a second check on their scales in the Autumn of 1969 which had been accepted as an annulus (Plate 1). The fish had been aged as two years old but retained in the 1968 year class on the assumption that they had formed their second annulus early. On a second reading of the scales and opercula it was discovered that a check which had not been accepted as an annulus could also be identified in a corresponding position on the scales of some of the other fish in the year class and that at least some form of irregularity could be found on the scales of most of them.

As the winter progressed the number of fish with an annulus near the scale edge became less. The shape of the frequency distribution changed and the mean number of rings outside the last annulus increased markedly (Fig. 1). In March/April the 'plus growth' on the scales was, on average, nearly 50% greater than in November/December, the mean number of rings outside the last annulus having increased from 16 to 24. This pronounced seasons of winter scale growth was reflected in a measurable increase in the length of the fish. The mean fork length ± standard error increased from 79.20 ± 0.73 mm in November/December to 84.42 ± 0.85 mm in March/April. From Fig. 2 it can be seen that most of this growth took place in the latter half of the winter. Similar growth has previously been recorded by Williams (1967) for roach from the River Thames. Data for the 1969 year class of roach was inadequate to demonstrate the pattern of scale growth in the winter of 1969/70. For the combined pre-1968 year classes, some fish had an annulus near the scale edge during the winter but the frequency distribution for the number of rings outside the last annulus was not bimodal and gave a mean value of 11 in both the early winter and the spring.

Fish of all age groups formed an annulus on their scales between May and July in 1970 (Fig. 1). As the pre-1968 year classes had not grown significantly during the 1969/70 winter, those fish which had a check at the scale edge during this period still showed only 1 annual check for the 1969-70 year. The autumn/winter formed check became part of the annulus formed in early summer when growth was resumed. As most of the 1968 fish had formed a check in the Autumn of 1969, followed by a period of fast scale growth, the check formed in May-June 1970 was at least the second formed in the 1969-70 year.

It has been shown that a large proportion of the autumn-formed checks were indistinguishable from true annuli and as a result of this many of the fish from the 1968 year class were initially over-aged after the true second annulus had been formed.

Autumn formed checks on roach scales have also been identified by Karpinska-Walus (1961) who gave the following explanation: 'As the formation of check on roach scale is connected with the increase of the rate of its growth, the annulus is formed every year, at the moment when the new current season growth starts. If, during the same year, the rate of growth is obviously increased again, for some reason, the false

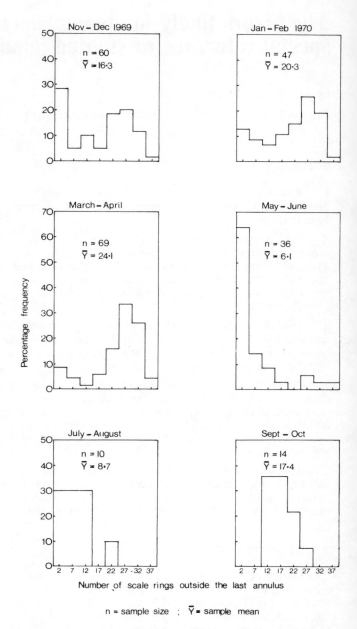

n = sample size ; $\bar{Y}$ = sample mean

Fig. 1. Scale growth in the 1968 year class of roach from Grey Mist Mere

check appears on the scale.' The data on the 1968 year class from Grey Mist Mere supports this view.

After completion of the second year's growth many fish in the 1968 year class could only be aged correctly because of chance circumstances surrounding the study. First, the project had been started at a time when it was possible to show that the fish had formed an autumn check in 1969 and that the formation of this check was followed by a season of pronounced winter scale growth. Secondly, the 1967 year class (and the 1966 class) was almost totally absent from the fishery and therefore doubts immediately arose about the true age of the large number of fish appearing in this class during 1970. Thirdly, through a combination of many factors the growth of roach in Grey Mist Mere improved dramatically after the winter of 1967/8 and the very few 1967 fish caught during the project could be distinguished from the 1968 fish because the length ranges of the two age groups did not overlap.

(a) 1968 year class, caught 21.11.69

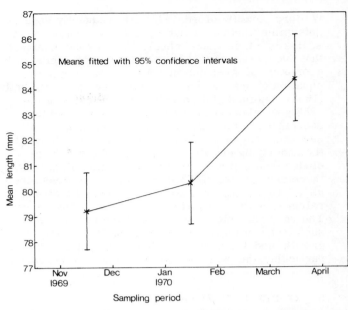

Fig. 2. Winter growth in the 1968 year class of roach from Grey Mist Mere

(b) 1969 year class, caught 11.6.70

Plate 1. Scales of roach from Grey Mist Mere

4. EFFECTIVENESS OF COMMONLY USED METHODS OF ERROR DETECTION

Having described how roach in the 1968 year class from Grey Mist Mere formed an extra check in their second year, it is interesting to consider how such a check might be correctly interpreted if it was formed in a population prior to the commencement of age and growth studies. It has been demonstrated that the standard practice of accepting only those checks which can be followed all around the scales, and which are constant features of all scales examined from any one fish, are not always effective in this respect. The autumn check in the 1968 year class could be satisfactorily matched up with a corresponding check on the opercula. Thus the combined use of more than one type of bony structure for ageing is of limited value in preventing this particular type of error.

The modes of a length frequency distribution (Petersen Method) can often be used to check the ages of at least the younger fish in a sample and this method is particularly useful for studies on fast growing populations. With stunted populations, however, it is of limited value because the length frequency distributions of all the age groups, except the first, overlap to such an extent that their modes cannot be identified. A sample of 258 roach taken from Grey Mist Mere in May 1969, before the improved growth rate had noticeably affected the population, had a unimodal length frequency distribution (Fig. 3). No one year old fish were included.

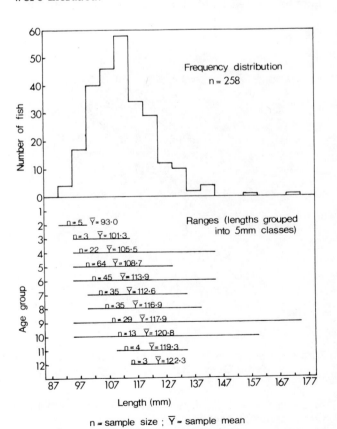

Fig. 3. Length data for roach from Grey Mist Mere in May 1969

Walford plots (Walford, 1946) are frequently used to determine whether or not a particular feature on the scales is a true annual check. The method assumes that successive annual length increments decrease in geometric progression in a pattern similar to the equation of organic growth derived by von Bertalanffy (1938). Walford plots carried out on scales of the 1968 year class of roach actually encouraged the acceptance of the autumn formed checks as annuli because many of the fish conformed more closely to the underlying growth model if the check was included than if it was omitted. In certain situations, therefore, the use of Walford plots can increase the difficulties in ageing roach correctly and a strong reliance on this method can lead to increased error. The very variable growth rate of the roach causes such frequent digressions from von Bertalanffy's growth model that, with stunted roach populations in particular, the value of Walford plots is questionable.

5.   OTHER CAUSES OF ERROR

(i)   The position of the first annulus

A common difficulty in ageing roach lies in establishing the position of the first annulus. This is very variable between year classes but fairly constant within any one year class.

In a poor summer, when breeding occurs late and the fry do not hatch until late June or early July, the first year's growth may be very poor, with only a few scale rings being formed inside the first annulus (Plate 2). In contrast, in a good year, when breeding occurs early and the growing season extends well into the autumn, the first year's growth may be considerably greater and more than twenty scale rings may be formed inside the first annulus (Plate 1).

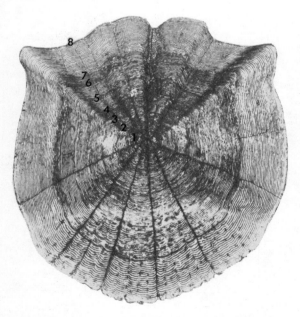

Plate 2.   Scale from a roach of the 1962 year class from Grey Mist Mere, caught 10.6.70

In a study where first year growth of one or both extreme types is encountered on the scales, two types of error can easily be made. First, an annulus very near to the centre may be dismissed as a false check if it is only encountered in one or two year classes.

This error is particularly likely to occur if the second year growth is poor. The alternative type of error may occur with fish that have formed their first annulus an exceptionally great distance from the scale centre. When compared with scales of fish from other year classes these fish will appear to have been too big for their apparent age when the first visible annulus was formed. The assumption is then likely to be made that the first visible annulus is in fact the second and, if the exceptionally good first year is followed by several poor ones, this assumption may be further encouraged by the use of Walford plots.

(ii)   The interpretation of two closely spaced checks

When an apparently poor year's growth is present on the scales of a roach population (Plate 2) the investigator has to make a decision on which of two possibilities to accept. Either, the two checks which appear close together are both annuli and the rings separating the two checks represent a whole year's scale growth, or, one of the two checks is a false check, formed either near the beginning or near the end of a relatively 'normal' year's growth. Unfortunately, when faced with this problem there is usually no way in which a worker can be sure of making a correct decision. Chance circumstances affecting a particular study may enable this to be done but more often than not the investigator is forced into making a decision based largely on intuition.

Practical circumstances usually dictate that a study of a particular fish population involves regular sampling for a relatively short period of time (rarely more than two years). If check formation is observed to be strictly annual during this period, acceptance of the validity of scale reading as a method of ageing will tend to lead to the acceptance as annuli of all scale checks resembling those formed during the sampling period. If it should happen that two pronounced checks are formed close together in the same year during a sampling period, then this observation will tend to encourage the belief that similarly spaced checks from previous years were formed in the same way. As the growth of roach may be highly variable from year to year, it does not follow that the pattern of check formation observed during the sampling period is necessarily identical to that of previous years. As the true pattern of scale growth in these years cannot always be assessed with confidence, the occurrence of closely spaced checks on roach scales presents a problem of interpretation that will inevitably lead to occasional errors in age and growth studies. This problem is illustrated, and has been discussed, in previous work by Cragg-Hine (1965) and Cragg-Hine and Jones (1969). The problem is most acute when working with scales from stunted populations because most of the annuli are laid down very close to one another (see below).

(iii)   Additional errors likely in ageing roach from stunted populations

The annual growth increments of fish from severely stunted populations can be so small in some years that the annuli become almost superimposed. In these circumstances severe erosion at the scale edge can result in the partial or even complete obliteration of several season's growth. Similar problems can also occur at the scale edge of exceptionally old fish from more 'normal' populations. Fortunately the opercular bones are not so susceptible to erosion and checks that might otherwise be missed can usually be identified by cross-matching the features to be found on the opercula with those on the scales (Plate 3).

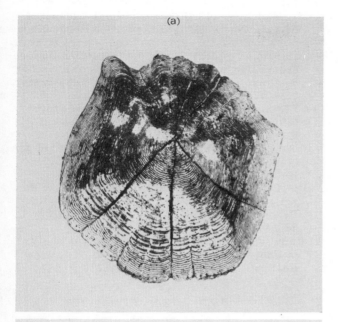

(a)

(b)

Plate 3. A scale (a) and an operculum (b) from a severely stunted roach (length 156 mm) from Grey Mist Mere. The fish was tentatively aged as 13[++]

False checks are common on the scales of stunted fish and their recognition is made particularly difficult by the fact that all the fish have a check near the scale edge throughout the year as a result of their very small growth increments. Although most false checks can be identified by their inconsistent appearance, it is difficult to be sure that the checks accepted as annuli have in fact been formed on an annual basis. Validity tests involving the progression of a dominant year class, or the sudden decrease in the average length of an age group after an annulus has been formed, cannot often be used with severely stunted populations. Several successive strong year classes are usually present (the overcrowding this produces being a con-

tributory factor to the cause of stunting) and their length frequency distributions may overlap to such an extent that their mean lengths are not significantly different (Fig. 3). Stunted populations therefore cause the most difficulties in ageing but it is interesting to note that errors in ageing such populations have far less effect on the final results of growth studies than similar errors made on 'normal' or fast growing populations. From about the third year of life the mean lengths of adjacent age groups in severely stunted populations differ so little that an error of one or two years in ageing many of the fish would make little difference to the overall results and the final conclusions. In fast growing populations a similar number of errors would have a much greater effect on the data and would therefore result in much greater errors being made when the final conclusions are drawn.

6. CONCLUSION

The variable growth rate of the roach produces irregularities in the annual pattern of scale growth which can lead to errors in ageing. The acceptance of false checks as annuli is considered the most likely error because such checks can be formed in ways which will not be shown up by standard techniques for error detection. Errors can also result from the rejection of annuli as false checks or from their being missed because they have become superimposed or obliterated. The non-formation of scale annuli has not been considered as a cause of error because it is not thought to be a common problem in ageing roach. The first annulus may sometimes be indistinct but is usually recognisable.

Stunted roach are particularly difficult to age but the final results from growth studies on stunted populations are less affected by errors than the results from studies on 'normal' or fast-growing fish. Currently used ageing technique may generally yield fairly accurate results in studies on roach populations but the method so often necessitates the making of decisions based on inadequate proofs of validity that the probable magnitude of resultant and undetectable errors can never be predicted. This is clearly unsatisfactory and underlines the value of long-term studies which enable the worker to study the formation of annuli and other scale checks over a period of many years. It is only from such studies that basic improvements in technique and interpretation can be made.

ACKNOWLEDGEMENTS

The work described in this paper formed part of a larger project financed by the Natural Environment Research Council and the Warrington Anglers Association. To both of these bodies I am very grateful. I am also indebted to Dr. J. W. Jones, O.B.E., for supervision of the work; Mr. T. B. Bagenal, for assistance in the preparation of slides and scale photographs; and to the Board of Glamorgan River Authority for permitting me to present the paper at the Symposium.

REFERENCES

Banks, J. W. (1970). Observations on the fish population of Rostherne Mere, Cheshire. Field Studies, **3,** 357-379.

Cragg-Hine, D. (1965). Age determination in coarse fish. Proc. 2nd Brit. Coarse Fish Conf., 3-6.

Cragg-Hine, D., and Jones, J. W. (1969). The growth of dace *Leuciscus leuciscus* (L.), roach *Rutilus rutilus* (L.) and chub *Squalius cephalus* (L.) in Willow Brook, Northamptonshire. J. Fish Biol., **1**, 59-82.

Hartley, P. H. T. (1947). The natural history of some British freshwater fishes. Proc. Zool. Soc. Lond., **117**, 129-206.

Jones, J. W. (1953). Part I. The scales of roach. Part II. The age and growth of the trout (*Salmo trutta*), grayling (*Thymallus thymallus*), perch (*Perca fluviatilis*), and roach (*Rutilus rutilus*) of Llyn Tegid (Bala) and the roach of the River Birket. Fishery Invest., Lond. (I), **5**, (7), 1-18.

Karpinska-Walus, B. (1961). The growth of roach (*Rutilus rutilus* L.) in lakes of Wegorzewo District. Roczn. Nauk. Roln., **77**-B-2, 329-398.

Le Cren, E. D. (1947). The determination of the age and growth of the perch (*Perca fluviatilis*) from the opercular bone. J. Anim. Ecol., **16**, 188-204.

Linfield, R. S. J. (1971). Observations relating to problems of fishery management at Grey Mist Mere. Proc. 5th Brit. Coarse Fish Conf., 78-88.

Linfield, R. S. J. (1973). Fishery studies at Grey Mist Mere. Proc. 6th Brit. Coarse Fish Conf., 166-173.

Masterman, A. T. (1923). Report on the scales of certain freshwater fish in relation to age determination. Fishery Invest., Lond., (I), **1**, (3), 1-16.

Segerstrale, C. (1932). Uber die jahrlichen Zuwachszonen der Schuppen und Beziehungen zwischen Sommer-Temperatur und Zuwachs bei *Abramis brama*. Act. Zool. Fenn., **13**, 1-42

Von Bertalannfy, L. (1938). A quantitative theory of organic growth (Inquiries on growth laws II). Human Biol., **10**, (2), 181-213.

Walford, L. A. (1946). A new graphic method of describing the growth of animals. Biol. Bull. Mar. Biol. Lab. Woods Hole, **90**, 141-147.

Wallin, O. (1957). On the growth structure and developmental physiology of the scale of fishes. Rept. Inst. Freshwat. Res. Drottningholm, **38**, 385-447.

Williams, W. P. (1967). The growth and mortality of four species of fish in the River Thames at Reading. J. Anim. Ecol., **36**, 695-720.

The problems of protracted check formation and the validity of the use of scales in age determination exemplified by two populations of dace *Leuciscus leuciscus* (L.)

by J. M. HELLAWELL

Natural Environment Research Council, Water Pollution Research Laboratory, Stevenage, Hertfordshire, SG1 1TH, England.

SUMMARY

1.   Samples of two populations of dace were taken each month for 13 consecutive months.

2.   Examination of the condition of the scale margin revealed a protracted period of check formation which complicated age determination.

3.   Examination of the scale margin by counting the number of rings since the last check, and an analysis of the length frequency distributions were not able to confirm age determinations in all cases.

4.   Walford plots were made which suggested that the early checks would be satisfactorily read.

5.   The anomalous delayed first check formation described by Mathews and Williams (1972) is attributed to a protracted period of check formation, discrepancies between the time of spawning and check formation and incorrect scale-reading.

6.   On reviewing all the available evidence it was concluded that the use of scales for age determination was valid.

INTRODUCTION

The data presented in this paper were obtained during a general study of the autecology of the dace *Leuciscus leuciscus* (L.) populations of two tributaries of the Herefordshire Wye (Hellawell, 1973) and describe the seasonal pattern of scale growth with particular reference to the validity of age determination. The evidence was appropriate for examination by two of Graham's (1929) criteria: the observation of annual, cyclical changes in scale morphology, and the occurrence of discrete length-frequency distributions which correspond with the determined age groups. The data were also appropriate for the examination of the Walford plot method of identifying suspected missing early rings.

The scales of dace were described and illustrated by Cragg-Hine and Jones (1969) and have been widely used for age determinations (Hartley, 1947a, 1947b; Healy, 1956; Cragg-Hine, 1964a, 1964b; Williams, 1967). In a recent paper, Mathews and Williams (1972) have suggested that the time of formation of the first check by dace in the River Thames may be as late as their third year of life. They also reviewed the published data and concluded that in at least one instance age determination was incorrect.

MATERIALS AND METHODS

Samples of dace were taken by electrofishing from the Afon Llynfi (Grid Reference SO 178389) and the River Lugg (Grid Reference SO 530509) each month from January 1964 to January 1965 (Table I). Full details of the sites, methods of capture, treatment of samples and definitions of terminology have been given elsewhere (Hellawell, 1971). The standard length of each fish was measured and scales were removed from the pectoral region above the lateral line. The scales were cleaned by soaking in dilute potassium hydroxide solution and examined in water under a low-power binocular microscope by transmitted light. The number of scale-checks present and the number of scale-rings along an anterior radius beyond the last scale-check were counted.

Table I.   Numbers of dace taken in each monthly sample from the Afon Llynfi and River Lugg, January 1964—January 1965

	Afon Llynfi	River Lugg
January 1964	381	71
February	171	31
March	159	91
April	217	58
May	315	4
June	120	44
July	206	84
August	90	30
September	151	30
October	174	110
November	332	116
December	102	303
January 1965	190	40
Totals	2308	1062

RESULTS

(1) Scale Morphology

Preliminary examination of scales from both populations revealed structures consistent with the descriptions of other workers (Plates I-V). The regular pattern of concentric rings was disturbed at intervals by clear checks. At each check there was a loss of complete rings along the posteriolateral margins, as though erased, before the next complete ring was formed. Indeed, the next complete ring appeared to cut over previously formed rings but there was no evidence for the origin of checks by erosion. The spacing of the rings was regular along the radii but closest on the anterior and widest on the posterior surfaces. Many rings present on the anterior and

173

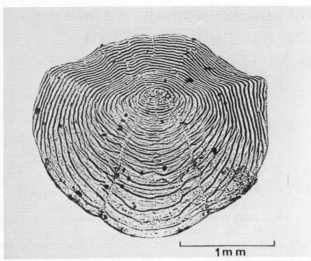

Plate I.   Scale of a 7.4 cm male dace taken in its first year of life (0+) from Afon Llynfi, November 1964. No check is visible; about 25 rings have been formed.

Plate II.   Scale of a 6.8 cm female dace taken at the end of its first year of life (0+) from the River Lugg, April 1964. No check is visible, 23 rings have been formed.

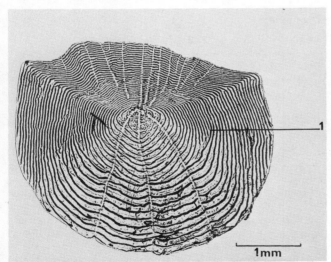

Plate III. Scale of dace from the River Lugg, taken in April 1964 at the end of its second year of life (1+). One check is visible about 18 rings from the centre and a further 20 rings have been formed beyond this.

lateral margins of the scale could not be traced completely around the posterior margin as they were terminated by the edge of the scale. This feature is evident on the photographs of scales published by Cragg-Hine and Jones (1969) and Mathews and Williams (1972) and suggests that growth does not proceed evenly around the scale perimeter. At the time of check formation it appears that scale growth stops and when growth resumes the first few rings are formed symmetrically but as growth proceeds new rings are initiated on the anterior margins at a greater rate than their completion at the posterior. Thus, each check is apparently derived from the incorporation of the edge structure when scale growth is arrested and restarted. If this interpretation is correct then, in practice, it will rarely be possible to determine the presence of a check at the edge of the scale but it will become evident when growth has restarted.

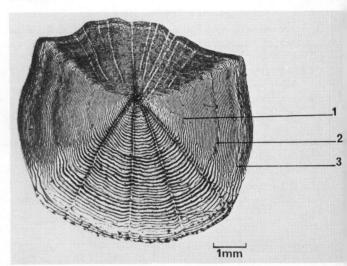

Plate IV.   Scale of a dace taken from the River Lugg in April 1964. Three clear checks are visible with 29 rings to the first check and six rings beyond the last. It is difficult to decide whether this fish formed the last check early in 1964 or whether the six rings represent the last year's growth.

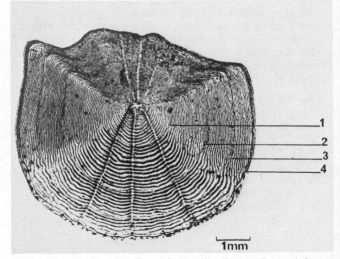

Plate V.   Scale of a dace from the River Lugg taken in April 1964 at the completion of its fourth year of life (3-4). Four checks are visible, the last almost at the scale edge with only two rings beyond it. There are about 17 rings to the first check.

Few dace had more than 7 checks and these were well spaced. This contrasts with the scales of sympatric chub *Leuciscus cephalus* (L) and roach *Rutilus rutilus* (L) with indicated ages of over 13 years and some crowding of the check towards the scale margin which reduced the precision of determinations (Hellawell, 1971, 1972). The difficulty of locating the position of the first scale-check which has been reported in chub (Leeming, 1967; Cragg-Hine and Jones, 1969; Hellawell, 1971) was not evident in the Wye dace populations and has not been recorded by other workers although failure to detect the first scale-check may explain some discrepancies in age and growth data in the literature which are discussed below.

(2) Seasonal Pattern of Scale Growth

The seasonal pattern of scale growth was investigated by computing the mean number of rings beyond the last scale check for the provisional 1959, 1960 and 1961 year-classes of the Afon Llynfi and the 1959 and 1960 year classes of the River Lugg and plotting these against the month (Fig. 1) to avoid the difficulty of detecting annual checks at the time of their formation (as explained in the previous section) since a reduction in the mean ring count would indicate, from the shape of the curve, the probable period of check formation. The technique has been applied sucessfully to other cyprinids (Hellawell, 1971, 1972) but in the two dace populations the pattern was less clearly defined although a depression, which probably indicated a period of protracted check formation, could be seen in some provisional year classes. The complete data for all year classes are given in Table II.

Frequency-distributions of the number of rings beyond the last scale-check in the combined provisional 2+ to 5+ age classes were prepared for each monthly sample from both rivers (Figs. 2 and 3). The Llynfi data and, to a lesser extent, the Lugg data show that ring

Table II.   Mean Number of Scale Rings beyond the last check in year class of Male and Female Dace of the Afon Llynfi and the River Lugg.

	Year Classes											
	Males						Females					
	1961	1960	1959	1958	1957	1956	1961	1960	1959	1958	1957	1956
Afon Llynfi												
Jan.		8.1	5.6	4.8	4.7	4.5	15.0	8.5	5.8	5.1	3.6	5.0
Feb.		11.2	5.5	4.1	4.8			9.9	5.5	3.4	4.0	
Mar.	18.2	14.1	7.0				20.0	14.2	6.7	5.5	6.0	3.0
Apr.			5.0	5.9	4.4	3.5		13.0	5.6	6.3	4.2	4.2
May	7.7	4.4	4.9	3.6	5.5	3.0	6.6	2.9	5.7	3.7	3.6	5.2
Jun.	4.7	5.2	3.5	3.3				5.4	2.9	4.8	6.0	
Jul.	4.3	4.3	3.2	2.7	4.0			3.6	3.7	3.2	2.5	3.0
Aug.	6.3	7.1	5.7	4.1				5.4	6.1	4.0	5.0	
Sep.	11.3	5.6	4.7				12.0	6.6	4.8	4.0	3.0	8.0
Oct.	11.7	5.2	4.0	4.0			11.5	6.2	4.5	3.4	4.0	
Nov.	9.3	6.2	3.7	4.5			9.9	6.8	4.1	3.7	5.0	
Dec.	6.5	6.6	5.5	5.6	4.0		11.0	6.7	6.3	5.0	5.0	6.0
Jan.	10.3	6.6	5.0	3.6			10.6	7.2	3.8	5.6	5.0	
R. Lugg												
Jan		9.1	4.1	3.6	7.5			7.8	4.8	6.0	5.0	
Feb.		5.0	4.4	4.7	5.0			6.5	3.5	5.6		4.5
Mar.		9.5	5.6	5.2	6.0	6.3		7.7	7.2	5.6	7.5	4.4
Apr.	24.0	10.9	5.4	7.0	5.0	8.0		9.3	8.0	7.0	5.0	5.0
May								6.0				1.5
Jun.		5.0	4.0	5.0		1.0	1.0	3.4	6.3	6.0		
Jul.	7.0	4.2	4.4	3.1	3.0		5.0	4.9	4.0	2.6		
Aug.		8.8	3.7	2.5				5.6	4.0	3.8	6.5	
Sep.		5.0	3.7	6.5	1.0		10.0	7.0	4.4	5.0	1.3	
Oct.		6.1	4.3	3.5	1.0		6.0	8.1	5.7	4.6	3.3	
Nov.	7.5	8.0	5.3	3.7	2.0			8.3	5.8	3.8	5.0	3.5
Dec.	10.0	7.4	4.8	4.4	3.8	4.0	6.0	7.7	5.6	5.5	4.9	4.3
Jan.		5.9	4.3	4.0				8.7	6.9	4.5	6.3	

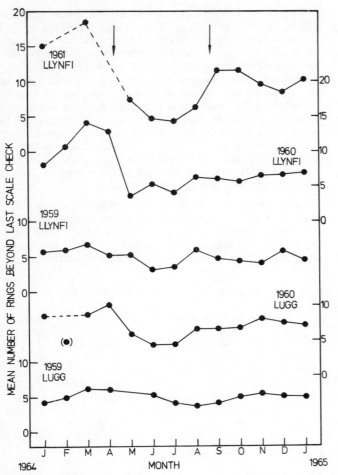

Fig. 1. Seasonal variation in the mean number of rings beyond the last scale check in the 1959, 1960 and 1961 provisional year classes of the Afon Llynfi and the 1959 and 1960 provisional year classes of the River Lugg, sexes combined. The vertical arrows indicate the probable period of check formation.

counts dropped in April and that the mode (and mean) advance, albeit irregularly, through the year. The clearest indication of the probable period of check formation is provided by the distribution of the maximum ring counts. The picture is, however, distorted by the variation in scale growth with advancing age. Highest ring counts were observed in small fish with fewest scale checks which, it may reasonably be assumed, are the youngest (Fig. 4). Some, if not most, of the apparent variation in ring counts may be attributed to variations in the proportional representation of smaller fishes in the samples.

(3) Length and Age Frequency Distributions.

Length-frequency distribution histograms of the monthly samples of both populations showed that almost all the Llynfi samples had a single mode in both sexes and the Lugg distributions were similar but less regular. Notable exceptions were the November sample from the Afon Llynfi, the December sample from the River Lugg and, to a much lesser extent, the April and November Lugg samples in which several modes were evident and probably indicative of discrete age-classes. A breakdown of the November Llynfi and December Lugg samples into provisional age-classes on the basis of scale checks is given in Fig. 5 together with an outline of the sample distribution. The discrete modes of the

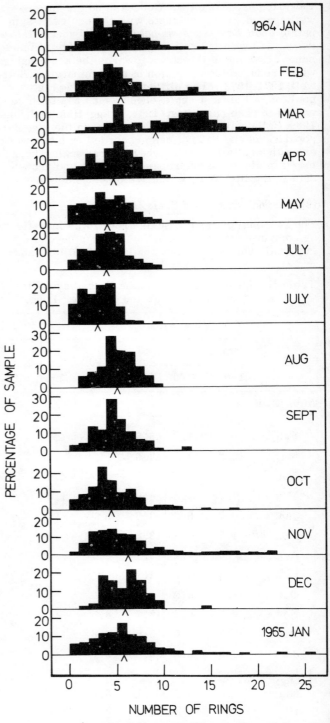

Fig. 2. Percentage-frequency distribution of the number of rings beyond the last scale check for each monthly sample of the provisional 2+ to 5+ age classes of the Afon Llynfi, sexes combined. Arrow heads indicate sample means.

youngest groups are evident but there is considerable overlap in the older groups.

It was not possible to follow the progress of dominant year-classes as the data were collected over only 13 months but partial support for the validity of age determinations was obtained by comparing the distribution of scale checks at the beginning and end of the year. A tentative conclusion that check formation was initiated in April or May was used to divide the samples into pre- and post-check groups. By taking the first three months and the last three months of the

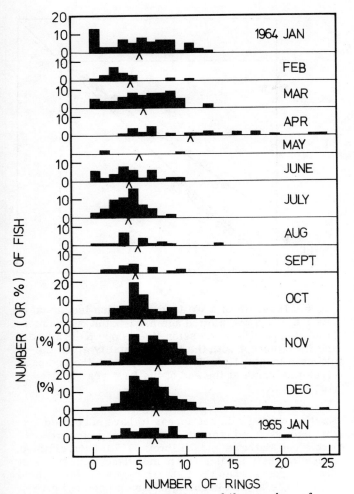

Fig. 3. Frequency distributions of the number of rings beyond the last scale check for each monthly sample of the provisional 2+ to 5+ age classes of the River Lugg, sexes combined. The large November and December samples are expressed as a percentage to match the scale of other months. Arrow heads indicate sample means.

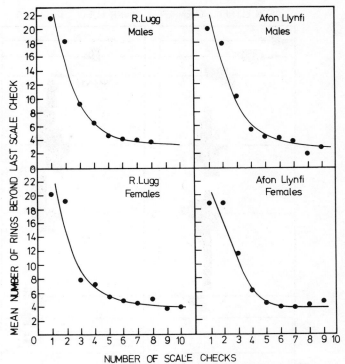

Fig. 4. Relation of mean number of rings beyond the last scale check and the number of scale checks in the combined samples (excluding May and June) of males and females of both populations. Lines fitted by eye to suggest trend of points.

thirteen samples and analysing the frequency-distributions of scale checks it was possible to test whether there was a shift of one age-class in the distribution after the period of check formation. The relevant data are given in Table III in which it is evident that the provisional age-class distributions advanced by one year between the first and second groups in both populations. To facilitate comparisons the provisional year-classes have been arranged on the same line.

(4) Walford Plots

The Von Bertalanffy growth model and the use of the Walford—plot technique are now well-known in fishery biology (Beverton and Holt, 1957; Dickie, 1971). When lengths are measured at equal time intervals, for example the end (or middle) of each year of life, it is possible to plot the length at a given age (L_t) against the length one year later (L_{t+1}) and, by fitting a line to the points, derive the theoretical ultimate length (L_∞) and an estimate of the length in the first year of life, assuming $L_0 = 0$ (Fig. 6). The point where the line meets the line of equality gives the value of L_∞ and the intercept with the L_{t+1} axis gives the estimate of the length at the end (or middle) of the first year of life. Thus one may check the validity of age determinations since the predicted and actual lengths assigned to the O+ age-class may be compared.

In practice, it is unnecessary to determine these values graphically since the relevant parameters may be calculated. Linear regression (Bagenal, 1955) may be used to fit a line to the paired values of the form

$$y = mx + c$$

where $x = L_t$

$$y = L_{t+1}$$

$$m = \text{slope}$$

$$c = \text{intercept}$$

At the point of intercept with the line of equality

$$y = x$$

Therefore, substituting and rearranging,

$$x = \frac{c}{1 - m}$$

or $$L_\infty = \frac{\text{intercept}}{1 - \text{slope}}$$

The slope of this equation $m = e^{-K}$ where K is the constant of the Von Bertalanffy growth model

$$L_t = L_\infty (1 - e^{-k - K (t - t_0)})$$

The intercept $c = L_{t1} - L_{t0}$ or the length at the end of the first year of growth.

The calculated parameters of Walford plots for male and female dace of both populations are given in Table IV where they may be compared with equivalent data provided by Mathews and Williams (1972). The results derived from the Wye dace populations are similar to those of Cragg-Hine and Jones (1969) and Mann (1967) but are quite dissimilar from those of Mathews and Williams (1972), Williams (1967), Hartley (1947a) and Healy (1956). Mathews and Wil-

177

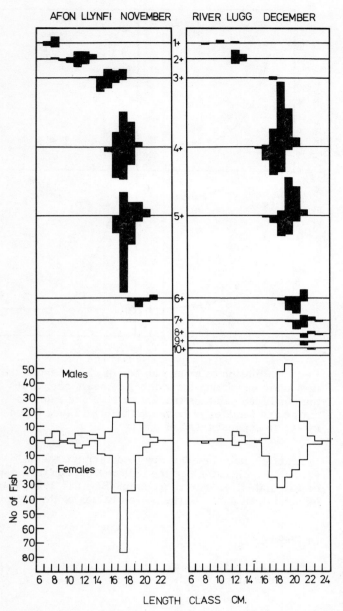

AFON LLYNFI NOVEMBER   RIVER LUGG DECEMBER

LENGTH CLASS CM.

Fig. 5. Length-frequency distributions of selected samples (November, Llynfi; December, Lugg) to show distribution within the provisional age-classes together with an outline of the sample distribution. Males above, females below the line. Indicated lengths are lower limits of 1 cm length-classes.

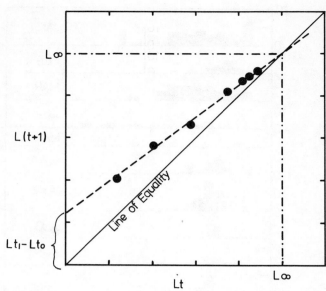

Fig. 6. Diagram of a Walford plot. Fish lengths at a given age (L_t) are plotted against lengths one year later (L_{t+1}). The regression line (slope K) is fitted and its intercept with the line of equality gives the ultimate length (L_∞). The intercept with the ordinate gives the length at the end of the first year of life ($L_{t1} - L_{t0}$).

Earlier workers do not appear to have suspected that ages derived from dace scales may be unreliable but Mathews and Williams (1972) have claimed, following their studies of Thames dace, that 'the first check appears when the fish are beginning their third year of life so that counting of annuli does not give the true age of the fish'. They subjected the data of previous workers to examination by Walford plots and concluded that Healy (1956) aged her dace incorrectly and aroused the suspicion that Hartley's (1947a) age determinations may be erroneous.

Although the evidence presented by a study of Wye dace populations was not absolutely decisive it seemed, on balance, reasonable to conclude that, used carefully, scale checks gave reliable age estimates. Comparable discrete length and age-frequency distributions were observed in some samples and the application of Walford plots suggested that neither the first (or second) age classes were missed nor that the length attained in the first year was unreasonably great. Weakest evidence was derived from consideration of the seasonal changes in scale morphology. Ideally, the formation of scale checks would be confined to an identical, short period each year; but while the seasonal variation in the distribution of scale-rings beyond the last scale-check was consistent with the hypothesis that check formation was annual and probably confined to a short period in individual fish it was not synchronous throughout the populations. At any given time during the greater part of the year each year-class within the population consisted of two groups: those which had formed their check with an indicated age of N years and new rings beyond the last check ('plus' growth = N+) and those approaching check formation with an indicated scale age of N — 1 years. Age determination is thus complicated by the necessity of distinguishing between fish which are approaching and fish which have passed their period of check formation on the basis of a subjective comparison with a theoretical expected ring-count, appropriate for the month and size of the fish.

liams (1972) have suggested that the high estimates of the first year's growth of Healy (1956) and Hartley (1947a) may be attributed to errors in age determination.

DISCUSSION

Reliable age determinations are essential for almost all aspects of fishery research but especially for studies of growth, production, population structure and dynamics (see papers by Hirschhorn, Le Cren and Brander, this volume). It is, therefore, imperative that the validity of the method of age determination is established in each population studies. The presence of clear checks on scales, operculars or other bony tissues is insufficient, in itself, and caution must be exercised since it is too easy to tentatively assume that a method is valid and retrospectively obtain apparent confirmation.

Table III. Distribution of age classes in samples taken during the early and later months. Year classes have been arranged on the same line to facilitate comparisons.

	Age Class	Jan.	Feb.	Mar.	Total	%	Nov.	Dec.	Jan.	Total	%	Age Class
Afon Llynfi	2+	1	1	14	16	2.2	39	7	21	67	11.5	3+
	3+	53	38	77	168	22.9	112	28	60	200	34.4	4+
	4+	230	129	61	420	57.2	128	36	94	258	44.4	5+
	5+	71	20	4	95	12.9	13	22	12	47	8.1	6+
	6+	28	6	1	35	4.8	1	7	1	9	1.6	7+
					734	100.0				581	100.0	
River Lugg	2+	0	0	0	0	0	2	2	0	4	0.8	3+
	3+	22	1	21	44	24.0	85	138	20	243	51.3	4+
	4+	34	14	30	78	42.6	52	90	11	153	32.3	5+
	5+	15	5	14	34	18.6	15	29	3	47	9.9	6+
	6+	9	6	12	27	14.8	6	18	3	27	5.7	7+
					183	100.0				474	100.0	

Table IV. Calculated parameters of Walford Plots compared with values provided by Mathews and Williams (1972) for several different populations.

Population	L_∞ cm	K^*	$L_{t1} - L_{to}$ cm
Afon Llynfi, males	23.99	0.728	6.524
females	23.77	0.751	5.908
River Lugg, males	23.75	0.727	6.494
females	22.61	0.697	6.855
Willow Brook (Cragg-Hine and Jones, 1969)	22.94	0.69	7.12
River Frome (Mann, 1967)	25.25	0.74	6.70
River Thames (Williams, 1967	20.18	0.82	3.58
River Cam (Hartley, 1947a)	22.83	0.57	9.65
River Funshion (Healy, 1956)	24.11	0.50	11.82
†River Thames (Mathews and Williams, 1972)	21.50	0.83	3.73

$^*K = e^{-K}$, where k is the constant in the Von Bertalanffy growth model

†Calculated from data provided in Mathews and Williams (1972)

Cragg-Hine and Jones (1969) have shown that the pattern of check formation varies between years. In 1961 check formation was protracted, although most fish appeared to form a check between May and September, while in 1962 check formation was confined almost exclusively to June. A period of protracted check formation may partly explain the delayed appearance of an annual check until the start of the third year of life in Thames dace described by Mathews and Williams (1972) on the basis of samples taken during July to September 1967 and in April and August 1968. Photographs of scales from the smallest group (about 3-4 cm) had between 8 and 10 rings but no evident check. In April the following year, just after completing their first year of life, no check was visible, but this is not unexpected since even if a check had been initiated it would not be evident until later. A scale from a 7 cm fish taken in August 1968 was claimed to show no check at an estimated age of 15 months but careful examination of the photograph reveals a check about 10-13 rings from the centre and a further 6 or 7 rings beyond it. An 8 cm fish taken in August 1967 shows a clear check, about 14 or 15 rings from the centre and a further 11 or 12 rings beyond, but it is claimed that such fish are too large to be 1+, aged 15 months and are thought to be 2+ fish, aged 27 months. Evidence of considerable variation in lengths within year-classes is presented by Mathews and Williams and it seems unreasonable to claim that a 7 cm fish taken in August 1968 is 15 months old (1+) while an 8 cm fish taken in August 1967 is too large and must be aged 27 months (2+).

In reporting apparent anomalies between the estimated ages of dace and the number of scale checks Mathews and Williams quite correctly drew attention to the need for a critical examination of check formation in each new habitat studied. The evidence presented in support of their claim that ages derived from scales are unreliable is unconvincing and the implication that the methodology of previous workers may be invalid is unjustified. Even when scale-checks are formed rapidly at the same time each year there may be discrepancies between the actual age of the fish and the indicated age simply because spawning and check formation are not synchronous. This problem has been discussed elsewhere (Hellawell, 1969) in relation to the determination of the age of the grayling *Thymallus thymallus* (L.). Cragg-Hine and Jones (1969) recorded check formation in Willow Brook occurred 3 months after the spawning season. Thus, some dace may be 15 months older than the age indicated merely by counting the *number* of scale-checks present. Clearly, reliable estimates may only be derived by a count of the number of scale checks; critical examination of the condition of the margin of the scale beyond the last scale check, especially at the time of check formation since this may be protracted; and knowledge of the probable spawning period.

ACKNOWLEDGEMENTS

I thank the Wye River Authority for assistance in sampling; Dr. J. W. Jones, O.B.E., for supervision of the work at the University of Liverpool; Mr. E. D. Le Cren for facilities at the River Laboratory; Mr. H. Leatham who drew the figures and Dr. W. P. Williams for an opportunity to discuss the problem of age determination in dace.

REFERENCES

Bagenal, T.B. 1955. The growth rate of the long rough dab *Hippoglossoides platessoides* (Fabr.) J. Mar. biol. Ass. U.K., **34**, 297-311.

Beverton, R. J. H. and Holt, S. J. (1957) On the dynamics of exploited fish populations. Fishery Invest., Lond, (2) **19**: 533 pp.

Cragg-Hine, D. (1964a) The biology of the coarse fish of Willow Brook, Northamptonshire. Ph. D. thesis, University of Liverpool.

Cragg-Hine, D. (1964b) An investigation into the biology of coarse fish of a lowland stream. Ann. appl. Biol., **53**: 498-501.

Cragg-Hine, D. and Jones, J. W. (1969) The growth of the dace *Leuciscus leuciscus* (L.), roach *Rutilus rutilus* (L.) and chub *Squalius cephalus* (L.) in Willow Brook, Northamptonshire. J. Fish Biol., **1**: 59-82.

Dickie, L. M. (1971) Mathematical models of growth, In: Ricker, W. E. (Ed) Methods for Assessment of Fish Production in Freshwaters, I.B.P. Handbook No. 3, 2nd edition, Blackwell (pp. 126-130).

Graham, M. (1929) Studies of age determination of fish. Fishery Invest. Lond. (2) **11**: 1-50

Hartley, P. H. T. (1947a) The natural history of some British freshwater fishes. Proc. zool. Soc., Lond., **117**: 129-206

Hartley, P. H. T. (1947b) The coarse fishes of Britain, being the final report of the coarse fish investigation. Scient. Publs. Freshwat. biol. Assoc., No. 12.

Healy, A. (1956) Roach and dace in the Cork Blackwater. Rep. Sea inl. Fish. Ire., Appendix No. 25, Dublin; 67-78.

Hellawell, J. M. (1969) Age determination and growth of of the grayling, *Thymallus thymallus* (L.) of the River Lugg, Herefordshire. J. Fish Biol., **1**: 373-382.

Hellawell, J. M. (1971) The autecology of the chub, *Squalius cephalus* (L.), of the River Lugg and Afon Llynfi. I. Age determination, population structure and growth. Freshwat. Biol., **1**: 135-148.

Hellawell, J. M. (1972) The growth, reproduction and food of the roach *Rutilus rutilus* (L.), of the River Lugg, Herefordshire. J. Fish Biol., **4**: 469-486.

Hellawell, J. M. (1974, In the press) The ecology of populations of dace, *Leuciscus leuciscus* (L.), from two tributaries of the River Wye, Herefordshire, England. Freshwat. Biol., 5:

Leeming, J. B. (1967) The biology of some coarse fish of the River Welland. Ph.D. thesis, University of Liverpool.

Mann, R. H. K. (1967) The production of coarse fish in some southern chalk streams. Proc. 3rd Br. coarse Fish Conf., 37-41.

Mathews, C. P. and Williams, W. P. (1972) Growth and annual check formation in scales of dace, *Leuciscus leuciscus* (L.) J. Fish Biol., **4**: 363-367.

Williams, W. P. (1967) The growth and mortality of four species of fish in the River Thames at Reading. J. Anim. Ecol., **36**: 695-720.

The effects of age-reading errors on the statistical reliability of marine fishery modelling

by KEITH BRANDER

Fisheries Laboratory, Ministry of Agriculture, Fisheries and Food, Lowestoft, Suffolk, England

SUMMARY

1. Handling of market sample information by computer allows more sophisticated use of the data on a routine basis, but it becomes increasingly important to ensure that the methods of calculation and of sampling are adapted to the uses to which the results are put.
2. A method for examining the way in which the rate of misallocation of otoliths into age groups increases with age is developed. It is shown, in two practical instances, that this misallocation has little effect on the estimated population parameters.
3. The statistical reliability of the age/length key method for converting length distributions into age distributions is investigated, and weighted mortality estimates with their associated confidence limits are produced for several stocks.
4. The use of polymodal length: frequency analysis for converting length distributions into age distributions is briefly discussed and an extension of the method is suggested.
5. The effect of errors in estimating mortality and recruitment on two models of cod populations is examined.

INTRODUCTION

The study of the dynamics of exploited fish populations is based on a knowledge of their growth rate, the mortality rate under exploitation and the strength of individual year-classes. The system for obtaining estimates of these parameters from samples taken on fish markets was investigated by John Gulland in the early 50s (Gulland, 1955) and his work forms the basis of the market sampling system used in England and Wales since that date and provides the background to the present study.

The aim of the market sampling system is to obtain the 'best' estimates of the above parameters for a given amount of sampling effort, i.e. estimates which are unbiased and of minimum variance. Over the years since the system was set up the processing of data has become increasingly automated and more sophisticated products can be obtained routinely by

AGE LENGTH KEY

Species/Year ...... COD 1971 Q.3 ......
Region ...... VII A ......
Port ...... FLEETWOOD ......
Hours fishing ... * 24242 3 ......

First age-group in A.L.K.	Mid point of length-group (cm)	Total No. of fish landed	Total No. of otoliths	1	2	3	4	5	6	7	8	9
1	27.5	3221	1	1								
1	32.5	26335	9	9								
1	37.5	16537	24	24								
1	42.5	5071	14	6	8							
1	47.5	8798	16	2	14							
2	52.5	12003	18		17	0	1					
2	57.5	7580	13		12	1						
2	62.5	5896	14		8	5	1					
2	67.5	4021	17		1	11	4	1				
3	72.5	2944	18			8	6	3	0	1		
3	77.5	1921	12			2	8	1	1			
3	82.5	1314	17			3	6	3	3	1	1	
4	87.5	654	11				1	4	3	3		
5	92.5	213	14					4	4	3	1	2
6	97.5	164	6						4	1	1	
7	102.5	129	1						1			
9	107.5	6	1								1	
7	112.5	52	2						1	0	1	
-1												

P08

Fig. 1. Age/Length Key.

adding to existing computer programs. This means that many of the tedious and repetitive calculations necessary for assessing the reliability of the data are carried out automatically, but it also means that the criteria used in deciding how to work up the data need to be examined so that where programming decisions are required they are made on a sound basis. In the present study certain aspects of the market sampling system over the past few years are examined and the reliability of the final products is investigated in relation to the uses to which they are put.

THE ESTIMATION OF POPULATION PARAMETERS FROM MARKET SAMPLING

Samples of most of the major commerically exploited species are measured on the fish markets of the large ports throughout England and Wales. The unit of sampling is generally the kit or box (weighing 6 to 10 stone) in which the fish are landed and sold. The fish are sorted into size categories before they are sold and the sampling system uses these categories as strata, raising either to the total weight landed by the sampled boat and thence to the total for the port or, where the categories are sufficiently uniform, to the total weight of each category for the port. Finally the length frequency distribution is calculated monthly, quarterly and annually for each region fished, and the record of the number of hours fished

is used to convert to numbers per 100 hours fished, the unit of catch per effort commonly used.

The samples of otoliths used for age determination are also collected at this time, in strata of 5 cm or 10 cm interval. Proportionally more are taken from the upper length strata where the spread of ages is greater. The otoliths are read (Williams and Bedford, this symposium) and grouped into quarterly and annual age/length keys (ALKs) which are used to convert the length distribution into an age distribution (Fig. 1 and 2). The final products of this process are estimates of the density of fish of each age (numbers per 100 hours) for each region for each quarter or year, and the mean length at age. These are used in order to estimate stock size, recruitment, mortality rate and growth. The reliability of these estimates will depend very largely on the correct determination of age from the otoliths and on the use of the otolith sample to convert the length distribution into an age distribution. We shall look first at the effect of errors in age determination and then at the statistics of the ALK.

ERRORS IN AGE DETERMINATION

When the age of a fish cannot be determined with certainty from the otolith or other marks it is the convention to record the age which it is believed to be with a question-mark, followed by the age which it is less likely to be. Thus a fish which is probably

```
COD   1971   Q3
V11   A
FLEETWOOD
```

LENGTH GROUP	YEAR CLASS	1	2	3	4	5	6	7	8	9	MEAN AGE
27.50		3221									
STD. DEV.		0									1.00
32.50		26335									
STD. DEV.		0									1.00
37.50		16537									
STD. DEV.		0									1.00
42.50		2173	2898								
STD. DEV.		671	671								1.57
47.50		1097	7681								
STD. DEV.		726	726								1.88
52.50			11336	0	667						
STD. DEV.			648	0	648						2.11
57.50			6997	583							
STD. DEV.			560	560							2.08
62.50			3369	2106	421						
STD. DEV.			780	755	406						2.50
67.50			237	2602	946	237					
STD. DEV.			229	466	414	229					3.29
72.50				1308	981	491	0	164			
STD. DEV.				345	327	259	0	159			3.89
77.50				320	1281	160	160				
STD. DEV.				207	261	153	153				4.08
82.50				232	464	232	232	77	77		
STD. DEV.				121	152	121	121	75	75		4.76
87.50					59	238	178	178			
STD. DEV.					57	95	88	88			5.73
92.50						61	61	46	15	30	
STD. DEV.						26	26	23	15	20	6.50
97.50							109	27	27		
STD. DEV.							32	25	25		6.50
102.50								129			
STD. DEV.								0			7.00
107.50										6	
STD. DEV.										0	9.00
112.50								26	0	26	
STD. DEV.								18	0	18	8.00
TOTAL NOS.		49364	32517	7151	4819	1418	741	647	120	62	
STD. DEV.		988	1540	1130	979	409	218	200	80	27	
NOS./100 HRS		203.6	134.1	29.5	19.9	5.8	3.1	2.7	0.5	0.3	
MEAN LENGTH		34.62	52.65	67.06	70.35	77.24	85.66	87.88	87.19	102.27	
UPPER LIMIT		35.04	53.37	69.59	77.93	84.41	93.15	105.92	80.63	121.60	
LOWER LIMIT		34.17	51.92	65.26	66.17	73.91	82.81	82.38	80.63	86.45	
S.D. OF MEAN		3.86	5.67	5.63	9.13	7.47	6.55	11.65	6.48	9.63	

Fig. 2.   Results from Age/Length Key including the standard deviation of the number at each age.

Table 1. Percentage of queried age determinations

	Age 1	2	3	4	5	6	7	8	9	10	11	12	13	14	15	16	17	18	19	20	21+	% Crystalline + Unreadable	Total Number
Cod																							
North Sea (N. Shields 1968–72)	10	3	4	2	6	6	8	18	21	17		40										0.1	4694
Irish Sea (Fleetwood 1968–71)	0	<1	<1	<1	3	4	7			8												0.04	2411
Iceland (Hull, Grimsby and Fleetwood 1969–72)		8	12	14	20	21	23	23	18	23	32	46	44	52	33			64				0.01	8068
Plaice																							
North Sea (Lowestoft 1970–71)	5	6	4	20	13	18	11	17	28	22	21	30	20	33	46	43	37	40	48	61	62	0.7	3647

Table 2. Comparison of results of normal ALK with one in which queried otoliths have been redistributed

(a) Iceland Cod 1971

	2	3	4	5	6	7	8	9	10	11	12	13	14	15+
Total Nos														
Normal	380345	6986464	16639785	20913158	11643073	6213607	3477640	1562251	724122	72680	2722	3487	3933	4177
Reassigned	464579	6797254	16703637	20781997	11639724	6385538	3479272	1565559	723028	71645	3799	4963	3165	3583
St. Deviation														
Normal	118508	544667	812320	883387	702154	361570	251262	182203	119548	32107	1184	1720	1376	1446
Reassigned	131910	540400	811230	882140	701610	374000	251900	180280	119950	31860	2100	1700	1320	1460

(b) North Sea Plaice ♀ 1971

	1	2	3	4	5	6	7	8	9	10	11	12	13	14	15	16	17	18	19
Total Nos																			
Normal	6213	492765	1909072	2528628	2512157	2507581	1601648	4356396	674979	604590	443575	570218	339523	210663	225427	52117	97543	109868	69127
Reassigned	6213	495970	1915133	2549600	2496314	2456149	1634454	4364780	654063	632774	448301	524870	385070	192427	216638	74196	95471	97483	70151
Std Deviation																			
Normal	4358	90408	188631	261132	276446	275692	226023	305553	124431	104985	90641	95954	56174	42072	49219	17054	32476	24964	19230
Reassigned	4360	92580	189290	261700	275710	273880	226650	307330	121200	108750	90440	90410	65530	36770	49340	24570	29820	23270	19280

	20	21	22	23	24	25	26	27	28	29	30	31	32	33	34	35	36	37
Total Nos																		
Normal	34129	13652	44314	25028	42039	52229	39764	35213	4551	4551	6826	0	0	0	2275	0	0	0
Reassigned	34796	15699	42949	28603	40674	48486	42998	33344	5054	5574	5461	683	683	1934	2275	1593	341	0
Std Deviation																		
Normal	8532	5503	11815	7371	11623	14190	11426	11014	3204	3204	3916	0	0	0	2271	0	0	0
Reassigned	9390	5890	11700	8280	11510	13420	12000	10520	4260	3540	3510	1250	1250	2090	1900	880	0	0

183

five, but may possibly be six is written 5 ? 6, or if it is thought to be six, but possibly five, 6 ? 5. If it is simply a doubtful reading it will be written 5? and in rare cases one may find 5?? or 6 ? 5 ? 7. The fact that the age of a fish is in doubt is ignored in constructing the ALK and the first age given is always used. Gulland (1955) has shown that if the probability of misclassifying the age is the same for all ages then the estimated survival rate is unaffected by the errors, but that if the probability of misclassification varies then a bias will be introduced. Since there is no absolutely certain way of ageing fish taken from commercial samples it is impossible to determine the proportion which are being misclassified, but one may determine the proportion of fish of each age which have been queried during age determination and examine the way in which the proportion queried varies with age. Since it is difficult to be completely objective about doubtful otolith readings, different readers may judge them in different ways and it is important to use stocks aged by one person as far as possible in order to maintain consistency (Gulland 1958).

Table 1 shows the percentage of queried age determinations for three cod stocks and one stock of plaice over a number of years. The results are shown graphically in Fig. 3 and it appears that the proportion queried increases with age and differs between different stocks of the same species. For example, the proportion of Iceland cod queried is higher at all ages than the proportion of North Sea cod. The majority of the age determinations of the oldest fish (above 29 for North Sea plaice, above 15 for Iceland cod) are to some degree doubtful, but the consensus of opinion among experienced otolith readers at this laboratory is that although the exact age may be difficult to specify with certainty the area of doubt is rarely more than two or sometimes three years.

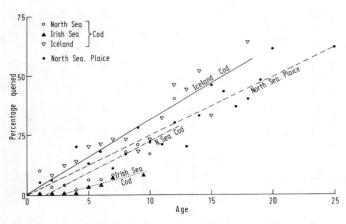

Fig. 3. Percentage of otoliths queried at each age.

One must make some assumption about the probability of misclassification in order to make use of the information on percentages queried. A reasonable assumption, which will be used in subsequent calculations, is that the probability of the first age quoted is 0.7 and of the second age 0.3, or where the age is queried, but no second alternative is given, that each adjacent age has a probability of 0.15. Crystalline and unreadable otoliths and other types of query are sufficiently rare to be ignored. The possibility that the age determinations and queries are completely wrong over part or all of the range has also not been considered.

The effect of reassigning otoliths which have been queried has been examined for the 1971 Iceland cod samples and the 1968 North Sea plaice sampled at Lowestoft. The routine ALK results and the results from the reassigned ALK are compared in Table 2 and, as can be seen, the differences in the estimated abundances are extremely small. The theoretical overestimate of survival produced if the proportion misallocated increases by 2.5% between successive ages is only between 0.1 and 0.2% and there is no evidence of any bias being introduced in the practical examples by not taking queries into account.

These two worked examples confirm the theoretical expectation that even a fairly high rate of misallocation will not materially affect estimates of survival rate if the misallocation does not alter suddenly and does not involve a systematic bias in ageing. Ricker (1969) examined the effect of inaccurate age determination on growth estimates and came to very similar conclusions.

ERRORS DUE TO THE AGE/LENGTH KEY

The ALK is used to convert the length frequency distribution into an age frequency distribution (Figs. 1 and 2).

If

N_i is the number of fish in length group i: n_i is the number examined for age in length group i; P_a is the proportion of n_i which are of age a;

then

$N_i P_a$ is the number of fish of age a in length group i and N_i var P_a is the variance of $N_i P_a$ due to the otolith sample, where

$$\text{var } P_a = \frac{P_a(1 - P_a)}{n_i}$$

There will also be a term of the variance of $N_i P_a$ due to the variance in the estimate of N (it will be var $N_i P_a{}^2$), but this term will be ignored here for three reasons:

1. we are principally concerned with errors in ageing;
2. the term is generally small compared with $N_i{}^2$ var P_a;
3. the variance of N_i is difficult to determine routinely.

Figure 2 shows the length frequency distribution split up into separate ages by means of the ALK, with the standard deviations of the individual estimates given. Also given are the numbers at each age per 100 hours fishing, the means and standard deviations of length at age, and the rough confidence limits of the mean length at age.

We are again concerned to determine the effects of these variances due to the ALK on the estimates of mortality used in population studies. In most assessment work one mortality estimate is obtained for each year and taken to represent the mortality on all fully recruited year-classes. The exact method of calculation may vary; for instance, it may be advantageous to look at mortality between each quarter of successive years in order to overcome the effect of seasonal changes in the fishery (Garrod, 1964). There may be evidence that mortality increase on the upper ages, in which case these may be excluded from the estimate or calculated separately. Whichever method is used, a series of mortality estimates can be obtained for each year-class between the two years, and the question then arises of how to combine these individual estimates into a single mortality figure for the year. The variances of the mortality estimate for each year-class may be calculated from the coefficients of variation of numbers at each age. Obviously those ages which are poorly sampled and have a high coefficient of variation will have a high variance on their mortality estimate and should be given a low weighting in the combined mortality estimate. Although we stated in an earlier section that proportionally more otoliths are taken from the larger fish, which will tend to even out the coefficient of variation over the age range, one finds that in practice the coefficient does increase with age and that weighting is therefore necessary.

Using Gulland's notation, let

$$_1n_x = \text{density index for fish aged x in year 1,}$$
$$_2n_{x+1} = \text{density index for fish aged x + 1 in year 2;}$$

$_1\sigma_x$ and $_2\sigma_{x+1}$ are their respective coefficients of variation.

$$m_x \text{ (mortality rate)} = \ln {}_1n_x - \ln {}_2n_{x+1}$$

and

$$\text{var } m_x = {}_1\sigma_x{}^2 + {}_2\sigma_{x+1}{}^2$$

If $x = 1, 2 \ldots k$ are the ages for which mortality rates can be determined, then

$$\overline{m} \text{ (combined mortality estimate)} = \sum_1^k w_x m_x,$$

where w is the weighting coefficient and $\sum_1^k w_x = 1$

(for equal weighting $w = \frac{1}{k}$);

$$\text{var } \overline{m} = \sum_1^k w_x{}^2 \text{ var } m_x,$$

assuming that the value of m are independent of each other.

It can be shown that a combined estimate of mortality with the smallest possible variance will be produced if the individual mortality estimates are weighted by the inverse of their variances (Aitken 1957, Bliss 1967), i.e. when

$$w_x = \frac{\text{var } \dot{m}_x{}^{-1}}{\sum_1^k \text{ var } m_x{}^{-1}}$$

Table 3a shows the average coefficient of variation for several years sampling at each age and the weighting coefficients for each pair of fully recruited ages for two stocks of coalfish, two of cod and one of plaice. The variances of the combined mortality estimates ($\overline{m}$) and the minimum confidence limits associated with them are shown in Table 3b.

The weighting factors are much higher on the younger, more abundant ages than on the older ones. For example, the weighting given to the mortality estimate for ages 5 to 6 in Iceland coalfish is nearly twenty times that given to the 13 to 14 mortality estimate.

Since the weighting factors derive from the coefficients of variation they will depend on the sampling scheme and will fluctuate from year to year. Abundant year-classes will generally maintain a lower than average coefficient of variation at all ages, which is why the coefficients for ages 5 and 8 for North Sea plaice are particularly low in 1968 and 1971: they both include the strong 1963 year-class.

In Fig. 4 the abundance of Iceland cod at each age is plotted, with 95% confidence limits for 1969 and 1970. The slope (mortality) for each year-class between the two years is shown and appears to be higher at greater ages, but the confidence limits on the mortality estimates are also far wider. For example, taking a combined mortality estimate on ages above 11, the minimum variance estimate is 0.0705, i.e. 95% confidence limits of ±0.531 on a total mortality of about 0.8. The actual variance on the combined estimate of mortality from the individual estimates for the 1955, 56, 57 and 58 year-classes is 0.2965, giving a 95% confidence limit ±1.089. Similarly, for female North Sea plaice sampled at Lowestoft the minimum estimate of the variance on the annual mortality calculated between the ages of 20 and 30 is 0.0229, i.e. 95% confidence limits of ±0.34 on a total mortality of about 0.3. It must be stressed that these estimates of variance and confidence limits only include the variance due to the ALK and assume that the individual mortalities for each year-class are independent They are calculated on the basis of the method of

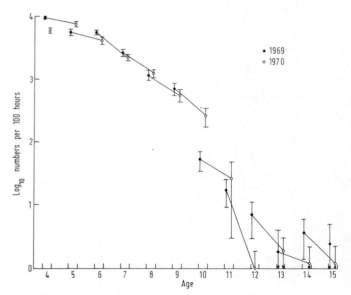

Fig. 4. Iceland cod 1969-70. Year class ±2 std. deviations. Lines joining the points represent the total mortality between the two years.

weighting by the inverse of the variance, which produces the minimum combined variance. Bearing this in mind it is obvious that conclusions about the mortality rates on older fish which are taken from the existing market sampling schemes are subject to very wide confidence limits and can only be tentative. Better estimates can only be obtained by increasing the number of otoliths taken from the larger fish and since these are generally more difficult to sample and age, such an increase or redistribution of sampling effort is difficult to justify on other grounds.

Where the main aim in calculating the age frequency distribution is to obtain a single combined estimate of the mortality rate it may be worthwhile to ignore all fish above a certain age, since they will contribute

Table 3a. Average coefficients of variation for all ages and weighting coefficients for all fully recruited ages (for North Sea Plaice the weightings have been calculated for ages 5-20 and 20-30 separately)

Coalfish

Iceland (Hull and Grimsby) 10 years sampled—690 otoliths p.a.

	2	3	4	5	6	7	8	9	10	11	12	13	14	15+
coeff of var.	0.4212	0.1201	0.0834	0.0793	0.0962	0.1248	0.1678	0.2429	0.2514	0.2787	0.3379	0.3493	0.4209	
weighting				0.3852	0.2411	0.1369	0.0687	0.0490	0.0425	0.0312	0.0253	0.0200		

Faroe (Hull and Grimsby) 11 years sampled—594 otoliths p.a.

	2	3	4	5	6	7	8	9	10	11	12	13	14	15+
coeff of var.	0.2066	0.0980	0.0875	0.0803	0.0998	0.1259	0.1524	0.1784	0.2310	0.3234	0.3107	0.3482	0.4176	
weighting				0.3493	0.2221	0.1467	0.1041	0.0673	0.0363	0.0285	0.0263	0.0194		

Cod

Iceland (Hull, Grimsby and Fleetwood) 4 years sampled—2032 otoliths p.a.

	1	2	3	4	5	6	7	8	9	10	11	12	13
coeff of var.	0.3000	0.0852	0.0420	0.0466	0.0565	0.0668	0.0391	0.1354	0.1822	0.2849	0.3731	0.4363	0.4021
weighting				0.3930	0.2754	0.1700	0.0802	0.0409	0.0184	0.0096	0.0064	0.0060	

North Sea (N. Shields) 8 years sampled—753 otoliths p.a.

	1	2	3	4	5	6	7	8	9	10	11	12
coeff of var.	0.271	0.067	0.074	0.083	0.104	0.155	0.212	0.282	0.438	0.542	0.627	0.925
weighting				0.411	0.287	0.146	0.074	0.041	0.019	0.010	0.007	0.004

Plaice ♀

North Sea (Lowestoft) 2 years sampled—1137 otoliths p.a.

	5	6	7	8	9	10	11	12	13	14	15	16	17	18	19	20
coeff of var.	0.1095	0.164	0.149	0.173	0.173	0.216	0.224	0.236	0.261	0.339	0.246	0.265	0.255			
weighting	0.076	0.108	0.124	0.129	0.200	0.143	0.097	0.071	0.069	0.058	0.046	0.036	0.033	0.028	0.019	0.020

	21	22	23	24	25	26	27	28	29	30
coeff of var.	0.267	0.295	0.276	0.272	0.287	0.313	0.704	0.704	0.704	0.574
weighting	0.403	0.295	0.276	0.272	0.287	0.313	0.027	0.025		

Table 3b. Variances of the combined mortality estimates (m) and the minimum confidence limits associated with them

	Mean value of m	Variance of m	95% Confidence limit
Coalfish			
Iceland	1.0-1.15	0.00599	±0.18
Faroe	0.7	0.00573	±0.17
Cod			
North Sea	0.6	0.00509	±0.16
Iceland	0.6-0.8	0.00210	±0.11
Plaice ♀			
North Sea			
(Ages 5-20)	0.3-0.4	0.00693	±0.18
(Ages 20-30)	0.3-0.4	0.02294	±0.34

very little to the combined estimate when a weighting factor is used.

THE USE OF TECHNIQUES FOR ANALYSING DISTRIBUTION MIXTURES

The method of obtaining age distributions by analysing length frequency distributions into their component ages (sometimes known as the Petersen method) has been widely described and used (Cassie 1963, Bhattacharya 1967),* and recently various computerized versions have been produced (Hasselblad 1966, Macdonald 1969). In a review of methods in fishery research Parrish (1958) states '... it is often possible to replace, either completely or partially, the more laborious scale or otolith method by Petersen's method, after the early exploratory phase of the investigation. Many workers today utilize Petersen's method on large samples of length data together with smaller check samples of scales or otoliths. This is the basis of the growing use of length age keys in routine age determination (Gulland 1955).'

The age/length key is not in any way based on the Petersen method and the fundamental difference between the two is that the Petersen method assumes that the distribution of length at age in the sampled population is normal, whereas the age/length key makes no such distributional assumption. Using the ALK, the estimate of the number of fish of a particular age in a particular stratum is independent of the number in every other stratum. We can use the length at age distributions obtained by means of ALKs to test whether the distribution of length at age in the sampled population of any particular stock is in fact normal. If it is normal then were are justified in drawing additional information from the ALK, using the assumption of normality.

TESTING THE NORMALITY OF THE DISTRIBUTION OF LENGTH AT AGE

Quarterly ALKs from North Sea trawl-caught cod sampled on the market at North Shields for the years 1963 to 1970 and ages up to 9 were tested for normality by estimating skewness (g_1) and kurtosis (g_2) using the formulae given by Fisher (1941). With some gaps in the data, mainly at the least and greatest ages,

Table 4.   Skewness (g_1) and kurtosis (g_2) of distribution of length at age of North Sea Cod, trawl caught, sampled at North Shields (1963-1970)

Age	Quarter	g_1 Quarterly mean	Annual mean	Std error of annual mean	g_2 Quarterly mean	Annual mean
1	3	−0.01	−0.23	0.16	−0.27	−0.65
	4	−0.45			−1.03	
2	1	0.40	0.26	0.11	−1.57	−0.70
	2	0.11			−0.48	
	3	0.39			−0.15	
	4	0.22			−0.61	
3	1	0.40	0.18	0.09	−0.60	−0.40
	2	0.47			0.02	
	3	−0.03			−0.72	
	4	−0.02			−0.29	
4	1	−0.30	−0.19	0.10	0.22	−0.20
	2	−0.07			−0.37	
	3	−0.64			−0.19	
	4	0.31			−0.45	
5	1	0.09	−0.34	0.15	−0.38	−0.16
	2	−0.34			−0.37	
	3	−0.87			0.63	
	4	−0.03			−0.51	
6			−0.85	0.18	0.47	0.47
7			−0.03	0.19	−0.70	−0.70
8			−0.48	0.41	0.51	0.51
9			−1.56	0.29	2.58	2.58

* Editor's note. See Mathews, C.P. 1974. This Symposium volume, Bagenal, T.B. (Ed.), Ageing of Fish, Unwin Brothers Ltd., 158-166.

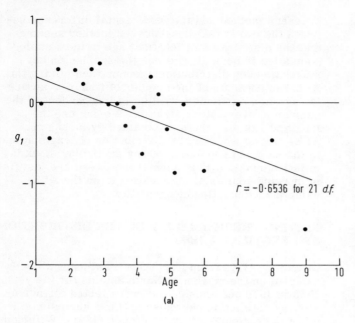

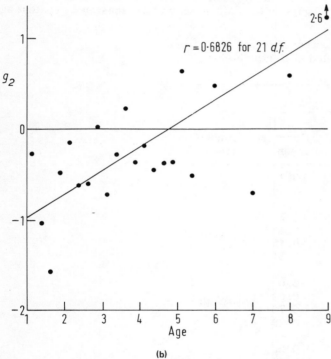

Fig. 5. Regression on age of (a) skewness (g_1) and (b) kurtosis (g_2) of the mean quarterly distribution of length at age for North Shields market sampled cod (1963-1970).

this gave a total of 128 distributions. Above the age of six it was necessary to combine the distributions into annual totals in order to reduce the sampling variance. The grouped results are given in Table 4 and are graphed in Figs. 5a and b.

The main features which emerge are:

1. Individual distributions cannot be shown to differ significantly from normal, but exact confidence limits are not obtainable, due to ignorance of the number of observations in ALKs.

2. The correlation between g_1 (skewness) and age is highly significant, and the regression lines plotted in Fig. 5a show a decline from slight positive values below about 4 years to negative

values above. The regression on the quarterly averages accounts for over 40% of the variance

3. Correlation between g_2 and age is highly significant and the regression (Fig. 5b) increases from slight negative values below about 5 years to positive values above. The regression on the quarterly averages accounts for 47% of the variance.

One may conclude that although the distributions of length at age in market samples of North Sea cod are approximately normal for the intermediate ages, the younger age groups tend to be positively skewed and platykurtic, whereas the older ones are negatively skewed and leptokurtic.

The computer programe used to analyse the polymodal length frequency distributions is a slightly modified version of one developed by Macdonald (1969), which fits a series of normal distributions by a maximum likelihood procedure. The version of the program most commonly used requires initial estimates of the proportions (π), means (μ) and standard deviations (σ) of all ages to be estimated, and allows only the proportions to vary. In this form it is useful where good estimates of the growth rate, including change in standard deviation, are available; it has been used in situations where there was an interruption in the otolith sampling, but not in length measuring, or where length measurements on a stock had been made for a number of years before otoliths were taken.

Table 5 shows input and output values for the program (MIXMLP) and a comparison with the results for the ALK. Underlined values had non-overlapping confidence limits. The agreement between the two methods is good, but the agreement between the values input and the ALK values is just as good.

These input values are crudely estimated by probability paper methods or by inspection. The main reason for preferring the output of MIXMLP to these values is that if a standard growth curve is used then the output from the computer will be repeatable and standardized and the subjective element is reduced. There is a gain in that MIXMLP can be used where no modes are evident in the length frequency distributions, but the element of 'poetic licence' which exists in the probability paper method is lost.

A possible extension of the method is suggested by the fact that it has been found for cod and haddock that for two fish of the same length but different ages the older will, on average, have a heavier otolith (Templeman and Squires 1956, Mina 1967). In these cases a two-dimensional separation, using otolith weight as well, may give a better separation of ages than length alone. Some preliminary tests on Irish Sea cod using discriminant techniques indicate that separation is improved. Table 6 shows values of

Table 6. Values of d/s (distance between ages) for Irish Sea cod, 1972

Ages	Sample sizes	d/s		
		Length	Otolith weight	Both
1-2	14, 44	3.311	3.143	4.186
2-3	44. 116	2.306	2.901	4.532
3-4	116.41	1.514	2.228	3.662

$^{d}/s$, the distance between means divided by the common standard deviation, for adjacent age groups (Snedecor and Cochran 1967).

The existing computer program could be amended by substituting the probability density function for a bivariate normal distribution in place of the single-dimensional one. This technique could be applied to populations for which length frequencies and otolith samples were available, but where the otolith could not be interpreted. In this case length/otolith weight modes might be evident where modes of either by itself were not. A further possibility is where large otolith samples were obtainable and could be weighed automatically.

THE EFFECT OF ERRORS IN DETERMINING THE AGE STRUCTURE OF POPULATIONS ON POPULATION MODELS

To summarize the conclusions so far reached about the determination of year-class strength and mortality from English and Welsh market samples:

1. The year-class strength of partially recruited year-classes is generally estimated with less accuracy than are the first fully recruited year-classes. They cannot be estimated accurately by Petersen methods because the distribution of length at age is not normal.
2. The intermediate ages are well estimated by both ALK and Petersen methods and common mortality estimates are generally obtained from them. Assuming that there are no trends in mortality and that it is valid to take a common value, the estimate with least variance is produced by weighting the individual estimates inversely by their variances.
3. The older ages are not well estimated by either

method, since the number of otoliths is lower and the distribution of length at age deviates from normal. The fact that there is increasing uncertainty about age reading must also be taken into account, although the overall estimate of mortality is little affected by high levels of uncertainty, provided that they are consistent.

The effect of the variance in the estimates of year-class strength and mortality can be examined for two population models. The first is a simple model of yield per recruit for cod in the northern North Sea (ICES Division IVa) (Holden and Flatman 1972), and the second is a multistock time-varied model of the North Atlantic cod fishery (Garrod and Clayden 1972).

Figure 6 shows a family of curves of yield per recruit against fishing mortality for different levels of

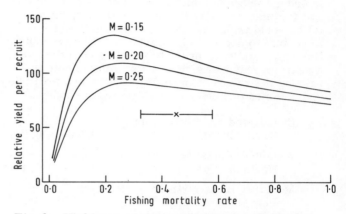

Fig. 6. Yield per recruit on fishing mortality for North Sea cod. The value of fishing mortality for 1968-69 is shown ±2 std. deviations. (Adapted from Holden and Flatman, 1972).

Table 5.

FD 1900	Input Values			Output Values		ALK Values			
	Initial estimated π	μ from growth curve	σ from growth curve	MIXMLP estimate of π	95% confidence limit	ALK estimate of π	95% confidence limit	μ from ALK	σ from ALK
Age									
1 {3						0.049	±0.031	38.8	3.25
4	0.31	39.0	3.8	0.377	±0.034	0.377	—	38.7	3.37
2 {1	0.30	44.0	5.0	0.310	±0.025				
2	0.45	47.5	5.2	0.454	±0.035	0.475	±0.059	47.2	5.15
3	0.66	50.0	5.3	0.666	±0.046	0.550	±0.056	50.9	4.68
4	0.47	54.0	5.4	0.475	±0.040	0.425	±0.045	53.4	4.40
3 {1	0.35	59.0	5.5	0.342	±0.034				
2	0.35	63.0	5.8	0.342	±0.045	0.322	±0.063	63.5	4.97
3	0.23	65.0	5.8	0.228	±0.051	0.318	±0.054	62.1	7.80
4	0.17	67.5	5.8	0.108	±0.032	0.140	±0.045	63.6	4.17
4 {1	0.25	70.0	5.8	0.234	±0.032				
2	0.10	73.0	5.8	0.017	±0.055	0.105	±0.036	76.9	4.27
3	0.11	75.0	5.8	0.107	±0.034	0.044	±0.014	76.6	4.86
4	0.05	76.5	5.8	0.039	±0.018	0.058	—	76.7	4.92
5+ {1	0.10	80.5	5.8	0.114	±0.018				
2	0.10	85.0	5.8	0.186	±0.041	0.098	±0.038	81.6	4.90
3						0.038	±0.012	81.1	5.58
4									

natural mortality for the northern North Sea cod. The average level of fishing mortality over the period 1968-1969 is marked, with the confidence limits on the weighted estimate of the annual total mortality for northern North Sea cod sampled at North Shields (Table 3). These confidence limits only include the variance due to the ALK and are the theoretical minimum values.

If more data on annual mortalities were included from other ports or other countries the limits might be reduced, but are unlikely to be much lower in practice.

If the objective of management is to secure the maximum yield per recruit, then the uncertainty due to ageing will be unimportant at these levels of fishing mortality, since yield per recruit varies very little over the range. If the fishing effort were reduced in order to secure a higher catch per effort (Holden and Flatman estimate that halving the fishing mortality would triple the catch rate), then it would be important to decrease the variance in the estimate of fishing mortality in order to regulate effectively on a year-to-year basis. It is interesting to note in passing the values of mortality of northern North Sea cod obtained for 1968/69 by different methods:

Unweighted mortality from North Shields c.p.u.e.	0.9384 ± 0.2410
Weighted mortality from North Shields c.p.u.e.	0.5286 ± 0.1075
Mortality from Virtual Population Analysis	0.6056 ± 0.0828

The virtual population estimate is based on total international catch and is the mean of the '68 and '69 values. The two North Shields estimates are based on the same set of catch per unit effort data and have non-overlapping confidence limits, but the confidence limits only take account of the ALK variance. Nevertheless this is a somewhat surprising result and it arises because some of the older ages produced very high mortality estimates (3.2834 ± 2.0326 in one case) which scarcely affected the weighted estimate, but raised the unweighted estimate considerably. If the increase in mortality with age is genuine, then it is not valid to calculate a common mortality in the first place.

In the multistock simulation model, Garrod and Clayden (1972, Table 2) have used two levels of fishing mortality ($F = 0.6$ and $F = 0.8$). These levels of mortality are translated into levels of fishing effort by means of the linear model $F = qf$, where q is the catchability coefficient and f is the fishing effort. Variances in estimating F are transferred directly to the estimate of effort.

Confidence limits are not available for all the stocks in the model; however the minimum confidence limit on mortality of Iceland cod sampled at Hull, Grimsby and Fleetwood is ± 0.11 (Table 3), so that Garrod and Clayden's values of $F = 0.6$ and 0.8 are a likely minimum confidence range for one year's sampling. The total catches obtained at these two levels of fishing mortality are almost identical (1670×10^3 and 1600×10^3 tons respectively), which is equivalent to the situation in the single stock model, but the total catches are calculated on the basis of known year-class strengths and, where prediction of future trends is required as part of the management policy, it will be necessary to know the strength of partially

recruited or pre-recruit year-classes. Naturally, only the former can be estimated from market samples and, as we have seen, estimates of partially recruited year-classes are subject to greater variances than are the first few recruited ages. Thus a prediction of the yield of the year-class of Iceland cod which is currently 2 years old will have a co-efficient of variation of at least 30%, but the coefficient of variation has dropped to 8.5% by the age of three (Table 3). This gives some indication of the rate at which uncertainty is likely to increase as predictions are pushed further into the future. The effects of errors of this kind on the setting of catch quotas or effort quotas, in order to regulate a fishery, have recently been investigated by Pope and Garrod (in press) and the more general problem of the effects on production studies is dealt with by Le Cren (this symposium).

Another most important effect of the high variances on younger age groups is in the study of the relation between stock and recruitment. As Garrod and Clayden remark in their discussion of biological overfishing, 'The form of the relationship (between stock and recruitment) is obscured by the obviously high variance'.

REFERENCES

Aitken, A. C. (1957). Statistical Mathematics. Oliver and Boyd Ltd., Edinburgh, 153 pp.

Bhattacharya, C. G. (1967). A simple method of resolution of a distribution into Gaussian components. Biometrics, **23** (1): 115-135.

Bliss, C. I. (1967). Statistics in Biology. McGraw-Hill, New York, 558 pp.

Cassie, R. M. (1963). Tests of significance for probability paper analysis. N.Z. Jl Sci., 6 (4): 474-482.

Fisher, R. A. (1941). Statistical methods for research workers. Oliver and Boyd Ltd, Edinburgh, 344 pp.

Garrod, D. J. (1964). Effective fishing effort and the catchability coefficient q. Rapp. P.-v. Réun. Cons. int. Explor. Mer, **155**: 66-70.

Garrod, D. J. and Clayden, A. D. (1972). Current biological problems in the conservation of deep sea fishery resources. Symp. zool. Soc. Lond., **29**: 161-184.

Gulland, J. A. (1955). Estimation of growth and mortality in commercial fish populations. Fishery Invest., Lond., Ser. II, **XVIII** (9).

Gulland, J. A. (1958). Age determination of cod by fin rays and otoliths. Spec. Publs int. Commn NW Atlantic Fish., (1): 179-190.

Hasselblad, V. (1966). Estimation of parameters for a mixture of normal distributions. Technometrics, **8**: 431-444.

Holden, M. J. and Flatman, S. (1972). An assessment of North Sea cod stocks using virtual population analysis. ICES CM 1972/F: 21, 4 pp. (mimeo).

Le Cren, E. D. The effects of errors in production studies. This Symposium volume, Bagenal, T. B. (Ed.), Ageing of Fish, Unwin Brothers Ltd., 221-224.

Macdonald, P. D. M. (1969). FORTRAN programs for statistical estimation of distribution mixtures: some techniques for statistical analysis of length-frequency data. Tech. Rep. Fish. Res. Bd Can., (129), 45 pp.

Mina, M. V. (1967). Study of the relation between the weight of an otolith (sagitta) and the length of an individual in the cod population of the Barents and White Seas. Nauch. Dokl. vyssh. Shr., (9), 26-31. (Transl. available, Fish. Res. Bd Can., (990)).

Parrish, B. B. (1958). Some notes on methods used in fishery research. Spec. Publs int. Commn NW Atlant. Fish (1): 151-178.

Pope, J. G. and Garrod, D. J. (in press). A contribution to the discussion of the effects of error on the action of catch quotas and effort quotas.

Ricker, W. E. (1969. Effects of size-selective mortality and sampling bias on estimates of growth, mortality, production and yield. J. Fish. Res. Bd. Can., **26**, 479-541

Snedecor, G. W. and Cochran, W. G. (1967). Statistical methods. Iowa State U.P., Ames, Iowa. 593 pp.

Templeman, W. and Squires, H. J. (1956). Relationship of otolith lengths and weights in the haddock to the rate of growth of the fish. J. Fish. Res. Bd Can., **13** (4): 467-487.

Williams, T. and Bedford, B. C. 1974. The use of otoliths for age determination. This symposium volume, Bagenal, T. B. (Ed.), Ageing of Fish, Unwin Brothers Ltd., 114-123.

The effect of different age ranges on estimated Bertalanffy growth parameters in three fishes and one mollusk of the northeastern Pacific Ocean

by GEORGE HIRSCHHORN

Northwest Fisheries Center, National Marine Fisheries Service, 2725 Mortlake Boulevard East, Seattle, Washington, U.S.A.

SUMMARY

The variation of Bertalanffy parameters (L_∞. k, t_0) with respect to age range used was examined in samples of walleye pollock *Theragra chalcogramma*, Pacific halibut *Hippoglossus stenolepis*, English sole *Parophrys vetulus* and razor clam *Siliqua patula*. While estimates of L_∞ are shown to increase and of k to decrease in the 3 fish species, trends opposite to these have been found in razor clams. The association of these trends with regard to allometry between width and length of the underlying age structures is discussed.

INTRODUCTION

In this Symposium the effects of errors in age determination on fishery management are considered by Brander and by Carlander (1974, this volume pages 181 and 200). The present paper considers the effects of different age ranges when used in estimating the Bertanlanffy growth parameters which are often basic to any rational fishery management policy. The ranges of ages used may differ through the exclusion of the mean lengths of older fish, since these are usually the most difficult to age, through excluding mean lengths based on few fish owing to their possible unreliability, or through abandoning the difficult outer rings when using back calculated lengths. It will be shown in this paper that the exclusion of older ages from data sets affects the estimation of Bertalanffy parameters and is therefore inadvisable.

The estimation of growth parameters is fundamental to much fishery work. For example, one of the main research activities of the Northwest Fisheries Center of the U.S. National Marine Fishery Service is the determination of ages of important groundfish species of the northwest Pacific and Bering Sea from otoliths.

Principal objectives of this research are to measure the relative strength of year classes, the effect of fishing or environmental changes on the stocks, growth and mortality rates, and biomass changes. In the development of growth formulations suitable for the study of yield relations, Bertalanffy parameters (L_∞, k, t_0) are estimated. For a recent discussion of Bertalanffy parameters in this context, see Alverson and Carney (1973).

In a detailed review of the Bertalanffy theory, Southward and Chapman (1965) noted systematic variations in parameter estimates of asymptote (L_∞) and curvature (K) for Pacific halibut *Hippoglossus stenolepis* with respect to the number of ages included in the age-length data set from which these estimates were obtained. They presented applications of a more generalized, 4-parameter equation developed by Chapman (1960) and Richards (1959)

which leads to a 'relative growth rate' (K/m) and a 'weighted mean growth rate' (K/2m + 2), with similar results as were obtained for K and regardless of whether the age-length data sets came from individual fish, or represented average lengths at age.

In this paper variations in parameters (L_∞, k, t_0) are examined with respect to age range used from data on 2 species of Pleuronectidae—Pacific halibut and English sole *Parophrys vetulus*; one species of Gadidae, the walleye pollock *Theragra chalcogramma*; and one species of mollusk, the razor clam *Siliqua patula*.

METHODS

The estimates of Bertalanffy parameters were obtained by the Walford method. Asymptotic linear regression estimates (Stevens, 1951) and Fabens estimates (Fabens, 1965) were also obtained since the computer program used performs all three estimations; the former is not given here because the fitting of the data is with respect to 3 parameters (L_∞, k, t_0) rather than 2, and the latter is equivalent to the Walford method when all ages in the data set are equidistant. Because the variation of curvature and asymptote is emphasized rather than 'goodness of fit' it was thought preferable to deal with the most direct estimates of k available. It should be mentioned that the asymptotic linear regression estimates lead typically to a better fit because of the additional parameter used in estimation. The estimation of t_0 from the 2-parameter equations, was based on the general algorithm of Fabens (1965), i.e.

$$t_0 = k^{-1} * l_n[\Sigma(l_\infty - l_i) * \exp(-kt_i)/\Sigma l_\infty * \exp(-2kt_i)]$$

where L_∞ and k are obtained from the Walford regression, l_i is observed length of t_i and the summations are taken over the entire data set.

MATERIALS

The presentation of results in Tables 1-3 follows the same order as the description of data sets below.

Walleye Pollock

Mean total lengths at age for samples of this species, collected in Bering Sea in 1973 and aged at the Northwest Fisheries Center.

A. Males
B. Females

Pacific Halibut

Fish from off Alaska—Area III of the International Pacific Halibut Commission. Data from page 11 of

Southward and Chapman (1965). Total lengths were estimated from otolith lengths as in Southward (1962a).

C. Specimen no. 1 of 1942 yearclass (16 years)
D. Specimen no. 2 of 1942 yearclass (16 years)
E. Average of five fish lengths of 16-year olds of 1942 yearclass.

Razor Clams

Clams from Hallo Bay, Alaska. Median lengths at age. Data from Weymouth and McMillin (1931).

F. Sexes combined
G. Males
H. Females

English Sole

Samples from Carr Inlet, Washington. Data from Holland (1969, Tables 2-4).

I. Males, observed lengths at age
J. Females, observed lengths at age
K. Males, fish length calculated from otolith length by semilogarithmic relation
L. Females, fish length calculated from otolith length by semilogarithmic relation
M. Males, otolith lengths at age
N. Females, otolith lengths at age
O. Males, otolith lengths at age, averaged over 1940-1950 yearclasses
P. Females, otolith lengths at age, averaged over 1940-1950 yearclasses

Data from Van Cleve and El-Sayed (1969, Fig. 7, lower)

Q. Measurements of outer annulus margins
R. Measurements of inner annulus margins

Table 1 contains the 18 age length data sets described above, with frequencies at age in parentheses when known.

Table 1. Age-length data sets A-R. For description of sets, see text. Frequencies in parentheses where known.

| Age | Walleye pollock | | Pacific Halibut | | | Razor clams | | |
| | | | Southward and Chapman (1965) | | | Weymouth and McMillin (1931) | | |
	A	B	C	D	E	F	G	H
1			7 (1)	7 (1)	7.4 (5)			
2	23.25 (24)	22.38 (34)	20 (1)	23 (1)	19.4 (5)	2.26 (226)	2.07 (111)	2.48 (115)
3	30.76 (21)	31.68 (25)	40 (1)	33 (1)	33.2 (5)	5.42 (229)	5.05 (113)	6.22 (116)
4	36.64 (14)	37.70 (10)	45 (1)	45 (1)	42.6 (5)	8.60 (229)	8.01 (113)	9.21 (116)
5	39.88 (8)	41.69 (13)	52 (1)	53 (1)	51.6 (5)	10.96 (228)	10.59 (112)	11.33 (116)
6	41.83 (6)	43.50 (2)	65 (1)	63 (1)	60.8 (5)	12.37 (227)	12.21 (111)	12.56 (116)
7	44.29 (7)	50.00 (9)	74 (1)	69 (1)	67.2 (5)	13.17 (211)·	13.10 (105)	13.27 (106)
8	50.00 (18)	52.83 (29)	86 (1)	77 (1)	74.4 (5)	13.65 (192)	13.56 (97)	13.76 (95)
9	48.00 (5)	55.13 (8)	93 (1)	84 (1)	79.8 (5)	14.06 (182)	14.05 (93)	14.07 (89)
10	58.00 (1)	66.00 (4)	100 (1)	89 (1)	86.4 (5)	14.44 (172)	14.44 (88)	14.46 (84)
11		·61.75 (4)	108 (1)	95 (1)	93.0 (5)	14.75 (138)	14.77 (73)	14.77 (65)
12			117 (1)	98 (1)	99.2 (5)	15.08 (111)	15.13 (57)	14.98 (54)
13			132 (1)	108 (1)	106.8 (5)	15.38 (77)	15.42 (42)	15.28 (35)
14			140 (1)	113 (1)	112.8 (5)	15.50 (52)	15.60 (28)	15.42 (24)
15			146 (1)	120 (1)	118.8 (5)	15.80 (27)	15.85 (15)	15.67 (12)
16			155 (1)	131 (1)	126.6 (5)	15.61 (7)		

Table 1. Age-length data sets A-R. For descriptions of sets, see text. Frequencies in parentheses where known. *Continued*.

	English sole									
Age	Holland (1969)							Based on Van Cleve and El-Sayed (1969)		
	I	J	K	L	M	N	O	P	Q	R
1	145	150	122	123	3.28 (243)	3.37 (127)	3.25 (1)	3.55 (1)	47.0 (1)	40.0 (1)
2	205	220	195	207	4.89 (181)	5.16 (98)	4.70 (1)	4.85 (1)	61.0 (1)	56.5 (1)
3	235	260	229	254	5.61 (150)	6.09 (78)	5.55 (1)	5.60 (1)	76.5 (1)	72.0 (1)
4	250	293	249	275	6.02 (83)	6.50 (60)	5.95 (1)	6.35 (1)	86.0 (1)	84.0 (1)
5	263	317	260	308	6.26 (52)	7.13 (39)	6.15 (1)	6.90 (1)	95.0 (1)	93.0 (1)
6	275	335	268	330	6.41 (42)	7.54 (32)	6.35 (1)	7.20 (1)	107.0 (1)	105.0 (1)
7	285	350	280	347	6.66 (22)	7.85 (27)	6.55 (1)	7.70 (1)	114.0 (1)	112.0 (1)
8	292	364	288	344	6.82 (21)	7.80 (27)	6.70 (1)	7.90 (1)		
9	298	376	285	358	6.76 (12)	8.04 (15)	6.85 (2)	8.05 (1)		
10	303	389	290	341	6.86 (8)	7.74 (7)	6.86 (8)	8.25 (1)		
11	307	400	317	382	7.40 (1)	8.48 (3)		8.48 (3)		

RESULTS

The frequencies of walleye pollock (Table 1) are bimodal, peaking at the lower end and near the upper end of the age range in both males (A) and females (B). Elimination of data points with average lengths from fewer than 5 ageings, or fewer than 10 (in males only), resulted in progressively better fits as judged by the reduced standard error of the residuals. Part A of Table 2 shows the reduction in standard error of fit from S.D. = 3.2 with age 10 included (n = 1), to S.D. = 1.7 without age 10. The exclusion of age frequencies under 5 in females (B) results in elimination of ages 6, 10 and 11 and the corresponding change in S.D. is from 3.4 (Table 2, B for upper age 11) to 0.76 (not shown). Table 1 (A, B) shows that the original data sets are poorly graduated at higher ages which could be due to small samples for some ages, or reading difficulties, or both. However, Fig. 1 (A, B) shows clearly that asymptote estimates (L_∞) increase and curvature values (k) decrease generally as the underlying age range of the data sets increases from ages 1-4 to ages 1-10.

Similar trends in L_∞ and k are obtained for the Pacific halibut series (C-E). The average fish lengths at age were estimated from otolith annuli and the resulting absence of negative length changes with age may be partly contributing to the smoother appearance of these trends in Pacific halibut than in walleye pollock where such changes are apparent (Table 1). The plots of halibut series C, D represent one specimen each, and series E represents curves fitted to averages of calculated fish length for 5 such

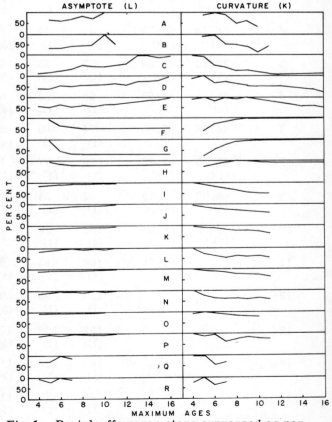

Fig. 1. Bertalanffy parameters expressed as percentages of series maxima. (See text for description of data, sets A-R)

Table 2. Bertalanffy parameters (L_∞, k, t_0) and standard error residuals from expectation. (see text for description of data, sets A-R).

(Part)		Upper limit of age range used												
		4	5	6	7	8	9	10	11	12	13	14	15	16
Walleye Pollock														
(A)	L_∞		47.82	46.32	48.08	59.72	50.49	70.08						
	k		.38	.41	.37	.21	.34	.15						
	t_0		.24	.32	.22	−.31	+.19	−.46						
	S.D.		.42	.39	.43	1.80	1.66	3.19						
(B)	L_∞		49.14	47.34	58.58	61.11	62.41	125.70	67.43					
	k		.43	.47	.27	.25	.23	.07	.21					
	t_0		.57	.65	.27	.17	.13	−.76	.21					
	S.D.		.03	.28	1.82	1.70	1.56	3.51	3.43					
Pacific Halibut[1]														
(C)	L_∞	66.00	70.00	106.00	125.00	187.00	174.00	175.00	189.00	214.00	368.00	363.00	322.00	356.00
	k	.34	.32	.12	.14	.08	.09	.09	.08	.07	.04	.04	.04	.04
	t_0	.70	.69	.66	.63	.60	.59	.59	.58	.56	.53	.53	.53	.52
	S.D.	5.49	3.80	3.91	3.65	3.88	3.51	3.26	3.05	3.00	4.32	4.10	3.82	3.74
(D)	L_∞	94.00	89.00	116.00	108.00	122.00	130.00	129.00	135.00	130.00	154.00	157.00	172.00	215.00
	k	.19	.21	.14	.16	.13	.12	.12	.12	.12	.10	.09	.08	.06
	t_0	.60	.61	.58	.58	.57	.56	.56	.55	.56	.55	.54	.53	.51
	S.D.	1.81	1.28	1.41	1.21	1.23	1.30	1.20	1.22	1.17	2.22	2.32	2.84	4.44
(E)	L_∞	130.00	123.00	142.00	124.00	131.00	127.00	135.00	145.00	154.00	173.00	181.00	190.00	215.00
	k	.11	.12	.10	.12	.11	.12	.11	.10	.09	.08	.07	.07	.06
	t_0	.48	.49	.47	.49	.48	.49	.48	.47	.46	.45	.44	.43	.41
	S.D.	1.50	1.09	.92	.86	.76	.70	.78	1.07	1.32	1.97	2.14	2.30	2.87
Razor Clams[2]														
(F)	L_∞		28.00	19.00	17.00	16.00	16.00	16.00	16.00	16.00	16.00	16.00	16.00	16.00
	k		.14	.23	.28	.31	.32	.32	.32	.32	.31	.31	.31	.31
	t_0		1.40	1.50	1.50	1.50	1.50	1.50	1.50	1.50	1.50	1.50	1.50	1.50
	S.D.		.21	.32	.37	.40	.39	.36	.34	.32	.31	.30	.30	.28
(G)	L_∞		47.00	23.00	18.00	17.00	16.00	16.00	16.00	16.00	16.00	16.00	16.00	
	k		.07	.17	.23	.27	.28	.29	.29	.29	.29	.28	.29	
	t_0		1.36	1.43	1.48	1.50	1.51	1.52	1.52	1.52	1.52	1.52	1.52	
	S.D.		.09	.27	.39	.46	.44	.42	.40	.37	.36	.34	.33	
(H)	L_∞		18.00	16.00	15.00	15.00	15.00	15.00	15.00	15.00	15.00	15.00	15.00	
	k		.27	.33	.36	.37	.38	.38	.37	.37	.36	.36	.36	
	t_0		1.47	1.49	1.51	1.52	1.52	1.52	1.52	1.52	1.52	1.51	1.52	
	S.D.		.08	.17	.21	.21	.21	.19	.19	.18	.20	.21	.19	
English Sole[3,4]														
(I)	L_∞	265.00	272.00	281.00	288.00	293.00	297.00	300.00	303.00					
	k	.69	.63	.56	.50	.47	.45	.42	.41					
	t_0	−.14	−.21	−.30	−.39	−.45	−.50	−.55	−.59					
	S.D.	0.00	2.26	3.97	5.11	5.60	5.96	6.23	6.42					
(J)	L_∞	347.00	362.00	370.00	377.00	386.00	394.00	403.00	411.00					
	k	.43	.38	.36	.34	.32	.30	.28	.27					
	t_0	−.32	−.39	−.43	−.47	−.52	−.57	−.62	−.68					
	S.D.	3.59	3.34	3.19	3.36	4.02	4.71	5.92	6.91					

Table 2. Bertalanffy parameters (L_∞, k, t_0) and standard error of residuals from expectation. (See text for description of data, sets A-R).—*Continued*.

(Part)		Upper limit of age range used												
		4	5	6	7	8	9	10	11	12	13	14	15	16
(K)	L_∞	266.00	269.00	272.00	280.00	285.00	284.00	287.00	300.00					
	k	.70	.66	.65	.59	.55	.56	.54	.46					
	t_0	.12	.09	.08	.03	−.02	−.01	−.03	−.14					
	S.D.	1.70	1.55	2.06	4.58	5.92	5.48	5.43	11.23					
(L)	L_∞	301.00	335.00	354.00	367.00	356.00	364.00	352.00	371.00					
	k	.65	.49	.42	.38	.41	.39	.43	.38					
	t_0	.19	.07	−.01	−.06	−.02	−.04	.02	−.04					
	S.D.	2.02	8.07	8.81	8.85	8.33	7.68	9.53	12.30					
(M)	L_∞	6.35	6.43	6.48	6.63	6.74	6.73	6.78	7.02					
	k	.74	.70	.68	.62	.58	.58	.57	.49					
	t_0	.01	−.02	−.04	−.10	−.15	−.15	−.17	−.28					
	S.D.	.04	.04	.05	.10	.13	.12	.12	.23					
(N)	L_∞	6.94	7.53	7.87	8.09	7.97	8.09	7.90	8.22					
	k	.70	.54	.47	.43	.46	.43	.47	.42					
	t_0	.05	−.09	−.18	−.24	−.20	−.24	−.18	−.25					
	S.D.	.03	.16	.18	.18	1.7	.16	.18	.23					
(O)	L_∞	6.49	6.43	6.50	6.60	6.69	6.78	6.80						
	k	.60	.62	.60	.56	.53	.51	.50						
	t_0	−.16	−.13	−.16	−.20	−.24	−.29	−.30						
	S.D.	.04	.03	.04	.07	.09	.12	.11						
(P)	L_∞	7.93	8.35	8.13	8.70	8.63	8.59	8.68	8.82					
	k	.34	.30	.32	.27	.27	.28	.27	.26					
	t_0	−.76	−.86	−.80	−.96	−.94	−.93	−.96	−1.01					
	S.D.	.11	.09	.07	.10	.09	.08	.07	.08					
(Q)	L_∞	144.00	143.00	199.00	175.00									
	k	.17	.17	.10	.12									
	t_0	−1.31	−1.29	−1.68	−1.53									
	S.D.	1.83	1.32	1.71	1.41									
(R)	L_∞	161.00	139.00	176.00	162.00									
	k	.15	.19	.13	.15									
	t_0	−.90	−.77	−.98	−.90									
	S.D.	.67	.80	1.30	1.05									

[1] Southward and Chapman (1965).
[2] Weymouth and McMillin (1931).
[3] Holland (1969), for series I-P.
[4] Van Cleve and El-Sayed (1969), for series Q and R.

Table 3. Residuals of length at age for data sets A-R. (See text for description of data, sets A-R.)

Age	A	B	C	D	E	F	G	H	I	J	K	L	M	N	O	P	Q	R
1	1.35		.79	.81	.38	.01	.01	.00	.03	.47	.39	2.68	.01	.04	.00	.01	.14	.07
2	2.05	1.07	1.21	4.77	.96	.01	−.47	−.18	6.90	8.73	7.97	7.76	.17	.16	.05	.12	−.73	−.30
3	2.05	1.55	9.08	3.42	3.97	−.46	−.12	.07	1.59	1.54	.59	.69	.00	.00	.05	−.05	1.64	.66
4	2.09	.44	2.39	4.72	3.17	.06	.48	.29	−6.88	−1.52	−5.59	−15.36	−.14	−.32	−.06	−.02	−.48	−.15
5	.30	−1.33	−1.88	2.64	2.53	.47	.62	.20	−9.48	−5.09	−11.16	−7.73	−.23	−.17	−.17	−.02	−1.75	−1.64
6	−2.05	−4.19	.25	3.14	2.62	.46	.62	−.01	−7.86	−8.15	−13.64	−3.12	−.29	−.07	−.16	−.15	1.17	1.07
7	−3.30	−1.46	−1.22	.19	.41	.21	.38	−.15	−4.75	−9.25	−8.26	1.97	−.16	.03	−.08	.02	.14	.07
8	−.76	−1.69	.68	−.25	−.52	−.07	.00	−.29	−2.53	−7.56	−4.46	−9.19	−.08	−.16	.00	−.04		
9	−5.49	−1.86	−2.05	−1.20	−2.81	−.22	−.15	−.20	.62	−4.97	−10.11	−.79	−.19	−.01	.11	−.09		
10		7.02	−4.44	−3.70	−3.48	−.25	−.28	−.20	3.60	.85	−6.79	−21.62	−.12	−.37	.10	−.04		
11	2.17	1.16	−5.49	−4.76	−3.74	−.24	−.19	−.05	6.25	6.35	19.15	16.76	.40	.33	.07	.07		
12			−5.21	−8.42	−4.03	−.13	−.19	−.05										
13			1.38	−4.70	−2.57	.01	−.11	.15										
14			1.27	−5.61	−2.36	.02	−.08	.22										
15			−5.39	−4.18	−1.84	.23	−.05	.02										
16			.93	1.56	.77	−.02												

individuals from the same yearclass, all collected as 16-year olds. In all 3 series there appear certain sequences of upper ages over which the parameter estimates obtained seem more or less steady. However, over the entire range of upper ages the variation is still large for each parameter equalling or exceeding a factor of 2 in both cases.

The razor clam series (F, G, H) differ sharply from those discussed so far, with no substantial variation evident when the upper ages of the data sets are above age 8, whether sexes are treated separately or combined. Below this age, each series forms curvatures whose concavities are reversed from those for the same parameters in walleye pollock and Pacific halibut.

The English sole series (I-P) display less overall variation than the 3 species discussed above. The changes appear continuous with respect to age range, particularly in k regardless of whether a data set refers to (i) observed fish lengths (I, J); (ii) fish lengths converted from otolith lengths on the assumption of a semilogarithmic relation (K, L); (iii) strict proportionality between fish length and otolith length (not shown); (iv) otolith lengths at age for composites of yearclasses (M, N); or whether (v) otolith lengths are based on a few specimens, or a single specimen (Q, P).

The residuals at age for the complete data sets (Table 1) are given in Table 3. For nearly all data sets the departures from expectation show similar patterns as those schematized in Fig. 1 of Southward and Chapman (1965) for halibut.

DISCUSSION

Figure 1 shows that in razor clams (F, G, H) the trends formed by age-range dependent estimates of asymptote (L_∞) are negative and of curvature (k) positive, and thus differ sharply from the patterns formed by walleye pollock, Pacific halibut and English sole data of length on age. For razor clams, Weymouth and McMillin (1930) demonstrated the absence of isometric relations between shell length and width, with relative width increasing curvilinearly between shell lengths of 4 and 16 cm. The corresponding allometric relationship is negative in otoliths of Pacific halibut, judging from Figure 1 in Southward (1962b). Whether English sole otoliths are similar in this regard is not known to the writer but interopercles of this species suggest similar relations from Fig. 7 of Van Cleve and El-Sayed (1969). The age dependence of parameters computed from measurements taken from the lower part of Fig. 7 of Van Cleve and El-Sayed (1969) is shown by series (P) of Fig. 1. It does not differ substantially from the other series, except those for razor clams.

The variation of the estimates of L_∞ and k for halibut, English sole and walleye pollock may be associated with similar allometric changes in otolith length and fish length (calculated or observed). In any event, as pointed out by Southward and Chapman (1965), and as indicated by Fig. 1, the dependence of estimates L_∞ and k on age represents a serious source of error in yield computations involving their use. It appears that no part of the age ranges shown can be considered as uniquely free of this defect, hence the exclusion of any ages from data sets seems inadvisable.

The points at which annular distances are usually

measured are naturally those of best visual definition, often at the outside margin of each annulus. An alternative set of points, measured at the inside margins of the specimen of English sole interopercle (Van Cleve and El-Sayed, Fig. 7) has been used to obtain series R in Fig. 1. Compared to series Q, which is based on radius lengths to the outer margins of the same annuli, the trends in L_∞, k and t_0, over age ranges from age 1 to upper ages 4-7, are substantially less pronounced in series R.

To the extent that conditions at time of annulus formation represent stress, differences of the kind encountered between series Q and R are not unexpected. Commenting on the effects of stress due to starvation, Bertalanffy (1951) pointed out that allometric reversals of body shape tend toward relations prevailing at earlier ages. In an Oregon population of razor clams, a study of relative shell width at 6-week intervals over the first 4 growth years showed that the general increase in relative width was reversed annually during the period of ring formation (Hirschhorn, 1962). As a result annulus width would be expected to be larger along the anteroposterior than the dorsoventral axis of the shell as can be seen e.g. in Fig. 1 of Weymouth and McMillin (1931). Similar differences in body and scale lengths of carp were discussed nearly 70 years ago (Hoffbauer, 1905). When ageing is from scales the types of device described by Fawell and by Mason elsewhere in this volume may be a valuable tool in the search for linear measures of size leading to more stable estimates of vital parameters than seem available at present.

LITERATURE CITED

Alverson, D. L. and M. S. Carney. In press. Growth and decay of population cohorts.

Bertalanffy, L. von. 1951. Theoretische Biologie. Zweiter Band: Stoffwechsel, Wachstum. A. Francke AG, Berlin. 418 pp., 117 graphs, 30 tables

Chapman, D. G. 1960. Statistical problems in dynamics of exploited fisheries populations. Proc. Fourth Berkeley Symposium on Math. Stat, and Probability, pp. 153-168. Univ. Calif. Press, Berkeley.

Fabens, A. J. 1965. Properties and fitting of the von Bertalanffy growth curve. Growth **29**, 265-289.

Hirschhorn, G. 1962. Growth and mortality rates of the razor clam (*Siliqua patula*) on Clatsop Beaches, Oregon. Fish Comm. Oreg., Contrib. 27. 25pp.

Hoffbauer, C. 1905. Weitere Beitrage zur Alters- und Wachstumsbestimmung der Fische, spez. des Karpfens. Z. Fisch., **12**, 111-142.

Holland, G. A. 1969. Age, growth, and mortality of races of English sole (*Parophrys vetulus*) in Puget Sound, Washington. Pac. Mar. Fish. Comm., Bull., 7, 35-50.

Mason, J. E. 1974. A semiautomatic fish scale reading machine for counting and measuring circuli. This symposium volume. Bagenal, T. B. (Ed), Ageing of Fish. Unwin Brothers, 87-102.

Richards, F. J. 1959. A flexible growth function for empirical use. J. exp. Bot., **10**, (29): 290-300.

Southward, G. M. 1962a. A method of calculating body lengths from otolith measurements for Pacific halibut and its application to Portlock-Albatross Grounds data between 1935 and 1957. J. Fish. Res. Bd Can., **19**, (2): 339-362.

1962b. Photographing halibut otoliths for

measuring growth zones. J. Fish. Res. Bd. Can., **19**, (2): 335-338.

Southward, G. M., and D. G. Chapman. 1965. Utilization of Pacific halibut stocks: study of Bertalanffy's growth equation. Rep. Int. Pac. Halibut Comm., **39**, 33 p.

Stevens, W. L. 1951. Asymptotic regression. Biometrics. **7**, 247-267.

Van Cleve, R., and S. Z. El-Sayed. 1969. Age, growth, and productivity of an English sole (*Parophrys vetulus*) population in Puget Sound, Washington. Pac. Mar. Fish. Comm., Bull., **7**, 51-71.

Weymouth, F. W. and H. C. McMillin. 1931. The relative growth and mortality of the Pacific razor clam (*Siliqua patula*, Dixon), and their bearing on the commercial fishery. Bull. U.S. Bur. Fish., **46**, 543-567.

Difficulties in ageing fish in relation to inland fishery management

by KENNETH D. CARLANDER

Iowa State University, Ames, Iowa U.S.A.

Although the separation of inland and marine fisheries for this topic is somewhat artificial, I believe that there are some differences which make the separation useful. Management of inland water depends less on catch regulation and utilizes a greater number of techniques related to habitat control than is possible in marine fisheries. Most marine age and growth studies are related to large commercial fisheries and made by fishery research laboratory staffs. On the other hand, in the United States at least, many inland studies are made by individual biologists, somewhat isolated from major fisheries investigations and not specifically trained for age and growth analysis.

Many of the studies are not undertaken with any specific management problem in mind but rather are made to provide biological background. Life history information on the various species is valuable but on many species the accumulation of age and growth data has reached the stage where mere addition of data hardly justifies the effort.

Even in management-related investigations, there often has been a failure to define the problem and to work out an adequate sampling program before the study. In most states, management has rarely been so intensive for fish in a given body of water as to require precise age and growth data. Emphasis is often more upon general habitat improvement and maintenance. The needs for intensive management are increasing, however.

The types of information which can be secured from ageing fish include growth rate, age at maturity, number of spawning periods per life span, age at harvest, age class composition of catch, abundance of year classes, longevity and mortality rate. These data can be used in fishery management

(1) to provide the general background needed for management decisions,
(2) to aid in diagnosis of management needs such as the recognition of overcrowding and stunting,
(3) to evaluate the effects of various environmental or hereditary factors by comparing growth rates and year class abundance,
(4) to evaluate the effects of management practices,
(5) through the use of growth and mortality rates to estimate optimum yields and the possible effects of catch regulations,
(6) to predict catch from year class abundance,
(7) with additional estimates of population numbers, to determine production rates,
(8) to separate populations, although further growth and scale analysis are often needed, rather than just ageing.

Age and growth may be determined by (1) direct observation including observation of tagged or otherwise identifiable fish, (2) length frequencies, or (3) interpretation of the rings on scales, otoliths, spines, or other hard structures. I will be concerned mostly with the interpretation of the rings on scales. Errors in determining the age from the rings may arise from failure of annual rings (annuli) to form and from difficulties in interpretation. Annuli may not form when the fish are so small at the first winter that the scales are just forming (Robertson 1947, Brown and Bailey 1952, Laakso and Cope 1956, Kruse 1959, Nordeng 1961, Regier 1962), when growth does not stop or slow down enough at any season to disrupt the scale pattern (Gray and Setna 1931, Surber 1937, Allen 1951, Nichols 1957, DeBont 1967), or when fish growth is so slow that the scale does not grow enough to show an annulus (Frey and Vike 1941, Frey 1942, Alm 1946, Bennett 1958, Hansen 1951, Alvord 1954, Reimers 1958, Kruse 1959, Nordeng 1961, Regier 1962, Buchholz and Carlander 1963). DeBont (1967) reviewed the factors which cause annulus formation and I will not try to add to that. Situations where the scales are too small to form annuli during the first winter are not common and can usually be recognized if fall collections are made or if it is known that hatching occurs late in the growing season. The second situation, where growth does not slow down, occurs mostly in tropical and subtropical climates or in constant temperature streams and thus would not be a source of error in most studies. Failure to grow enough to separate the annuli occurs rarely in young fish but may be fairly common in older fish. The 1952 year class of yellow bass *Morone mississippiensis*, in Clear Lake, Iowa, formed the first three annuli but did not grow the next year and formed its 4th annulus when 5 years old and grew no more the next 3 years (Buchholz and Carlander 1963). The 1948 year class formed 6 annuli before stopping growth and the 1949 class formed 5 annuli and showed no further growth until age IX when some individuals added a 6th annulus. In the years when these year classes did not grow, the younger yellow bass grew enough to form normal annuli. If we had collected fish only in 1957 and took what might be a good sample, we would think that we had representatives of ages I-VI showing slower than average growth. Actually we had ages I, II, III, V, VIII and IX with ages IV, VI and VII missing. The growth was slower than we would have known and the missing year classes would not have been detected. The slow growth was related to a high population density aggravated by a drop in water level and volume.

Aass (1972) found that annuli were often missing on scales of cisco *Coregonus albula*, probably the result of slow growth after reaching maturity at age II or III. Beyond this age otoliths often indicated that the fish were older than the scales would suggest, even though the scale characteristics seemed very clear and readily interpreted. In some cases otoliths indicated as much as 7 years more than the scales. Missing year classes, not readily detectable from the scale readings were obvious in the otolith interpretations.

Brook trout *Salvelinus fontinalis,* in Bunny Lake, California (Reimers 1958, McAfee 1966), and grayling *Thymallus arcticus,* in Grebe Lake, Wyoming (Kruse 1959), failed to form more than two annuli although many lived 6-15 years. Returns on tagged walleyes *Stizostedion vitreum,* in Clear Lake indicate that some of the walleyes live live longer than scale examination indicates. One walleye, tagged in April 1953 when 365 mm and probably age IV was caught 15 years later at 555 mm. Unfortunately, scales were not collected but of 3094 scales examined from the population, none was listed as over age XII and only 5 beyond age X (Carlander and Whitney 1961).

Except for the very old fish, failure to grow enough to form annuli probably occurs only in populations that show slow growth upon scale examination. The errors are thus ones of underestimating the degree to which growth is slowed rather than the recognition of slow growth which may be the necessary information for management decisions. (The paper by Aass (1972), not found until after the above statement was made, indicated that failure to form annuli after reaching maturity may be more common than I thought).

Interpretation difficulties can usually be traced to (1) the formation of false annuli (disruptions in the scale pattern caused by the cessation or slowing of growth at some time other than the time of annulus formation), (2) incomplete or indistinct development of annuli, (3) failure to distinguish whether the growth beyond the last annulus represents the current year's or the previous year's growth, and (4) inadequate experience or care in defining and recognizing the annuli. The formation of false annuli probably occurs more frequency on fast-growing scales, which thus have a greater space between annuli for false checks, than on scales from slow-growing fish. Bennett (1948), Burris (1949) and Sprugel (1954, 1955) reported more false annuli on bluegill scales when they were growing faster, and Carlander (1961) reported more difficulty in interpreting the scales of a fast-growing year class of walleyes than a slower-growing year class. Bennett (1948) also found false annuli to be common in slow-growing populations. Indistinct annuli may be formed on fast-growing or slow-growing fish.

Hatch (1961) reported that 60-90% of the brook trout in four New York lakes showed false annuli, not detectable except by position and the knowledge that the fish could not be as old as indicated.

The first annulus is often especially difficult to interpret, particularly when the spawning season may extend through much of the growing season. Special care is therefore needed in establishing criteria for the first annulus. The age 0 dace scale in Dr. Hellawell's paper shows a small check which might give some problems in interpretation, but which would indicate a fish at a size which probably could not overwinter. Such checks, sometimes referred to as 'fry checks', are fairly common and are often interpretted as a change in feeding habits from plankton organisms to larger items. In fish such as the bluegill sunfish *Lepomis macrochirus,* with extended spawning seasons, these 'fry checks' are particularly confusing.

Spawning checks may sometimes be misidentified as annuli or spawning checks may otherwise interfere with the recognition of annuli. Spawning checks

of anadromous salmon may involve so much scale erosion that annuli are actually lost, but such scale erosion is less common in freshwater fish. Resorption of two or three annuli from the lateral fields of yellow bass scales when growth conditions were poor was reported by Buchholz and Carlander (1963). Age determination of rainbow trout over age II or III was not considered satisfactory in Lake Lyndon, New Zealand, because of scale erosion (Percival and Burnet 1963).

Loss of scales and scale regeneration may also interfere with ageing of older fish. In the Au Sable River, Michigan, 26% of the scales from 102-203 mm brown trout were regenerative and 94% of those from trout over 500 mm (Williams 1955, quoting W. Tody 1949 mss).

Everyone that has read scales recognizes that it is an art that develops with experience. There is danger of it becoming a routine with decreased discrimination. Many errors of interpretation can be avoided by careful definition of the criteria used in recognizing annuli for each species.

Probably the best method of reducing errors of interpretation and of recognizing situations where annuli have not been formed is to examine adequate collections made at intervals in several consecutive growing seasons. Then the scale interpretations can be verified by checking for consistency in the relative abundance and in the growth patterns of year classes. It was only this type of comparison that permitted the recognition of the failure of annulus formation in the Clear Lake yellow bass.

Length-frequency analysis also often gives a method of verifying scale readings and of clearing up some difficulties in interpretation. I found recently that in most years I could follow the growth of the Clear Lake yellow bass just as well from length-frequency analysis as from scale analysis (which took longer). In fact, the length-frequency analysis was not hindered by the failure of annulus formation which complicated the scale analysis. This length frequency analysis was helped by the fact that there were big differences in the abundance of year classes, with some missing. When annual year classes of about equal abundance occurred in the 1960's, the separation of age groups by the length frequency method was almost impossible after age III or IV.

In many studies, scales are independently read two or more times to eliminate some errors of interpretation. Tabulation of the frequency of disagreement between readings of scales of the same fish gives a measure of the difficulty and of the frequency of error in age determination (Tables 1 and 2). Although there was some disagreement in the readings of age I and II, their frequency was much less than with older fish. The practice by some scientists of disregarding the readings on which agreement is not secured introduces a bias by eliminating many of the older fish—a bias which is very important when estimating mortality rates but probably less significant when describing growth rates.

Age determination from scales of Age I to IV *Salmo trutta* agreed with ages determined by tagging in over 90% of the cases in a study by Sych (1967). Triple reading eliminated most errors. Tabulation of the degree of doubt felt about the readings proved to give a measure of the accuracy of age determination.

Table 1.   Number of fish assigned to each age class and percentage disagreement between two readings in some studies.

| | Morone mississippiensis | | Pomoxis nigromaculatus | | Stizostedion vitreum | |
| | Skillman, 1965 | | Vanderpuye, 1968 | | Carlander, 1961 | |
Age group	No.	%	No.	%	No.	%
0	—	—	—	—	6	0
1	69	1	188	11	31	13
II	158	2	242	14	132	16
III	416	7	135	25	174	14
IV	524	15	78	47	121	39
V	291	22	56	38	107	50
VI	288	15	38	45	50	66
VII	123	24	34	59	33	60
VIII+	11	64	10	60	17	35

Table 2.   Number of fish aged, percentage disagreement between two readings, and percentage of sample in age III or older (in most of these the percentages were not given by age class).

	Number	Percentage	Percentage age III or older
Perca flavescens, Hervey 1963	848	4	5
Stizostedion canadense, Vanicek 1963	531	4	32
Micropterus dolomieu, Reynolds 1965	308	5	23
Esox lucius, Ridenhour 1955	390	9	25
Morone mississippiensis, from Table 1	1880	14	88
Pomoxis nigromaculatus, from Table 1	781	24	45
Stizostedion vitreum, from Table 1	671	31	75

Sockeye salmon *Oncorhynchus nerka* scales were read independently by two biologists (Koo 1962). The scales were read in seven batches totalling 1,167 fish, all with 2 or 3 marine annuli. On the first batch of 85 scales, they disagreed on almost 1 in 4. They then jointly examined the scales on which they disagreed, and discussed the source of disagreement. On the last batch of scales, they disagreed on only 3.4%. Agreement in the readings does not necessarily mean that the ages were properly determined. Koo developed a graphic method wherein the distances between circuli were plotted and annuli were detected as valleys in the graph. The graphic method gave results with the sockeye salmon scales which were more consistent and apparently more accurate than the visual examination. In one sample of 39 fish classed visually as having 2 annuli, 8 were found by the graphic method to have 3 annuli and examination of their lengths indicated that they probably were of the latter age group. Annuli too poorly defined to pick up visually were detected by the graphic method. On the other hand, of 43 classed visually as having 3 annuli, graphic analysis indicated that a false annulus was classified as a true annulus on two fish.

I do not know of any similar comparison of the graphic method and the visual method with freshwater fishes. The graphic method was used for rainbow

trout by Gray and Setna (1931) and Bhatia (1932). It has been used for a variety of marine fish, cod (Hjort 1914, Winge 1915, Dannevig 1925), plaice and flounders (Cutler 1918), albacore (W. F. Thompson reported by Koo 1962) and salmon (Mathisen 1966).

Since the graphic method depends upon only the spacing of circuli, and leaves out other criteria, such as anastomosis, used in visual interpretation, electronic scanners have been developed to read the scales (Kuroki et al. 1965, Koo and Isarankura 1968, and Griffiths 1968).

If we accept the concept that ageing errors are relatively infrequent in younger year classes, e.g. to ages III or IV, but fairly frequent as age increases, with errors not at random but fairly consistent in one or the other direction, we can speculate on approaches which will provide the necessary information with minimum effort. The more difficult scales take much more time to interpret and may give differing results upon duplicate reading. Is it better to read all scales at least twice to seek agreement or to read scales from twice as many fish? The availability and cost of securing larger samples may be an important consideration. In many cases, maximum information from the available samples is desirable. Double reading of at least part of the sample gives clues as to difficulties and accuracy of ageing.

If agreement on double readings is not secured, should the data on these fish be disregarded, as has often been done, or should continued effort be made to assign the most likely age? If the difficult scales are mostly from older fish or from slower-growing individuals, disregarding the data introduces a bias which is particularly serious in estimates of age-class composition, longevity, and mortality rates. Increasing the sample size may do nothing toward eliminating the bias. Assigning the most likely age will not necessarily eliminate the bias either. It may be possible to disregard the difficult scales and the older age groups to get good estimates of early growth rate, age at maturity or first harvest, and year class abundance (if the sampling of the year classes in the first years of life is adequate). Whenever possible, other estimates of mortality, such as from tagging, should be secured to replace, supplement, or verify the mortality estimates from scale analysis.

I believe that the use of age data to provide general background for management decisions has been quite successful. Errors in ageing have probably not significantly affected our knowledge of average growth rates, ages at maturity or harvest, and variations in abundance of year classes. Our concepts of longevity may be somewhat biased because of difficulties in recognizing ages of older fish, but from a management standpoint this underestimate of longevity is probably not very important because so few fish reach the maximum age.

In diagnosis of management needs on individual bodies of water the growth rate may be compared to some norm. If the growth rate is above average, techniques of increasing population numbers might be recommended; if growth rate is slow, attempts should be made to determine the cause of slow growth—overpopulation being a common cause. Growth during the first 3 or 4 years may be the most important and then only the younger, more easily read, scales need be included. In many species most of the annual production is contributed by these younger year classes. Growth in later years of life much below the norm may indicate the need to improve conditions for the larger fish, and this information will be missed if only data from younger age groups are included. Errors of interpretation of growth of the older fish are probably much more frequent and thus particular care should be taken in the analysis.

In Clear Lake, Iowa, yellow perch (*Perca flavescens*) over 180 mm total length have been rarely taken since 1940. Parsons (1950) found the growth rate to be about average but the life span to rarely exceed 2.5 years. After learning that the yellow bass did not grow sufficiently to form a detectable annulus after the 3rd to 5th year in Clear Lake, we wondered whether the same situation might be true of the perch. Hervey (1963) tried to detect annual differences in growth rate or year class abundance which would determine whether the perch were rapid growing but short-lived or rapid growing for 2 years with no further growth although surviving longer. He was unable to find clear evidence to decide this question. Since the perch is a minor species in the Clear Lake fisheries, the question did not involve a serious management decision.

Age class composition of the catch and mortality rates may also be involved in diagnosis of management needs, particularly with relation to catch regulations. These data may be seriously biased if only the easily read scales are included.

In the evaluation of the effects of various environmental or hereditary factors or of management practices, data from only the younger age groups may often be most significant, permitting the elimination of the older age groups. One common error has been to try to evaluate effects by comparing average sizes of fish at various ages before and a year or two after an environmental or management change when the effects can be more precisely evaluated by comparing the growth increments for the specific years involved.

The evaluation of effects upon year class abundance is more difficult than detecting changes in growth rate. In an evaluation of stocking to supplement natural reproduction in Clear Lake, Iowa (Carlander *et al.* 1960), walleye fry were stocked only in alternate years for 10 years and the relative abundance of year classes was determined by catch per effort data on fingerlings and by scale analysis of fish caught in experimental gillnets and by anglers. The rankings of the year classes by the two methods were similar but not identical. Correlation coefficients between indices of abundance of fingerlings and of the older fishes were 0.59 and 0.46, not high enough to be significant at the 95% level of confidence (Carlander 1971). The rankings by either system for the years of no stocking were significantly lower than the years when fry were stocked. The fingerling indices were lower for all 5 years without stocking than for any year when fry were stocked. The adult rankings were 1, 3, 4, 5, and 7 for years of no stocking compared to 2, 6, 8, 9, 10, and 11 for years with stocking. The fry stocking therefore appeared to have an effect on walleye abundance in Clear Lake although such fry stocking to supplement natural reproduction has had no measurable effect on several other lakes.

Walleye scales are among the more difficult to interpret, particularly with older fish. Double reading of the scales showed considerable disagreement (Table 1). Only ages I-VI were used in computing the indices, but misinterpretation of a relatively small number of scales might shift the rankings of some year classes so that the importance of the fry stocking might be different than indicated. I am going to have a student work on the graphing method of annulus detection in the analysis for a continuation study. It was suggested that the alternation of abundance in year classes might be partly a function of a very successful year class in 1950 (the year after the first year without stocking) rather than entirely to the fry stocking. A new experiment was therefore initiated with the numbers of fry to be stocked each year on a predetermined schedule varying from 1200 to 37,000 fry per hectare and not in an alternate high-low sequence. It was hoped that this might also give clues as to the optimum number to stock. This schedule ended this year but analysis of the scale data has not yet been made.

In the use of growth and mortality rates to estimate optimum yields or effects of fishing pressure, elimination of data from difficult scales could seriously affect mortality estimates. The effects of ageing errors in such cases is discussed by Mr. K. Brander, (1974, this volume) and Mr. E. D. LeCren (this volume) discusses the effects upon determination of production rates.

One of the most important parts of an age and growth study for fisheries management is the planning. If the questions to be asked and the information needed are carefully delineated, more efficient sampling designs and types of scale examination can be selected. The size of sample needed to get estimates with the desired degree of accuracy (or probability of error) can be determined from variances in pre-samples or approximated with data from similar studies. I have not discussed the difficulties which arise from poor sampling. It might be mentioned, however, that many sampling methods tend to catch fish of an intermediate size and that this overestimates the growth rate of the younger age groups and overestimates the mortality rate.

As the data are analysed, the results should be examined for internal consistency and inconsistencies and for possible independent evidence on the validity of the ageing. As already indicated, data collected over several seasons and several years gives much greater opportunity to detect errors than 'one-shot' investigations (see Linfield, 1974, This Symposium volume).

I have no doubt that most published age and growth data, and probably most studies now in progress, could be improved if the goals had been well defined, the sampling designed, and more thought given to the analysis. (Computors are marvellous in production of more data and in shortening the time spent on computation, but is the freed time being used for more thought?)

REFERENCES

Aass, P. 1972. Age determination and year class fluctuations of cisco *Coregonus albula* L. in the Mjsa hydroelectric reservoir. Rep. Inst. Freshwat. Res. Drotningholm, **52**, 5-22.

Allen, K. R. 1951. The Horokiwi stream; a study of a trout population. Fish. Bull. N. Z., **10**, 1-231.

Alm, G. 1946. Reasons for the occurrence of stunted fish populations. Meddn St. Unders.-o FörsAnst Sötvattfisk. No. 25: 1-146.

Alvord, W. 1954. Validity of age determinations from scales of brown trout, rainbow trout, and brook trout. Trans. Am. Fish. Soc., **83**, 91-103.

Bennett, G. W. 1948. The bass-bluegill combination in a small artificial lake. Bull. Ill. St. nat. Hist. Surv., 24: 377-412.

Bhatia, D. 1932. Factors involved in the production of annual zones on the scales of the rainbow trout (*Salmo irrideus*). J. exp. Biol., **9**, 6-11.

Brander, K. 1974. The effects of age-reading errors on the statistical reliability of marine fishery modelling. In this volume, Bagenal, T. B. (Ed.), Unwin Brothers, 181-191.

Brown, C. J. D. and J. E. Bailey. 1952. Time and pattern of scale formation in Yellowstone cutthroat trout, *Salmo clarkii lewisii*. Trans. Am. Microsc. Soc., 71: 120-124.

Buchholz, M. M. and K. D. Carlander. 1963. Failure of yellow bass, *Rocais mississippiensis*, to form annuli. Trans. Am. Fish. Soc., 92: 384-390.

Burris, R. M. 1949. The growth rate of bluegills and largemouth black bass in fertilized and unfertilized ponds in central Missouri. M. Sc. thesis. Univ. of Missouri. Columbia.

Carlander, K. D. 1961. Variations on rereading walleye scales. Trans. Am. Fish. Soc., **90**, 230-231.

———. 1971. Methods of evaluating stocking success. pp. 57-64. Proc. North Central Warmwater Fish Culture-Management Workshop. Iowa Coop. Fishery Unit, Ames, Iowa.

———. and R. R. Whitney. 1961. Age and growth of walleyes in Clear Lake, Iowa, 1935-1957. Trans. Am. Fish. Soc., **90**, 130-138.

———. R. R. Whitney, E. B. Speaker and K. Madden. 1960. Evaluation of walleye fry stocking in Clear Lake, Iowa, by alternate-year planting. Trans. Am. Fish. Soc., **89**, 249-254.

Cutler, D. W. 1918. A preliminary account of the production of annual rings in the scales of plaice and flounders. J. mar. biol. Ass. U. K., N. S. **11**, 470.

Dannevig, A. 1925. On the growth of the cod and the formation of annual zones in the scales. FiskDir. Skr. (Ser. Havunders.) **3** (6): 23 pp.

DeBont, A. F. 1967. Some aspects of age and growth of fish in temperate and tropical waters. pp. 67-88 in 'The biological basis of freshwater fish production' edited by S. D. Gerking. J. Wiley & Sons. N. Y.

Frey, D. G. 1942. Studies on Wisconsin carp. I. Influence of age, size, and sex on time of annulus formation by the 1936 year class. Copeia 1942. 214-223.

Fry, D. G. and L. Vike. 1941. A creel census on Lakes Waubesa and Kegonsa, Wisconsin in 1939. Trans. Wis. Acad. Sci. Arts, Lett. 33: 339-360.

Gray, J. and S. B. Setna. 1931. The growth of fish. 4. Effects of food and supply on scales of *Salmo irrideus*. Br. J. exp. Biol., **8**, 55-62.

Griffiths, P. G. 1968. An electronic fish scale proportioning system. J. Cons. perm. int. Explor. Mer. **32**, 280-282.

Hansen, D. F. 1951. Biology of the white crappie in Illinois. Bull. Ill. St. nat. Hist. Surv., **25**, 211-265.

Hatch, R. W. 1961. Regular occurrence of false annuli in four brook trout populations. Trans. Am. Fish. Soc., **90**, 6-12.

Hervey, J. B. 1963. Growth of yellow perch in Clear Lake, Iowa, 1950 to 1962. M. S. thesis. Iowa State Univ. Library. Ames. 67 p.

Hjort, J. 1914. Fluctuations in the great fisheries of northern Europe. Rapp. P.-v. Réun. Cons. perm. int. Explor. Mer. **20**, 1-228.

Koo, T. S. Y. 1962. Age and growth studies of red salmon scales by graphic means. pp. 49-121 In 'Studies of Alaska red salmon' edited by T. S. Y. Koo. Univ. Wash. Press. Seattle.

———. and A. Isarankura. 1968. Objective studies of scales of Columbia River chinook salmon, *Oncorhynchus tshawytscha* (Walbaum). Fishery Bull. Fish Wildl. Serv. U. S., **66** (2), 165-180.

Kruse, T. E. 1959. Grayling of Grebe Lake, Yellowstone National Park, Wyoming. Fishery Bull. Fish Wild. Serv. U. S., **59** (149), 307-351.

Kuroki, T., K. Kyushin, R. Kawashima and O. Sata. 1965. A trial setup of the semi-authomatic scale reading recorder. Bull. Fac. Fish. Hokkaido Univ., **16** (2), 83-113.

Laakso, M. and O. B. Cope. 1956. Age determination in Yellowstone cutthroat trout by the scale method. J. Wildl. Mgmt, **20**, 138-153.

Le Cren. E. D. 1974. The effects of errors in ageing in production studies. In this volume, Bagenal, T. B. (Ed.), Unwin Brothers, 221-224.

Linfield, R. S. J. 1974. The errors likely in ageing roach *Rutilus rutilus* (L.), with special reference to stunted populations. In this volume, Bagenal, T. B. (Ed.), Unwin Brothers, 167-172.

Mathisen, O. A. 1966. Some scale characteristics of the Ozernaya sockeye salmon. J. Fish. Res. Bd. Can., **23** (3), 459-462.

McAfee, W. R. 1966. Eastern brook trout. pp. 242-260 In A. Calhoun 'Inland Fisheries Management.' Calif. Dept. Fish & Game. Sacramento.

Nichols, A. G. 1957. The Tasmanian trout fishery. I. Sources of information and treatment of data. Aust. J. mar. Freshwat. Res., **8**, 451-475.

Nordeng, H. 1961. On the biology of char (*Salmo alpinus* L.) in Salangen, North Norway. I. Age and spawning frequency determined from scales and otoliths. Nyt. Mag. Zool., **10**, 67-123.

Parsons, J. W. 1950. Life history of the yellow perch, *Perca flavescens* (Mitchill), of Clear Lake, Iowa. Iowa St. J. Sci., **25**, 83-97.

Percival, E. and A. M. R. Burnet. 1963. A study of the Lake Lyndon rainbow trout (*Salmo gairdnerii*). N. Z. Jl. Sci., **62**, 273-303.

Regier, H. A. 1962. Validation of the scale method for estimating age and growth of bluegills. Trans. Am. Fish. Soc. **91**, 362-374.

Reimers, N. 1958. Conditions of existence, growth, and longevity of brook trout in a small, high-altitude lake of the eastern Sierra Nevada. Calif. Fish Game, **44**, 319-333.

Reynolds, J. B. 1965. Life history of smallmouth bass, *Micropterus dolomieui* Lacepede, in the Des Moines River, Boone County, Iowa. Iowa St. J. Sci., **39**, 417-436.

Ridenhour, R. L. 1955. The northern pike, *Esox lucius* L., population of Clear Lake, Iowa. M. S. thesis. Iowa State Univ. Library. Ames. 67 p.

Robertson, O. H. 1947. An ecological study of two high mountain trout lakes in the Wind River Range, Wyoming. Ecology, **28**, 87-112.

Skillman, R. A. 1965. Increased growth of yellow bass in Clear Lake, Iowa, 1959-1964. M. S. thesis. Iowa State Univ. Library. Ames. 57 p.

Sprugel, G. Jr. 1954. Growth of bluegills in a new lake with particular reference to false annuli. Trans. Am. Fish. Soc. 83 : 58-75.

——. 1955. The growth of green sunfish (*Lepomis cyanellus*) in Little Wall Lake, Iowa. Iowa St. Coll. J. Sci. 29 : 707-719.

Surber, E. W. 1937. Rainbow trout and bottom fauna production in one mile of stream. Trans. Am. Fish. Soc., **66**, 193-203.

Sych, R. 1967. Confidence estimation of a fish age determination from scales as exemplified by sea-trout (*Salmo trutta* L.). Roczn. Nauk Roln., **90**(H2): 281-303

Vanderpuye, C. J. 1968 Age and growth of black crappie, *Pomoxis nigromaculatus* (LeSueur), in Lewis and Clark Lake, Missouri River. M. S. thesis. Iowa State Univ. Library. Ames. 68pp.

Vanicek, C. D. 1963. Life History studies of the sauger, *Stizostedion canadense* (Smith), in Gavins Point Reservoir. M. S. thesis. Iowa State Univ. Library. Ames. 56pp.

Williams, J. E. 1955. Determination of age from the scales of northern pike (*Esox lucius* L.). Ph. D. dissertation. Univ. Mich. 185pp.

Winge, Ö. 1915. On the value of the rings in the scales of the cod as a means of age determination, illustrated by marking experiments. Meddr Kommn Havunders. Ser. Fiskeri, **4**(8), 1-21.

The application of age determination in fishing management

by A. E. HOFSTEDE

Oosterbeek, The Netherlands

SUMMARY

1. A method for a rapid and practical 'appraisal of fishing waters and their fish populations' was developed for the purpose of being able to deal efficiently and quickly with the many requests for advice in The Netherlands from the managers of the 1,000 to 2,000 units of management. The present article deals with the appraisal of fish stocks.

2. Almost all inland waters (345,000 ha) can be classified in the bream zone. Most of these waters are eutrophic, even hypertrophic, due to excessive pollution originating from abroad down the rivers Rhine and Meuse, as well as from The Netherlands itself.

3. Consequently, most of the freshwater fish species (appr. 40) are those belonging to the bream zone. A small number only demands management. This concerns species that are important to recreational and/or professional fishing and also species that may become a nuisance due to excessive numbers, competition for food, etc.

Species in demand by both recreational and professional fishermen, are pike, pike-perch and perch. which are therefore often overfished. Cyprinids (in particular bream, roach and rudd, but also carp, white bream, etc.) are highly appreciated by sport fishermen who, usually, return them to the water. There is only little commercial fishing of these species. As a consequence, they are underfished in many waters which results in stunted growth, low catchability, etc. Bream and roach need special attention in the first place on account of their excessive reproduction which often leads to a stunted over-population

4. Two theories trying to explain the dynamics of fish populations and the effects of certain management policies, namely the fishing theory of Russel and the production theory of Walter are discussed. It is concluded that the growth is the most important management tool for the characterization of the fish stock, but for a correct diagnosis one must have growth standards at ones disposal. Against the background of Walter's production theory such standards were determined for bream and roach by which the growth in subsequent years should be as follows, provided that the milieu is suitable:-

roach   6 — 11 — 15 — 18 — 21
bream   7 — 14 — 21 — 27 — 32 — 36 — 40 —
        44 — 47 — 50

5. With the purpose of eliminating imperfections regarding the ageing as much as possible, various means are tried to determine the 'general trend of the growth' of the population under consideration. This procedure includes:

(1)   Collection and evaluation of general indications on the growth. These can be derived from length
f   frequency standards, the length frequency curves, the proportion of males to females, the first spawning maturity in females, the readability of the scales, the condition of the fish and the occurence of fish disease.
(2)   Direct ageing by means of bony structures of the body from which the actual age composition can be derived, while back-calculation shows the growth of the subsequent year classes.

From such information the general trend of the growth can be found and this growth trend has to be compared with the standard.

While discussing this procedure examples are given from appraisals carried out in several inland waters.

INTRODUCTION

An attempt was made to develop a method for a rapid and practical appraisal of fishing waters and their fish stocks to be able to cope efficiently and quickly with the many requests for advice concerning fisheries management. This method which is, of course, adapted to the situation in The Netherlands is primarily divided in two parts, namely

(1)   characterization of the ecosystem (the biological appraisal of fishing water), and
(2)   characterization of the fish stock (the practical appraisal of fish stocks) mainly with regard to the important species.

The word 'characterization' is purposely used because it is considered irrelevant to classify either the water or the fish stock: they almost all belong to the bream zone. The method tries to characterize the situation by carrying out a certain number of diagnostic observations and by comparing the data obtained with suitable standards. On the basis of such characterization a policy leading to improvement can be advised.

The present article deals with the practical appraisal of fish stocks by which ageing plays the important part It treats the subject in the following sections:-

1.   The Netherlands' inland waters.
2.   The fish species in The Netherlands' inland waters.
3.   The fishing and the production theory.
4.   Determination of some growth standards.
5.   Determination of the growth

I am much indebted to Mr. B. Steinmetz with whom I could frequently discuss all problems regarding this subject and, in particular, also to Mrs. I. J. de Vries-Williams who kindly and accurately studied and read the manuscripts prepared for this symposium and rectified the errors and mistakes in the English language.

THE NETHERLANDS' INLAND WATERS

The following summary was given by Hofstede and Blok (1972)from the data regarding the present situation derived from a study of Blom (1967, 1968).

The areas are given in hectares.

Present situation

Lake IJssel		200,000
Polders, reservoir systems (lakes etc.)	85,600	
Main rivers (Rhine, Meuse, etc.)	18,600	
Small rivers	2,500	
Delta waters	26,000	
Marginal lakes	10,000	
Various other waters	2,300	
Total	145,500	200,000

Estimated situation after 1980

Lake IJssel		120,000
Polders, reservoirs, etc	85,600	
Main rivers	18,600	
Small rivers	2,500	
Delta waters	61,000	
Marginal lakes	21,500	
Various other waters	2,300	
Total	191,500	120,000

Delta waters are lakes reclaimed from the sea, mainly in the south-west of The Netherlands. They are expected to become fresh but at the present time Lake Veere (2,000 ha; reclaimed in 1961) is still brackish and the water of the Grevelingen (11,000 ha; reclaimed in 1971) has a salinity almost equal to sea water.

The inland waters, which include a great variety from small (also drainable ponds) to large waters, are intensively used for sport fishing by appr. 1½ million fishermen, and other forms of recreation. This recreational use is intensified by their location: mainly in and around the western part of The Netherlands where one finds the greatest population density. In addition there is often professional fishing which is still important. Furthermore, taking into consideration the hydrological and hydrobiological features of these waters one can distinguish 1,000 to 2,000 units of management. If one now wants to give advice about certain types of management in which it is often essential to keep oneself informed on progress and improvements resulting from the advice given, it is of prime importance to have rapid methods of appraisal and diagnosis in particular with regard to the fish stocks.

When appraising waters and their fish stocks or diagnosing certain problems there are a few points to keep in mind with regard to the situation in The Netherlands:

(1) Almost all waters can be classified in the bream zone and are sluggish or stagnant, shallow waters. This also refers to the delta system of the river Rhine which always has been classified in this zone. Apart from these, several large barrages have been constructed on the river in recent years. The river Meuse originally belonged to the barbel zone. As a consequence of the construction of seven barrages in the 1920's and 1930's the water is almost stagnant during the greater part of the year, which brings this river also into the bream zone.

(2) Consequently, the fish species of The Netherlands are mainly those belonging to the bream zone. There are approximately 40 freshwater species of which only a few are of real interest to recreational and professional fishing.

(3) There exists a high degree of pollution in almost all inland waters which is due to the heavily polluted Rhine entering the country from Germany and the ever increasing pollution of the Meuse coming from Belgium. These two rivers contribute the greatest part of the water supply to The Netherlands. In addition, also in The Netherlands itself domestic and industrial pollution is excessive. As a consequence, most of the inland waters are eutrophic, even hypertrophic and phenomena resulting from the secondary pollution are common.

(4) The great importance of recreational fishing was recognized by the Government and lead to a policy of high priority to the development of sport fishing. It has to be kept in mind in this connection that sport fisheries and professional fisheries may have different aims.

THE FISH SPECIES IN THE NETHERLANDS' INLAND WATERS

There are approximately 50 species: 40 freshwater species and some migratory and some seawater species in the salt and brackish water lakes.

A small number only demands management *sensu stricto*. This concerns species that are important for recreational and/or professional fishing and also some species that may become a nuisance through excessive numbers, stunted growth, food competition, etc. The most important and/or interesting species are the following:

1. Salmonidae

In recent years rainbow trout *Salmo gairdneri* (Richardson), and brown trout *Salmo trutta fario* (L.) have been used on a fairly large scale for stocking brackish and salt water lakes (Lake Veere since 1968, the Grevelingen since 1971). Growth in these waters is excellent but these species will not reproduce. Practical research is centred on (1) angling results by means of creel census, (2) growth and migration by means of tagging, (3) the occurrence of diseases, etc. Despite periodical stocking, catches in Lake Veere have declined during the last few years. This is now being investigated.

In fresh inland waters (for instance Lake Brielle) the size of the trout stocked should be, or exceed, the legal minimum size of 25 cm as growth is normally negligible in these waters.

Smelt, *Osmerus eperlanus* (L.), which maintains itself in fresh water is an important food fish for predators but is of little importance to professional fishermen and anglers and, therefore, not subject to management of any kind.

2. Cyprinidae

Of the 20 species represented in The Netherlands only six always need attention

Bream *Abramis brama* (L.) in many waters has a tendency to become excessive in numbers which results in retarded or even stunted growth. Food competition may exercise unfavourable influence upon other bottom fish species, such as eel and carp. Therefore the management must prevent over population of many waters.

In roach *Rutilus rutilus* (L.) the same tendency to stunted growth is found quite often. The absence of fish of larger size than 25 cm is often correlated with absence of *Dreissena* and other molluscs. Prevention of growth retardation due to over population is often an important concern of the management.

White bream *Blicca bjoerkna* (L.) is very similar to bream and roach. There is a tendency to overpopulation and food competition with other bottom fish species. Considering its general occurrence white bream is about the third fish after bream and roach.

Rudd *Scardinius erythrophthalmus* (L.) is less common than bream and roach but particularly appreciated by sport fishermen on account of its fighting quality and its taking flies.

Ide *Leuciscus (Idus) idus* (L.) is a fish from large lakes and running water. It is being regularly introduced in most smaller inland waters mixed with professionally caught Cyprinids (mainly roach) supplied for restocking.

Common carp *Cyprinus carpio* (L.) only maintains itself in inland waters in lower numbers. Stocking of two or three year old fish particularly in smaller closed waters gives satisfactory results.

Other Cyprinids like tench *Tinca tinca* (L.), dace *Leuciscus (Leuciscus) leuciscus* (L.), chub *Leuciscus (Squalius) cephalus* (L.), crucian carp *Casassius carassius* (L.) and *Carassius auratus gibelio*, and barbel *Barbus barbus* (L.) do appear in catches and are often of local significance but in general are relatively unimportant. Therefore, only little incidental management practices are encountered. There is, however, a certain export of commercially caught tench.

3. Anguillidae

Eel *Anguilla anguilla* (L.) is the most important and often the only fish for professional fishing. In some parts of The Netherlands sport fishermen also concentrate on the catch of eel.

Management is focussed on various important problems, such as (1) the passage through or around dams, barrages and sluices to allow elvers and/or juvenile eels to enter the inland waters and to move up stream, (2) the additional stocking of elvers imported from abroad and of juvenile eels, and (3) the dangers of overstocking probably causing slower growth, the predominance of smaller male eels, unfavourable influence by food competition, and detrimental effects on other fish species such as feeding on roe.

4. Esocidae

In waters fished by sport fishermen or by professional fishermen in combination with recreational fishing, overfishing of pike *Esox lucius* (l.) is a common phenomenon. The virtual disappearance of the most favoured spawning sites (flooded meadows in early spring) and a lowered fecundity probably due to DDT (research not included) decrease the resilience of this species. It often appears to be very difficult to realize that even in a normal situation only a few sizeable pike per ha per year can be taken without danger for overfishing (a production of 10-20 kg/ha per annum has to be considered very good). Management, therefore, has to be focussed on the decrease of fishing pressure, on protection of spawning sites and on additional stocking of fingerlings.

5. Percidae

Pike-perch *Stizostedion lucioperca* (L.) is of interest to both catagories of fishermen, recreational and professional. An uncertain rate of reproduction and a low production capacity (5 kg/ha per annum is a good production) are a permanent danger for overfishing.

Perch *Perca fluviatilis* L. is a relatively slow-growing but prolific predator. It is of interest to both professional and recreational fishermen. In waters with lush underwater vegetation where the small size food fish can hide, its growth is often stunted. In that case it can happen that females of around 10 cm already propagate intensively while one rarely finds perch larger than about 16-17 cm. Management should include eradication of too abundant submerged vegetation and prevention of too heavy fishing pressure.

Ruffe *Acerina cernua* (L.) has neither commercial nor recreational value. It may exercise unfavourable influence by food competition with eels, carp and bream, particularly as a consequence of its frequent mass occurrence. As a food fish for pike-perch, eel and perch it only has secondary importance.

THE FISHING AND THE PRODUCTION THEORY

1. As a consequence of the increase of sport fisheries' interests and, concurrently, the decrease of the importance of professional fishing, great changes took place with regard to the fishing intensity. The facts causing the decline of commercial fishing were, and still are, (1) the water pollution, and (2) a serious decline of the market value of cyprinids, mainly bream and roach, which occur abundantly in the bream zone. Inland fish species in demand for commercial fishing are eel, pike, pike-perch and perch.

Sport fishermen are interested in almost any species of fish which has sporting qualities. Cyprinids are fished intensively, in particular roach and bream, but also rudd, carp, white bream, etc. However, these species find little appreciation as food and are, therefore, almost always returned to the water. The acquired hook-avoidance diminishes the catchabiliy. This has been proved in The Netherlands by Beukema (1967, 1970a, 1970b) with regard to carp and pike and by Hofstede (1972) also with regard to carp (experiments in the years 1959 and 1960). Thus, there is not any fishing intensity worth-while mentioning from sport fisheries with regard to cyprinids. On the other hand, sport fishermen, as well as commercial fishermen, are highly interested in the predators pike, pike-perch and perch. These are taken home in most cases although there is an intensive propaganda to put them back in the water because of their smaller abundance and their qualities with regard to checking the mass occurrence of cyprinids.

As a consequence one can expect the following situation in inland waters with respect to the development of fish stocks.

(1) Underfishing of cyprinids because these species are insufficiently removed from the water. In

most cases this refers to bream but also to roach.

(2) Overfishing of predators which are removed from the water by both professional and recreational fishermen.

The appraisal of fish stock in a certain water has to take these facts into consideration. When advising for improvement attention should be given to the wishes of the manager because (1) different exploitation systems can be practised, and (2) there may be a clear difference between the aims of recreational and professional management.

2. There are two theories which try to explain the dynamics of fish populations and the effects of a certain management policy, namely the fishing theory and the production theory.

The theoretical background of fishing was clearly defined by various sea fisheries biologists, for example Russell (1931, 1939, 1942), Hjort (1933), and Graham (1935, 1939, 1944).

In The Netherlands it was Baerends (1946, 1947) who drew attention to it and discussed it in detail. It is the opinion of the present author that the theory also holds good for large inland waters. It appears to be interesting, furthermore, to consider and to study the applicability in a range of ever smaller and finally very small waters. At the end of this series of water bodies fish ponds are found. In this latter type of waters all factors influencing the production can be controlled. Here a link can be established with Emil Walter's production theory (1934, 1937). It is also the opinion of the author that Walter's rules are applicable for large inland waters and that both ways of approaching problems with regard to fishing and production touch and overlap each other and can be complementary.

3. According to the fishing theory size and composition (in general the character) of fish stocks are determined by 4 factors.

Increase of fish stock
   (1) reproduction; i.e. an increase in numbers
   (2) growth; i.e. an increase in weight.

Decrease of fish stock
   (3) natural mortality; i.e. a decrease in number and weight.
   (4) fishing mortality; i.e. also a decrease in number and weight.

If the fertility of the water and the climate remain reasonably invariable the nature of the fish stock is determined by these 4 factors. If all these factors remain constant no marked changes take place in the stock. The purpose of a management is to get optimal results which also remain constant. Therefore the manager must execute appropriate measures by which influence is exercised upon one or more of the factors mentioned.

With regard to inland fisheries it certainly is possible to exercise influence upon these factors by which the character of the stock (e.g. size, composition, or selected species) can be directed towards a preconceived goal.

Reproduction means the supply of small fish to the stock. It is primarily an increase in numbers which can be regulated, for instance, by extension, or by limitation of spawning sites. The result of the propagation in natural undrainable waters can never easily and rapidly be expressed in exact numbers. Nor is it

possible to bring about such a propagation that the exact number of young fish wanted is added to the stock.

On the other hand it is practicable in fish culture with drainable ponds to count exactly the number of, for instance, the fry obtained from the propagation and also to count the number to be stocked into growing ponds, etc.

It must be kept in mind that if one wants to exercise influence upon the number of fish by means of 'birth control' in natural or undrainable inland waters it can only be done in broad outline.

Natural mortality and fishing mortality diminish the fish stock in number and weight.

The natural mortality can be influenced to a certain extent (e.g. control of diseases and plagues, increase or decrease of the stock of predators, etc.). However, the extent of the natural mortality is difficult to assess accurately or rapidly.

In the case of fishing mortality certain quantities of fish are consciously removed from the water. With commercial fisheries, if there is an efficient marketing organization, the amounts in weight are accurately registered, and the numbers can be calculated with sufficient accuracy. With regard to the sea fisheries and to the inland fisheries in some great lakes, e.g. Lake IJssel, marketing systems, giving adequate statistics on landings are organized in The Netherlands. However, there does not exist such a system for the rest of the inland waters which cover an area of at least 100, 000 ha.

In the case of recreational fishing one can only roughly assess the amount, number and weight, removed from the water (for example by a creel census). But reliable and accurate data about all fish removed from all the waters by recreational fishing can not be expected.

Nevertheless, it must be well understood that by means of removing fish from the stock great influence can be exercised upon the fish remaining in the water. This removal of fish cannot be done unrestrictedly. The question arises how the remaining stock should be evaluated. The theory of fishing states that somewhere between the under- and the over-fishing the point of optimal fishing is found. And this point by which a certain amount of fish is allowed to be caught without depleting the stock has to be determined by trial and error on the basis of landing statistics, information on fishing effort, etc. It is a laborious method and not applicable in the case of sport fisheries because of the impossibility to collect the reliable and accurate data needed.

Growth of fish, i.e. increase in length and weight, is primarily subject to the amount of food available per fish during the period of favourable temperature. The production of food depends on the fertility of the water and the climate. The climate can not be influenced and the fertility only to a small extent in natural waters by fertilization. Therefore, it can be said that the production of food is a rather constant factor in such waters so that the amount of food available per fish is determined by the number of fish. It has been said before that in natural, undrainable large waters this number is difficult to determine. On the other hand, growth, which can be considered a relative measure for the amount of food available per fish and also a relative measure for the number of fish, can often be easily determined by means of ageing. If such a growth determination will be of any use for fisheries management there must be available growth standards which concur with the aims of a certain exploitation. Such a desired growth must then be approached by manipulating with the unknown number of fish by thinning out or additional stocking, increasing or decreasing of fishing intensity, etc. The growth rate has to be determined at regular intervals for the purpose of registering progress.

If on the basis of a well-organized marketing system which made available statistics covering many years the optimal production of a water area has been established the corresponding growth rate to it can be found and be used as a standard for the fishing intensity. A treatment of the applicability of such standards in the practise of sea fisheries falls beyond the scope of this article but in inland fisheries it is a highly practical method.

The situation of under- and over-fishing was mentioned earlier. There are a few points which must be remembered in particular in connection with recreational fishing management in inland waters. In the case of overfishing anglers only catch small numbers of small fish because there are only low numbers of fish in the water which do not get the time to grow to larger sizes. In the case of underfishing the fish caught are similarly small size. They cannot grow to larger sizes because of the small amount of food available per head. In other words, the growth is stunted. Experience has shown that in such underfished populations anglers' catches are also low. It means that in both situations, the underfished and the overfished fish stocks, the anglers catch low numbers of small fish. As a consequence it has often been thought that the poor catches in an underfished stock indicated overfishing. An attempt was then made to improve the stock by means of additional, even heavy, stocking. This, of course, worsened the situation and the result was no improvement.

It became clear from many practical experiments and observations that a thorough thinning-out of the underfished stock improved the catches considerably, while concurrently, growth was augmented. To diagnose the unsatisfactory situation it is only necessary to determine the age since in the overfished stock growth is quick and in the underfished stock it is slow.

In the many underfished cyprinid stocks in The Netherlands ageing turned out to be an important and practical diagnostic tool.

It is remembered here that different American experts studied the relation between the development of the fish population and the results of catches on hook and line. Bennet (1943) formulated his conclusions very clearly. Good catches can only be expected 'when adequate numbers of fast growing fish are present'. This is a clear characterization of the fish population by means of a growth standard which fulfills the demands of recreational fisheries.

Summarizing these views with regard to the theory of fishing it can be stated that under influence of 4 factors—reproduction, natural and fishing mortality and growth—the fish population attains a certain character. This character can be changed into a certain, wanted, direction by exercising influence upon one or more of these factors. It is concluded that the growth is, or can be a reliable indication for the development. Moreover, it is easily determined in many, if not most, cases. For a correct diagnosis

growth standards are needed. Dependent upon different circumstances and conditions these standards can, or have to be, adapted to the character of the water and the water body and to the wishes of the manager concerning the desired fish species and product.

4. Walter (1933, 1937) studied, in pond experiments mainly with carp, the interrelation between stocking density (= number of fish), growth (= individual increase in weight and length) and production (= increase in weight of total stock). These conceptions are also found in the theory of fishing. However, these factors can be expressed or determined in exact figures in drainable fish ponds. This enables us to observe to what extent changing but known conditions manifest themselves in the rate of growth.

Walter has formulated his conclusions in a number of rules which serve our purpose of evaluating and managing fish stocks to a great extent. With regard to their pond culture the Organization for Improvement of Inland Fisheries (O.V.B.) drew attention to it in the annual report 1961/62 while the present author after some earlier publications in Dutch treated it with regard to the management of fish population in inland waters in English (1971, 1972).

Rule 1. Increase of stocking density diminishes the individual increase in weight (= growth) and vice versa.
Rule 2. The maximum increase in weight of the total stock corresponds with moderate increase of weight (growth) per individual fish.
In other words: The highest production in kg/ha per unit of time is obtained in a density of stock that allows moderate growth (i.e. not very rapid and not very slow, but somewhere in between).

The curves in Fig. 1 demonstrate these rules in a graph which is the result of the experiments. Furthermore, a summary of the relation density—growth—production is shown in Fig. 2.

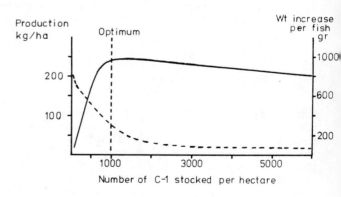

Fig. 1. (After Emil Walter). Interrelation between number stocked, growth per fish and production per hectare. The upper continuous line indicates the production per hectare and the lower dotted line represents the growth increase per fish.

It is remarked that sport fishermen are not much interested in a high or the highest production expressed in kilograms per hectare. Their primary interest is in large fish and preferably in great numbers.

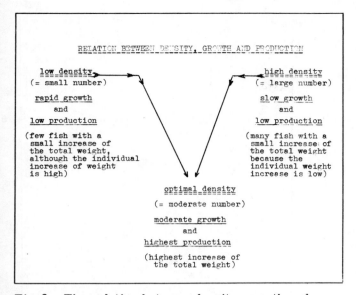

Fig. 2. The relation between density, growth and production.

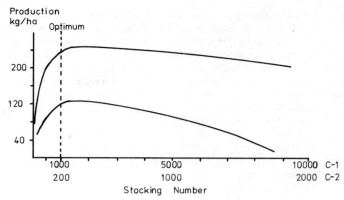

Fig. 3. (After Emil Walter). The differences in the production in connection with the number and size of the carp stocked. The graph shows the stocking number of one and two year old carp plotted against the production in kg/ha. The upper curve shows C-1 to C-2 and the lower curve C-2 to C-3.

However, to assure the presence of large fish, the fish must have the opportunity to grow fast. And this does not happen if their number is too great. Therefore, if the average size of the fish obtained on the basis of the formula 'optimal density—moderate growth—highest production' does not satisfy the demands of sportfishing a lower density should be established so that rapid growth of a smaller number of fish guarantees fish of bigger size.

Rule 3. The higher the individual weight of the fish, the lower the production capacity, of the water.

This very important rule can best be illustrated with the example given by Walter. In the case of growing carp from one-summer to two-summer fish and from two-summer to three-summer fish the following figures ensuring the maximum production were found (C—1, C—2, etc. means one year (summer), two year old , carp; etc.)

	growth from	
	C—1 to C—2	C—2 to C—3
Stocking density (No.)	1000 C—1	200 C—2
Individual weight increase	275 grams	600 grams
Production per hectare	240 kg.	120 kg.

Figure 3 shows the curves resulting from the experiments.

This part of Walter's experiments clearly shows that if one wants large fish one has to stock low numbers. It can now also be concluded that every year class (or size of fish) has its own optimal density by which the average (= optimal) growth takes place. The bigger the fish, the smaller should be their number in order to maintain a satisfactory growth. This means that every year class has to be either thinned out adequately or, alternatively, stocked up. If natural and fishing mortality turns out to be inadequate a well planned additional fishing out of all year classes

has to be carried out. Checking on the development easily can be done by determination of the average length of every year class and comparing it with the standards of growth.

Rule 4. The higher the production capacity of a water, the smaller the difference between the total production of smaller and bigger fish. This means that in case of lower fertility one cannot expect to come up to the growth standards.

DETERMINATION OF SOME GROWTH STANDARDS

It was stated in the preceding paragraphs that in The Netherlands predators are usually overfished and cyprinids underfished.

Within the programme the practical appraisal no ageing with the purpose of characterizing the stock of predators has been carried out because (1) ageing is difficult in a field programme, and (2) there are other methods which give sufficient insight into the development of these stocks.

The problems regarding ageing and growth of the predators were investigated by Willemsen, biologist of the Government Institute for Fisheries Investigations in recent years, and his information regarding the general averages in The Netherlands are given in Table 1 (personal communication).

Table 1

GROWTH RATE PREDATORS (in cm) (after Willemsen)

predator	age in years			
	1	2	3	4
pike	20	35	50	60
pike-perch	14	27	40	50
perch	7	13	19	24

Ageing of pike is questionable, of perch it is sufficiently reliable when using spines (no back calculation possible) and ageing of pike-perch is considered reliable by means of scales.

Other methods for the appraisal of predator stocks in clude (1) the number caught (which is mainly a matter of experience), the relation of predators to non-predators expressed in weight, and (2) information derived from the frequency curve with regard to the distribution of the sizes (see table 5) and the Petersen curve which in normally growing pike-perch (see table 5) and perch give adequate information. Due to the great range of length in the age classes in pike no meaningful Petersen curves are found. The overpopulation and the stunted growth of perch in densely vegetated waters are easily recognized by its predominant small size and blackish appearance (see also page 208.)

In the case of Cyprinids the situation is different. In particular with regard to bream and roach it was said that these species can increase in numbers to such an extent that their own growth becomes stunted, and, furthermore, that for an adequate appraisal ageing is essential by which the results have to be compared with standards. Walter showed the way to find a moderate growth by which the highest production is obtained and by which the population has a certain density. From our side it was remarked that the growth rate can be increased by diminishing the population density. As a result the fish can grow to larger sizes. Figure 1 clearly demonstrates this principle. It is evident that the optimal growth needed for the establishment of a population with a certain desired character must be found somewhere between the maximum and a poor rate of growth.

With regard to roach, a growth standard was suggested between a maximum growth found in pond experiments (Hofstede, 1963b) and a poor growth often encountered in practise. This is shown in the upper part of Table 2, and in Fig. 4. The practical definition reads as follows: The optimal growth must reach the length of 15 (males 14, females 16) cm at the end of the third growing period.

Table 2

ROACH: growth standard					
growth rates in cm					
maximum	11 — 22 — 26 — 30				
poor	5 — 8 — 10 — 12 — 14 — 15				
suggested parameter	6 — 11 — 15 — 18 — 21				

De Biesbos (not published)

males	6.4 — 10.9 — 14.5 — 17.7 — 19.2 — 20.5
females	6.3 — 11.8 — 15.7 — 18.5 — 20.8 — 22.1

Lake IJssel (Havinga, 1945)

6 — 11 — 16 — 21 — 25 — 28

This, or even a greater rate of growth may actually be found in larger waters, as shown in the middle and lower parts of Table 2.

No similar pond experiments could be carried out with bream before 1967. However, in that year, Steinmetz was able to start a similar programme with bream and rudd in the newly built experimental station (see his contribution to the present Symposium). Before that it was too dangerous on account of diseases, to introduce this fish species in the carp

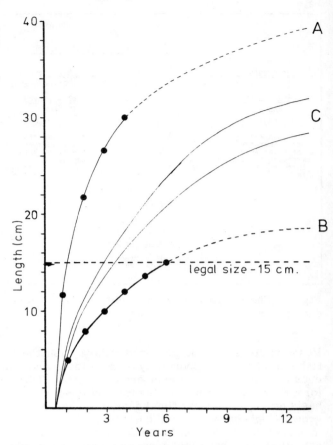

Fig. 4. The growth standard of roach. The points indicate growth observations. Curve A represents maximum growth, curve B poor growth and C optimal growth.

production establishment of the Organization for Improvement of Inland Fisheries. Roach used for the experiments entered the ponds with the water supply. For the determination of the 'moderate' growth of bream foreign literature, i.e. Wagler (1948/51), Järnefelt (1921), Bauch (1953), who are cited by Heuschmann (1941), and Dutch literature, Redeke (1923), Havinga (1945), were used in addition to observations and experiments in various inland waters in The Netherlands (most of them not published). All these rates of growth are shown in Fig. 5 on the basis of which the growth standard given in Table 3 was recommended with regard to the management of sport fishing waters. This means that bream should reach a length of 50 cm in 10 years and after that the growth curve must still run upwards.

Table 3

BREAM: growth standard
7 — 14 — 21 — 27 — 32 — 36 — 40 — 44 — 47 — 50

DETERMINATION OF THE GROWTH

It can be remembered from the preceding paragraphs that it was concluded that the growth is an indirect measure of the amount of food available per fish. When the amount of food produced in a certain water is a rather constant supply, be it within certain limits, the growth is a relative measure for the number of fish (one or more species) feeding on this

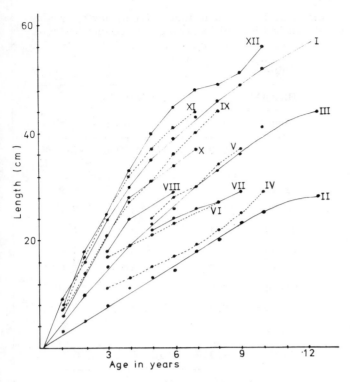

Fig. 5. Growth of bream in various waters.

I. South German lakes (Wagler, 1948/51)
II. Tuusulasee (Järnefelt, 1921)
III. North German lakes (Bauch, 1953)
IV. Lakes of Langeraar (Redeke, 1923)
V. Het Wijde Blik (Redeke, 1923)
VI. Lakes of Langeraar (Hofstede and Blok, 1961)
VII. Oude Gaasterbrekken (Hofstede unpublished)
VIII. River Rotte (Hofstede, 1965)
IX. Lake IJssel (Havinga, unpublished)
X. Biesbos (Hofstede, unpublished)
XI. Forest of Amsterdam (Hofstede unpublished)
XII. Forest of Amsterdam, maximum growth of one fish (Hofstede unpublished)

food. Then the growth can be influenced by manipulating with the number of fish (thinning-out, additional stocking, etc.). Therefore, within the framework of the 'Practical appraisal of fish stocks', determination of the rate of growth is of fundamental importance because the character of the stock can be clearly described and the effects of measures aiming at changes in a certain direction can be easily tested.

Growth can be determined by means of correlating the length of the fish with the age. The length (total, standard, etc.) is easily determined while different methods can be used to determine the age: scales, finrays, otoliths, etc. They all have in common that they react on differences in growth. When these growth changes are brought about be periodical influences (cold seasons, spawning migration, etc.) the differences in the structure can be used to determine the age. In our climate we have the winter ring or annulus. It has been stated before that, when appraising fish stocks in The Netherlands' inland waters it is of particular importance to determine the age of bream and roach. For these species the scales turned out to be very suitable (Hofstede, 1963b, 1974; Steinmetz, 1974). Growth can also be assessed by means of tagging which seems almost the only reliable method for pike. It must be realised, however, that certain methods of tagging may have an unfavourable influence upon the growth (e.g. with carp: Hofstede, 1972).

As is the case with many biological methods the ageing may have imperfections which may well lead to misinterpretation. Therefore, the determination of the growth should not only depend on the reading of scales, finrays, etc. Fortunately there are other indications which may also give information on the growth, even if only in a more general way. These should be taken into account. In doing so it seems possible to formulate a method which includes more safety and which gives a reliable and practicable conclusion with regard to the trend of the growth. The procedure recommended in The Netherlands is described below. It is admitted that it looks rather laborious in its complete form but it can often be considerably facilitated in practice. This has to be decided from case to case.

Whilst discussing the procedure some examples derived from fisheries investigations, including from the River Rotte (Hofstede, 1968), will be given. This river is a slow flowing river-like water (length appr. 15 km; area appr. 175 ha) which receives its water from surrounding polders; it therefore acts as a drainage canal.

1. The basis of the appraisal of a fish stock is the collection of information from commercial statistics (some times also available from the private bookkeeping of the professional fisherman), and by means of experimental fishing. The experimental fishing has to be carried out with different types of gear (Hofstede and Blok, 1972) with the purpose of landing adequate numbers of all fish species and of all length classes of these fish. The choice of the gear to be used must take into consideration the applicability in the water concerned, the selectivity of the gear, the possibility of gear avoidance known from some species and other factors. From the point of view of ageing, the catch of one-year-old fish is important because the first year ring is sometimes difficult to locate. This was also emphasized by Chugunova (1963). Considering the execution of experimental fishings preference is given to the cold season, November to April, when the fish are concentrated and less active, and because at that time they have completed a growing period. If special attention has to be paid to the time of first spawning preference might be given to the months around March. Eel is usually sampled in spring and around September and trout in the months May to August. This sampling gives a rough insight into the composition of the fish stock (species, numbers, weights) and points out clearly the important and predominant fish species.

With regard to the Rotte there are available commercial statistics collected over many years. Table 4 gives information on the period 1960 to 1964. The average landing per year amounted to 22, 000 kg; i.e. 127.7 kg/ha/year.

Predators and non-predators are in the proportion of 1—19. The great predominance of bream with roach (often mixed with white bream) as second fish, a most common phenomenon in The Netherlands' inland waters, is clearly shown.

Because in 1966 the management of all fish except eel came into the hands of a sport fishing association advice was asked regarding the execution of measures to adapt the fish stocks to recreational fishing. To do so additional information was derived from five experimental fishings: one in March 1965 and four from the months December and January 1966/67. With regard to the composition of the stock, they all gave the

Table 4

River Rotte—Commercial Catches in the Period 1960-64

fish species	kg/ha/year		% of total weight	
bream	108.2		84.7	
roach, white bream	12.5	121.2	9.8	94.9
carp	0.5		0.4	
pike-perch	3.1		2.4	
perch	2.5	6.5	2.0	5.1
pike	0.9		0.7	
Total	127.7		100	

same picture: i.e. great predominance of bream, and roach as second fish while predators were found in a similar proportion as in the commercial catches.

2. The second step is the construction of length frequency curves, in particular with regard to the important fish species. As additional evaluation of the growth there are some useful standards. The length frequency curve should show the presence of adequate numbers of fish in the various length classes and approximately in the ranges as shown in Table 5. If fish are present divided over these ranges it is an indication of a probably satisfactory growth.

Table 5

Length Frequency Standards

fish species	approximate range (cm)
pike	15—60 and some larger specimen
pike-perch	12—70
perch	6—35
eel	10—60
bream	7—50 and preferably larger specimen
roach	7—35
rudd	7—35

With regard to the River Rotte, in which bream is by far the predominant species, Table 6 gives the division into length groups of this species.

It is noted that very few bream larger than 40 cm are found in the catches. Because no indication of over-fishing could be traced it is concluded that there must be something wrong with the growth; it is either poor or it is retarded somewhere around the length of 35 cm.

Furthermore, the frequency curve may show clear peaks indicating year classes (Petersen principle). In Fig. 6 pronounced peaks representing the ages of 3 and 4 years (checked by means of the scales) can be seen in the catch of 15-3-1965 (curve A.). The ages of 5 years and older can not be reliably distinguished by well-separated peaks. The catch of 7-12-1966 (curve B) does not show a reliable sequence of separated peaks. Considered by its shape, the only peak in curve B is very probably a mixture of different year

classes. It is evident that in frequency curves as shown in Fig. 6 all peaks have to be checked with other ageing methods.

Table 6

BREAM—length groups River Rotte

Length (cm)	Experimental fishings		
	15-3-1965 %	7-12-1966 %	5-1-1967 %
11-15	—	—	5.9
16-20	14.2	33.2	47.1
21-25	7.1	57.8	11.2
26-30	17.6	4.2	4.3
31-35	39.7	3.5	15.0
36-40	17.2	1.0	12.8
41-45	3.0	0.3	3.7
46-50	1.1	—	—
Total	99.9	100.0	100.0
Total no. measured	267	313	187

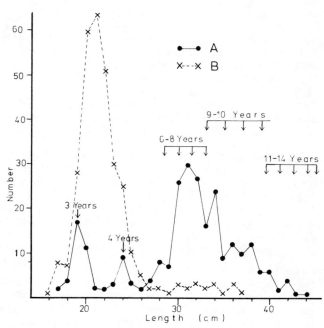

Fig. 6. The length frequency of bream from the River Rotte. Graph A (solid line between dots) is based on 267 fish caught on 15-3-65 and graph B (interrupted line between crosses) is based on 313 fish caught on 7-12-66. The mean lengths of various age groups as determined by scale samples are shown for the 15-3-65 fish (Graph A).

Nevertheless, it is a fact that in stocks of well-growing fish, by which the annual increase in length amounts to at least 4 to 5 cm, pronounced peaks occur which in the case of bream can be found well separated up to the length of about 40 cm. Thus, as can be seen in Fig. 6, curve A, when there are no more well separated peaks in the length groups over 26 cm this is an indication that the growth is unsatisfactory and that the curve between the lengths of 26 to about 40 cm is a mixture of age groups with a small difference of their average length.

It stands to reason that the number of fish upon which such a frequency curve is constructed should not be too low.

The frequency curve of normally growing roach shows clear peaks by which, however, a complication may occur. There is a difference in growth rate between males (which is somewhat slower) and females, which already manifests itself at the end of the second year. As a consequence, the peaks of 3- and 4- year-old roach may be deformed in such a way that they look like a mixture of more than one-year class. By dividing the sample into males and females normal peaks will appear.

In larger inland waters, such as Lake IJssel and other lakes, which have a suitable milieu, pike-perch and perch show reliable Petersen curves if sufficient numbers are measured. Information on pike-perch is given by Havinga (1945), Willemsen (1969), Steinmetz (1969) and Steinmetz and Oudelaar (1971a and b). The information can be summarized as in Table 7.

Table 7

Pike-perch Petersen curves (length in cm)

age in years	1	2	3	4
Havinga year class 1937	14-18	30-34	44-46	appr. 52
Willemsen year class 1966	14	32.5	44.5	
general average	12	28	40	
Steinmetz Inland waters	5-20	20-30	30	45
Oudelaar (Lake IJssel	5-20	20-35		>35

Normally growing perch shows clear peaks around the averages 7-13-18-24. The stunting of this fish species in densely vegetated waters was mentioned before. The result is an irregular frequency curve between 6 and roughly 16 cm and not fish of greater size.

The general conclusion is that, if one realizes the pro's and con's, frequency curves can be of good use for the determination of, or for a check on the growth.

3. The frequency curve can be determined immediately after the landing of the catch. Then it is possible to measure a great number of fish. Although it could also be done in the field, it is preferable to carry out the sexing and the sampling of ageing material as soon as possible in the laboratory. In this connection it is recommended to take home 10 fish of each size group.

4. The 10 fish of each size group are sexed for the determination of

(1) The proportion of males to females with the purpose of being able to break down the frequency curves, and

(2) The lengths of first spawning maturity in females. The female is considered ripe for spawning in the coming season when the abdominal cavity is full of eggs.

The proportion of males to females, in particular in the larger size classes of the stock under consideration, can also give some information of the growth. For instance, it is most common to discover the absence of male roach larger than about 20 cm in many, mainly smaller, inland waters while at the same time larger females do occur. It is known, however, that males can also grow to larger sizes (e.g. up to 25-30 cm) although the growth is slower than in females (Hofstede, 1963). In this connection also the following example is instructive. An experimental fishing was carried out in the southern part of Lake IJssel on 16-3-1965 the results of which were never published. Of each size group of roach between 25 and 30 cm four scale samples from 2 males and 2 females, were collected. Determination of the age gave the information shown in Table 8.

Table 8. Growth of roach in Lake IJssel

age (years)	lengths (cm)	
	males	females
5		25-25
6		28
7		26-26-27-27-28
8	25-25-26-26-27	29-30-30
9		
10	27-28-29-30	

Females attained the lengths of 29 and 30 cm in 8 years and males in 10 years. Back-calculation gave the growth rates shown in Table 9

Table 9. Back-calculated growth of roach in Lake IJssel

age	1	2	3	4	5	6	7	8
males	5-6	9	14	17	20	22	24	26
females	5-6	10	16	20	23	25	27	—

It is a fact (1) that males lag behind, and (2) that they can also grow to sizes well over 20 cm. If it now happens that no males occur at a certain length while there are females of much larger sizes, it indicates that the growth curve of the males is already flattened down to such an extent that no further increase in length can take place. If this happens at lengths of around 20 cm it is another indication of a too slow, a retarded or poor growth. In the River Rotte roach grow reasonably well during the first three years. After that the growth declines to such an extent that males longer than 17 cm do not occur, while females are present up to about 23 cm.

The first spawning maturity in females can also give a general idea of the growth. Although it is often reported that the first year of maturity correlates with the rate of the growth it is the opinion of the present author that the age is an important, if not the most important, factor determining the first spawning maturity of the female. Of course this may be different in various fish species but as far as the Dutch experience goes it is closely linked to the age in bream, roach and perch.

With regard to the River Rotte Table 10 gives information on age and length of the first spawning maturity in male and female bream.

Table 10.

BREAM: length and age at maturity (River Rotte)

age in years	males		females	
	mature	lengths	mature	lengths
3	none	under 18	none	under 17
4	majority	20.5-25.0	small part	20.5-25
5	all	23.5-29.0	50%	23.5-29
6	all	over 27	all	over 27

It can be seen that 50% of the females (lengths 23.5 to 29.0 cm) spawn for the first time in the beginning of the 6th year and that all females propagate in the beginning of the 7th year. This happens as from the length of 27 cm.

Havinga (1945) reported on rapidly growing bream in Lake IJssel: females reach the first maturity at the age of 6 years at an average length of 35 cm. This means that this rapidly growing female bream propagate for the first time in the beginning of the 7th year.

The experimental fishing of 16-3-1965 in Lake IJssel (already mentioned before) landed 182 bream consisting of 82 males and 80 females. The ages and the corresponding lengths are given in Table 11.

Table 11. Growth of Bream in Lake IJssel

age	5	6	7	8	9
males	30-31	32-37	33-38	32-43	38-44
—average	31	34.7	35.6	38.6	40.0
females		30-36	32-38	33-46	38-49
—average		33.6	35.1	38.6	42.8

Maturity of the females started at a length of 32 cm. Between 32 and 35 out of 19 females 15 (= 80%) were mature and from 36 cm upwards all females (60 fish) were ripe. These data give the same picture of the first maturity, that is almost all mature in the beginning of the 7th year.

These facts can be used in practice. For instance, it can be said with regard to bream that the first spawning takes place at the age of 5 or 6 years. According to the growth standard bream have at that age an average length of 32 and 36 cm respectively. When female bream are sexed in the field (this can be easily done by means of a slight pressure in caudal direction in the months March and April) and it turns out that all females of, for instance, 27 cm in length release their eggs it means that these bream are already 5 or 6 years old. This is an indication of a slower growth rate than given by the standard.

Similar observations were made with regard to roach and perch which reach their first maturity in the beginning of the 4th year at lengths averaging 16 cm for roach and 18 cm for perch. In stunted populations of both species it can be seen that the eggs are abundantly released at lengths of around 10 cm.

We can therefore, conclude that determination of the length of the first maturity in females, which can be done in the field, is another means of estimating the rate of growth.

5. It was recommended in paragraph 3 of this section to take a random sample of 10 fish per length class for further laboratory examination. This includes determination of the proportion of males to females per length class and of the length of first spawning maturity in females (paragraph 4).

For the purpose of determining the ages it is also recommended to take three scale samples of both males and females, per length class.
They serve to determine:

(1) the actual age composition of the population, and
(2) the course of the growth of each year class.

It is endeavoured to determine the general growth trend of the stock by which it is assumed that, by using a sufficient number of samples, incidental misinterpretations are eliminated.

Scale samples are mentioned because they serve their purpose excellently in bream and roach. However, in general terms one could say 'ageing material' rather than scales. There are biologists who categorically reject the reliability of scales and who are of the opinion that only finrays give the correct age and that they do not show false rings. This may be true with regard to ageing in some species but it certainly is not with bream and roach. Nevertheless, such problems ought to be studied more thoroughly by making use of fish of known age.

One scale sample (scales taken from one fish) consists of at least 5 scales. They are taken from the left side of the body and, with regard to bream and roach, just above the lateral line somewhat in advance of the dorsal fin. After a superficial cleaning the scales are pressed between glass slides. When they are still slightly moist they stick to the glass and will not move.

The scales are examined with a stereo microscope with magnifications of 25 and 50 (ocular: 12.5; objective: 2 and 4) and mainly with transmitted light which is partly and intermittently screened off with the hands. The microscope must be provided with an ocular micrometer for the execution of measurements.

For the determination of the age as many scales as possible of one sample are scrutinized. In case of measurement 3 normally shaped scales are selected. They should clearly show all particular characteristics which also ought to be present in the other scales of the sample. Scale measurements should be carried out in caudal direction.

With regard to the River Rotte the bream was thoroughly studied (Hofstede, 1968). This investigation will be used to demonstrate the present procedure. Some useful general information is summarized below.

(1) The experimental fishings landed bream of 13-46 cm; there were only a few fish of over 40 cm in length (see Table 6).
(2) These experimental fishings were carried out on different spots of the river; there was no local difference in growth rate. Also no difference in growth could be proved between males and females. Consequently, all scale samples could be mixed.

(3) Table 12 shows neither a great nor a regular difference in the numbers of males and females.

The fish in the experimental catch of 15-3-1965 had a length frequency between 18 and 46 cm (see Table 6 and Fig. 6) and included 6 males and 3 females larger that 40 cm. The landings of 7-12-1966 and 5-1-1967 had a frequency curve of 13 to 45 cm (Table 6 and Fig. 6); all the fish between 37 and 45 cm, 8 bream were females.

The actual age composition is given in Table 13.

Table 12

BREAK: (sex ratio in River Rotte)

sample from exp. fish.	males		females		unknown	
	nr	%	nr	%	nr	%
15-3-1965	61	41.5	81	55.1	5	3.4
7-12-1966) 5- 1-1967)	85	51.2	79	47.6	2	1.1
mean percentage	46.6		51.1		2.2	

This leads to another general rule based on experience: scales of adequately growing fish are transparent and easily read. And the reverse: when scales are difficult to read and are much less transparent, in short, if they don't look attractive, it is an indication of poor growth.

Scale measurements (caudal direction) to determine the growth curve of each year class were carried out on about 90 samples; that means a total of 270 scales. The scales belonged to fish in the length classes 13-40 cm: i.e. there were 27 length classes. Thus, 3-4 samples per length class were treated. On this basis the growth data shown in Table 14 could be formulated.

This table clearly shows that up to the 4th year growth is retarded, although still acceptable. After that, a further decrease in growth manifests itself with the same conclusions that there appear to be 5 year classes between the lengths of 30 to 40 cm, as stated before. It all indicates a poor growth when compared with the standard.

The course of the growth of 10 year classes, 1955 to 1964, is given in Fig. 7. The growth curves based on back-calculations of the year classes 1959 to 1962, (for which the stock was sampled in March 1965 and

Table 13

BREAM: age composition (experimental fishing on 15-3-1965)

age (years)	3	4	5	6	7	8	9	10	11-14
scale samples (number)	9	8	2	10	4	2	3	10	4
mean length (cm)	19.1	24.1	25.5	29.5	30.7	32.5	37.0	36.7	44.0

It is remarked that from the age of 8 years upwards the scales are gradually more and more difficult to read because the growth zones on the scales become narrow. This indicates an increasing retardation of the growth between 30 and 40 cm. The complete set of data prove that there are 5 year classes (6-10 years) between 30 and 40 cm which brings the average growth back to about 2 cm per year. In this case the annuli are difficult to discern.

Table 14

BREAM: growth rate in comparison to standard (River Rotte)

age in years	lengths cm	standard cm
1	4 - 7.5	7
2	10.5-13	14
3	16 -19.5	21
4	20.5-25	27
5	23.5-29	32
6	28.5-32	36
7	30.5-34	40
8	32.5-36	44
9	34 -38	47
10	35 -40	50

in December and January 1966/67) closely coincide. Back-calculations of the year classes 1957 and 1958 are equal up to the age of 5 years. In the years after

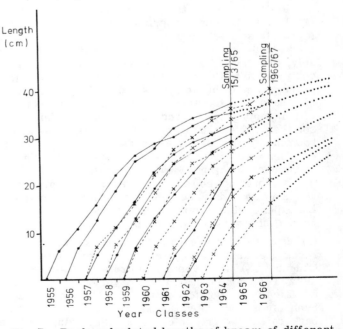

Fig. 7. Back-calculated lengths of bream of different year classes in the River Rotte, calculated from two sampling dates: 15-3-65 shown as solid line and dots; and 1966/67 shown as interrupted line and crosses.

that there are irregularities perhaps due to mis-interpretations in the periods of very low increase in lengths. However, the most important result of this graph is the general growth trend shown. This trend was theoretically extrapolated with interrupted lines. It is evident that this trend did not alter since 1955 and, furthermore, that the growth curves flatten down in such a way that the maximum length the fish can attain can not be more than about 45 cm. Proof of this fact was given with the experimental catches which always landed very few bream of more than 40 cm in length.

It turned out to be effective to have available data regarding two experimental fishings with a period of two years (summers) between. It might be advisable to include such a procedure in the appraisal programme.

Finally, there are a few remarks which ought to be made with regard to the problem of age determination.

(1) Scale reading and measuring are primarily a matter of thorough study and experience. Studies should be made by means of material (scales, fin ray, otoliths, etc.) of known age and of which the growth history is also given. In addition, it must be remembered that all fish species differ from each other and so do their scales. Experience and knowledge of one species do not provide that needed for other species.

(2) Knowledge of the milieu in which the fish lived is of fundamental importance. The character of the water concerned should be known and also many 'historical' events from about the last 20 years. This includes calamities (heavy fish kills, water shortage, etc.) as well as other events such as a long and hot summer, the change from saline into brackish or fresh water, etc. These all comprise influences which may have (or have had) harmful effects but also which may be favourable to the fish remaining in the water. All such happenings may have their effects upon the scales. For instance, Hofstede (1974, contribution to this Symposium about roach and dace) reported the formation of a false ring in the scales of dace. In his opinion, this was due to the long, hot and dry summer of 1959. In the same experimental pond roach did not form a false ring. Apparently, the river fish dace was not at home in a pond with stagnant water with, probably, also too high temperatures. Steinmetz (1974, contribution to this Symposium) reports a false ring in the scales of bream. This happened in a pond which may have been too small with submerged vegetation which completely covered the bottom. For this reason the pond was drained and the fish transplanted to two other ponds. It seems essential to experiment in a milieu which is to a high extent suitable for the fish under consideration. Furthermore, such experimental ponds should not be too small. Perhaps it might be worth-while considering the execution of such growing experiments in large ponds in addition to the normal stock of fish (e.g. carp).

(3) It is, of course, extremely important to be able to recognize false rings. As well as other authors Chugunova (1963) gives certain rules and also Steinmetz (1974, contribution to this Symposium) paid attention to it. Hofstede (1974, contribution to this Symposium) suggested that an irregular course of a back-calculated growth curve of fish originating from a rather regular habitat might indicate a false ring. At all events, it is a subject which needs much efficient experimenting including artificially induced false rings and thorough study.

(4) With regard to measuring the scales preference is given to the caudal direction. As far as present knowledge goes this method does not need any correction when applied for practical purposes. For the practical research it is sufficiently accurate and it is also convenient with roach, dace, bream and rudd. However, often the annuli are far better discernable in other directions. To meet the demands of practice (dealing with great numbers of measurements) it is worth-while to consider the set-up of correction tables.

6. Summary of the procedure regarding growth determination. The procedure described and discussed in the preceding paragraph includes:

(1) information/observations giving general indications on the growth, and
(2) direct determination of the growth.

It is intended to find a method by which various imperfections regarding the age determination are eliminated and to establish the general trend of the growth which is sufficiently accurate to be used in practice.

General information on the growth can be obtained from the following observations.

(1) length frequency standards (see Table 5) from which it is concluded that the length frequency should show adequate numbers of the fish species concerned varying from small to large sizes.

(2) The length frequency curves should show clear and well separated peaks indicating the year classes. This is possible in roach, bream, perch, pike-perch (and also other Cyprinids but certainly not in pike). If they do not show peaks it is an indication of a too slow growth.

(3) The proportion of males to females may give information on the growth. For instance, roach which has a clear difference in growth rate between males and females. Absence of males over a certain length (e.g. 20 cm which is often encountered in practice) while females occur in much larger size may indicate retardation of the growth.

(4) The first spawning maturity in females which is to a high extent linked to the age can give an idea of the growth rate in bream, roach and perch.

(5) The readability of the scale (at first sight). Scales of well-growing fish are almost always transparent, clear and easily read. Scales of poor growing fish are less transparent, are read with difficulty, or not readable at all, and do not look attractive.

(6) There are a few other indications not mentioned before. Fish in poor conditions (length-weight relation, condition factor) do not grow well. However, a good condition factor does not indicate a good growth, as for instance is the case with carp. Sometimes fish diseases may give information on the condition of the stock. In The Netherlands' inland waters this mainly refers to the so-called *Aeromonas* infections. When the symptoms are widely spread through the whole stock (very often of one species, such as bream or roach) it indicates that the population is too dense. When such stocks are properly thinned out the growth increases and the symptoms disappear.

Direct ageing is carried out by means of scales, fin rays, otoliths and other bony parts of the body. By means of determining the actual age composition and the growth of the year classes (back-calculation) a conclusion can be made regarding the general trend of the growth which must fall in line with the 'general indications on the growth'.

This general trend of the growth has to be compared with growth standards of the fish species concerned.

REFERENCES

Baerends, G. P. 1946, De werkwijze van het biologisch zeevisserijonderzoek en de betekenis ervan voor het visserijbedrijf. Vakbl. Biol., 26, 5-6

Baerends, G. P. 1947. De rationeele exploitalie van de zeevischstand, in het bijzonder van de vischstand in de Noordzee. Versl. Meded. Afd. Vissch. No. 36, 99pp.

Bauch, G., 1953. Die einheimischen Süsswasserfische. Radebeul und Berlin. 187 pp. (cited by Heuschmann, 1962).

Bennet, G. W. 1943. Management of small artificial lakes. Bull. Ill. St., nat. Hist. Surv., 22, (3) 357-376.

Bennet, G. W. 1962. Management of Artificial Lakes and Ponds. New York: Reinhold. 357 pp.

Beukema, J. J. 1967. Hook resistance. Annual Rep. 1966/67. Organisation for Improvement of Inland Fisheries. (In Dutch).

Beukema, J. J. 1970a. Angling experiments with carp Cyprinus carpio L. Neth J. Zool., 20, 81-92.

Beukema, J. J. 1970b. Acquired hook-avoidance in the pike Esox lucius L., fished with artificial and natural baits. J. Fish. Biol., 2, 155-160

Blom, B. 1967. Het gebruik van de Nederlandse rivieren en overige binnenwateren als viswater per 1 januari 1965. Documtie Rapp. Afdeling Sportvisserij en Beroepsbinnenvisserij, Utrecht. No. 5.

Blom, B. 1968. The use of fishing waters in The Netherlands. EIFAC/68 Sc 1-9.

Chugunova, N. I. 1963. Age and growth studies in Fish. Jerusalem. 132 pp. Translation of Chugunova N. I. 1959. Rukovodstvo po izucheniyu vozrasta i rosta ryb. Moscow.

Deelder, C. L. 1951. A contribution to the knowledge of the stunted growth of perch in Holland. Hydrobiologia, 3, (4), 357-378.

Graham, M. 1935. Modern theory of exploiting a fishery and application to North Sea trawling. J. Cons. perm. int. Explor. Mer, 10, 264-275.

Graham, M. 1939. The sigmoid curve and the overfishing problem. Rapp. P.-v. Réun. Cons. perm. int. Explor. Mer, 110, 17-20.

Graham, M. 1943. The Fish Gate. London. 196 pp

Havinga, B. 1945. Rapport betreffende de visscherij en de vischstand op het IJsselmeer. Unpublished.

Heuschmann, O. 1962. Die Weiszfische (Cyprinidae). Handbuch der Binnenfischerei Mitteleuropas. 3B. Ed. Demoll, R., Maier H. N. and Wundsch, H. H. Stuttgart. 23-199.

Hjort, J. J., Jahn, G. and Ottestad, P. 1933. The Optimum catch. Hvalråd. Skv., No. 7. 92-128.

Hofstede, A. E. 1963a. Bestandsregeling in Nederlandse Binnenwateren. Viss. Nieuws 16, (7)

Hofstede, A. E. 1963b. Groeiwaarnemingen van blankvoorn en serpeling in karpervijvers. Documtie Rapp. Afdeling Sportvisserij en Beroepsbinnenvisserij, No. 2, 60 pp.

Hofstede, A. E. 1968. Visserijkundig onderzoek van de Rotte. Documtie Rapp. Afdeling Sportvisserij en Beroepsbinnenvisserij, Utrecht. No. 8, 76 pp.

Hofstede, A. E. 1970a. Visserijkundig onderzoek van de Rotte. Visserij, 23, No. 2.

Hofstede, A. E. 1970b. Scale reading and back-calculation (roach and dace of known age). Documtie Rapp. Afdeling Sportvisserij en Beroepsbinnenvisserij, Utrecht, No. 11, 15 pp.

Hofstede, A. E. 1971a. Some observations with regard to roach and dace. Visserij, 24, (7), 424 (In Dutch: English summary)

Hofstede, A. E. 1971b. De Beoordeling van de Brasemstand. Documtie Rapp. Afdeling Sportvisserij en Beroepsbinnenvisserij, Utrecht, No. 12, 36 pp.

Hofstede, A. E. 1972. Angling experiments in 1959 and 1960; hook avoidance and retardation of growth in tagged carp. Visserij, 25, (7), (In Dutch: English summary)

Hofstede, A. E. 1974. Studies on growth, ageing and back-calculation of roach Rutilus rutilus (L,), and dace Leuciscus leuciscus (L.). In this volume Bagenal, T. B. (Ed.), Ageing of Fish, Unwin Brothers, 137-147.

Hofstede, A. E. and Blok, E. 1964. Visserijbiologische warnemingen in de Langeraarse Plassen. Documtie Rapp. Insp. Viss. Utrecht., No. 4. 75 pp.

Hofstede, A. E. and Blok, E. 1972. Appraisal of fishing waters and their fish populations. EIFAC 72/SC-1.

Järnefelt, H. 1921. Untersuchungen über die Fisch und ihre Nahrung im Tuusulasee. Acta Soc. Fauna Flora Fenn., 52, No. 1 (cited by Heuschmann, 1962).

Neubaur, R. 1926. Biologisches und Wissenschaftliches von Blei im Stettiner Haff und seinen Nebengewässern. Z. Fisch., 24.

O. V. B. 1963. Jaarverslag, 1961/62. 56-68.

Redeke, H. C. 1923. Rapport van onderzoekingen aangaande de groei van brasem in verschillende wateren. Verh. Rapp. Rijksinst. Visschonderz, 1, (2).

Russell, E. S. 1931. Some theoretical considerations on the over fishing problem. J. Cons. perm. int. Explor. Mer., 6, 3-21.

Russell, E. S. 1939. An elementary treatment of the overfishing problem. Rapp. P.-v. Réun. Cons. perm. int. Explor. Mer, 110, 5-15.

Russell, E. S. 1942. The overfishing problem Cambridge, 130 pp.

Schäperclaus, W. 1938. Die Schädigungen der Deutschen Fischerie durch Fischparasiten und Fischkrankheiten. Fischeriezeitung, Neudemn, 41, 22.

Schäperclaus, W. 1940. Seenverschlechterung. Z. Fisch., 38, 345-375.

Schiemenz, P. 1916. Ueber das Mindesmasz der Fische. D. Fisch. Korresp. 20.

Steinmetz, B. 1969. 1966, a strong year class of pikeperch, I. Visserij, 22, (3). (In Dutch)

Steinmetz, B. 1974 Scale reading and back-calculation of bream Abramis brama (L.) and rudd Scardinius erythrophthalmus. In this volume, Bagenal, T. B. (Ed.), Ageing of Fish, Unwin Brothers, 148-157.

Steinmetz, B. and Oudelaar, H. G. J. 1971a. Experimental trawl catches in Lake IJssel in the years 1966-69. Documtie Rapp. Afdeling Sportvisserij en Beroepsbinnenvisserij, Utrecht, No. 13. (In Dutch).

Steinmetz, B. and Oudelaar, H. G. J. 1971b. Experimental trawl catches in Lake IJssel in the year 1970. Documtie Rapp. Afdeling Sportvisserij en Beroepsbinnenvisserij, Utrecht. No. 14 (In Dutch).

Wagler, E. 1948-1951 Fische und Fischerei in den bayerischen Voralpenseen. Series in/Allg. Fisch.

Z. tg. from 1948 to 1951. (cited by Heuschmann, 1962)

Walter, E. 1934. Grundlagen der allgemeinen fischereilichen Produktionslehre. Handbuch der Binnenfischenerei Mitteleuropas, **4**, Ed. Demoll, R. and Maier, H. N. Stuttgart. 481-662.

Walter, E. 1937 Sachgemäsze Bewirtschaftung kleiner Teiche. Arb. Reichnährbestandes. **33**.

Willemsen, J. 1969 1966, a strong year class of pikeperch II. Visserij, **22**, (3).

The effects of errors in ageing in production studies

by E. D. LE CREN

Freshwater Biological Association, Windermere Laboratory
The Ferry House, Ambleside. LA22 0LP, England

SUMMARY

Production estimates are based on measures of abundance, mortality and growth. Of five methods of estimation those using yield and P/B ratios are approximate but need no age data. Allen survivorship-growth curves and the Ricker method do not necessarily need age data if cohorts can otherwise be distinguished and a time scale is available. Mathematical models normally depend upon ageing for growth and mortality parameters. Unbiased errors in ageing, especially for older fish, will have little effect on production estimates. Estimates of juvenile production require data that will reveal errors in interpreting the first annulus. The unlikely systematic errors arising from doubling or halving the true age will halve or double the production estimates. For most production estimates inaccuracies are caused much more by errors in the measurement of abundance than by ageing errors.

INTRODUCTION

Production, in the ecological sense in which it is used in this paper, can be defined as the total quantity of fish flesh produced in a given area in a given time regardless of whether it all survives to the end of that time. It should not therefore be confused with yield. The production of natural populations of fish was first measured by Allen (1946, 1951) and Ricker and Foerster (1948) but the whole concept has recently had stimulus under the auspices of the International Biological Programme.

Production can be usefully considered as an epitome of the whole population ecology of the fish being studied and is of relevance to both the understanding of fish ecology and to the management of fisheries (Ivlev 1966, Gerking 1967, Le Cren 1972). It is important to remember, however, that production is only one parameter, albeit a key one, in population dynamics, and obtains its real value only in comparative studies or in relation to other population parameters such as growth, mortality, fecundity, recruitment and food consumption.

The following paper attempts a brief exploration of some of the methods of estimating production, discusses the need for age determinations in such estimates and what the effects will be of either no age determinations or inaccurate or biased ones.

METHODS FOR ESTIMATING PRODUCTION

There would appear to be five distinct but related techniques for estimating production, two of which do not involve age determinations but are very approximate or applicable only in special circumstances.

1. *Yields.* In well managed fish ponds natural mortality is negligible so that yield is nearly as large as production and can be taken as a measure of it. This does not pertain to natural situations where production will never be less than the yield unless an accumulated stock is being fished out.

2. *P/B ratios.* Where data from other similar situations are available, very approximate estimates of production can be obtained by multiplying a biomass determination by the probable ratio between biomass and production. Such estimates have very little value but do not, of themselves, require age determinations.

3. *'Allen' curves* (Allen 1951). Allen curves are plots of survivors against mean weight for cohorts (broods or year-classes) throughout life. The area beneath the curve is a measure of production. This simple technique is a good way to present the concept of production graphically and even if one of the two following methods are used for the actual calculation of production, drawing an Allen curve is an excellent visual check on the validity and plausibility of the estimates. Allen curves will be discussed in detail below in relation to the other two methods and age determinations.

4. *The 'Ricker' method* (Ricker and Foerster 1948). This method involves the estimation of the growth and mortality rates for a series of time periods over the life of the cohort, together with an estimate of population density or biomass at at least one point in time. In many situations it is a computational version of the Allen curve, and should produce the same estimate.

5. *Mathematical models.* This method involves the modelling of the growth and mortality processes and the calculation of production from a formula derived in a way similar to the familiar yield formulae (e.g. Beverton and Holt 1957). It will usually be necessary to have good age determinations to estimate the parameters of the model but this is not absolutely essential.

THE ESSENTIAL REQUIREMENTS FOR PRODUCTION ESTIMATION

It will be realised, from the brief description of the three methods generally applicable, that the basic data required relate to population or biomass density, growth and survival (or mortality). The use of these for production estimation can be illustrated by reference to the Allen curve.

Allen curves are plots of numbers against weight, and are graphs of the survivors still alive and the mean weights of these survivors all of whom represent one cohort or year-class. The area beneath the curve is equivalent to the production. Allen curves, and their interpretation are discussed by Allen (1951) Chapman (1971) and Le Cren (1972), but, as it is necessary to fully understand what they represent before considering the role of age determination in their construction, I will discuss them in further detail.

The total area beneath an Allen curve for a cohort from hatching until the death of the last survivor accurately represents the total production of that cohort throughout its life. If, as is usually the case, there is an annual spawning resulting in one annual cohort—a 'year-class'—and the population is in a steady state with constant annual recruitment, the total production throughout life of any one cohort will be equivalent to the total annual production of all cohorts present in any one year. In practice, it is rare to follow any one cohort throughout its whole life but more usual to plot an Allen curve based on a 'composite' cohort built up with data from the series of cohorts (age-groups) present in one, or a short series of years. This can give rise to problems caused by the variation in strength of cohorts from year-to-year and adjustments may have to be made to compensate for this. Ideally a thorough study will extend over a series of cohorts over several years. The production achieved by cohorts of differing initial size or early survival may, in itself, be a valuable study.

The other major problem in making production estimates is to relate the production for the population sampled to the whole area or stock being studied, or to some standard area such as m² or ha. Population estimates to achieve this are usually the weakest part of the whole production estimate and estimates may be expressed in terms such as 'per recruit' in an attempt to avoid relating the production estimate to any particular total population.

An Allen curve can also be regarded as an accumulated histogram, each horizontal bar of which represents an individual fish at the time of its death; the length of the bar representing the weight on death. Such a graph for a hypothetical cohort is shown in Fig. 1. It will be seen that the cohort started with thirty fish each weighing 0.5g on hatching, and ended when the last survivor died weighing 28g. Two fish died before putting on any weight, the next two when they weighed 0.6g, the fifth and sixth at 0.7g, the seventh at 0.8g and so on.

Rarely is it possible to know the weight of fish on death (unless this is due to capture) and the data that are available usually consist of numbers of survivors and their mean weight at intervals of time. Four such points in time are shown on Fig. 1 by t_0, t_1, t_2 and t_3; t_0 being the time of hatching. The numbers and mean weights would be, respectively:

t_0	30	0.5 g
t_1	10	4.0 g
t_2	3	16.5 g
t_3	1	27.0 g

The actual total production for this cohort can be exactly calculated by summing the weights on death and comes to 158.8g. If the four points t_0-t_3 are plotted separately, and a smooth curve drawn between them the area beneath the curve is equivalent to about 155g; a close enough approximation.

The important point about this example, either as Fig. 1 or as its smoothed approximation, is that no information on age has been required, only (a) the knowledge that the cohort studied has been a typical one inhabiting a known area of water, and (b) that the survivors sampled at times t_0-t_3 did belong to the same cohort. In order to relate the production as measured to a time scale, so that the production per year or other appropriate time interval could be calculated, some measure of time must be made; in this case the mere dates of sampling would be adequate.

We can thus conclude that the prime need for age determinations will be as a means to identify cohorts and distinguish them from other cohorts a year or two younger or older. Thus means of identification other than age determination might be just as suitable.

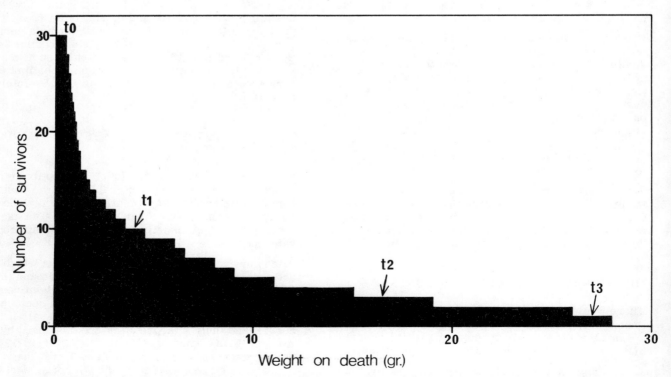

Fig. 1. Allen curve for a hypothetical cohort of fish. The number of survivors is plotted against the weight of each fish on death. $t_0 \ldots t_3$ are times of sampling. (see Text).

If, for example, the eggs of Fig. 1 had been marked with a stain (Bagenal, 1967) the resultant cohort might have been identifiable throughout its life.

In fact cohorts can be identified without using any of the normal methods of age determination such as scales. With young fish, in situations where there is a relatively short spawning season, size alone is an adequate identification especially if sampling can be carried out throughout the year. The analysis of length-frequency data has been widely used for tracing the survival and growth of fish and other organisms by identifying cohorts or age groups. Even if the normal distributions of age-groups overlap, the mean lengths and approximate numbers of each can often be determined with sufficient accuracy. A large batch of fish belonging to a particular age-group can often be marked (e.g. when young enough to be distinct), so that it can continue to be identified after its mode in a length-frequency graph has ceased to be distinguishable.

It is important to realise that time, as such, does not appear on an Allen curve. Successive points along the curve from top left to bottom right are points in time but their spacing is unlikely to be equal and indeed mortality can occur with passage of time without any growth and thus progress of the graph along the abscissa. The spacing of sample data in time should obviously be as frequent as possible especially during periods when rates of growth or mortality are high or changing rapidly, as they are in early life. The lines joining the points on the curve are then shorter and more accurate simulations of reality. Frequently, however, for long-lived fish, data are available at only yearly intervals. Production estimates will then be approximations only, though often reasonably accurate ones, especially if the seasonal variations in growth and mortality rates tend to be correlated.

It is important to realise that, as production is a product of growth (or mean size) and numbers, the errors in production estimates will be products of the errors in each of the two components. Provided the age determinations (and/or back calculations) are reasonably accurate, mean weights can be estimated with a coefficient of variation of the order of 1%, while a population estimate from a mark-recapture experiment might have a coefficient of variation of the order of 10%. Clearly the population estimates are likely to contribute the major share to the errors in production estimates.

The Ricker method of estimation (Ricker and Foerster 1948, Ricker 1958) is based on estimating the mean growth and mortality rates and population density for a series of time intervals. Production for each period is then calculated from:

$$P = \overline{B}G$$

where P = production, B = biomass and G = the instaneous relative growth rate. The production is then summed over all the time intervals. This method will give virtually the same results as an Allen curve if it is based on the same data. Growth rates will normally be estimated from observed differences in mean size (or possibly back calculations using scales, etc.). Mortality rates will often be estimated from observed decreases in population estimates, or observed decreases in relative abundance. Ricker type estimates are likely to be affected by the same errors as those influencing Allen-curve estimates; predominantly those arising from errors in population rather than size estimates.

With the mathematical model methods it will, again, usually be easier to estimate growth parameters reasonably accurately than mortality parameters, especially natural mortality rates. The models are unlikely to be realistic for the younger stages of life when growth and mortality especially will be changing rapidly. It is possible to obtain reasonable estimates of both growth parameters and mortality rates from marking experiments without involving any age determinations, especially when the population being studied is also being heavily fished or intensively sampled. Usually, however, an ability to make reasonably accurate age determinations will allow more accurate and easier production estimates.

JUVENILE PRODUCTION

The estimation of production in the young stages of a cohort usually involves methods rather different from those used for older fish. Sampling techniques may be different; capture of unselected samples is often difficult. As mortality and growth rates tend to be high and to be changing rapidly with time, frequent sampling is desirable and often essential. Usually it will be easy to recognise and follow a cohort from size-frequency data and normally no age-determination from scales, etc., is required. (There may indeed be a need for length-frequency analyses to check the accuracy of age and growth determination from the scales of older fish). Problems can arise when spawning or hatching periods are prolonged or occur more than once a year. It may also be important to follow changes in habitat with growth; constant sampling in one habitat may merely sample successive cohorts who each occupy that habitat for a particular phase of their development.

Production in the first few months of life may constitute a major part of the total production (e.g. Le Cren 1962) and any realistic study of fish production should include the young stages and also small species, even though they are of negligible direct fishery importance (Mann 1971).

GONAD PRODUCTION

Production can take two forms; somatic and gonadic. In juvenile fish all production results in an increase in body weight but in adult fish some of the increase in body weight is shed at spawning as eggs and milt. For older, slow-growing fish gonadic production may be as large as somatic production (Le Cren 1962) and in some species, such as the stickleback *Gasterosteus aculeatus* (L.) which lays a succession of egg batches, much larger (Wooton 1973). Estimates of gonadic production would not seem to require age determination, though the age at first spawning may be valuable supplementary information.

THE EFFECTS OF ERRORS IN AGE DETERMINATION

Errors in age determination will affect production estimates either through errors in growth-rate determinations (e.g. in the mathematical model or Ricker methods) or because an Allen curve estimate is not correctly related to the time scale or the cohorts involved.

Errors in age determination can take several forms. Unbiased errors in a proportion of the fish where the age is designated one or two years less or greater than it really is will often cancel each other out and have little combined effect. Moreover such errors are most commonly made when ageing older fish. These are usually few in number and relatively slow growing and so contribute little to the total production. The underestimation of age when the fish was growing too slowly to register discernible growth rings on its scales will similarly cause little bias in production estimates.

A common problem in scale interpretation arises at the centre where the first annulus may be missed thus giving rise to ages a year less than they should be. If production is being estimated only for fish after they have been recruited, and juvenile (pre-recruit) production is excluded, then errors arising before recruitment will have no effect on production estimates. A missed first annulus could give rise to errors in an estimate of juvenile production because the time over which the growth and production occurred would be underestimated. But any serious study of juvenile production would involve a frequency of sampling which would reveal the missing annulus and the correction of the error in ageing.

There is the possibility of systematic errors arising from the ages being read as twice or half what they should be. (Though such errors are unlikely in normal temperate conditions they might arise in subtropical situations where fish spawn twice a year or there are two rainy seasons). If the ages tend to be twice what they really are, there would appear to be alternately strong and weak year-classes with most of the fish belonging to even-numbered age groups. As the production measured (e.g. by an Allen curve) would appear to have occurred in twice the true time the production estimate would be half what it should be. In the reverse case, when every other annulus was missed, the production estimate would be twice the true one.

DISCUSSION AND CONCLUSIONS

It should be clear from the above discussion that production estimates will be made usually only as part of rather intensive and detailed comparative studies in fish population dynamics. In such studies some effort will be made to provide checks on age determinations and there will usually need to be sampling throughout the year for production data which will incidentally provide data for such checks. When production by young stages is being estimated, frequent sampling will be essential and age determination from scales of only supplementary value. Young stages often contribute a major part of the production.

Where production estimates for the adult or recruited stages of the life are being made using annual growth and survival data the production estimates will be approximate only but, especially for long-lived species, of some value. In such situations systematic errors in age determination could give rise to serious errors. Apparent ages double the

real ones would give a production estimate half what it should be, but such errors in ageing should be readily apparent. Apparent ages half the real ones are unlikely to occur but if they did would give a production estimate twice what it should be. Errors in the ageing of old slow growing fish will make little difference to production estimates. An error in the early ages will make no difference to a production estimate for older fish.

It can also be concluded that many estimates of production may be possible without recourse to ageing, provided cohorts can be otherwise identified, or growth and mortality estimates made from marking experiments.

Even if ageing is subject to some errors the accuracy of production estimates is likely to depend mainly on the precision with which population or biomass estimates can be made.

REFERENCES

Allen, K. R. 1946. The trout population of the Horokiwi River. Rep. Fish. N.Z., 1945 Appendix, 33-40.

Allen, K. R. 1951. The Horokiwi Stream: a study of a trout population. Fish. Bull. N.Z., **10**, 1-238.

Bagenal, T. B. 1967. A method of marking fish eggs and larvae. Nature, Lond., **214**, 113.

Beverton, R. J. H., and Holt, S. J. 1957. On the dynamics of exploited fish populations. Fish. Invest., Lond., (2) **19**, 1-533.

Chapman, D. G. 1971. Production. In Methods for the assessment of fish production in freshwaters. IBP Handbook No 3., 182-196 (Ricker, W. E. ed.) Oxford: Blackwell.

Gerking, S. D. 1967. (Ed.) The biological basis of freshwater fish production. Oxford: Blackwell, 495 pp.

Ivlev, V. S. 1966. The biological productivity of waters. J. Fish. Res. Bd Can., **23**, 1727-1759. (Translation of Ivlev, V. S. 1945. Biologicheskaya productionost' vodoemov. Usp. sovrem. Biol., **19**, 98-120.)

Le Cren, E. D. 1962. The efficiency of reproduction and recruitment in freshwater fish. In The exploitation of natural animal populations, 283-296 (Le Cren, E. D., and Holdgate, M. W., eds). Oxford: Blackwell.

Le Cren, E. D. 1972 Fish production in freshwaters. In Conservation and productivity of natural waters (Edwards, R. W., and Garrod, D. J., eds). Symp. zool. Soc. Lond., **29**, 115-133.

Mann, R. H. K. 1971. The populations, growth and production of fish in four small streams in southern England. J. Anim. Ecol., **40**, 155-190.

Ricker, W. E. 1958. Handbook of computations for biological statistics of fish populations. Bull. Fish. Res. Bd Can., **119**, 1-300.

Ricker, W. E., and Foerster, R. E. 1948. Computation of fish production. Bull. Bingham Oceanogr. Coll., **11**, 173-211.

Wootton, R. J. 1973. The effect of size of food ration on egg production in the female three-spined stickleback, *Gasterosteus aculeatus* L. J. Fish Biol., **5**, 89-96.

List of Participants

AASS, Dr. Per. Freshwater Fisheries Laboratory, Ministry of Environment, Dept. of Fish and Game, Fellesbygget, 1432 ÅS-NLH, Norway.

ABEL, Mr. R. Zoology Department, South Parks Road, Oxford University, Oxford, OX1 3PS, England.

ALLARDI, Mr. J. Centre Technique du Génie Rural des Eaux et des Forêts, Division Qualité des Eaux, Pêche et Pisciculture, 14, Avenue de St. Mandé, 75012 Paris, France.

ARMSTRONG, Mr. D. W. Department of Agriculture and Fisheries for Scotland, Marine Laboratory, P. O. Box 101, Victoria Road, Aberdeen, Scotland.

ARNTZ, Dr. W. E. Institut fur Meerskunde, University of Kiel, 1, Wischofstrasse, 2300 Kiel., 14, Federal Republic of Germany.

BACKIEL, Prof. T. Inland Fisheries Institute, Zabieniec, 05-500 Piaseczno, Poland.

BAGENAL, Mr. T. B. Freshwater Biological Association, Windermere Laboratory, Ambleside, Westmorland, LA22 0LP, England.

BANKS, Dr. J. W. Freshwater Fisheries Unit, Life Sciences Building, Liverpool University, P. O. Box 147, Liverpool L69 3BX, England.

BARBER, Mr. W. J. Biological Sciences Dept., City of London Polytechnic, 31, Jewry Street, London, E. C. 3, England.

BARR, Miss C. D. Freshwater Fisheries Unit, Life Sciences Building, Liverpool University, P. O. Box 147, Liverpool L69 3BX, England.

BEAMISH, Dr. R. J. Freshwater Institute, 501 University Crescent, Winnipeg, R3T 2N6, Mannitoba, Canada.

BEDFORD, Mr. B. C. Fisheries Laboratory, Ministry of Agriculture, Fisheries and Food, Lowestoft, Suffolk, England.

BELLAMY, Mr. G. C. Zoology Department, Reading University, Whiteknights Park, Reading, RG6 2AJ, England

BERRIE, Dr. A. D. Freshwater Biological Association, River Laboratory, East Stoke, Wareham, Dorset, BH20 6BB, England.

BIERNAUX, Dr. J. Faculte des Sciences Agronomiques de l'Etat, 5800 Gembloux, Belgium.

BILTON, Mr. H. T. Pacific Biological Station, Fisheries Research Board of Canada, Nanaimo, B. C., Canada.

BLACKER, Mr. R. W. Fisheries Laboratory, Ministry of Agriculture, Fisheries and Food, Lowestoft, Suffolk, England.

De BONT, Prof. A. F. Walenpotstraat I. A., Berten, B-3060, Belgium.

BOYD, Mr. J. C. Institut d'Ecologie, Service Chasse et Pêche, Place de Tunnel 19, 1005, Lausanne, Switzerland.

BROWN, Mr. V. M. Water Pollution Research Laboratory, Elders Way, Stevenage, Herts, SG1 1TH, England.

CANE, Mr. A. Freshwater Fisheries Unit, Life Sciences Building, Liverpool University, P. O. Box 147, Liverpool, L69 3BX, England.

CARLANDER, Prof. K. D. Zoology and Entomology Dept., Science Building, Iowa State University, Ames, Iowa, 50010, U.S.A.

CASSELMAN, Mr. J. M. Zoology Department, Toronto University, 25, Harbord Street, Toronto, Ontario, Canada, M5S 1A1.

CAZEMIER, Mr. W. G. Government Institute for Fisheries Research, Waalstraat 34, Ymuiden, The Netherlands.

CHAMP, Mr. T. Inland Fisheries Trust Inc., Mobhi Boreen, Glasnevin, Dublin 9, Ireland.

CHURCHWARD, Mr. A. S. Severn River Authority, Church Street, Malvern, Worcestershire, WR14 2AN, England.

CLARKE, Mr. D. A. J. Moreton Cottage, Compton Martin, Bristol, England.

CRAGG-HINE, Dr. D. Ministry of Agriculture for Northern Ireland, Fisheries Research Laboratory, The Cutts, Coleraine, Co. Londonderry, N. Ireland.

CRAIG, Mr. J. F. Freshwater Biological Association, Windermere Laboratory, Ambleside, Westmorland, LA22 0LP, England.

CUBBY, Mr. P. R. Freshwater Biological Association, c/o Nature Conservancy, Moor House, Alston, Cumberland, England.

DAHL, Dr. J. Danmarks Fiskeri-og Havundersøgelser, Charlottenlund Slot, DK-2920 Charlottenlund, Denmark.

DAVAINE, Mr. P. Institut National de la Recherche Agronomique, Station d'Hydrobiologie, BP 79, 64 Biarritz, France.

EASTON, Mr. K. The Polytechnic, Walfruma Street, Wolverhampton, WV1 1LY, England.

ERIKSSON, Mr. L. Biology Department, Section of Ecological Zoology, Umeå University, S-90187 Umeå, Sweden.

EVERSON, Mr. I. British Antarctic Survey, Monks Wood Experimental Station, Abbots Ripton, Huntingdon, England.

FAGADE, Dr. S. O. School of Biological Sciences, Lagos University, Lagos, Nigeria.

FAWELL, Mr. J. K. Inveresk Research International, Inveresk Gate, Musselburgh, Midlothian EH21 7UB, Scotland.

FITZMAURICE, Mr. P. Inland Fisheries Trust Inc. Mobhi Boreen, Glasnevin, Dublin 9, Ireland

FRAKE, Mr. A. A. Avon and Dorset River Authority, County Gates House, 300 Poole Road, Parkstone, Poole, Dorset, BH12 1AU, England.

FROST, Dr. Winifred E. Ferry House, Ambleside, Westmorland, England.

GASSER, Mr. M. Zoologisches Institut, Univesitatsstrasse 4, A-6020 Innsbruck, Austria.

GEE, Mr. A. S. Biology Department, Sir John Cass College, City of London Polytechnic, 31, Jewry Street, London, EC3, England.

GORDON, Dr. J. D. M. Scottish Marine Biological Association, P. O. Box 3, Oban, Argyll, Scotland.

GREEN, Mr. G. P. Zoology Department, Reading University, Whiteknights Park, Reading, RG6 2AJ, England.

GREENWOOD, Mr. J. H. Avon and Dorset River Authority, County Gates House, 300, Poole Road, Parkstone, Poole, Dorset, BH12 1AU, England.

GROSS, Mr. H. P. Zoology Department, Animal Ecology Research Group, Oxford University, South Parks Road, Oxford, OX1 3PS, England

HAMMOND, Mr. R. W. R. Biology Department, Bognor College of Education, Sussex, England.

HANCOCK, Mr. R. S. Freshwater Fisheries Unit, Life Sciences Building, Liverpool University, P. O. Box 147, Liverpool, L69 3BX, England.

HARAM, Dr. John. Biology Department, Liverpool Polytechnic, Byrom Street, Liverpool, L3 3AF, England.

HARCUP, Mr. M. F. Applied Biology Department, University of Wales Institute of Science and Technology, Cathays Park, Cardiff, Wales.

HARTLEY, Mr. W. G. Freshwater Fisheries Laboratory, Ministry of Agriculture, Fisheries and Food, East Block, 10, Whitehall Place, London, SW1A 2HH, England.

HELLAWELL, Dr. J. M. Water Pollution Research Laboratory, Stevenage, Herts, SG1 1TH, England.

HOFSTEDE, Mr. A. E. Graaf van Rechterenweg 27, Oosterbeek, The Netherlands.

HOLDEN, Mr. M. J. Fisheries Laboratory, Ministry of Agriculture, Fisheries and Food, Lowestoft, Suffolk, England.

HOPKINS, Mr. D. G. Zoology Department, Royal Holloway College, 'Alderhurst', Bakeham Lane. Englefield Green, Surrey, TW20 9TY, England

HUET, Prof. M. Station de Researches des Eaux et Forêts, Ministry of Agriculture, Avenue Général Derache 104, 1050 Bruxelles, Belgium.

HUGGINS, Mr. R. G. Bristol Avon River Authority, Green Park Road, Bath, Somerset, BA1 1XG, England.

HYND, Mr. I. J. R. Freshwater Fisheries Laboratory, Department of Agriculture and Fisheries for Scotland, Faskally, Pitlochry, Perthshire, Scotland.

JOHNSON, Mr. S. P. Zoology Department, University College, Lee Maltings, Prospect Row, Cork, Ireland.

JOLLY, Mr. D. W. Huntingdon Research Centre, Huntingdon, PE18 6ES, England.

JONES, Dr. J. W. Freshwater Fisheries Unit, Life Sciences Buildings, Liverpool University, P. O. Box 147, Liverpool, L69 3BX, England.

KIPLING, Miss C. Freshwater Biological Association, Windermere Laboratory, Ambleside, Westmorland, LA22 0LP, England.

KNIGHT, Dr. M. J. British American Optical Co. Ltd. 820, Yeovil Road, Slough, Bucks, England.

LAIRD, Miss L. M. Freshwater Fisheries Unit, Life Sciences Building, Liverpool University, P. O. Box 147, Liverpool, L69 3BX.

LAMP, Dr. F. Institut für Küsten- und Binnenfischerie der Bundesforschungsanstalt für Fischerie, 2, Hamburg 50, Palmaille 9, Federal Republic of Germany.

LANGHELT, Mr. P. National Museum of Wales, Zoology Department, Cardiff, CF1 3NP, Wales.

LAURENT, Dr. M. L. Institut National de la Recherche Agronomique, Station d'Hydrologie, BP 79, 64 Biarritz, France.

LAWS, Dr. R. M. British Antarctic Survey, Monks Wood Experimental Station, Abbots Ripton, Huntingdon, England.

LE CREN, Mr. E. D. Freshwater Biological Association, Windermere Laboratory, Ambleside, Westmorland, LA22 0LP, England.

LIE, Mr. S. F. Biological Sciences Department, Hatherly Laboratories, Exeter University, Prince of Wales Road, Exeter, EX4 4PS.

LIEW, Mr. P. K. L. Biology Department, Ottawa University, Ontario, Canada.

LINFIELD, Mr. R. S. J. Glamorgan River Authority, Tremains House, Coychurch Road, Bridgend, Glamorgan, Wales.

McCARTHY, Mr. D. T. Department of Agriculture and Fisheries, Fisheries Division, 3, Cathal Brugha St., Dublin 1, Ireland.

McDONALD, Mr. I. Thames Conservancy, River Purification Department, Reading Bridge House, Reading, England.

MANN, Mr. R. H. K. Freshwater Biological Association, River Laboratory, East Stoke, Wareham, Dorset, BH20 6BB, England.

MASON, Mr. J. E. National Marine Fishery Service, 2725, Montlake Boulevard East, Seattle, Washington 98112, U.S.A.

MATHEWS, Dr. C. P. Escuila Superior de Ciencias Marias AP 453, Ensenada, Beja California Nortre, Mexico.

MOORE, Mr. D. E. Freshwater Fisheries Unit, Life Sciences Building, Liverpool University, P. O. Box 147, Liverpool, L69 3BX, England.

MORIARTY, Dr. C. Department of Agriculture and Fisheries, Fisheries Division, 3, Cathal Brugha St., Dublin 1, Ireland.

NAIKSATAM, Mr. A. S. Division of Ichthyology, Zoological Institute, Charles University, Vinična-7, Praha-2, Czechoslovakia.

NIELSEN, Mrs. E. Danmarks Fiskeri og Havundersøgelser, Charlottenlund Slot, DK-2920, Charlottenlund, Denmark.

NWAUZO, Mr. E. E. Zoology Department, Chelsea College, University of London, Hortensia Road, London, SW10 0QX.

O'HARA, Mr. K. Freshwater Fisheries Unit, Life Sciences Buildings, Liverpool University, P. O. Box 147, Liverpool, L69 3BX, England.

PANELLA, Mr. G. Geology Department, C.A.A.M., University of Puerto Rico, Mayaguez, Puerto Rico, 00708, U.S.A.

PARNELL, Mr. W. C. Fisheries Laboratory, Ministry of Agriculture, Fisheries and Food, Lowestoft, Suffolk, England.

PARRY, Mr. M. L. Yorkshire River Authority, 21, Park Square South, Leeds, LS1 2QG, England.

PEDLEY, Miss R. B. Freshwater Fisheries Unit, Life Sciences Building, Liverpool University, P. O. Box 147, Liverpool L69 3BX, England.

PETRICHENKO, Dr. I. All Union Research Institute of Inland Fisheries, Dmitrov, Moscow Region, U.S.S.R.

PRITCHETT, Mr. R. S. Freshwater Fisheries Unit, Life Sciences Building, Liverpool University, P. O. Box 147, Liverpool L69 3BX, England.

RAUCK, Dr. G. Bundesforschungsanstalt für Fischeri, 2 Hamburg 50, Palmaille, Federal Republic of Germany.

REAY, Dr. P. J. Department of Environmental Sciences, Plymouth Polytechnic, Drake Circus, Plymouth , PL4 8AA, England.

RIAZANTSEV, Mr. Y. B. All Union Research Institute of Marine Fisheries and Oceanography (VNIRO) Moscow, U.S.S.R.

RIEMENS, Dr. R. G. Organisatie Verbetering Binnenvissery, Stradhouderslaan 53, Utrecht, The Netherlands.

ROBINSON, Mr. J. F. Cumberland River Authority, Chertsey Hill, London Road, Carlisle, Cumberland, England.

RUFLI, Mr. H. Federal Institute for Water Resources and Water Pollution Control, CH-8600 Dubendorf-Zurich, Switzerland.

RUSSELL, Sir F. S. 'Wardour', 295, Tavistock Road, Plymouth, PL6 8AA, England.

SALMBERG, Miss K. H. Odense University, Smedevaenget 2, 5700 Svenborg, Denmark.

SCOTT, Dr. J. S. Biological Station, Fisheries Research Board of Canada, St. Andrews, New Brunswick, Canada.

SHEARER, Mr. W. M. Department of Agriculture and Fisheries for Scotland, 6, California Street, Montrose, Scotland.

SHEARMAN, Mr. H. B. Brencroft Ltd., P. O. Box 8, Princes Risborough, Aylesbury, Bucks, England.

SHILLOCK, Dr. D. J. Yorkshire River Authority, 21, Park Square South, Leeds, LS1 2QG, England.

SIMKISS, Prof. K. Zoology Department, Reading University, Whiteknights Park, Reading, RG6 2AJ, England.

SIMMONS, Mr. J. R. Ministry of Agriculture, Fisheries and Food, Veterinary Investigation Centre, Madingley, Cambridge, CB3 0ER, England.

SOLBE, Mr. J. F. Water Pollution Research Laboratory, Elders Way, Stevenage, Herts, SG1 1TH, England.

STOTT, Mr. B. Freshwater Fisheries Laboratory, Ministry of Agriculture, Fisheries and Food, East Block, 10, Whitehall Place, London, SW1A 2HH, England.

STOTT, Dr. F. C. Back of Beyond, Winter Hill, Cookham Dean, Berks, SL6 9TW, England.

STEINMETZ, Mr. B. Ministry of Agriculture and Fisheries, Meentsteeg 2, Maarn, The Netherlands.

SYCH, Dr. R. Inland Fisheries Institute, Zabieniec, 05-500 Piaseczno, Poland.

TEMPLETON, Mr. R. G. Hampshire River Authority, South Side Office, The Law Courts, Winchester, England.

THORPE, Mr. J. E. Freshwater Fisheries Laboratory, Department of Agriculture and Fisheries for Scotland, Faskally, Pitlochry, Perthshire, Scotland.

THUROW, Mr. F. Bundesforschungsanstalt für Fischerei, Labor Kiel, Wischhofstr. 1-3, 23 Kiel 14, Federal Republic of Germany.

TWELVES, Mr. E. L. British Antarctic Survey, Monks Wood Experimental Station, Abbots Ripton, Huntingdon, England.

WELCOMME, Mr. R. L. Inland Fisheries Resources Branch, Fishery Resources Division, F.A.O. Via Delle Terme Di Caracalla, Rome, Italy.

WENT, Dr. A. E. J. Salmon Research Trust of Ireland Inc., 3, Cathal Brugha St., Dublin 1, Ireland.

WILKINSON, Mr. D. R. Freshwater Fisheries Unit, Life Sciences Building, Liverpool University, P. O. Box 147, Liverpool, L69 3BX, England.

WILLEMSEN, Mr. J. Government Institute for Fisheries Research, Maasstraat 19, Ymuiden, The Netherlands.

WILLIAMS, Mr. R. Applied Biology Department, University of Wales Institute of Science and Technology, Cathays Park, Cardiff, Wales.

WILLIAMS, Mr. T. Fisheries Laboratory, Ministry of Agriculture Fisheries and Food, Lowestoft, Suffolk, England.

WOODIWISS, Mr. F. Trent River Authority, Meadow Lane Laboratories, Meadow Lane, Nottingham, England.

YOUNG, Dr. May R. Zoology Department, Nottingham University, Nottingham, NG7 2RD, England.

Demonstrations

With the kind permission of Professor Simkiss demonstrations were set out in the Zoology Department of the Reading University for the evening of Thursday, 19th July 1973. The following demonstrations were well attended by the participants. The name of the person responsible for setting out the exhibit where it involved the work of a group, is given in brackets.

1. Brencroft Ltd. Projectina Projection microscopes and other equipment were exhibited by Mr. H. B. Shearman.

2. British American Optical Company Ltd. The Reichert Visopan projection microscopes and other equipment were exhibited by Mr. M. Knight.

3. E.I.F.A.C. Subcommission III Working Party on Ageing. (Professor T. Backiel). A manuscript dealing with *Coregonus* spp. scales was exhibited as an example of the proposed 'Atlas of Freshwater Fish Scales'.

4. The River Laboratory of the Freshwater Biological Association demonstrated the work on the fish of the River Stour. (Mr. R. H. K. Mann)

5. The Zoology Department Reading University demonstrated some aspects of the Fish Investigations on the River Lambourne (Dr. A. D. Berrie) particularly

    (a) Diet Studies
    (b) Population Studies

6. The Lowestoft Laboratory of the Ministry of Agriculture Fisheries and Food arranged the following exhibits:

    (a) Marine teleost fish otoliths
    (b) The use of Tetracycline for age validation (Mr. Bedford)
    (c) Electronic flash photography of gadoid otoliths (Mr. Blacker)
    (d) An electronic fish scale proportioning system (Mr. W. C. Parnell)

7. The Inland Fisheries Trust Inc. (Mr. P. Fitzmaurice and T. Champ) exhibited the use of scales in the age determination of rudd, bream, gudgeon, grey mullet, bass and pike.

8. The Department of Biological Studies, City of London Polytechnic (Dr. Anne M. Powell) illustrated aspects of studies particularly with roach and bream, on gravel pit populations.

9. Dr. J. W. Banks, Freshwater Fisheries Unit, Liverpool, showed the use of scales in age determination of pike *Esox lucius* L. from Mortons Mere (Isle of Ely)

10. Dr. D. Cragg-Hine, Ministry of Agriculture, Northern Ireland, demonstrated some erosion problems with Lough Erne roach scales.

11. Dr. W. E. Frost exhibited some scales of char in Windermere and the char populations.

12. Mr. R. S. J. Linfield, Glamorgan River Authority, exhibited scales from tagged mirror carp from Grey Mist Mere.

13. Mr. G. N. Swinney, Freshwater Fisheries Unit, Liverpool, demonstrated variations in size and ring composition of scales from different regions of the body of salmon *Salmo salar* (L) parr.

Index

Acellular bone	6, 9, 19
Acetate replicas of otoliths	29-39, 125-133
Age at first spawning	201, 215, 218
determination by otoliths	28-39, 108-113, 114-122, 124-135, 158-166
scales	137-142, 148-157, 200-204, 216-219, 167-171, 173-180
for fisheries management	181-190, 200-204, 206-219
production studies	221-224
distributions	182-190
length keys	162-166, 182-190
Ocean, of Pacific salmon	87-102
ranges and growth parameters	192-198
reading as a language	78-85
terminology	29, 114, 129, 167, 173
validation	78, 113, 119, 132, 171, 173-179, 201-202
Ageing American eels	124-135
and calcium metabolism	1-12
as a communications system	79
bream	148-157
by graphical methods	158-166, 187
Petersen method	160-166, 169, 176, 187, 214
dace	137-147, 173-179
errors due to ALKs	184-185
in freshwater fishery management	200-204, 206-219
marine fishery modelling	181-190
otolith reading	109-113
production studies	221-224
stock assessment	166, 206-219
stunted roach populations	167-177
fish, Information obtainable from	200
roach	137-147, 167-177
rudd	148-157
for stock assessment	166, 206-209
structures and allometric growth	198
tropical and subtropical fish	31-39, 158-166
ALKs	162-166, 182-190
Allen curves	221-224
Allocation of birthday	120-121
Allometric growth and ageing	198
American eel	124-135
Annual checks	
Annuli, *see also* Checks, Circuli and Rings	
False	40-70, 130-135, 169, 201-204
Failure to form	200-204
in otoliths	124-135
on bream and rudd scales	148-157
dace scales	137-142, 173-180
Oncorhynchus scales	40-70
pike cleithra	13-25
roach scales	137-142, 167-177
tropical fish opercular bones	60-76
otoliths	37, 158-166
Machines for counting	87-102, 103-107
Time of formation of in eel	131
Apatite	8
Aragonite	8, 20, 28-39, 126-134
Ash content of cleithra	14-27
Automatic machines for age determination	87-102, 103-107, 122, 181
Automation, Advantages and disadvantages of	106-107
Back-calculation	132, 217-218
of bream and rudd growth	148-157
dace and roach growth	137-147
Bertalanffy growth equation	158-166, 170, 176-179, 192-198
'Best' age	108-112
Bias in age determinations (*see also* Errors)	87, 201
Bimonthly otolith patterns	28-39
Birthday allocation	120-121
Black box principal	79
Blood, Calcium in	1-2

Bones, Calcium content of   6-7, 13-17
     Growth of in pike   13-27
Brackish water and ring formation   71-75
Breaking otoliths   109
Bream, Ageing, growth and back-calculation of   148-157
     of known age   148-157
Burning otoliths   105, 118-119

Calcite   8
Calcitonin   8-9
Calcium content of bone and cleithra   13-27
     in blood and plasma   1-2
     ion transport by various organs   2-5
     metabolism   1-12
     stores in various body tissues   6-8
Cassie curves   158-166, 185-187
Cellular bone   6, 9, 19
Checks *see also* Annuli, Circuli and Rings   120

     Estuarine   60
     Formation of   25, 40-70, 173-179
         and food   40-70, 73, 134-135
            handling   135
            temperature   134
     Fry   60
     Number of   40-70
     and spawning   73, 179, 201
     Supplementary   60
Circuli *see also* Annuli, Checks and Rings
     Counting   87-102
     Formation of   40-70
     Measurement of   87-102
     Number and spacing of   40-70, 106
Cleithra, Ageing pike with   13-27
     Chemical analysis of   13-27
     Specific gravity of   14-27
Coded information on scales   80-85
Cod otolith exchange scheme   108-113
Communications analysis   78-85
Computers   88-102, 103-107, 122, 158-166, 181-189, 192-198, 201

Cosmoid scales   7
Counting circuli   87-102
Crichton effect   7
Crystalline otoliths   184
Ctenoid scales   7
Cumulative length frequencies   158-166
Cutting over   167
Cybernetical approach to age reading   78-85
Cycloid scales   7

Dace age, growth and back-calculation   137-147, 173-179
     of known age   137-147
Daily growth patterns in otoliths   28-39
Day length, Effects of   40, 71
Decision theory in age determination   78-85
Dermal skeleton   1
Doubt indices   83-84
Doubtful age readings   109-113, 158-166, 167-171, 182-184, 200-202

Eel ageing   124-135
Egg size and scale nucleus   53
Elver otoliths   125-135
Electron microprobe X-ray analyser   13-27
     scanning microscope   28-39, 125-135
Erosion of scales   167-170, 174
Errors in ageing, Reduction of by exchange scheme   109-113
     Detection of   108-113, 120-122, 130-135, 158-166, 167-177, 201
         Effects of in fishing management   200, 206-219
            marine fishery modelling   181-190

Errors in ageing, Effects of in a multistock model   190
         on abundance estimates   184
         growth parameters   192-198, 200-201
         mortality estimates   184
         population models   198-190
         production studies   221-224
       due to age length keys   184-185
       exclusion of some ages   198, 200-204
       protracted check formation   173-179
       Elimination of by graphical methods   158-166, 202
       Sources of   78-85, 132-135, 142, 169-171, 200-204
       with stunted roach populations   167-177
       tropical fish   71-77, 158-166
     growth rate affecting production estimates   223
Exchange schemes   108-113

False annuli, checks or rings   40-70, 107, 120, 130-135, 141-142,
                 152-157, 167-177, 201-204, 216-218

Feeding, Effects on check formation in eel otoliths   134-135
       Pacific salmon scales   40-70
Fibrillar plate   7
Fin rays   148-157, 218
First annulus   170, 200-201, 224
Fish of known age   124-135, 137-142, 148-157
Fishery management   200-204, 206-219
Floods affecting growth rings   71-75
Fry checks   60, 201
     Size of affecting scale nucleus   61

Geographical differences in ageing   113
         otoliths   119
       origin determined from scales   87
Ganoid scales   7
Gills and calcium transport   5
Gonad production   223
Graphical ageing methods   95, 158-166, 169, 176-180, 185-187, 202,
                 214

     methods of production estimation   221-224
Growth of bream and rudd   148-157
     dace   137-147, 173-179
     Mexican marine fish   158-166
     otoliths   114-122
     roach   137-147, 167-171
     scales   40-70, 173-179, 200-204
    determination for fishery management   212-219
    parameters   192-198
    rate errors affecting production studies   223
    rings and salinity   73-75
      Factors affecting   73-75, 200-203
    Seasonal   175
    standards and stock appraisal   200-204, 206-219

Handling fish, Effects on check formation   40-70, 135
Hyalodentine layer of scales   7

I.C.N.A.F.   108
Illumination   29, 104-105
Image analysis   103-107
Imanco Ltd.   103-107
Intercirculus space   87-102
Intestines and calcium transport   2
Instrumentation   87-102, 103-107

Juvenile production   223

Kidney and calcium transport   4
Known age, Bream of   148-157
     Dace of   137-147
     Eels of   124-135
     Importance of fish of   216
     Roach of   137-147
     Rudd of   148-157

Lamellar layer in scales	7
Larval check ring	112
otolith	114
Length as a criterion of age	113, 121
Length frequency	138-146, 148-157, 159-166, 200-201
Leptocephalus	129
Machines for ageing	87-102, 103-107, 204
Mathematical models for production estimates	221-224
Measurement of circuli	87-102, 138-142, 148-157
otoliths	119, 125
Methods of estimating production	221
Misclassification of ages	109-113, 182, 202-204
Models, Mathematical, or marine fisheries	181-190
Monthly otolith patterns	28-39
Mortality rates in production estimation	221-224
Mouth brooding and growth rings	73
Multiple annuli	28-39, 71-75, 120, 158-166, 170-171
Nitrogen content of cleithra	14-27
Normality	187-189
NORMSEP	158-166
Nucleus of otoliths	114-121, 124-135
scales	40-70, 200
Objectivity	182
Ocean age of *Oncorhynchus* spp	87-102
Opercular bones	71-75, 167-177
Organic content of otoliths and bone	13-24, 126
Otolin	126
Otoliths, Acetate replicas	29-39, 125-133
Age determination from	114-122, 124-135, 200
Bimonthly patterns in	28-39
Breaking of	109, 115-118
Burning of	118-119
Cassie curves and	158-166
Calcium stores in	7-8
Collection of	115, 125
Crystalline	184
Cutting of	109
Daily growth patterns in	28-39
Descriptions of	114-118, 125-135
Differences between pairs of	122
Edges of	110
Electron scanning microscope and	124-135
Examination of	115-119, 125-135
exchange scheme	108-113
False zones in	128-131
Growth of	29, 114-122
Growth patterns in	28-39
Interpretation of	108-113
Lengths of	115, 198
Measurements of	119, 125
Methods of viewing	115
Mounting of small	115, 125
Nucleus of	114-121, 124-135
of different species	114, 121, 124-135, 158-160
larvae	114
tropical and subtropical fish	158-160
Organic constituents of	126
Particular year marks in	121
Photographing for error elimination	108-113
Preparation of	115-118, 125
Removal of	125
Resorption of	8
Sampling of	182-190
Sectioning of	115-118
Shapes of	114-122
Spawning zones in	121-122
Staining of	125
Stock recognition by	121

Otoliths, Structure of	28-39, 126-135
Terminology of growth structures in	29-30, 129
Timing of annulus formation in	131
Treatment of small	115
Unreadable	184
Weight of	189
Parathyroid	8-9
Parents affecting scale features	40-70
Petersen method	160-166, 169, 176, 185-187, 214
Placoid scales	7
Plasma, Calcium in	2
Plumbicon	104-107
Polarising stage	106
Population models and effects of ageing errors	189-190
Production studies and effects of ageing errors	221-224
Programs for computers	87-102, 103-107, 158-160, 181-188, 192-198
Protracted check formation	173-179
Quantimet 720	103-107
Queried ages	158, 182-184
Radius of opercular bones	71-72
Refractive liquids	105-106, 115
Reliability of fishery models with age errors	181-190
Reproducibility	78
Resorption of otoliths	8
scales	7, 25, 167, 201
Ricker production estimates	221
Rings *see also* Annuli, Checks and Circuli	
Factors affecting	73-75, 200-201
False	120, 200-201
Floods affecting	73-75
on scales	173-179, 200-202
Salinity changes producing	71-75
Sea, in scales of anadromous and catadromous fish	87-102, 129
Secondary	120
Spawning	37, 73, 201
Split	120
Roach, Ageing and back-calculation of	137-147, 167-177
Rudd, Ageing and back-calculation of	148-157
Rules for ageing	81, 201-203
Sacculith	30
Sacculus	115-122
Sagitta	30, 125
Salinity and growth rings	71-75
Sampling, Effects on ageing structures	40-70, 135
Scales as calcium stores	7
Checks on	25, 168-171, 173-179, 200-203
Cleaning of	173
Effects of starvation and feeding on	40-70
Examination of	216-219
Growth of	40-70, 173-179
Impressions of	42, 91, 106
Measurement of	138-141, 150-155, 218
Methods of ageing with	138, 148, 173, 216-219
Morphology of	173-175
Nucleus of	40-70
and egg size	53
of bream	148-157
dace	137-147, 173-179
eels	124-135
roach	137-147, 167-177
rudd	148-157
Position on fish for sampling from	148
Preparation of	216
Radius of	40-70
reading	137-147, 148-157
Rings on	168, 173-179, 200-203
Used for fish origin determination	87
Scanning electron microscope	29-39, 125

Sea rings in eel otoliths — 129
Seasonal growth — 114, 175
Secondary rings — 120
Semi-automatic machines for age determination — 87-102, 103-107
Sexual maturity marks on ageing structures — 37, 87, 110, 121-122, 201
Size of egg affecting scale nucleus — 53
       fry affecting scale features — 61
Skeleton as calcium store — 6-7
Skin and calcium transport — 5
Sockeye salmon — 40-70, 87
Sources of errors in ageing — 78-85, 114-122, 130-135, 158-166, 167-171, 173-180, 181-190

Spawning marks on ageing structures — 37, 71-75, 106, 110, 121, 179, 201
Specific gravity of cleithra — 14-27
Split rings — 120
Starvation effects on ageing structures — 25, 40-70, 134-135
Stock appraisal, Ageing for — 200-204, 206-219
      recognition from ageing structures — 87, 121
Stratified sampling of otoliths — 182-190
Stunted populations — 167-177
Subtropical fish, Ageing of — 158-166
Sulcus acusticus — 109
Supplementary checks — 60

Tropical fish, Ageing of — 28-39, 71-77, 158-166
Television scanners — 103-107
Temperature affecting check formation — 25, 134
Tetracycline — 6, 14, 119

Unreadable otoliths, Effects of on results — 158, 184
      scales, Effects of on results — 202-203
Ultimobranchial gland — 8-9

Validation of age determinations — 113, 119, 132, 167, 171, 173-179, 201
Variations in age readings — 108-113, 202-203
Vaterite — 8
Verification of ageing by graphical methods — 158-166, 202
      with fish of known age — 124-135, 137-147, 148-157
Vidicon — 104-107
Vitamin D — 8, 9
Von Bertalanffy *see* Bertalanffy

Walford plots — 162, 170, 176-179, 192
Water transparency affecting ageing structures — 73-76

Year classes and allocation of age — 120, 138-142, 148-157, 201-203